AT THIS THEATRE

AT THIS THEATRE

100 YEARS OF BROADWAY SHOWS, STORIES AND STARS

LOUIS BOTTO

edited by
ROBERT VIAGAS

APPLAUSE
THEATRE & CINEMA BOOKS

PLAYBILL®

NEW YORK

At This Theatre: *100 Years of Broadway Shows, Stories and Stars*
By Louis Botto
Edited by Robert Viagas

Except where otherwise noted, all photographs in this book are from the archives of the Theatre Collection, Museum of the City of New York. These include the following photographs by Martha Swope: Pg. 24: *Your Arms Too Short To Box With God* and *Morning's at Seven*; Pg. 32: *Oh! Calcutta!; Ain't Misbehavin'*; Pg. 41: *Peter Pan; Private Lives*; Pg. 49: *Cats*; Pg. 68: *Applause*; Pg. 78: *Ain't Misbehavin'; Children of a Lesser God*; Pg. 86: *A Chorus Line*; Pg. 95: *Butterflies Are Free*; Pg. 96: *For Colored Girls Who Have Considered Suicide/When the Rainbow Is Enuf*; Pg. 107: *Dancin'*; Pg. 116: *Plaza Suite*; Pg. 117: *Piaf*; Pg. 130: *A View From the Bridge*; Pg. 144: *Lena Horn: The Lady and Her Music*; Pg. 155: *Side by Side by Sondheim*; Pg. 164: *Pippin*; Pg. 165: *Dreamgirls*; Pg. 176: *The Little Foxes*; Pg. 186: *1776*; Pg. 193: *Candide; Evita*; Pg. 227: *Same Time, Next Year; The Dresser*; Pg. 237: *Joseph and the Amazing Technicolor Dreamcoat*; Pg. 255: *The Wiz; The Act*; Pg. 274: *Annie*; Pg. 297: *Sugar Babies*; Pg. 316: *The Man Who Came To Dinner*; Pg. 317: *The Caine Mutiny Court-Martial*; Pg. 324: *The Pirates of Penzance*.

Editor's note: All PLAYBILL covers in this book are from the magazine's archives or the private collections of the author and editor. Unfortunately, the people at PLAYBILL had no sense that someday these covers would be used in a book and stamped some with dates and other marks. We show the covers exactly as they appear in our archives.

Design: Julie Meridy
Art Direction: Michelle Thompson
Published in the United States of America by Applause Books and PLAYBILL Books
Printed in Hong Kong

Library of Congress Cataloguing-in-Publications Data
Library of Congress Card Number: 2002105517

ISBN 1-55783-566-7

Applause Theatre & Cinema Books
19 West 21st Street, Suite 201
New York, NY 10010
Phone: (212) 575-9265
Fax: (212) 575-9270
Email: info@applausepub.com
Internet: www.applausepub.com

Applause books are available through your local bookstore, or you may order at www.applausepub.com or call Music Dispatch at 800-637-2852

Sales & Distribution:

North America:
  Hal Leonard Corp.
  7777 West Bluemound Road
  P.O. Box 13819
  Milwaukee, WI 53213
  Phone: (414) 774-3630
  Fax: (414) 774-3259
  Email: halinfo@halleonard.com
  Internet: www.halleonard.com

Europe:
Roundhouse Publishing Ltd.
Millstone, Limers Lane
Northam, North Devon EX 39 2RG
Phone: 01237-474474
Fax: 01237-474774
Email: roundhouse.group@ukgateway.net

PUBLISHER'S WORD

Dear Friends of the Theatre,

At This Theatre is the culmination of our sincere and passionate devotion to bring to you vivid and memorable glimpses into the histories of the theatres that are Broadway. It would be a terrible oversight to allow this work to be distributed without properly acknowledging the two individuals who made this revival better than our original effort. The cast has been enlarged and, as you will read, the results are a collection of forty wonderful journeys into the theatres that have filled our memories with experiences that we treasure for a lifetime.

Louis Botto, our author, has brought to life another generation of tenants of these special theatres. We are thankful and admire greatly his work and talent. Robert Viagas, our editor, brought a level of devotion and energy that in fact made this book possible. He was our captain and led the process with thoughtful, subtle leadership.

All chapters of our book have been updated to reflect our hope of encapsulating the most memorable shows of the 20th century in an informal history. We made many decisions and no doubt some will argue that a few worthy efforts have been overlooked. But the story hasn't ended. We hope in future editions to continue chronicling the ongoing story of Broadway as it continues to flourish. As my father always taught me, "It's a long game."

We would like to thank our partners and colleagues at Applause Theatre & Cinema Books for their stewardship of the publishing process. Their patience and flexibility made this process effortless and a rewarding experience.

Philip S. Birsh
President & Publisher
PLAYBILL Magazine

PREFACE

Brian Stokes Mitchell has starred in Broadway productions of Ragtime *at the Ford Center,* King Hedley II *and* Jelly's Last Jam *at the Virginia Theatre,* Kiss of the Spider Woman *at the Broadhurst,* Mail *at the Music Box,* Oh, Kay! *at the Richard Rodgers, and* Do Re Mi *and* Carnival *at City Center. He won the Tony Award as Best Actor in a Musical for his performance in a revival of* Kiss Me, Kate *at the Martin Beck Theatre.*

A theatre is a living thing.
It is born, it breathes, it eats, it communicates,
It grows old
And like all things in our universe,
It eventually dies.

Each theatre even has its own distinct personality—some are friendly, some brooding, some cozy, some expansive, some formal, some flamboyant. Its personality is initially defined by the entrepreneur who envisions it, the architect who designs it and the artisans who build it.

It is further shaped by the people and productions that take temporary residence in the theatre's heart. Together, over time, this fusion of wood, metal, plaster, stone, sound, ideas, artists and audiences shape its spirit.

One might even say spirits.

The concept of spirits and theatre intermingled is part of the history, tradition and superstition of the theatre that follow us into this 21st century. Every night, after the audience has left and the stage lights and houselights are extinguished, the house electrician places a single light onstage. It is usually a large black lamp about five feet tall with a single bare light bulb on top. It is there to illuminate the way for the actors who are yet removing makeup and costumes and crewmembers that are per-forming their final duties of the evening. It remains on throughout the night and next day and is not turned off until the stage lights are once again brought to life in preparation for the next show.

It is called the ghost light.

There is debate on exactly how it got its name. Some say it is because of its ghostly glow and the long shadows it casts. Others say it is there to keep away certain mischievous spirits that may lurk in aisles or dressing rooms or backstage nooks. Still others say it is there as a beacon to the ghosts of the theatre who wish never to be left in darkness. I like to think it is a beacon.

I am generally one of the last people out of the the-atre. I love crossing the dimly lit stage while making my way to the final exit of the evening out the stage door. Oftentimes I stop at the center of the stage while bathed in the soft glow of the ghost light and I stand silently for a few minutes, staring out into an empty house that fades into darkness. That's when I can best feel the spirit of the theatre and the ghosts that reside there. In those quiet moments, one can't help but hear the echoes of voices long gone—the words and music and laughter and applause that once resounded within those same walls.

I can nearly hear the excited backstage whispers of "Merde" and "Break a leg." I can almost feel the footfalls of other performers that once walked those same boards. I can smell the paint and sawdust and the burnt gels of the lights; the pipe and cigar smoke that once emanated from the lobby. I catch a fleeting glimpse of something beautiful trying to escape notice in the wings. These are the ghosts that become illuminated for me.

There is a magical time during the creation of a Broadway show when a company finally leaves the famil-iarity of a rehearsal hall and moves for the first time to the theatre. It is a time of anticipation and optimism, of apprehension and excitement. The shows I have been a part of have always marked this significant first day with a ritual.

Everyone is invited to gather onstage—cast, crew, creators, musicians, producers—anyone present that is taking part in the collaborative effort that is a Broadway show. We encircle the ghost light and instinctively clasp the hands nearest us. We ask the spirits there to welcome us. We invoke them by recalling past shows that played there and the people that filled the same space. Stories are shared from actors who have previously performed there, or crewmembers that have sometimes spent decades there. We pay homage to the people that tempered and seasoned the same wood and metal and plaster and stone that now embrace us. We ask the spirits of the theatre to welcome and support us as we endeavor to honor the tradition of those who came before us, for we are aware we are just passing through. We are itinerant storytellers in a long line of itinerant storytellers.

My first time on the Ford Center stage was particularly momentous. As the first chapter of this book describes, the Ford Center is the merging of modern theatrical architecture with the parts and parcels of two historic theatres, the Lyric and the Apollo. This new theatre holds a special place in my heart, for not only did I participate in its inaugural show, I was privileged to be the first to sing on its stage at its opening ceremony. For most performers, the theatre is a kind of church, I suppose—and to be present at its consecration, to be among the chosen few that are able to feel the power of its first heartbeat is among the rarest of honors in the theatre.

Perhaps one day my spirit will join my fellows
Released from the wood and metal and plaster and stone,
Summoned by the ghost light
And the optimistic hearts that beckon us
As we welcome and support a new Act
In the continuing story of body and mind and heart and soul
That once again plays
"At this theatre."

Brian Stokes Mitchell
April 2002

FOREWORD

One of the first emails I received after putting PLAY-BILL ON-LINE on the web in 1994 was a query about how the emailer could order a copy of Louis Botto's book *At This Theatre*.

The book had special meaning for me. The first time I had ever set foot in the PLAYBILL office was years earlier, as a member of the public, trying to buy a copy as a gift for my brother.

To answer the email, I went down the hall to Mr. Botto's office. You could hear him in the distance, singing showtunes in his quasi-operatic tenor, as he sometimes likes to do. The main feature of his office was shelves from floor to ceiling loaded with reference books, theatre biographies, playscripts, bound volumes of newspaper reviews, and the flotsam and jetsam of six decades hobnobbing with the nabobs of Broadway. His desk was a Himalaya of more books, clippings, souvenir programs, sheet music, press releases, and correspondence, all threatening to bury the typewriter that he resolutely refuses to replace with a computer.

Generally smiling and genial, his face fell a little when I asked about ordering *At This Theatre*. Every copy had been sold or given as prizes and gifts, he explained. But surely there were some in a warehouse? No. Surely he had a carton or two at home he could crack open? Again, an apology, no. The author himself possessed only a single copy, which he used as a resource for the columns he wrote each month in the PLAYBILL programs.

He gestured to the heap of letters. "Every day I hear from someone who says, 'Where can I buy it? Where can I find it?'" He shook his head. "People are clamoring for it. We really need to bring out a new edition."

I thanked him. "You're vellcome!," came his trademark cheery reply.

That was eight years ago.

Originally published in 1984 to mark the one-hundredth anniversary of PLAYBILL itself, *At This Theatre* took the unusual tack of telling the history of Broadway from the point of view of its great playhouses. The theatres themselves are the main characters, huge ornate creatures whose dreams are our entertainment. They proudly stand more or less unchanged as New York has continued to grow around them. The format of *At This Theatre* based on the columns of the same name Mr. Botto writes in each theatre's PLAYBILL, briefly summarizing its history. Readers would sometimes remark one favorite show or another had been omitted (usually owing to space limits in the program), and how nice it would be to have a complete history of each theatre. The book was simply a compendium of those detailed histories.

At This Theatre was widely praised on its first publication and quickly became a favorite of researchers and writers around the world. It brought back memories for those who had seen or worked on the shows, and made a world come alive for those who hadn't. A few reviewers complained about the lack of an index; the new edition remedies that with an index of more than 5,000 entries. One hundred new images have been added to a text that's greater than 25 percent longer.

The book is a product of both Mr. Botto's tireless research, and his detailed memory. As host of PLAYBILL's monthly Spelvin Lunches for theatre insiders at the Algonquin Hotel or Sardi's restaurant, Mr. Botto has always drawn on an amazing stock of theatre anecdotes involving the great, the noteworthy and the scandalous —preferably those who are all three. Having seen his first Broadway show in 1937, he was able to pick up where Damon Runyon, Franklin P. Adams, Cholly Knickerbocker,

Dorothy Kilgallen, and the Algonquin Round Tablers had left off.

PLAYBILL publisher Philip S. Birsh initiated this second edition of *At This Theatre* in 2000, with the hook that it would serve as a comprehensive record of Broadway in the 20th century. Not only does it chronicle the intervening years, busy years of transition and renewal for the Great White Way, but adds chapters on six more theatres that were refurbished, newly openend, or returned to life during that time.

The theatres of Broadway stand as majestic monuments of the past, but still full of light and music and ideas in the present. Take a moment to steal out on their stages, and you're standing where Merman proclaimed "Everything's Coming up Roses" (the Broadway), where the dancers of *A Chorus Line* once poured out their life stories (the Shubert), where the *Follies* girls once descended staircases wearing little but stardust and giant headdresses (the New Amsterdam), where the Marx Brothers clowned and where Judy Garland broke hearts (the Palace).

Theatres are giant musical instruments—the only instruments that the audience sits inside. The auditorium is the bell, and what is vibrating is not so much the air, as the hearts and the minds of the audience. Theatres become seasoned with use, and improve with age as long as they are cared for.

They're especially precious when you consider how close we came to losing them. The theatres in this book are survivors of the 1930s-70s holocaust of parking lots and skyscrapers that saw half of New York's classic playhouses fall to the wrecking ball. Gone forever: the Casino, the Empire, the Center (where Mr. Botto saw his first show), the Hippodrome, the Maxine Elliott, the Playhouse, the Cohan, the Waldorf, the Morosco, the Bijou, and many more. In a book that celebrates the living theatres, it's worth taking a moment to recall the ones that are gone.

We're lucky enough to live in an age, when New York is trying to preserve and renovate those still in operation, and even to resurrect those that had fallen into decay or were diverted to other uses. The playhouses lining Forty-second Street between Broadway and Eighth Avenue—the Acropolis of American theatre—lay in ruins for three generations. When the first edition of *At This Theatre* came out, they were still being used for cheapo action movies, or pornography, or had been gutted as stores. A determined alliance of public and private entities decided to repair these temples of theatre and restore them to their intended purpose. This second edition of *At This Theatre* celebrates that renaissance with fresh-minted chapters on the New Amsterdam, the American Airlines (formerly the Selwyn) and the Ford Center (a combination of the Lyric and Apollo), among others.

In addition to everything else, *At This Theatre* serves as a record of PLAYBILL covers through the century, to give a sense of what theatregoers of the past held in their hands as they took their seats. We're always amazed at how many people collect PLAYBILLS, even frame them. Program covers are works of popular art, too often used and forgotten, like posters, but often quite interesting or beautiful, sometimes even historic. As you flip these pages you'll see how PLAYBILL evolved from its early art nouveau days, faded into sepia utilitarianism in the middle of the century, then burst back into color in the later decades. Think of *At This Theatre* as your own private collection.

As a private note, I brought out some of my oldest recordings and played them as I was editing. The voices of Broadway's titans were in my ears as I was reviewing their memorable exploits. In a very real sense, they hovered over me throughout the project and I thank them.

Special thanks also to the following for their help in creating this new edition: Brian Stokes Mitchell, Gary Pearce, Julie Meridy, Pat Cusanelli, Michael Taratuta, Joan Marcus, Carol Rosegg, Catherine Ryan, and the folks at Applause Theatre & Cinema Books.

Robert Viagas
April 2002

CONTENTS

INTRODUCTION

At This Theatre is an expanded version of the popular feature of the same name that has appeared since the 1930s in PLAYBILL Magazine, which serves as the program of the professional legitimate theatre in the United States. While attending a Broadway show, theatregoers are fond of reading this page to discover the names of other production an stars they have seen in the past at this same theatre. The feature offers instant nostalgia and that is the primary purpose of this book.

It was the idea of Joan Alleman, former Editor-in-chief of PLAYBILL, to expand "At This Theatre" to book form as one of the observances of the magazine's centennial in 1984. PLAYBILL, which was founded by Frank Vance Strauss, an Ohio advertising man, has brought a century of playgoing pleasure to theatregoers by combining magazine features with a theatre program, offering a rich memento of the show they have seen.

This expanded *At This Theatre* contains the informal history of forty theatres that were built, as either legitimate houses or movie palaces and that are currently operating as legitimate theatres. The only exception is the Mark Hellinger, a theatre with a rich history, currently leased as a church. Theatres that were formerly night clubs are not included, nor are theatres that have been demolished or that have reverted to showing films or other uses, such as the Eltinge on Forty-second Street.

Even in this expanded form, *At This Theatre* is not a complete history of all shows that these forty theatres have housed. Hundreds of short-lived productions are omitted. Some shows have moved from theatre to theatre; these productions are listed at the theatre where they first played and also in other theatres if they had extended runs after they moved.

A number of legitimate theatres have had name changes in their long years of operation. The names that appear in the chapter headings are the current names of these theatres, but all significant name changes are included in each history.

It has not been possible to chronicle ownership changes of every house. The original builders and owners are noted, as well as the current owners, but many who came in-between are not mentioned.

The entire cast of a show is not listed, unless the production had a very small cast. Other credits—author, director, producer, set designer, composer, lyricist, librettist, costume and lighting designers, choreographers, et al—are listed when their contribution was notable.

Unfortunately, due to a fire, PLAYBILL magazine's "theatre-by-theatre" listing of productions that have played in each house goes back only as far as 1924. To determine shows that played in theatres before that year, it has been necessary to refer to the following sources: *Notable Names in the Theatre*; *The New York Times Theater Reviews*; *The Best Plays* annuals edited by Burns Mantle and his successors; *A Pictorial History of the American Theatre* by Daniel Blum; *Twentieth Century Theatre* by Glenn Loney; *American Musical Theatre* by Gerald Bordman; *Encyclopedia of the Musical Theatre* by Stanley Green; *Broadway* by Brooks Atkinson; *The City and the Theatre* by Mary C. Henderson; *Documents of American Theater* by William C. Young; and *Our Theatres Today & Yesterday* by Ruth Crosby Dimmick.

Other sources include: the *Theatre World* annuals, edited successively by Daniel Blum and John Willis; the *Best Plays* annuals, edited successively by Burns Mantle, John Chapman, John Kronenberger, Henry Hewes, Otis L. Guernsey Jr. and Jeffrey Sweet; *The World of Musical Comedy* and *Ring Bells! Sing Songs!* both by Stanley Green;

The Tony Award by Isabelle Stevenson, and the www.Tonys.org website; *The Magic Curtain* by Lawrence Langner; *Vintage Years of the Theatre Guild 1928-1939* by Roy S. Waldau; *A Pictorial History of the Theatre Guild* by Norman Nadel; *Revue* by Robert Baral; *Complete Book of the American Musical Theater* by David Ewen; *Matinee Tomorrow* by Ward Morehouse; *Stage* and *Theatre Arts* magazines; *The Rodgers and Hammerstein Fact Book*, edited by Stanley Green; and *The Passionate Playgoer* by George Oppenheimer.

All PLAYBILL magazines are from the files of PLAYBILL or from my own collection, or the collection of my editor, Robert Viagas. Souvenir programs, sheet music, "heralds" (inserts placed in theatre programs to advertise a show playing in another theatre) are from my own collection.

All photographs are from the collection of The Museum of the City of New York. Unfortunately, not all actors are credited on some photographs and, in some cases, it has proven impossible to verify their names. Some actors changed the spelling of their names or changed their named entirely. These changes have been noted.

I am grateful to Arthur, Philip, and Joan Birsh for the completion and publication of this book. I appreciate the hard work of graphic artists Julie Meridy and Michelle Thompson in bringing its look up to date. Pat Cusanelli and Gary Pearce deserve thanks for their work in saving and processing the artwork, and treating the delicate original pieces from my collection with such care. I thank the team at Applause Theatre & Cinema Books for being so supportive in returning this volume to print. Most of all I wish to thank Philip Birsh, president and publisher of PLAYBILL for securing the services of Robert Viagas as editor of this book. He has been a diligent aide and helpful deadline taskmaster, and has also provided a sorely-needed index.

Louis Botto
Senior Editor, PLAYBILL

FORD CENTER

The Ford Center for the Performing Arts, now under the direction of the Clear Channel Entertainment Group, opened in 1998 after a miraculous restoration that combined two adjacent, historic Forty-second Street theatres—the Lyric and the Apollo.

In 1995, the Toronto-based Livent company announced that the Ford Motor Company would grant its name and financial support to a new, 1,839-seat theatre, combining features of the Lyric (built in 1903) and the Apollo (1910). Although the two vintage theatres were destroyed, landmark elements of their buildings, both interior and exterior, were retained and combined in the new structure. This included ceiling domes, the proscenium arch, sail vault and side boxes, all of which were expanded to fit the scale of the new, larger theatre. An elliptical dome from the Lyric Theatre was reproduced and now forms the centerpiece of a magnificent two-story atrium design with a majestic limestone staircase. In the atrium's floor there is a spectacular mosaic design featuring masks of comedy and tragedy inspired by similar designs that adorn the Forty-third Street facade retained from the Lyric Theatre. At the top of the stair is a medallion with the head of Zeus, also taken from the Lyric Theatre.

The Ford Center was baptized in starlight at a special Dec. 18, 1997, ceremony, attended by stars and writers from previous Livent shows, including Chita Rivera, Christopher Plummer, Colm Wilkinson, Elaine Stritch,

Harold Prince, Terrence McNally, Marvin Hamlisch, E.L. Doctorow, Vanessa Williams, John Guare, Stephen Flaherty, Lynn Ahrens, James Hammerstein, and many more. Marin Mazzie and Brian Stokes Mitchell sang "Wheels of a Dream" from the forthcoming inaugural production, *Ragtime*, and Ms. Mazzie alone sang the hymn "Bless This House" with new lyrics by Marty Bell and Ms. Ahrens. Led by Livent's Garth Drabinsky, the assembled stars used multiple sets of scissors to cut a red ribbon across the stage, and declared the house christened.

The opening of the new theatre on January 18, 1998 was a gala event afforded much media attention. Fortunately, *Ragtime* equaled the splendor of the theatre. Based on the novel and film of the same name by Mr. Doctorow, adapted by Mr. McNally with a score by Mr. Flaherty and Ms. Ahrens, the musical boasted a stellar cast that included Ms. Mazzie, Mr. Mitchell, Audra McDonald, Mark Jacoby, and Judy Kaye. Graciela Daniele staged the musical segments and Frank Galati directed the book, which featured personages of the past (Booker T. Washington, Harry Houdini, J.P. Morgan, Henry Ford, Evelyn Nesbit, Stanford White, Harry K. Thaw, Emma Goldman, and others) in a fictional story.

Racial discrimination was a strong element of the plot and some critics and theatregoers felt that the musical's second act was too long and depressing. *Ragtime* lost to *The Lion King* for the Best Musical Tony Award, but it

BEFORE

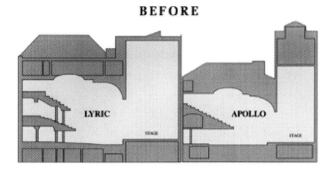

AFTER

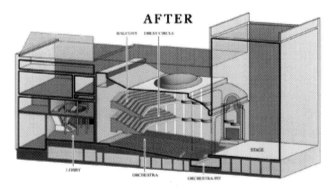

SHOWBILL
FORD CENTER FOR THE PERFORMING ARTS *Ford*

Top: Plans for combining the Lyric and Apollo Theaters into the Ford Center for the Performing Arts. *Center:* Auditorium of the Ford Center under construction combines preservation with state-of-the-art new construction. *Left:* PLAYBILL for the opening show to the Ford Center, *Ragtime* (1998).

won the following Tonys: Best Musical Book (McNally), Best Score (Flaherty and Ahrens), Best Featured Musical Actress (McDonald), and Best Orchestrations (William David Brohn). It also received seven other Tony Award nominations. The musical ran for 861 performances and was hailed by The Drama League as "One of the 20 greatest musicals of the 20th Century." It got the Ford Center off to a flying start.

In 1999, the financially troubled Livent included the Ford Center among assets sold to the SFX Theatrical Group. Parent company SFX Entertainment was the largest diversified promoter, producer and venue operator live entertainment events in the United States at that time. SFX also bought The Ford Center For The Performing Arts in Chicago.

The Ford Center's second production was a spring 2000 revival of Andrew Lloyd Webber's *Jesus Christ Superstar*, which ran 161 performances. It was followed by a no-expenses-spared revival of *42nd Street*, which enjoyed the publicity value of putting the show of that name on the street of that name. It won the 2001 Tony Award as Best Revival of a Musical.

Since the Ford Center in New York combined elements of both the Lyric Theatre and the Apollo, a brief history of each is in order. The Lyric Theatre at 213 West Forty-second Street was built in 1903 by the Shuberts and composer Reginald De Koven to house the type of operettas DeKoven composed. The Lyric was noted for its magnificent turn-of-the-century Forty-second Street and Forty-third Street facades which have been splendidly restored. The Lyric was one of the few Broadway theatres that had two entrances—one on Forty-second Street and one on Forty-third Street. The theatre was designed by Victor Hugo Koehler and was criticized because posts supporting the two balconies obstructed the view from some seats. Also, there were too many boxes (18) for a theatre this size.

The Lyric opened on October 12, 1903, with a play called *Old Heidelberg* starring the distinguished actor Richard Mansfield.

The Shubert brothers established their first New York producing headquarters above the theatre. In 1905, Douglas Fairbanks Sr., starred there in the hit musical *Fantana*, whose producer and co-librettist was Sam S.

Above: Program cover for *Her Family Tree* (1921). *Top Right*: Program cover for *The Three Musketeers* starring Dennis King (1928).

Shubert. Oscar Straus's *The Chocolate Soldier*, a musical version of Shaw's play *Arms and the Man*, proved to be a huge hit in 1909. Another operetta hit was Rudolf Friml's *The Firefly* (1912). In 1911, Henrik Ibsen's *The Lady From the Sea* had its New York premiere here.

In its heyday, the Lyric enjoyed such delights as Fred and Adele Astaire in the 1922 musical *For Goodness Sake*. Bedlam ensued in 1925 when the four Marx Brothers (Harpo, Groucho, Chico, and Zeppo) wreaked havoc on the Lyric in their lunatic musical *The Cocoanuts* with a book by George S. Kaufman and a score by Irving Berlin. In the cast was also the stately dowager Margaret Dumont who was to become the victim of Groucho's insults in many of their shows and films. There is an amusing anecdote about Berlin's score. Kaufman, who hated love songs, forced Berlin to take his song "Always"

out of the musical. The lyric, which stated "I'll be loving you, always," bothered Kaufman, who insisted that you can't love someone always. He argued that if the lyric was "I'll be loving you, Thursday," he might accept it. The song was dropped, but it soon swept the country and was the only song from the score that became a huge hit. *The Cocoanuts* ran for 375 performances—spectacular for the 1920s.

In 1926, the popular comedy team of Bobby Clark and Paul McCullough romped successfully in a musical called *The Ramblers*. In 1928, Florenz Ziegfeld produced a hit musical version of *The Three Musketeers* with a score by Rudolf Friml, P.G. Wodehouse, and Clifford Grey, and a book by Anthony Maguire. The stellar cast included Dennis King, Vivienne Segal, dancer Harriet Hoctor, Reginald Owen, and Clarence Derwent. It was one of

Program cover for *Her Family Tree* (1921).

Ziegfeld's last hits.

The following year, Cole Porter enjoyed an early hit with the musical *Fifty Million Frenchmen,* starring William Gaxton, Helen Broderick, Genevieve Tobin, and Evelyn Hoey. "You Do Something To Me" was the show's hit song, and the score also contained several numbers that are still heard in nightclubs: "You've Got That Thing," "Find Me A Primitive Man," "I Worship You," and the clever "The Tale of an Oyster," which, unfortunately, was cut from the show after the opening night.

The book, by Herbert Fields, dealt with Americans in Paris and in particular with wealthy playboy Peter Forbes (Gaxton) pursuing a beautiful American blonde named Looloo Carroll (Tobin) in such exotic locales as Longchamps, the Ritz Bar, Cafe de la Paix, and the American Express Company—all brilliantly designed by Norman Bel Geddes. Helen Broderick amused with her perusal of "feelthy French postcards." Despite the stock market's crash just a month before this show opened, the musical ran for a healthy 254 performances.

Sadly, after a series of flops in the early 1930s, the Lyric became one of Forty-second Street's notorious movie houses and showed films until 1992 when it closed for good.

The adjacent Apollo Theatre began its life in 1910 as a movie and vaudeville house. In 1920, the Selwyns, notable Broadway producers, took it over, renamed it the Apollo and converted it to a legitimate theatre. Its first production, on November 17, 1920, was the unsuccessful musical *Jimmie* by Oscar Hammerstein II and Herbert Stothart. The following year, Lionel Barrymore also failed, as Macbeth. First-nighters had their eyes on Lionel's sister, Ethel, seated in a box, and wondered what she thought of her brother acting Shakespeare.

The house's first big hit was a musical called *Poppy* (1923) starring the great comic W.C. Fields. The book was by Howard Dietz and Dorothy Donnelly, the lyrics by Ms. Donnelly, and the music by Stephen Jones and Arthur Samuels. Fields played a traveling showman named Professor Eustace McGargle who tarries long enough in a Connecticut town to install his daughter (Madge Kennedy) as a long lost heiress. Also in the cast was Robert Woolsey, later to become half of the popular comedy team known as Wheeler and Woolsey.

Fields was hailed by critics for his skillful juggling, his bouts with inanimate objects, and his verbal acrobatics. *The New York Times* proclaimed that it was the best performance he ever gave. The musical ran for 346 performances and was later made into a movie, also starring Fields.

Beginning in 1924, the Apollo became famous as the home of six editions of the glittering *George White's Scandals* revues, starring such luminaries as Jimmy Durante, Ethel Merman, Rudy Vallee, Ray Bolger, Eugene and Willie Howard, and, in the chorus, Alice Faye. The *Scandals* were noted for their dazzling dances performed by Ann Pennington and Mr. White, who was a gifted tap dancer, and by Tom Patricola. George Gershwin contributed hits to the *Scandals* including "Somebody Loves Me," and "I'll Build A Stairway To Paradise." The two biggest *Scandals* editions were produced in 1926 and 1931. During the 1920s this theatre occasionally showed silent films.

Left: PLAYBILL cover for *George White's Scandals of 1931*, starring Ethel Merman, Ray Bolger, Rudy Vallee, Willie and Eugene Howard, and, in the chorus, Alice Faye. *Right:* Sheet music for "Eadie Was a Lady" sung by Ethel Merman in *Take a Chance* (1932).

In 1930 Bert Lahr and Kate Smith had a huge hit in the musical *Flying High*. One of that era's most successful musical comedy writing teams—DeSylva, Brown, and Henderson—collaborated with John McGowan. With aviation much in the news (Charles Lindbergh and Amelia Earhart), Broadway embraced the flying theme. Mr. Lahr played a goofy plane mechanic who establishes an all-time endurance record in the air because he doesn't know how to land the plane. The show's most fondly remembered scene was one in which Lahr must give a doctor his urine specimen and he pours scotch into the container. Asked what nationality he is, he replied, "Scotch—by absorption."

Two popular songs were sung in the show—"Thank Your Father" and "Red Hot Chicago," the latter a show-stopper belted by Ms. Smith. This laugh fest ran for 355 performances.

Another big hit opened at the Apollo on November 26, 1932. With a book by B.G. DeSylva and Laurence Schwab, music by Nacio Herb Brown and Richard A. Whiting, and lyrics by DeSylva, the show had flopped in Pittsburgh, where it was called *Humpty Dumpty*. It was rewritten as *Take A Chance*, with five new songs by Vincent Youmans, and had this superlative cast: Ethel Merman, Jack Haley, Sid Silvers, Jack Whiting, Mitzi Mayfair, and "Rags" Ragland. The plot dealt with the production of a revue called *Humpty Dumpty*, scenes and songs from which were incorporated into the story. Merman and Haley stopped the show with the catchy song, "You're an Old Smoothie." In fact, they sang it in a saloon setting with a swinging door. Sid Silvers was supposed to come in via these doors when they finished singing, but the opening night audience demanded four encores and the singers were forced to push Silvers offstage through the doors to sing another encore. It was one of the evening's biggest laughs. Merman had another show-stopper with "Eadie Was A Lady," which became one of her standards. She also sang two Youmans numbers that critics loved: "Rise 'n' Shine" and "I Got Religion." This rowdy musical was an enormous audience pleaser for 243 performances. The last legit show at the Apollo was the short-lived revue *Blackbirds of 1934* with Bill Robinson.

From 1934 to 1938, the Apollo housed burlesque. Then, for 40 years, it became a movie house. In the late 1970s the Brandt Organization, which owned the theatre, closed it and beautifully restored it to legitimacy. It reopened in 1979 with the warmly received play, *On Golden Pond* with Tom Aldredge and Frances Sternhagen, followed by two hits, *The Fifth of July* with Christopher Reeve, and *Bent* with Richard Gere, plus the flop *The Guys in the Truck*.

After a period as the Academy Theatre for rock and jazz concerts, the theatre closed in 1992. In 1995, the Livent company announced that the Lyric and Apollo would be razed and transformed into one state-of-the-art theatre, which brings us back to the present incarnation. The Ford Center for the Performing Arts is one of the most beautiful theatres in Manhattan and is gracing its splendors with impressive bookings.

NEW AMSTERDAM THEATRE

When this magnificent theatre was opened in 1903 by producers Klaw and Erlanger it was described as "the house beautiful." The entire building, which also housed offices, was designed and decorated in lush Art Nouveau style by architects Herts and Tallant.

The opening production on October 26, 1903 was an appropriately lavish staging of Shakespeare's *A Midsummer Night's Dream* featuring music by Mendelssohn and star turns by popular performers of that day, Nat C. Goodwin and William Farnum. The production was only a moderate success, with the best reviews going to the theatre itself, for its classic splendor.

The eleven-story building contained two theatres, including one on the roof, and the most elaborate lobby, staircases, murals, lounges, and even elevator doors seen in any Broadway theatre. The media devoted unprecedented space to its glories. The predominant color scheme of the theatre was green, mother of pearl, and mauve. The seating capacity was 1,750 in the orchestra, two balconies, and twelve boxes.

Among the great stars of that era who appeared on the New Amsterdam stage were James O'Neill (Eugene O'Neill's father), Lillian Russell, comics Weber and Fields, Grace George, Mrs. Patrick Campbell, and Richard Mansfield.

Musicals and classic repertory were the staples of this

theatre in its early years. George M. Cohan wrote book, music, and lyrics for his 1906 musical *Forty-five Minutes from Broadway* which starred Fay Templeton, Victor Moore, and Donald Brian. Shaw's *Caesar and Cleopatra* had its world premiere in 1906 and starred Johnston Forbes-Robertson and Gertrude Elliott. Winchell Smith and Byron Ongley's comedy *Brewster's Millions* arrived on New Year's Eve 1906 and ran for just 64 performances, but was constantly revived.

The New Amsterdam's first real megahit arrived on October 21, 1907, when Franz Lehar's beloved operetta *The Merry Widow* opened, starring Ethel Jackson and Donald Brian. With its enchanting waltz, *The Merry Widow* played here for 416 performances in an age when any show that played more than 100 performances was considered a hit.

In 1910, a melodrama called *Madame X* opened here and became a favorite for revivals and movie versions.

Another popular operetta, *Madame Sherry*, was booked here in 1910, starring Lina Abarbanell, and ran for 231 performances, to be followed by an even bigger hit, *The Pink Lady*, starring Hazel Dawn and William Elliott, which delighted audiences for 312 performances.

A spectacular adaptation by William Young of Lew Wallace's epic novel *Ben Hur* opened in 1911, starring Richard Buhler and Edward H. Robbins. There were many productions of this classic at different theatres at

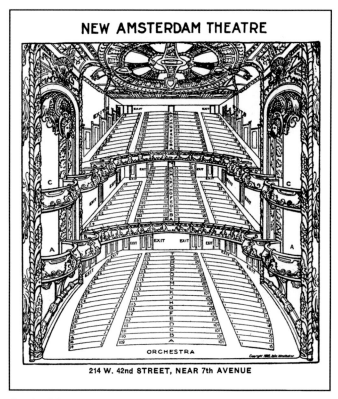

NEW AMSTERDAM THEATRE

ORCHESTRA

214 W. 42nd STREET, NEAR 7th AVENUE

Sketch of the seating arrangement of the New Amsterdam Theatre.

this time. Treadmills were used for the exciting chariot race scene.

Two operettas were popular here in 1912: Reginald De Koven's *Robin Hood* and the American premiere of Lehar's *The Count of Luxembourg*.

On June 16, 1913, an event occurred that came to define the New Amsterdam, and, indeed, an entire era. Florenz Ziegfeld began producing his annual *Ziegfeld Follies* revues at this theatre. He had produced six of them before at other theatres, but the jewel-like New Amsterdam seemed to have been custom-made for these superlative revues which showcased the funniest comedians, the sweetest singers, the most sparkling of melodies by the era's top songwriters, and the most stunning American beauties in the most gorgeous and scanty gowns on the most opulent sets. The annual editions were the last word in class and talent, and their magic resonated years after the lights went out on the series, in shows like Stephen Sondheim's *Follies* and Cy Coleman's *The Will Rogers Follies*. The New Amsterdam was the natural home of the *Ziegfeld Follies*. The 1913 *Follies* had

Leon Errol, dancer Ann Pennington, and Frank Tinney in the cast and played for 96 performances.

The Roof Theatre of the New Amsterdam was first called Aerial Gardens, but when Ziegfeld started presenting his *Midnight Frolic* there in 1915, it was changed to Dance de Follies. The space was successively rechristened Dresden Theatre and the Frolic Theatre in later years. This theatre contained a glass balcony, and Peeping Toms got their thrills looking up for an intimate view of the ladies dining above.

Victor Herbert's *Sweethearts* was a hit in 1913 and so was Hazel Dawn in a musical adapted from the French called *The Little Cafe*. The *Ziegfeld Follies of 1914* starred Ed Wynn, Bert Williams, Leon Errol, and the dynamic dancer Ann Pennington and played for 112 performances.

On December 8, 1914, a dance sensation opened at the New Amsterdam. It was Irving Berlin's first complete score for Broadway, in a ragtime musical called *Watch Your Step*, subtitled *A Syncopated Musical Show*. The program stated "plot—if any—by Harry B. Smith." The show, which was really a revue, starred that great dance team of that era, Vernon and Irene Castle. Forty years later, one of the show's songs, "Play A Simple Melody," finally gained popularity. Frank Tinney and a *Follies* beauty, Justine Johnson, were also in the cast. The jazzy musical played for 175 performances.

The *Ziegfeld Follies of 1915* boasted a number of outstanding attributes. It was the first *Follies* with sets by the famed European designer Joseph Urban (who would later design the glorious Ziegfeld Theatre, the Central Park Casino and the St. Regis Hotel Roof). The revue starred W.C. Fields, Ina Claire, Ed Wynn, Bert Williams, Leon Errol, and Billie Burke (Ziegfeld's second wife).

In 1916, Sir Herbert Tree and Company played Shakespeare's *Henry VIII, The Merchant of Venice*, and *The Merry Wives of Windsor* at this theatre. His company included Constance Collier, Henrietta Crosman, and Elsie Ferguson. This was followed by *The Ziegfeld Follies of 1916*, which had Fanny Brice (in her third Follies appearance), surrounded by the revue's usual beauties. Among the Ziegfeld glorified girls: the actress Marion Davies, who also gained fame as the mistress of William Randolph Hearst.

Miss Springtime, a 1916 musical by Guy Bolton and

Emmerich Kálmán, starring Ada Mae Weeks and Charles Meakins, delighted audiences for 224 performances. The *Ziegfeld Follies of 1917* was distinguished by the first appearance of Will Rogers in the series, surrounded by Eddie Cantor, Fanny Brice, W.C. Fields, Peggy Hopkins, Lilyan Tashman, and Ann Pennington.

The Cohan Revue of 1918 had book, music, and lyrics by George M. Cohan, with additional songs by Irving Berlin. Starring Nora Bayes, Charles Winninger, and Frederic Santley, it ran for 96 performances. Sydney Greenstreet and Laura Hamilton appeared next in a musical called *The Rainbow Girl* by Rennold Wolf and Louis A. Hirsch, which played for 87 performances.

Will Rogers's monologues, which he delivered while displaying his agility with a lasso, were so topical and popular that he appeared again in the *Follies of 1918* and in many succeeding editions. Another bright star to grace this revue was the lovely dancer/singer Marilyn Miller. Two musical hits followed the *Follies*. *The Girl Behind the Gun*, with book and lyrics by the popular team of Guy Bolton and P.G. Wodehouse, and music by Ivan Caryll, played for 160 performances. *The Velvet Lady*, with music by Victor Herbert book by Frederick Jackson and lyrics by Henry Blossom, lasted for 136 performances.

The *Follies of 1919* was considered by critics to be the finest of the series. It introduced an Irving Berlin song

View of West 42nd Street, looking west from Seventh Avenue toward Eighth Avenue in 1931 near the end of its heyday. The New Amsterdam marquee is visible at left, above trolley.

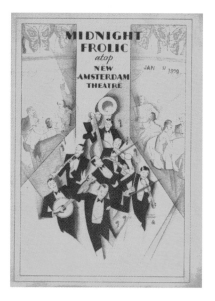

Images from "souvenir postal cards" reproducing murals from the New Amsterdam's smoking room. *Top:* "Governor Andrus Takes the City for the English." *Bottom:* "Landing of Stuyvesant." *At Right:* program from the *Midnight Frolic* in the New Amsterdam Roof (1929).

that was to become the signature number not only for the *Follies*—but also for endless beauty pageants: "A Pretty Girl Is Like a Melody." The show's other hits included "Mandy," "You'd Be Surprised," and "You Cannot Make Your Shimmy Shake On Tea." It was the last *Follies* in which the popular comic Bert Williams and Marilyn Miller (soon to become Broadway's greatest musical comedy star) appeared. It ran for 171 performances.

In 1919, a musical version of Booth Tarkington's short story *Monsieur Beaucaire* played for 143 performances, followed by *Ed Wynn's Carnival*, a revue that starred Mr. Wynn and Marion Davies. Mr. Wynn not only starred in it, but also wrote the dialogue and songs. It ran for 64 performances. The 1920 *Follies* starred Fannie Brice and comedienne Ray Dooley, who really originated the baby-talk character of Baby Snooks, later immortalized by Brice both in the *Follies* and on the radio. Joseph Urban's elaborate settings were becoming works of art and Ben Ali Haggin's tableaux (featuring near-nude showgirls in historic settings) were the talk of Broadway.

On December 21, 1920, one of the New Amsterdam's most illustrious hits arrived. It was *Sally* with music by Jerome Kern and Victor Herbert, book by Clifford Grey, and starring the luminous Marilyn Miller in her greatest success. It made her the queen of Broadway musicals in the 1920s. She played a poor girl who worked as a waitress, and while she washed dishes she sang one of Kern's most enduring songs: "Look For the Silver Lining." Since Ziegfeld was the producer, the waitress ended up as a glamorous *Follies* girl. This gem ran for 570 performances —just two fewer than Ziegfeld's masterpiece, *Show Boat.*

The 1922 *Follies* introduced the comedy team of Gallagher & Shean, who stopped the revue with their comic routine of smart-alec questions and answers in thick accents. Dancer Gilda Gray and Will Rogers also starred in this edition. The 1923 edition of the annuals was considered one of the weakest by the critics, but, surprisingly, it ran for 333 performances. (Tallies of the performance totals for *Follies* editions vary.) Perhaps the fact that Paul Whiteman and his Orchestra were in the pit hyped its popularity.

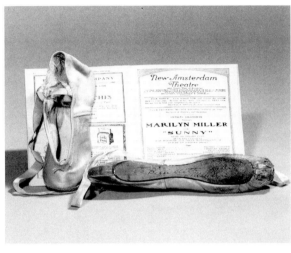

Left: Marilyn Miller and friends in *Sunny* (1925). *Above:* Ms. Miller autographed the dancing shoes she used in the show.

In 1924 the popular singer Vivienne Segal joined the *Follies*. Strangely, although it was neither a critical, nor artistic success, it enjoyed the longest run (401 perform-ances) of any *Follies* produced by Ziegfeld himself. (In 1943, the *Follies* produced by the Shuberts at the Winter Garden broke all records for this revue series, running 553 performances. It starred Milton Berle, Ilona Massey, Jack Cole, and Arthur Treacher.)

In 1925, singer Ethel Shutta joined the revue. (She would stop Sondheim's 1971 *Follies* with her rendition of the song "Broadway Baby.") Also in this production was the exotic Louise Brooks, who was to become a ravishing cult movie star. On September 22, 1925, Marilyn Miller returned to this theatre in another Jerome Kern/Otto Harbach/Oscar Hammerstein II triumph. Produced by Charles Dillingham, the musical was titled *Sunny*—obviously trading on the success of *Sally*. This time Miss Miller played a British circus rider who stowed away on a boat bound for the U.S. to be with her lover. Others in

the cast: Jack Donahue, Paul Frawley, and the dance team of Clifton Webb and Mary Hay. The show's hit song was Kern's "Who?" sung by Miss Miller. The musical was the season's hot ticket and ran for 517 performances.

A curious musical opened in 1926. Called *Betsy*, it had a book by Irving Caesar and David Freedman and a score by Rodgers and Hart (with an interpolated number by Irving Berlin, "Blue Skies," that turned out to be the show's only hit.) In fact, one critic was so tone deaf that he recommended Hart get a new composer, since Rodgers's music wasn't as fine as Hart's lyrics. The show starred Belle Baker and Al Shean and closed after only 39 performances.

Another curiosity was a 1927 musical called *Lucky,* by Otto Harbach, Bert Kalmar and Harry Ruby, with a score by Jerome Kern. Ruby Keeler and Walter Catlett starred in it and the program lists a song sung by Miss Keeler with the eyebrow-raising title "The Man in the Moon is a Coon." In later years, Miss Keeler denied

Sheet music from the Irving Berlin hit "Shaking the Blues Away," introduced by Eddie Cantor in the *Ziegfeld Follies of 1927*.

singing this politically incorrect number. The show ran for just 71 performances.

The *Ziegfeld Follies of 1927* was the last of this revue series to play at the New Amsterdam Theatre. Eddie Cantor not only starred in it, but also wrote most of the script, while Irving Berlin composed the score. It cost a then-staggering $289,000 to mount. Chiefly remembered about the spectacle was the sight of dancer Claire Luce making her startling entrance riding a live ostrich with a bejeweled collar across a jungle setting. Ruth Etting sang the catchy "Shaking the Blues Away" and Cantor did his customary numbers in blackface. Since he was doing so many numbers in the revue and had written much of it, he felt he should be paid more. He quit the show, was hauled before Actors Equity and lost his case. The show closed after 167 performances. He and Ziegfeld later made up.

Marilyn Miller returned to the New Amsterdam in the new musical, *Rosalie*, with a score by George and Ira Gershwin, Sigmund Romberg, and P. G. Wodehouse. The book was by Guy Bolton and William Anthony McGuire. Miss Miller played a princess studying at an American college, who falls in love with a West Point lieutenant. Since it was a Ziegfeld production, the musical was opulently produced. Frank Morgan played her father, a comic king, a role he repeated in the movie version with a score by Cole Porter. Two Gershwin songs are remembered from the score: "How Long Has This Been Going On?" and "Oh, Gee! Oh, Joy!" It ran for 327 performances.

One of the 1920s's most cherished musicals came to this theatre on December 4, 1928: *Whoopee*, which proved to be Eddie Cantor's greatest hit. The show was based on a hit play, *The Nervous Wreck*, by Owen Davis. The hero (Cantor's role) was an extreme hypochondriac who got into all sorts of comic situations because of his imaginary affliction. The book was by one of Ziegfeld's favorite writers, William Anthony McGuire, and the great score was by Walter Donaldson and Gus Kahn. Supporting Cantor were Ruth Etting, Ethel Shutta, and, in a small role, Buddy Ebsen. The title song, "Makin' Whoopee!" became Cantor's signature tune. Other hits from the show: "Love Me Or Leave Me" and "I'm Bringing a Red Red Rose." The show's Wild West locale inspired Ziegfeld to bring his glorified girls to ride real horses and Joseph Urban to design memorable sets, including one of the Grand Canyon. John Harkrider's costumes also stunned the audience. This musical comedy gem ran for 379 performances. Ziegfeld teamed with Sam Goldwyn to make a Technicolor movie (one of the first) of the show—also a big hit.

The next tenant at the New Amsterdam was a revival of *Sherlock Holmes* written by and starring William Gillette. Mr. Gillette made this play a perennial of his, just as James O'Neill (Eugene's father) made *The Count of Monte Cristo* his annuity.

The popular Stone family—Fred, his wife and his daughter Dorothy—starred next in a musical called *Ripples*. Fred played the great-great-grandson of Rip Van Winkle, who is an alcoholic. The book was written by William Anthony McGuire and the score was by Oscar

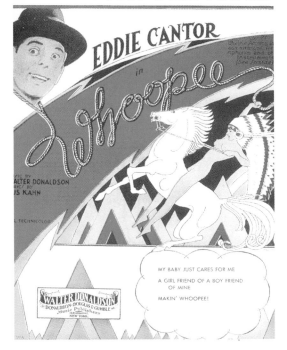

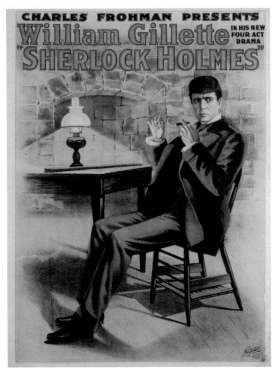

Top: Sheet music for "My Baby Just Cares for Me" by Walter Donaldson and Gus Kahn "with ukelele accompaniment," from *Whoopee* (1928). *Bottom:* William Gillette's perennial favorite, *Sherlock Holmes* (1929).

Levant and Albert Sirmay, with lyrics by Irving Caesar and Graham John. There were interpolated songs by Jerome Kern, Fred Coots, Howard Dietz, and Arthur Schwartz. Despite all these noteworthy contributors, the musical died after 55 performances.

In July, 1930 one of Ziegfeld's arch rivals, Earl Carroll, opened one of his celebrated *Vanities* revues at the New Amsterdam. (Ziegfeld had meanwhile erected his magnificent Ziegfeld Theater on Sixth Avenue and Fifty-fourth Street in 1927 and was producing his shows there—including his last *Follies* in 1931.)

Stars in the *Vanities* included Jack Benny, Jimmy Savo, and Patsy Kelly. The songs were written by Harold Arlen, E.Y. Harburg, Jay Gorney, and Ted Koehler, and the sketches were by Eddie Welch and Eugene Conrad. The costumes were by Vincente Minnelli and Charles Le Maire and the scenery by Hugh Willoughby. The revue was extremely vulgar and ran into censorship problems. The first act finale featured a huge glass swimming tank in which a male swimmer pursued two showgirls who appeared to be nude. Carroll was forced to launder this scene and some of the blue sketches, but the revue benefitted from all the publicity and ran for 215 performances.

Next at this theatre was a revival of J.M. Barrie's popular play *The Admirable Crichton* with a sterling cast: Walter Hampden, Fay Bainter, Estelle Winwood, and Effie Shannon. It played for 56 performances.

On June 3, 1931, a great event occurred at the New Amsterdam: the opening of *The Band Wagon*. To this day it is considered one of the two greatest revues produced on Broadway. (The other was the Moss Hart/Irving Berlin *As Thousands Cheer* in 1933). With a brilliant score by Dietz and Schwartz and hilarious sketches by George S. Kaufman, the stellar cast headed by Fred and Adele Astaire (her last Broadway appearance), Frank Morgan, Helen Broderick, and the enchanting Austrian dancer Tilly Losch thrilled critics and audiences with the artistry and intelligence of their work. Albert Johnson's magnificent sets (two revolving stages and a carousel) garnered raves, as did Hassard Short's staging and Albertina Rasch's choreography. The memorable score included "Dancing in the Dark," "I Love Louisa" (sung by the principals on a revolving carousel), "New Sun In The Sky," and "High and Low." The Astaires performed a

Sheet music for Schwartz and Dietz's "Love Louisa," a hit from *The Band Wagon* (1931).

witty song called "Hoops" while rolling hoops on the revolving stage and Fred and Tilly Losch dazzled in a ballet called "The Beggar's Waltz." Kaufman's sketches were models of hilarity and the entire production was a theatrical highlight of the 1930s. It ran for 260 performances.

Next came Irving Berlin and Moss Hart's musical *Face the Music*, their first collaboration. It was a political satire with Mary Boland as the filthy rich Mrs. Meshbesher, married to a policeman whose wealth was achieved by graft. In one scene, Boland arrived onstage riding a gigantic papier-mâché elephant. A clever scene showed social figures burned by the Wall Street crash, eating at an automat and singing one of the show's hit songs, "Let's Have Another Cup of Coffee." Another hit was "Soft Lights and Sweet Music." Staged by Hassard Short and George S. Kaufman, the musical ran for 165 performances.

Walter Hampden, who had played *Cyrano de Bergerac* for years in New York and on tour, revived it once again at this theatre in 1932. Another revival, Eva Le Gallienne's Civic Repertory Theatre production of *Alice in Wonderland*, moved here from downtown and played for 64 performances. In addition to Miss Le Gallienne, the outstanding cast included Alla Nazimova, Burgess Meredith, Joseph Schildkraut, and Josephine Hutchinson. This same company appeared in a revival of *The Cherry Orchard* which followed *Alice in Wonderland*. Both these productions had sets by the famed designer Aline Bernstein.

Earl Carroll returned to the New Amsterdam in 1933 with a novelty. Called *Murder At The Vanities*, it depicted a series of murders backstage at the opening night of a *Vanities* revue. The book was by Mr. Carroll and Rufus King, and the score by no fewer than nine writers. In the cast were future movie star Robert Cummings, James Rennie, Jean Adair, and horror film idol Bela Lugosi. One of the songs—"Weep No More My Baby" by John W. Green and Edward Heyman—became popular. The show ran for 298 performances.

The next musical at this theatre proved that a hit song can turn a lukewarm show into a hit. This was the case of *Roberta*, with Jerome Kern and Otto Harbach's immortal "Smoke Gets In Your Eyes" radiantly sung by Tamara. Kern supplied other gems: "The Touch of Your Hand, "Yesterdays," and "You're Devastating." The superlative cast in addition to Tamara included Bob Hope, George Murphy, Fred MacMurray, Fay Templeton, Ray Middleton, Alan Jones, and Sydney Greenstreet. The plot by Otto Harbach was considered weak. It was based on Alice Duer Miller's novel *Gowns by Roberta* and told of an American halfback (Ray Middleton) who inherits his Aunt Minnie's haute couture shop in Paris and goes there with his friends (including comic Bob Hope) to run it. He falls in love with his aunt's assistant, a Russian princess (Tamara), and starts to run the shop with her until complications set in. The show cost a staggering $115,000 in Depression dollars to mount and featured an elaborate fashion show that helped the box office. It ran for 295 performances. On its opening night, Noël Coward walked up the aisle and spotted Max Gordon, the producer of the musical.

From left: Bob Hope, Ray Middleton, Lyda Roberti, and Sydney Greenstreet in *Roberta* (1933).

Coward, with his usual bitchiness shouted, "It stinks, Max."

The next musical at the New Amsterdam arrived with a touch of scandal. It was called *Revenge With Music* by Howard Dietz and Arthur Schwartz. It starred torch singer Libby Holman, who had been accused of fatally shooting her wealthy husband, a Reynolds tobacco heir, but was acquitted. This was to be her Broadway comeback after having scored in such lauded revues as *The Little Show* and *Three's A Crowd*. Although the score included such hits as "You And The Night And The Music" and "If There Is Someone Lovelier Than You," the book's libretto was criticized. Ms. Holman was supported by Charles Winninger, George Metaxa, and Ilka Chase.

The spicy tale told of Winninger trying to woo Holman away from her new husband on their wedding night, and the groom (Metaxa) seeking revenge by having a romance with Winninger's wife (Chase). The musical

played for 158 performances and, despite its cost, recouped its investment.

Another Ziegfeld rival—George White—came to the New Amsterdam with one of his *Scandals* series in 1935. This one starred Rudy Vallee, Bert Lahr, Willie, and Eugene Howard. The revue format was beginning to wane and the critics were not enchanted with this latest example. There were no hit songs and much of the comic material had been seen before in other revues. It nevertheless had a run of 110 performances.

Walter Hampden once again brought his production of *Cyrano de Bergerac* to the New Amsterdam in 1936. This time it ran for 40 performances.

Unfortunately, the last two legitimate shows to play the New Amsterdam before it became a movie theatre were not successful. On November 2, 1936, *Forbidden Melody*, an operetta by Sigmund Romberg and Otto Harbach, limped into the theatre and was judged old-fashioned and maudlin by the critics. Operettas, like revues, were becoming passé.

The last production at this theatre for many years should have been outstanding. It was *Othello* with Walter Huston as the Moor of Venice, his wife Nan Sunderland as Desdemona, and Brian Aherne as Iago. Despite the fact that the eminent scenic designer Robert Edmond Jones designed and directed the production, it was not well received. Mr. Huston's Othello was considered weak. Mr. Aherne's Iago received better notices—but not good enough to save the show. The revival opened January 6, 1937, and closed after just 21 performances.

The Depression took a heavy toll on the once-glittering acropolis of theatres on West Forty-second Street. Most had switched to burlesque or movies. By 1937 the New Amsterdam was the last legitimate house on the block—and then it, too, succumbed, and its bright

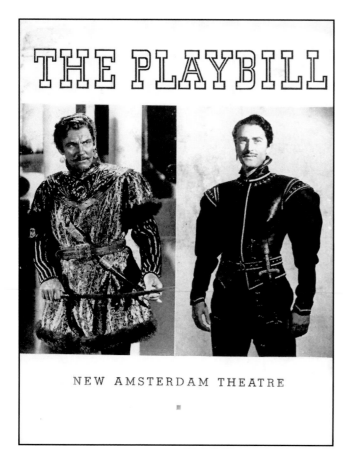

Walter Huston and Brian Aherne as Othello and Iago in *Othello* (1937), the final legitimate production at the New Amsterdam for 60 years.

history as a Broadway theatre seemed to come to an end. The Abe Erlanger estate, probably for financial reasons, turned the theatre over to the Dry Dock Savings Bank which sold it to Max A. Cohen, with the proviso that the theatre was never to house burlesque. It never did. After extensive renovations and a new marquee, the theatre's first film booking was ironic. In 1903 the New Amsterdam had opened with a live production of *A Midsummer Night's Dream*. Its first film was Max Reinhardt's movie of the Shakespeare comedy. It had an all-star Warner Brothers cast: Mickey Rooney, James Cagney, Joe E. Brown, Olivia De Havilland, and countless others, along with Mendelssohn's familiar score.

The deterioration of the New Amsterdam over the ensuing half century was one of Forty-second Street's greatest tragedies. In 1979, after decades of showing action films (but no pornography), the interior and exterior of the theatre were declared New York City landmarks, but the decline continued. In 1982 the Nederlander Organization bought the theatre, hoping to restore it and stage lavish musicals there. Meanwhile, the rooftop theatre was being used to rehearse Broadway plays. There were plans to restore the theatre and producer Alexander H. Cohen stated that his production of *La Tragédie de Carmen* would open there. However, it was discovered that the rooftop theatre had structural flaws and Mr. Cohen had to move his production to Lincoln Center. It looked like only a miracle would ever save the New Amsterdam and its neighbors.

With the redevelopment of the Times Square area, the miracle happened. The New Amsterdam had decayed miserably and was closed for ten years. But in 1992 the 42nd Street Development Project bought the theatre and Hardy Holzman Pfeiffer Associates was hired to restore the house to soundness. The Walt Disney Company began to eye the theatre as a possible venue for its planned spectacular Broadway musicals. Walt Disney CEO Michael Eisner took a now-legendary tour of the New Amsterdam and was so impressed (and saddened) by what he saw that he resolved that the former "House Beautiful" must be restored. Combining with the 42nd Street Development Project (which contributed a loan of $26 million), Disney kicked in with $36 million. Disney also received a 49-year lease on the theatre. Famed

Left: View of the Grande Promenade in 1997 after Disney's restoration. Photo by Whitney Cox. *Right:* Program from *The Lion King* (1997).

architect Hugh Hardy was engaged to achieve the restoration and a large crew of workers was assembled. For a complete report on this epic restoration, read Mary C. Henderson's magnificent book, *The New Amsterdam: The Biography of a Broadway Theatre* (Hyperion), the most beautiful book on a Broadway theatre ever published.

On May 18, 1997, with much media hoopla, the House Beautiful, restored to its original splendor, reopened for 9 performances of *King David* (a concert) by Alan Menken and Tim Rice. The high praise in the press was for the stupendous restoration of the theatre, but not for *King David*. This was followed by a short debut engagement of the animated Disney film, *Hercules*.

On November 13, 1997, Disney's magnificent production of *The Lion King* opened to jubilant reviews. Ziegfeld would have been proud. Brilliantly directed by Julie Taymor, with costumes, masks and puppet designs by her, the production was a magical adaptation of the popular Disney animated film of the same name. The book was by Roger Allers and Irene Mecchi and the score was by Elton John and Tim Rice. The highest praise went to Ms. Taymor for the enchanting parade of faux animals down the aisles at the show's opening, a sight never before staged in a Broadway theatre.

For her artistic triumph, Ms. Taymor won two Tony Awards: one for her direction and another for her costumes. *The Lion King* also won the Best Musical Tony Award; Best Scenic Designer (Richard Hudson); Best Lighting (Donald Holder) and Best Choreographer (Garth Fagan). The musical also received these Tony Award nominations: Featured Musical Actor (Samuel E. Wright); Featured Musical Actress (Tsidii Le Loka); Musical Book (Allers and Mecchi); Best Score (Elton John, Tim Rice, Lebo M, Mark Mancina, Jay Rifkin, Julie Taymor and Hans Zimmer).

The Lion King immediately became the hottest ticket in town and will undoubtedly still be running long after this book is published. And the House Beautiful,

Tony Award nominee Tsidii Le Loka as Rafiki in *The Lion King* (1997).

having risen from its ashes like the proverbial phoenix, will continue to dazzle playgoers for decades to come.

Two postscripts to the history of this theatre must be added. First is the legend that it is a haunted house. In his book, *Ziegfeld*, Charles Higham reported that in 1952, a handyman at the theatre was alarmed by the appearance of a beautiful, ghostly show girl in a white dress with a gold sash on which appeared the name "Olive." When he followed her, she vanished. Two weeks later, the apparition returned. Another worker identified her as Olive Thomas, a statuesque *Follies* girl whom he knew and adored. She had committed suicide in Paris after discovering that her husband, Jack Pickford (Mary's brother), had given her syphilis. During the restoration of the New Amsterdam in the 1990s a workman on the project called PLAYBILL and stated that there had been spooky incidents in the theatre while he worked. Things moved mysteriously backstage and a woman's voice behind him

asked, "Hey—how're you doin'?" He turned around and no one was there.

Reports of ghosts in theatres are not unusual. The ghost of David Belasco was often said to have been spotted in the Belasco Theatre, and the ghost of Enrico Caruso has been seen in the Brooklyn Academy of Music. Fortunately, they do not disrupt performances.

A much happier reappearance of *Follies* alumnae will bring the history of the New Amsterdam full circle. On April 13 and 14, 1998, five original *Follies* showgirls, Nona Otero Friedman, Yvonne Arden Hyde, Lucile Layton Zinman, Eleanor Dana O'Connell, and Doris Eaton Travis, some in their nineties, returned to the New Amsterdam stage as special guests of that year's Broadway Cares/Equity Fights AIDS Easter Bonnet Competition. Ms. Travis led a company of young gypsies in performing the original choreography from "Mandy," and became a fixture of the event in ensuing years.

LYCEUM THEATRE

When the famed impresario Daniel Frohman opened the Lyceum Theatre on November 2, 1903, on West Forty-fifth Street, east of Broadway, he called it the New Lyceum to distinguish it from the old Lyceum that he formerly owned on Fourth Avenue. The opening of his new theatre brought much publicity, and the day before its premiere *The New York Tribune* ran a feature article on the splendors of the new house. One of the unusual features was a ten-story tower at the rear section of the theatre containing such departments as a carpenter shop, scene building and painting studios, wardrobe sections, and extra dressing rooms.

The paper praised the theatre's decorative scheme by architects Herts and Tallant; its gray limestone façade with Roman columns; the marble staircases in the lobby; the width of the auditorium, which brought seats closer to the stage; the absence of posts, giving all theatregoers an unobstructed view of the stage; and Mr. Frohman's elegant quarters above the theatre with a concealed window that permitted him to supervise rehearsals from above and to telephone directions to his stage manager below.

Ideal for dramas and comedies, the New Lyceum opened with *The Proud Prince,* starring the distinguished American actor E.H. Sothern, who had appeared in many fine plays at the downtown Lyceum. Later in 1903 another illustrious star, William Gillette, sparkled in James M. Barrie's *The Admirable Crichton.*

In 1905 a tremendous hit came to the Lyceum. Charles Klein's *The Lion and the Mouse* was an attack on big business and in particular on John D. Rockefeller. The drama was about a judge whose career was unjustly ruined by a tycoon named John Burkett Ryder (the Rockefeller character, played by Edmund Breese). The judge's daughter, who exposes the injustice (a character based on the real-life Ida Tarbell), was acted by Grace Elliston. Her boyfriend was played by Richard Bennett, father of the future stars Constance and Joan Bennett. The play caused a sensation and ran for 686 performances.

In 1907 Daniel Frohman presented his wife, Margaret Illington, and Kyrle Bellew in Henri Bernstein's play *The Thief.* During the run of this hit, Frohman and his wife discovered a way to control her performance in the explosive second act. Margaret would look up, and if she was overacting Frohman would wave his handkerchief frantically from his secret window above the stage.

During the early years of the Lyceum, the theatre presented a parade of ravishing stars in plays that were regarded more as star vehicles than as great dramas. Billie Burke, a Virginia beauty, soon became a Lyceum fixture in a series of these vehicles, many produced by Daniel Frohman's celebrated brother, Charles Frohman. Among these plays were *Love Watches* (1908); *Mrs. Dot* (1910); *Suzanne* (1910); *The Runaway* (1911), with C. Aubrey Smith and Henry Miller, Jr.; and *The "Mind the Paint" Girl*

(1912). The beautiful young Ethel Barrymore starred in *Our Mrs. McChesney* (1915), by Edna Ferber and George Hobart; the steamy Lenore Ulric heated the house with Pedro de Cordoba in David Belasco's *Tiger Rose* (1917); and the coruscating Ina Claire made sparks in *The Gold Diggers* (1919), another hit Belasco production. It ran for 720 performances.

The Roaring Twenties continued to bring hits to the Lyceum. In September 1921 Belasco revived Eugene Walter's shocker *The Easiest Way,* starring the revered actress Frances Starr. In his autobiography, *Present Indicative,* Noël Coward relates how he attended this opening night while on his first visit to New York. He was introduced to the acerbic critic Alexander Woollcott, and Coward confessed to the critic that he found the performance of one of the actresses in the cast "vexing." Woollcott thought the remark hysterically funny and he and Coward became lifelong friends.

David Belasco continued to provide the Lyceum with hits. In November 1921 he presented actor Lionel Atwill and popular Lina Abarbanell in one of Sacha

Guitry's romantic comedies, *The Grand Duke,* about royalty mingling with peasantry. It worked for 131 performances. In the summer of 1922 Belasco produced a naval comedy, *Shore Leave,* starring James Rennie as a romantic gob and Frances Starr as his girl in a New England port. This amusing comedy later was turned into the smash musical *Hit the Deck,* and still later into the enchanting Rogers/Astaire film musical *Follow the Fleet.*

Belasco's 1924 hit was *Ladies of the Evening,* a Pygmalion tale about a man (James Kirkwood) who makes a lady out of a prostitute (Beth Merrill) and then falls in love with her.

Charles Frohman returned to producing at the Lyceum in 1925 and presented *The Grand Duchess and the Waiter,* with Elsie Ferguson as the royal dame who falls for a waiter (Basil Rathbone) who turns out to be the son of the president of the Swiss Republic. Later in the year, Frohman produced another continental comedy, *Naughty Cinderella,* with the vivacious French star Irene Bordoni as an amorous secretary.

In 1926 revue genius Fanny (she spelled it Fannie at

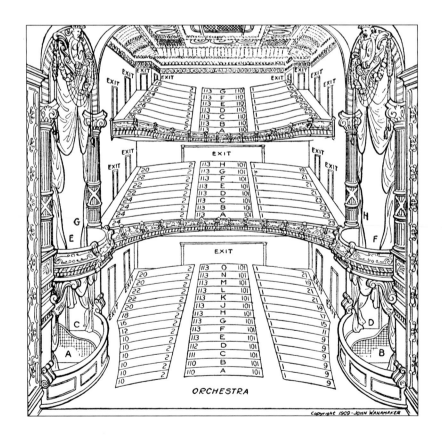

Left: Sketch of the Lyceum Theatre in 1909 from *The Wanamaker Diary. Above:* Daniel Frohman, original owner-manager of the theatre.

Clockwise from top left: E.H. Sothern in *The Proud Prince* (1903). Lenore Ulric in the sultry hit *Tiger Rose* (1917). Billie Burke, a Lyceum favorite, in *Mrs. Dot* (1910). Regal Ethel Barrymore in *Our Mrs. McChesney* (1915).

that point) Brice starred in a comedy called *Fanny* with Warren William, but despite the Belasco production and Brice's clowning, it lasted only 63 performances. In 1928 Walter Huston gave a comical performance as baseball pitcher Elmer Kane in Ring Lardner's *Elmer the Great,* produced by George M. Cohan, but the unpopularity of baseball as a stage topic resulted in only 40 performances.

One of 1929's ten best plays (as chosen by critic Burns Mantle for his annual *Best Plays* volumes) opened at the Lyceum and became one of its most fondly remembered experiences. The prestigious producer Gilbert Miller and actor Leslie Howard co-produced a fantasy called *Berkeley Square* by John L. Balderston. It starred Mr. Howard as a contemporary American whose spirit is transported back to his ancestors' home in London in 1784, where he engages in a fateful romance with a lovely British woman (Margalo Gillmore). The enchanting play ran for 227 performances and was made into a successful film with Mr. Howard.

The Depression had its effect on the Lyceum as

Clockwise from right: Patricia Peardon, Lenore Lonergan, and their boyfriends in *Junior Miss* (1941). Paul Douglas and Judy Holliday battle over gin rummy in *Born Yesterday* (1946). Sir Edward Lutyens' set for *Berkeley Square*. Leslie Howard travels back in time in the memorable *Berkeley Square* (1929).

Daniel Frohman's career declined, and he was threatened with eviction in the early 1930s. In 1939 the Lyceum was in danger of being demolished, but a group of theatre titans, who loved the old playhouse, banded together and bought it the following year. They were playwrights George S. Kaufman and Moss Hart, producer Max Gordon, and others. They bought the Lyceum with the stipulation that Daniel Frohman be permitted to live in his quarters above the house for one dollar a year. It was a fitting gesture for the aged impresario, who died on December 16, 1940. The Kaufman/Hart group sold the Lyceum at a profit in 1945 and it is currently owned by the Shubert Organization.

Highlights of the 1930s at this theatre included the American debut of Charles Laughton with his wife, Elsa Lanchester, in a murder thriller, *Payment Deferred*

(1931). Laughton was hailed for his performance. In 1933 a raucous naval comedy called *Sailor, Beware!* made critics blush and ran for 500 laugh-provoking performances. The glittering Ina Claire returned to the Lyceum in 1934 with Walter Slezak in *Ode to Liberty;* Jessie Royce Landis had a hit in *Pre-Honeymoon* (1936); Maurice Evans was an admired Napoleon in *St. Helena* (1936); Arthur Kober's charmingly ethnic *Having Wonderful Time,* starring Jules Garfield (later, John) and Katherine Locke, was a huge hit in 1937; a British hit, *Bachelor Born,* moved here from the Morosco and played for many months in 1938; and the decade ended with J.B. Priestley's *When We Are Married.*

Kaufman and Hart's *George Washington Slept Here* was one of their lesser hits, in 1940; Saroyan had a fanciful fling with *The Beautiful People* (1941); and a marvelous comedy called *Junior Miss,* about adolescence, was expertly staged by Moss Hart and romped for 710 performances.

The authors of *Junior Miss*—Jerome Chodorov and Joseph Fields—came up with another winner for the Lyceum in 1942 when their wartime comedy *The Doughgirls* opened. Arlene Francis was the hit of the show as a Russian guerrilla fighter sharing a Washington apartment with two other women. It was good for 671 performances, thanks to George S. Kaufman's dazzling direction.

Kaufman also co-wrote, with John P. Marquand, and directed *The Late George Apley,* based on Marquand's Pulitzer Prize novel of the same name. The play, a warm chronicle about a Boston Brahmin (brilliantly played by Leo G. Carroll) and his family, opened on November 21, 1944, and stayed for 384 performances.

A Sound of Hunting (1945) was not a hit, but it served as the Broadway debut of Burt Lancaster (billed as "Burton"), who promptly went to Hollywood and made a fortune. In 1946 Garson Kanin wrote a comedy called *Born Yesterday* about a dumb blonde and her uncouth keeper, a loudmouth junk dealer. The morning after it opened at the Lyceum, the blonde—Judy Holliday—and the junk dealer—Paul Douglas—were famous. It was the Lyceum's longest-running show, chalking up 1,642 performances.

The Lyceum's next hit occurred in 1950 when Clifford Odets returned to Broadway with *The Country Girl,* starring Uta Hagen as the courageous wife of an

Top: Shelley Winters and her junkie husband (Ben Gazzara) in *A Hatful of Rain* (1955). *Above:* Alan Bates, Mary Ure, and Kenneth Haigh clash in *Look Back in Anger* (1957).

Top left: *Your Arms Too Short to Box with God* (1976). *Right: Three Men on a Horse* with (from left): Zane Lasky, Jack Klugman, Jerry Stiller, Joey Faye, and Tony Randall. *Above:* (From left): Nancy Marchand, Elizabeth Wilson, Maureen O'Sullivan, and Teresa Wright in *Morning's at Seven* (1980).

alcoholic actor (Paul Kelly) who has to contend with a tough stage director (Steven Hill). Mr. Odets directed his successful drama.

Melvyn Douglas starred in two fluffy comedies at this theatre: *Glad Tidings* (1951), with Signe Hasso, and *Time Out for Ginger* (1952), with Nancy Malone as his daughter, Ginger, who tries out for her high school's football team. Another light comedy, *King of Hearts* (1954), by Jean Kerr and Eleanor Brooke and directed by Mrs. Kerr's husband, critic Walter Kerr, starred Jackie Cooper and Donald Cook and featured Cloris Leachman.

Anastasia (1954), a fascinating drama about a woman who claims to be the daughter of the last Russian czar and to have survived the family's massacre, was brilliantly acted by Viveca Lindfors as the claimant and by Eugenie Leontovich as the dowager empress.

Another powerful drama, *A Hatful of Rain* (1955), by actor Michael V. Gazzo, dramatized the anguish of a wife (Shelley Winters) married to a drug addict (Ben Gazzara). Harry Guardino and Anthony Franciosa were also in the cast.

Comedy returned to the Lyceum in 1956 when Walter Pidgeon arrived as *The Happiest Millionaire,* based on the life of millionaire Anthony J. Drexel Biddle. In sharp contrast to this high society romp was a 1957 drama from England, John Osborne's *Look Back in Anger,* starring Kenneth Haigh, Alan Bates, and Mary Ure. This lashing protest against the genteel Britain of yesteryear started a new school of playwriting called "kitchen sink drama." Its vitriolic antihero, Jimmy Porter (Mr. Haigh), became the dramatic symbol for the "angry young man."

Another fine drama from Britain, *A Taste of Honey,* by young playwright Shelagh Delaney, started the Lyceum off with a hit in 1960. It starred Angela Lansbury as the mother of a pregnant, unmarried daughter and it was written in the "kitchen sink" style. Britain sent still another excellent play in 1961 called *The Caretaker* by Harold Pinter, starring Alan Bates and Robert Shaw as brothers who make the charitable error of taking in a homeless, ominous stranger (Donald Pleasence).

After a number of short runs, the Lyceum had a mild hit in *Nobody Loves an Albatross* (1963), a comedy about an overpowering TV personality (said to be inspired by Lucille Ball) and her coworkers. It starred Robert Preston and Constance Ford.

From 1965 to 1969, the Lyceum became the home for the Phoenix Theatre and the APA Repertory Company with Ellis Rabb as artistic director. During these years, the combined companies staged a rich variety of theatre, including a highly successful revival of *You Can't Take It with You*, *War and Peace*, Helen Hayes in George Kelly's *The Show-off, The Cherry Orchard, The Cocktail Party, The Misanthrope,* and *Hamlet.*

In the 1970s the Lyceum housed a number of productions, none of which ran very long, except for the gospel musical *Your Arms Too Short to Box with God.* Worthy of mention is *Borstal Boy,* Frank McMahon's adaptation of Brendan Behan's book about his early years in prison. Although the play only ran a few months, it won a Tony Award and a New York Drama Critics Circle

Award. Also admired in the 1970s was *Cold Storage*, with Len Cariou and Martin Balsam as patients in a hospital terminal ward, and Arthur Kopit's *Wings*, a harrowing study of a woman who suffered a stroke. Constance Cummings's performance won her a Tony Award.

In 1980 a play called *Morning's at Seven* by Paul Osborn, which had flopped on Broadway in 1939, was beautifully revived with an all-star cast and turned into a belated hit. It won a Tony as the season's best revival and additional Tonys for its director, Vivian Matalon, and David Rounds for best featured actor.

This was followed by Jules Feiffer's *Grown Ups* (1981) with Bob Dishy, Frances Sternhagen, and Harold Gould; Athol Fugard's powerful racial drama *'MASTER HAROLD'... and the boys* (1982); Edward Albee's *The Man Who Had Three Arms* (1983); Whoopi Goldberg in a one-woman show that won her a Theatre World Award and a Drama Desk citation (1984); *As Is*, William M. Hoffman's powerful play about AIDS (1985); *A Little Like Magic*, the Canadian life-size puppet theatre presented by Famous People Players (1986); *Safe Sex*, three one-act plays by Harvey Fierstein on Gay themes (1987); *Michael Feinstein in Concert* (1988); and the Lincoln Center Theatre's revival of Thornton Wilder's classic *Our Town*, which won a Tony as the season's Best Revival (1988).

As it had housed the APA-Phoenix Rep in the 1960s, the Lyceum spent most of the 1990s as home to Tony Randall's National Actors Theatre. NAT inaugurated its tenancy in 1992 with three revivals: *The Seagull* with Tyne Daly, Jon Voight, Maryann Plunkett, Tony Roberts, and John Beal; *Saint Joan* with Ms. Plunkett in the title role; and *Three Men On A Horse* with Mr. Randall, Jack Klugman, and Joey Faye.

The National Actors Theatre returned to the Lyceum in 1994 with revivals of Shakespeare's *Timon of Athens*, *The Government Inspector* and *The Flowering Peach*, the latter starring Eli Wallach and Anne Jackson.

In 1995 the company presented revivals of *Gentlemen Prefer Blondes* and Sheridan's *School for Scandal*. The company scored two hits in 1997: *The Gin Game* starring Julie Harris and Charles Durning and *The Sunshine Boys* starring Mr. Randall and Mr. Klugman.

In March of that year, *Mandy Patinkin in Concert* played a limited engagement.

In 1999, Randall's troupe scored another hit with a revival of the suspense play, *Night Must Fall*, starring Matthew Broderick and Judy Parfitt, which moved to the Helen Hayes Theatre to make way for Irish playwright Martin McDonagh's *The Lonesome West*, an unsuccessful follow-up to his 1998 hit, *The Beauty Queen of Leenane*.

Lincoln Center Theatre's production of Martin Sherman's one-woman play *Rose*, starring Olympia Dukakis, allowed her to recreate her London success with this drama about a woman recalling the Holocaust. Produced by arrangement with The Royal National Theatre, the play ran for a limited engagement.

BELASCO THEATRE

The history of the Belasco Theatre on Forty-fourth Street, between Broadway and Avenue of the Americas, can be very confusing. David Belasco, the flamboyant playwright/actor/producer/director and set designer, who was called "the bishop of Broadway" because he always dressed in priestly garments, had two Belasco Theatres at different times. The first, located on Forty-second Street, was Oscar Hammerstein's Republic Theatre until Belasco leased it and named it for himself. On October 16, 1907, the impresario opened his own theatre on Forty-fourth Street, but he called it the Stuyvesant. In 1910, when the Forty-second Street theatre reclaimed its Republic name, Belasco renamed his Forty-fourth Street theatre the Belasco, and that name has remained ever since.

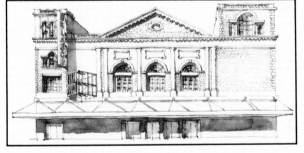

Because Belasco was more interested in spectacular, realistic stage sets than in great plays, he made certain that his theatre, designed by architect George Keister, was a marvel of technical wizardry. It cost $750,000 and had a permanent dimmer board with sixty-five dimmers, an elevator stage that could be lowered for set changes, space for set and lighting studios, and a private backstage elevator that ascended to his sumptuous apartments for himself and his leading ladies. Belasco may have worn clerical garments, but there is no evidence that he practiced celibacy.

Our Theatres Today and Yesterday, published by Ruth Crosby Dimmick in 1913, had this description of the Belasco Theatre: "This was the first theatre to be built in an enclosed rectangular court. It is broad and shallow, seats about 1,100 persons and allows each a clear view of the stage at such close range that opera glasses are superfluous. The decorations are artistic to the Belasco degree. No chandeliers or brackets are visible, the lights being enclosed between the roof and almost flat ground glass globes. A feature of the house is the absence of an orchestra and the unique manner in which the rising of the curtain is announced by the sounding of a muffled gong."

The Stuyvesant Theatre's opening bill was a new play by Belasco and two collaborators, Pauline Phelps and Marion Short, titled *A Grand Army Man* (1907). The interesting cast included David Warfield, Jane Cowl, and Antoinette Perry (the actress for whom the Tony Awards are named).

In September 1908 Belasco had a big hit in *The Fighting Hope*, starring Blanche Bates, But in 1909 he topped this with a shocker called *The Easiest Way*, by Eugene Walter. As critic Brooks Atkinson said years later, "*The Easiest Way* was a scandal, a sensation, and a success—the three bright 'S's' of show business." Frances Starr played a mediocre actress of loose morals who tries to reform but finds virtue dull and vice exciting. Her famous curtain line to her maid, "Dress up my body and paint my face. I'm going back to Rector's to make a hit and to hell with the rest," caused women in the audience to faint and priests to denounce the play from their pulpits.

On September 17, 1910, Belasco rechristened the

Program Cover for the Belasco's first musical success, Vincent Youmans' buoyant *Hit the Deck* (1927).

Stuyvesant Theatre in his own name. A hit soon followed: On October 4 he had another success with a German play, *The Concert*. Leo Ditrichstein, who translated the play, also starred as a violinist whose wife cures him of his amorous adventures. The play ran for 264 performances.

Belasco wrote his own next hit, *The Return of Peter Grimm*, starring David Warfield as a man who returns from the dead. The fantasy ran for 231 performances, but Warfield almost drove the cast insane with his onstage practical jokes. One night he secreted Limburger cheese in a bowl of tulips, and when actress Janet Dunbar buried her face in the flowers during the play's climax, she almost passed out.

During these early years of the Belasco Theatre, its

owner was celebrated for his development of such stars as Blanche Bates, Frances Starr, Lenore Ulric, Ina Claire, Katharine Cornell, and Jeanne Eagels. He was also famed for his insistence that if a play called for a scene in a laundry, the set designer had better provide a real laundry where people could actually take clothes to be washed and ironed. For one play he duplicated a Child's Restaurant.

In 1917 Ina Claire scored a tremendous success in a Cinderella play, *Polly with a Past*, that ran for 315 performances. Jeanne Eagels, who would later achieve immortality as Sadie Thompson in *Rain*, proved an instant hit in *Daddies* (1918) with George Abbott, and played for 340 performances. The sexy Lenore Ulric was good for 223 performances in *The Son-Daughter* (1919), a play about China by Belasco and George Scarborough.

Miss Ulric became a big Belasco star in the 1920s, featured in such seamy dramas as *Kiki* (1921), *The Harem* (1924), *Lulu Belle* (1926), and *Mima* (1928). Other celebrated stars who played the Belasco at this time were Lionel Barrymore in *Laugh, Clown, Laugh!* (1923) and Katharine Cornell in *Tiger Cats* (1924).

Surprisingly, the Belasco Theatre booked a musical in 1927 and it was one of the theatrical highlights of the 1920s. *Hit the Deck* had a captivating score by Vincent Youmans and it brightened the Belasco for 352 performances. Louise Groody, Charles King, and Brian Donlevy were in the cast.

Two more hits played the house before the end of the decade: *The Bachelor Father*, with C. Aubrey Smith and June Walker, and *It's a Wise Child*, starring Humphrey Bogart. The latter was a bright comedy that amused for 378 performances.

David Belasco's last production at his theatre was a success. In November 1930 he presented Melvyn Douglas and Helen Gahagan in a continental romance called *Tonight or Never*. The stars fell in love not only onstage, but offstage as well. They married and remained husband and wife for the rest of their lives.

David Belasco died in New York on May 14, 1931, at age seventy-one. His theatre was then leased to Katharine Cornell Productions, Inc., and her husband, Guthrie McClintic produced and directed the first play under the new management. It was S.N. Behrman's witty comedy *Brief Moment*, but it must have caused the

David Belasco always wore priestly garb but was not known to practice celibacy.

Melvyn Douglas and Helen Gahagan married after appearing in Belasco's last production, *Tonight or Never* (1930).

ghost of David Belasco (often seen in the theatre) unrest because it numbered among its cast the vitriolic critic Alexander Woollcott, who had panned many of his plays. Woollcott played himself in *Brief Moment*—a fat, lazy, snippy dilettante—and one of the biggest laughs in the show occurred when an actress had this line to say to him: "If you were a woman what a bitch you would have made."

Miss Cornell appeared in two plays under her own management at this theatre: *Lucrece*, translated from the French by Thornton Wilder (1932), and Sidney Howard's *Alien Corn* (1933). The Belasco was next leased to Mrs. Hazel L. Rice, wife of playwright Elmer Rice, who provided the theatre with two plays, *Judgment Day* (1934) and *Between Two Worlds* (1934), neither of which succeeded.

The famous Group Theatre's association with the Belasco began in December 1934, when it moved its production of *Gold Eagle Guy* there from the Morosco. Some of the Group's illustrious members who appeared in this play included Clifford Odets, Morris Carnovsky, Luther and Stella Adler, Sanford Meisner, and J. Edward Bromberg. On February 19, 1935, the Group Theatre made theatrical history with its production of Odets's *Awake and Sing*, featuring its acting company (including Jules Garfield). The Odets sting was at its sharpest in this

Left: Luther Adler, Elia Kazan, Roman Bohnen, and Francis Farmer in the Group Theatre's *Golden Boy* (1931). *Right:* Jules (John) Garfield and Morris Carnovsky in Odets's *Awake and Sing* (1935).

chronicle of the volcanic life of a Jewish family living in the Bronx.

On the evening of October 28, 1935, a play opened at the Belasco that would have delighted David Belasco. It was Sidney Kingsley's *Dead End* and it ran for 684 performances, the longest-running play in the Belasco's history to this day. Produced and designed by the famed Norman Bel Geddes, it featured a realistic set of a dead-end street on Manhattan's East River that Belasco himself would have cheered. The Dead End Kids, unknown young actors who became famous overnight and later made endless films in Hollywood, actually dove into the orchestra pit, where the East River supposedly flowed. The play, which was a social tract on how dead-end boys grow up to be gangsters, featured a short, haunting performance by Marjorie Main as a notorious gangster's mother. She repeated her role in the superb movie version of the play.

Another memorable play came to this theatre in 1937 when the Group Theatre presented Odets's *Golden Boy*, starring Luther Adler as the boxer/violinist and Frances Farmer as his unlucky girlfriend. Expertly directed by Harold Clurman, the play ran for 248 performances. Two more Group Theatre productions followed: Odets's *Rocket to the Moon* (1938) and Irwin Shaw's *The Gentle*

People, starring Sylvia Sidney, Franchot Tone, Lee J. Cobb, Sam Jaffe, Karl Malden, and Elia Kazan.

A sorry spectacle in 1940 was a comedy called *My Dear Children*, starring a weary and shamelessly ad-libbing John Barrymore in his last Broadway appearance. A more rewarding play was *Johnny Belinda* (1940), with Helen Craig giving a moving performance as a deaf-mute. Amusement was provided by *Mr. and Mrs. North* (1941), about a husband/wife detective team, and by *Dark Eyes* (1943), a comedy about Russian expatriates by Eugenie Leontovich and Elena Miramova, who also starred in the hit play.

A cause célèbre occurred at the Belasco in 1944. A play called *Trio*, with Richard Widmark, Lois Wheeler, and Lydia St. Clair, dealt with lesbianism. For some bizarre reason, no theatre wanted this drama, although it was written with taste. It finally opened at the Belasco on December 29, 1944, but its troubles were not over. The critics did not think it was a very good play, but they agreed that it was not lurid in its approach and that it deserved to have a hearing. Unfortunately, public officials disagreed and *Trio* was forced to close after two months when the owners of the Belasco refused to renew the producer's lease.

Baby Face Martin is gunned down on Norman Bel Geddes's massive waterfront set for Sidney Kingsley's *Dead End* (1935).

Kiss Them for Me in 1945 was notable as the first play in which the great talents of Judy Holliday were noticed. Her performance as a tramp with an honest approach to her profession helped to land her the lead in *Born Yesterday* (1946) that would make her a star. Other 1940s highlights included Arthur Laurents's *Home of the Brave* (1945); a rollicking revival of *Burlesque* (1946), starring Bert Lahr and Jean Parker; Gertrude Berg in *Me and Molly* (1948); and Alfred de Liagre, Jr.'s mesmerizing production of *The Madwoman of Chaillot* (1948), with gloriously loony performances by Martita Hunt and Estelle Winwood.

From mid-1949 until November 1953, the Belasco Theatre was leased to NBC as a radio playhouse. On November 5, 1953, it returned to the legitimate fold with a glittering hit, George S. Kaufman and Howard Teichmann's comedy *The Solid Gold Cadillac*, starring the incomparable Josephine Hull as a small stockholder who causes a big ruckus at a shareholders's meeting. The satire ran for 526 performances.

Shows worthy of mention in the 1950s include Odets's *The Flowering Peach* (1954), with Menasha Skulnik as Noah, *Will Success Spoil Rock Hunter?* (1955), starring Jayne Mansfield, Orson Bean, Martin Gabel, and Walter Matthau; Noël Coward's return to Broadway in a thin play of his own, *Nude with Violin*, alternating (1957-58) with some performances of *Present Laughter* to relieve the tedium.

In November 1960 a beautiful play came to the Belasco. Tad Mosel's *All the Way Home*, adapted from James Agee's novel *A Death in the Family*, starred Arthur Hill, Lillian Gish, Colleen Dewhurst, and Aline MacMahon. It etched with feeling the impact of a young father's death on his family. It was awarded the Pulitzer Prize and the New York Drama Critics Circle Award as the best play of the season.

Write Me a Murder (1961), by Frederick Knott, was an offbeat thriller with Denholm Elliott, Ethel Griffies, and Kim Hunter; Sam Levene was his Seventh Avenue best in a popular comedy, *Seidman and Son* (1962); Nicol Williamson gave a lacerating performance in John Osborne's *Inadmissable Evidence* (1965).

The Killing of Sister George (1966)—which was much more explicit about lesbians than the exiled *Trio*—ran for 205 performances unmolested. *Does a Tiger Wear a Necktie?* (1969) offered the Broadway debut of Al Pacino as a drug addict, and his electrifying performance won him a Tony Award.

Top Left: Tad Mosel's play caught on after it won a Pulitzer Prize. *Right:* Dorothy Chansky and John Hammil in their *Oh! Calcutta!* duet (1971). *Above:* The cast of *Ain't Misbehavin'*, which moved from another theatre to the Belasco in 1981.

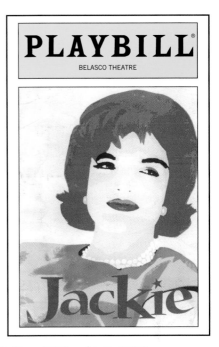

PLAYBILL covers from the original Broadway *The Rocky Horror Show* (1975), Janet McTeer's revival of *A Doll's House* (1997), and *Jackie* (1997).

Oh! Calcutta!, which moved to the Belasco in 1971 from the downtown Eden Theatre, had the entire cast in the nude and also featured the most explicitly sexual revue sketches and dances ever performed in the legitimate theatre.

For the next two decades, the Belasco's most successful tenants were long-run musicals that moved there from other theatres. In 1980, *Your Arms Too Short to Box with God* moved in from the Ambassador; and in 1981 *Ain't Misbehavin'* transferred from the Plymouth to run for an additional year at the Belasco.

For years, actors who appeared at this theatre and backstage personnel claimed that they saw the ghost of David Belasco in his priestly garb, usually sitting in an unoccupied box at opening nights. A caretaker at the theatre also told newspapers that he sometimes heard the creaky elevator chains rattling backstage, although Mr. Belasco's private elevator hasn't worked for years. But according to an article that appeared in *The New York Times*, the Belasco ghost has never been seen in the theatre since *Oh! Calcutta!* played there. This nude show may have been too much realism, even for Belasco.

Kept in pristine condition by its owner, the Shubert Organization, the Belasco housed the original 1975 production of the British import, *The Rocky Horror Show*; Colleen Dewhurst in *An Almost Perfect Person*; Uta Hagen and Charles Nelson Reilly in *Charlotte*; Elizabeth Ashley in *Hide and Seek*; Jonathan Pryce in Dario Fo's *Accidental Death of an Anarchist*; the New York Shakespeare Festival Repertory of *Macbeth/As You Like It/Romeo and Juliet*; the musical, *The Prince of Central Park*; and Len Cariou starring as a troubled Vietnam veteran in Steven Tesich's *The Speed of Darkness.*

During the 1991-1992 season, Tony Randall's National Actors Theatre inaugurated its first season here with three revivals: Arthur Miller's *The Crucible*; Feydeau's *The Little Hotel on the Side* and Ibsen's *The Master Builder.* The puppet show, *A Little More Magic*, produced by the Famous People Players of Canada, played a limited engagement there in 1994.

The following year, British actor Ralph Fiennes played Hamlet and won a Tony Award for his performance. Later in 1995, Alexander H. Cohen and Max Cooper presented Ellen Burstyn in a religious drama called *Sacrilege.* Nicol Williamson starred in *Jack*, a one-man show about John Barrymore in 1996. In 1997, Margaret Colin played Jacqueline Kennedy in a cartoon-like satire on the Kennedy family, called *Jackie.* That

Above: Christopher Walken in the musical *James Joyce's The Dead* (2000). *Top Right:* Margaret Colin and Thomas Derrah satirize the Kennedys in *Jackie* (1997). *Right:* The company recaptures the past in the "Loveland" number from *Follies* (2001). Photos by Joan Marcus.

same year, a stunning production of *A Doll's House* won a Best Actress Tony Award for British actress Janet McTeer as Nora and a Best Supporting Actor Tony for Owen Teale. In 1998, Jane Alexander returned to the stage in the play *Honour*. In 1999, Lincoln Center Theater presented a new production of Anouilh's *Ring Round the Moon* with Toby Stevens, Marian Seldes, Fritz Weaver, Simon Jones, and Joyce Van Patten.

A famous James Joyce short story served as the basis for an unusual musical that transferred from Off-Broadway's Playwrights Horizons to the Belasco on January 11, 2000. *James Joyce's The Dead* painted a portrait of a group of Dubliners who gather on a snowy Christmas Eve to sing together. Like the story, the musical

revealed the powerful emotions moving just below the surface of the merry proceedings. Among the stellar cast were Blair Brown, Christopher Walken, Sally Ann Howes, Daisy Eagan, Alice Ripley, Emily Skinner, Stephen Spinella, and Marni Nixon. The musical received five Tony Award nominations.

The Belasco greeted the Millennium in April 2001 with a revival of the Stephen Sondheim's and James Goldman's musical, *Follies*, starring Blythe Danner, Treat Williams, Judith Ivey, and Gregory Harrison. Though paying tribute to David Belasco's contemporary, Florenz Ziegfeld, that musical brought the playhouse full circle: Ziegfeld's *Follies* were inaugurated the same year that the Belasco (née Stuyvesant) opened its doors, 1907.

LUNT-FONTANNE THEATRE

This beautiful theatre opened on January 10, 1910, as the Globe, named after Shakespeare's theatre in England. It was built by the illustrious producer Charles B. Dillingham and originally had its entrance on Broadway between Forty-sixth and Forty-seventh streets. Dillingham, who spared no expense on his projects, hired the famed architects Carrère and Hastings to design his theatre. According to a report in the New York *Dramatic Mirror* on January 22, 1910, the new theatre had a large stage, a compact auditorium, Italian Renaissance decor with draperies of Rose du Barry and walls of old gold, blue, and ivory white. One feature of the theatre that attracted much attention was a large oval panel in the ceiling that could be opened when the weather permitted. The *Mirror* called this "a complete novelty in American theatrical design."

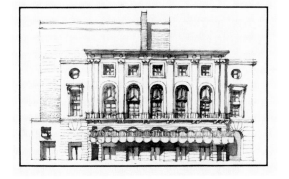

Another unusual feature was the theatre's principal façade on West Forty-sixth Street (which today is used as the entrance). The Globe used this side entrance for its carriage patrons. Above the entrance was an outdoor balcony that theatregoers could visit during intermissions, weather permitting.

For his premiere attraction, Dillingham wisely chose a lavish musical for two of that era's most popular musical comedy stars, Dave Montgomery and Fred Stone. The show was called *The Old Town* and had a book by George Ade and music by Gustav Luders. The two comics won raves and the hit show got the new Globe Theatre off to a rousing start.

In 1911 the popular Elsie Janis amused audiences in a sappy musical called *The Slim Princess* in which she played a princess too slim to attract suitors, often stepping out of character to do her famous impersonations of Sarah Bernhardt, Ethel Barrymore, Eddie Foy, and George M. Cohan. In recent years, it has been discovered that Victor Herbert wrote some of the music for this show.

Elsie Janis teamed up with Montgomery and Stone in *The Lady of the Slipper* (1912), and the Victor Herbert musical proved to be a smash.

Montgomery and Stone scored still another triumph in 1914 when they opened in *Chin-Chin*, a Chinese fantasy about Aladdin and his two slaves, played by the comedy team. The musical was a sellout and ran for 295 performances.

Irving Berlin's *Stop! Look! Listen!* brought ragtime to the Globe in 1915, plus Ziegfeld Follies beauty Justine Johnstone, comic Joseph Santley, and Harland Dixon in a popular show.

In 1916 the Globe had a dramatic change of pace. The great American actress Laurette Taylor, who had been acting in England, returned to Broadway in a play called *The Harp of Life*, written by her husband, J. Hartley Manners. The New York *Dramatic Mirror* reported that Miss Taylor "has made a triumphant return to her native stage." Also in the cast: young Lynn Fontanne, a name later to have great significance for the theatre.

One of the Globe's favorite performers, Dave

Standard program cover for Globe Theatre shows in the 1920s.

playing in drag and the Duncan Sisters doing their vaudeville act. The musical ran for 120 performances and would have continued except for the famed actors' strike, which forced it to close.

The Roaring Twenties at the Globe brought a very mixed bag of material. In June 1920 George White presented his second edition of *George White's Scandals.* It had a score by George Gershwin, lyrics by Arthur Jackson, and sketches by George White and Andy Rice. The headliners were Mr. White, tapping furiously, Ann Pennington as a mechanical piano doll, and Lou Holtz providing the low comedy.

In sharp contrast to the worldly outlook of the Scandals was the return of Fred Stone in still another innocent musical involving children, a fantasy fairyland, and "family" entertainment. This one was called *Tip Top* (October 5, 1920) and it was written by Globe veterans Anne Caldwell and composer Ivan Caryll. Fred Stone's popularity triggered the musical's run of 241 performances.

Since Ziegfeld's New Amsterdam Theatre was occupied by one of his greatest hits, *Sally,* he presented his *Ziegfeld Follies* of 1921 at the Globe. It had much to recommend it. Joseph Urban's sets and James Reynolds's costumes were so extravagant that this was Flo's most expensive *Follies,* costing over a quarter of a million dollars. The cast was stupendous. Fanny Brice sang two of her most memorable numbers: "Second Hand Rose" and "My Man," a radical departure for her. And the great comics W.C. Fields, Raymond Hitchcock, and Ray Dooley joined Miss Brice in sketches that became immortal.

The end of 1921 brought an endearing Jerome Kern show to the Globe, *Good Morning, Dearie,* starring Louise Groody and Oscar Shaw.

George White staged his 1922 *Scandals* at the Globe and it is still remembered today for George Gershwin's "I'll Build a Stairway to Paradise" and for "Blue Monday Blues," a twenty-five-minute jazz opera that was cut after the opening. It was a work that would influence Gershwin to write his full-scale opera *Porgy and Bess.* W.C. Fields and Paul Whiteman and his orchestra were among the luminaries in the cast. In June of 1923 another *Scandals* with a Gershwin score opened at the Globe, but it was one of the least successful in the series.

Montgomery, died in the spring of 1917, but his partner, Fred Stone, returned to the theatre on his own and scored a triumph in the musical *Jack o' Lantern* in October of that year. Written by the same team that had created *Chin-Chin,* and produced by Dillingham, the show had sumptuous sets by Joseph Urban of *Ziegfeld Follies* fame and a perfect role for Stone as a loving man who saves two children from a wicked uncle.

The most interesting thing about The Canary (1918) was that it had songs by Irving Berlin, Jerome Kern, Harry Tierney, and Ivan Caryll. It starred the beautiful Julia Sanderson and comic Joseph Cawthorn and it was about a man who swallowed a diamond.

Mr. Kern had his own show, *She's a Good Fellow,* written with Anne Caldwell, in 1919, with Joseph Santley

In 1923 Fred Stone returned to the Globe in *Stepping Stones*, and this time he brought his stunning, dancing daughter Dorothy along to make her Broadway debut. Dad and daughter were a hit. The memorable score was by Jerome Kern and Anne Caldwell and the plot was an adaptation of *Little Red Riding Hood*, allowing Fred Stone to play his usual role of a good man who this time saves a little girl from the big bad wolf.

Ed Wynn, the lisping comic billed as "The Perfect Fool," brought one of his ingenious shows—*The Grab Bag*—to the Globe in 1924. The Wynn formula was to present a revue in which he would barge in on other acts and amuse the audience with his ludicrous comments and insane inventions, such as a typewriterlike device for eating corn on the cob without getting his fingers full of butter. The revue was a hit and ran for 184 performances.

On the evening of September 16, 1925, the audience attending the opening night of a new musical at the Globe entered the theatre humming two of the show's hits—"Tea for Two" and "I Want to Be Happy"—*before* they even heard the overture. The show was *No, No, Nanette,* and it had a curious history. It had already played in London (although it was strictly an American musical), had played for one year in Chicago, and had several road companies touring the country before the Broadway opening. The musical was a hit.

The Globe's next tenant also had a strange history. It was supposed to be the *Ziegfeld Follies of 1926*, but because Flo had ended his partnership with Klaw and Erlanger, he was not permitted, by court decision, to use the Follies name. Therefore, he called this edition *No Foolin'* for its Globe opening, but very quickly changed the title to *Ziegfeld's American Revue of 1926*. It was not one of his best revues, but it had young Paulette Goddard and Louise Brooks in the chorus and featured the beautiful Claire Luce (the dancer, not the playwright).

Left: Raymond Hitchcock and Betty Carsdale in the 1921 edition of the *Ziegfeld Follies. Above:* Sheet-music cover for the Jerome Kern hit *The Stepping Stones*, starring Fred Stone (1923).

Above: Ona Munson in the 1925 smash *No, No, Nanette. Right:* Georges Metaxa and Bettina Hall in the memorable musical *The Cat and the Fiddle* (1931).

Fred Stone and his daughter Dorothy appeared in *Criss Cross* at the Globe in 1926 and the musical had practically the same plot as Stone's 1917 musical *Jack O'Lantern*. In this one, he saves a child (his daughter) from being swindled out of her inheritance. It was another Jerome Kern/Anne Caldwell show, with Otto Harbach collaborating on book and lyrics. This was to be Fred Stone's last show at the Globe. He and his daughter were supposed to appear in another Globe musical in 1928, called *Three Cheers*, but he was not well, and was replaced by Will Rogers. At the opening night performance, Rogers said to the audience: "I don't know one thing that Fred does that I can do." Dorothy Stone was featured in the cast and she drew raves for her singing and dancing.

In December 1926 Beatrice Lillie starred in Vincent Youmans's musical *Oh, Please!*, but it failed. The only thing that survived was the hit song "I Know That You Know."

The last legitimate show to play the Globe Theatre was the memorable musical *The Cat and the Fiddle.* Jerome Kern provided one of his best scores (including "The Night Was Made for Love," "Try to Forget," and "She Didn't Say Yes"). Book and lyrics were by Otto Harbach. The leads in this Brussels operetta were played by Georges Metaxa, Odette Myrtil, Bettina Hall, and Eddie Foy, Jr. It ran for 395 performances.

The stock market crash in 1929, which caused some Broadway theatres to remain dark during the Depression years, had a tragic effect on producer Charles B. Dillingham. He was wiped out financially and lost the Globe Theatre. When *The Cat and the Fiddle* closed in mid-1932, his theatre, like so many elsewhere in the theatre district, was converted to a movie house. It continued to show films until 1957.

Fortunately, Roger Stevens and Robert W. Dowling of the City Investing Company rescued the old house by buying it and spending a fortune to reconstruct it. Dowling chose to redo the theatre in an elegant eighteenth-century style. A new stage was built, the second balcony removed, and a cantilevered mezzanine added. Blue damask walls, crystal chandeliers, and a 100-foot mural on the ceiling depicting the theatrical muses added to the house's new opulence, and, most impressive of all, it was renamed the Lunt-Fontanne in honor of America's foremost husband/wife acting couple, Alfred Lunt and Lynn Fontanne.

Appropriately, on May 5, 1958, the Lunts opened their new house with one of their best plays, *The Visit*, a stark, harrowing drama of revenge by Friedrich Duerrenmatt. Tickets were printed in gold for the gala opening night, and the celebrity-studded audience gave the Lunt-Fontanne Theatre and the Lunts a clamorous welcome. The critics also loved the new house and the new play, which, unfortunately, proved to be the Lunts's Broadway swan-song.

After 1958 the Lunt-Fontanne enjoyed a parade of hits. Some highlights: John Gielgud and Margaret Leighton in *Much Ado About Nothing* (1959); the last Rodgers and Hammerstein musical, *The Sound of Music*, starring Mary Martin, which played for 1,443 performances (including some at the Mark Hellinger) and won six Tony Awards, including Best Musical, Best Score, and Best Performance in a musical (Martin).

The 1960s brought Sid Caesar in Cy Coleman and Carolyn Leigh's marvelous musical, *Little Me* (1962), which should have run longer but was hampered by a newspaper strike; Martha Graham and her Dance Company (1963); Richard Burton in a commendable *Hamlet*, attended at each performance by his then wife, Elizabeth Taylor (1964); Julie Harris in her first musical,

Top: Alfred Lunt and Lynn Fontanne in *The Visit*, their last Broadway appearance (1958). *Above:* Mary Martin in Rodgers and Hammerstein's last show, *The Sound of Music* (1959).

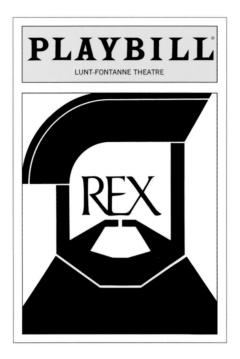
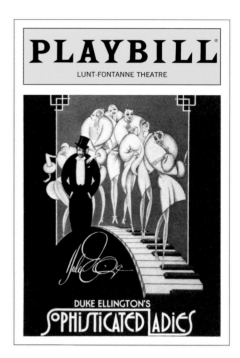

PLAYBILL covers for the Richard Rodgers musical *Rex* (1976) and the long-running revue *Sophisticated Ladies* (1981).

Skyscraper (1965); the British comic Norman Wisdom in *Walking Happy* (1966), a musical version of the novel *Hobson's Choice*; Marlene Dietrich making her Broadway debut in dazzling fashion, singing her famous songs and backed by Burt Bacharach and his huge orchestra (1967); a musical about Wall Street called *How Now, Dow Jones* (1967); and Nicol Williamson in another *Hamlet* (1969).

The Rothschilds (1970) was a musical success about the famed Jewish banking family. Hal Linden won a Tony as Best Actor in a Musical, and Keene Curtis won the same award as Best Featured Actor.

Several famous musicals were revived at the Lunt-Fontanne during the 1970s, including *A Funny Thing Happened on the Way to the Forum* (1972), starring Phil Silvers; an interracial production of *The Pajama Game* (1973) with Hal Linden, Barbara McNair and Cab Calloway; the lavish twentieth-anniversary production of *My Fair Lady*, which moved to the Lunt-Fontanne from the St. James in December 1976; and Carol Channing in a revival of her signature show, Jerry Herman's *Hello, Dolly!* (1978). In the middle of all these revivals, a Richard Rodgers/Sheldon Harnick/Sherman Yellen musical about King Henry VIII, called *Rex* (1976), was beheaded by the critics. Nicol Williamson starred as the king.

In 1979 Sandy Duncan brightened the Lunt-

Fontanne by flying all over the house in *Peter Pan*. In 1981 the elegant Duke Ellington revue, *Sophisticated Ladies*, moved into the Lunt-Fontanne, starring Gregory Hines and Judith Jamison, and thrilled theatregoers for 767 performances with its silken Ellington melodies and sparkling choreography.

In 1983, Zev Bufman produced two revivals at this theatre: Noël Coward's *Private Lives*, starring Richard Burton and Elizabeth Taylor, and *The Corn Is Green*, starring Cicely Tyson. These were followed by Peggy Lee in her autobiographical musical Peg, a one-woman show backed by a large band.

The remainder of the 1980s brought revivals of *The Wiz*, O'Neill's *The Iceman Cometh*, and rock star Sting in *The 3 Penny Opera*. There were also some new musicals —*Uptown... It's Hot*, *Smile* and *The Gospel at Colonus*; and such entertainments as *Doug Henning & His World of Magic*; *Jerry Garcia on Broadway*; *Joan Jett and the Blackhearts On Broadway*; and *Freddie Jackson: Up Close and Personal*.

Cathy Rigby starred in a successful revival of *Peter Pan* in 1990; *An Evening With Harry Connick, Jr.* proved popular that same year; in 1991, the hilarious *Catskills On Broadway* played to enthusiastic audiences.

In 1993, *Ain't Broadway Grand*, a musical about Mike

Todd, opened here. Mike Burstyn played Todd, with Debbie Shapiro Gravitte as Gypsy Rose Lee, Maureen McNamara as actress Joan Blondell (one of Todd's wives), and Gerry Vichi as comic Bobby Clark. The musical had a score by Mitch Leigh, lyrics by Lee Adams, and a book by Adams and Thomas Meehan. The show managed only 25 performances.

In 1994, *Best Little Whorehouse Goes Public* (a sequel to the hit musical *The Best Little Whorehouse in Texas*) went nowhere, running for only 15 performances despite the presence of classy Dee Hoty. This was followed by another flop—*Comedy Tonight*—a vaudeville-type show with Mort Sahl, Dorothy Loudon, Joy Behar, and Michael Davis which lasted for only 8 performances.

In 1995, Carol Channing returned to this theatre in still another revival of *Hello, Dolly!* Once again the critics raved and the musical had a run of 188 performances. The Royal Shakespeare Company's production of *A Midsummer Night's Dream* directed by Adrian Noble

opened at the Lunt-Fontanne in March 1996, and it received 8 positive reviews which helped it to run for 65 performances. In November of that year, the Moscow Theater Sovremennik performed Chekhov's *The Three Sisters* and *The Whirlwind* by Eugenia Ginsburg, performed in Russian, with simultaneous English translation via headphones. The company gave 8 performances.

The musical *Titanic* opened to mixed reviews after severe technical mishaps during previews with a set that recreated the tipping of the decks on the doomed ocean liner. Nevertheless, Peter Stone's story and the choral score by Maury Yeston struck a chord with audiences, and the show went on to win five Tony Awards, including Best Musical of the season. It sailed on for 804 performances.

After *Titanic* disembarked for the last time, the theatre was closed from spring through fall 1999 for extensive renovations made by the theatre's owner, The Nederlander Organization, and executed by the Sachs

Left: Sandy Duncan flying high in the 1979 revival of the musical *Peter Pan.*
Above: Elizabeth Taylor and Richard Burton in the 1983 revival of Noël Coward's durable drawing room comedy *Private Lives.*

Morgan Studio (SMS). The aim was to make the orchestra section seem more intimate and to brighten the house's decor. Improved restroom facilities were installed and the

second floor lobby was completely redone.

On November 12, 1999, the Disney superhit *Beauty and the Beast* moved from the Palace for a long run.

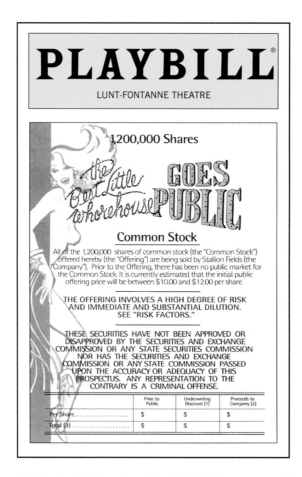

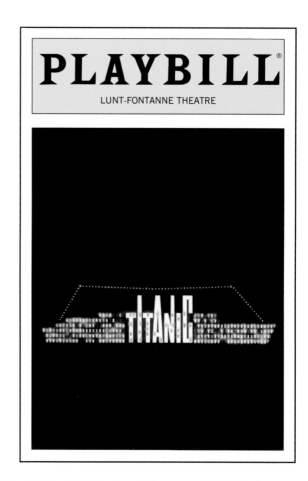

Left: The Best Little Whorehouse Goes Public (1994), an unsuccessful sequel to *The Best Little Whorehouse in Texas*, issued PLAYBILLs that resembled stock certificates for the namesake brothel. *Right:* The opening night program for Tony-winner *Titanic* (1997).

CADILLAC WINTER GARDEN THEATRE

On the blustery evening of March 20, 1911, the Messrs. Shubert unveiled on Broadway at Fiftieth Street the Winter Garden, a lavish music hall "devoted to novel, international, spectacular and musical entertainments."

Built on the site of the former American Horse Exchange owned by W.K. Vanderbilt, the theatre was designed by architect William Albert Swasey to resemble an English garden, with lattice work on the walls and a trellised ceiling. Roof gardens were a popular motif on Broadway at this time, especially on top of such theatres as the Casino, the Olympia, the American, the Victoria, the Century, and the New Amsterdam. Despite the Winter Garden's ambience of an outdoor roof garden, some unkind critics claimed they could still smell the horses whenever a flop show opened there.

Unmarred by a marquee, the original Winter Garden had a classical façade with Palladian arches and columns, and contained, besides the auditorium, a "promenoir" in the rear of the house, extending from Broadway to Seventh Avenue for intermission processions "which are joined in by everyone of prominence," an early program proclaimed.

The Winter Garden's opening production, *La Belle Paree* (1911), was composed of two parts. Part one was a one-act "Chinese opera" called *Bow Sing*; part two was a lively vaudeville, *Jumble of Jollity*, with songs by Frank Tours and Jerome Kern. The hit of this segment was singer Al Jolson, who for many years would be the Winter Garden's biggest star.

The Winter Garden was an instant hit ("New York's latest plaything, a very flashy toy, full of life and go and color and with no end of jingle to it!" wrote one critic). Two of the theatre's most talked about features in its early days were a series of Sunday night concerts, in which new talent such as Jolson and Marilynn (later shortened to Marilyn) Miller were brilliantly promoted and a structural innovation that became a Winter Garden trademark: the "runway." On a European trip, Lee Shubert had met the great German producer/director Max Reinhardt, who broke down the invisible wall between actors and audience with a thrust stage that jutted out into the orchestra section of the theatre. The Shuberts borrowed this idea and built a bridge over the tops of orchestra seats from the stage to the rear of the house. On this bridge, Jolson pranced into the audience, belting his songs and communicating with his delirious fans. Eighty near-nude show girls also paraded on the runway, which soon became known as "the bridge of thighs."

Though it was subsequently removed, the "bridge" would return to the Winter Garden some sixty years later

Left: Standard Winter Garden program cover before 1930. *Above:* Al Jolsen, who serenaded Winter Garden audiences from a specially-built runway.

when director Hal Prince installed a Japanese Kabuki-style *hanamichi* runway through the Winter Garden (sans thighs) for the musical *Pacific Overtures*.

Just as the New Amsterdam Theatre became identified with the *Follies* and the Apollo with the *Scandals*, the Winter Garden became the home of a rowdy revue series called *The Passing Show*. From 1912 through 1924 there was an annual edition, except in 1920. Among the luminous stars who appeared in these shows were Fred and Adele Astaire, Marilyn Miller, Willie and Eugene Howard, Charlotte Greenwood, Ed Wynn, Frank Fay,

John Charles Thomas, Marie Dressler, the Avon Comedy Four, Fred Allen, George Jessel, and James Barton.

The major song contributors were Sigmund Romberg and Jean Schwartz; the gilded sets were mostly by Watson Barratt, and the silken costumes mostly by Cora McGeachey and Homer Conant.

The Passing Show revues were less subtle than those produced by the Shuberts's arch rival, Florenz Ziegfeld. One wonders what women's lib would have said to a bizarre "Rotisserie" scene in which show girls were roasted on a spit and then placed on tables like well-done

44

Left: A sextet of chorines from one of the *Greenwich Village Follies* revues in the 1920s. *Right:* Eddie Cantor appeared in two Winter Garden shows.

chickens. In *The Passing Show of 1924* (the last of the series), a chorus cutie named Lucille Le Seur portrayed a "Beaded Bag" and "Miss Labor Day." The chorine went to Hollywood and became better known as Joan Crawford.

Al Jolson never appeared in a *Passing Show,* but he headlined some of the Winter Garden's biggest hits. He first appeared in blackface (which became his specialty) in *Vera Violetta,* a 1911 musical in which he co-starred with the French singer Gaby Deslys and a sexy newcomer named Mae West. He again appeared with Deslys in *The Honeymoon Express* (1913), with a funny girl in the cast named Fanny Brice. In 1918 Jolson took Broadway by storm in *Sinbad,* a fantastic musical in which he belted out some interpolated numbers that were forever identified with him: "My Mammy" (sung on the runway in blackface and white gloves), "Rock-a-Bye Your Baby with a Dixie Melody," and "Chloe." When the show went on tour, Jolson added a song called "Swanee," which made George Gershwin famous overnight. In many of his

shows, Jolson played the same character, a smart-aleck blackface servant named Gus. In his last Winter Garden show, *Big Boy* (1925), the singer made Gus a stableboy who suddenly finds himself riding as a jockey in the Kentucky Derby.

After *The Passing Show* series was through, the Winter Garden staged other revues such as *Artists and Models* and *The Greenwich Village Follies,* studded with tall, medium, and "pony"-size showgirls and low comics. Eddie Cantor appeared in two Winter Garden shows, *Broadway Brevities of 1920* and *Make It Snappy,* and Martha Graham danced in the 1923 edition of *The Greenwich Village Follies.*

During the 1920s, the Winter Garden was redesigned as it appears today by architect Herbert J. Krapp, and an enormous marquee was added. But to Broadway's dismay, from 1928 to 1933 the theatre was leased by Warner Brothers and converted into a Vitaphone (talking pictures) temple. Aptly, the first movie shown there was Al Jolson in *The Singing Fool.*

Bert Lahr, Luella Gear, and Ray Bolger clown in the 1934 revue hit *Life Begins at 8:40.*

After a shaky return to legitimacy with Joe Cook in a mediocre musical, *Hold Your Horses* (1933), the Winter Garden embarked on its golden era of glittering revues, noted for their beauty and sophistication. It all began when the Shuberts and Billie Burke (Ziegfeld's widow) combined to present a posthumous *Ziegfeld Follies* (1934), starring Fanny Brice, Willie and Eugene Howard, Vilma and Buddy Ebsen (who stopped the show with their dancing), and Jane Froman.

In 1934 Ray Bolger, Bert Lahr, Luella Gear, and Frances Williams brightened the house in *Life Begins at 8:40,* a breathtaking revue with mechanical sets and a hit tune—"Let's Take a Walk Around the Block." This was followed by the racy *Earl Carroll Sketch Book,* starring Ken Murray.

In 1935 Vincente Minnelli began his splashy tenure as revue master of the Winter Garden and he came up with *At Home Abroad,* a travelogue starring Beatrice Lillie, Ethel Waters, Eleanor Powell, and Reginald Gardiner. Minnelli designed eye-filling sets of foreign ports, Lillie did her hilarious "Dozen Double Damask Dinner Napkins" sketch, Gardiner imitated wallpaper and trains,

Powell tapped up a storm, and Waters sang Dietz and Schwartz gems.

Another *Ziegfeld Follies* arrived in 1936 with Minnelli sets and costumes, Fanny Brice doing Baby Snooks, Bob Hope singing "I Can't Get Started" to Eve Arden, Josephine Baker singing and dancing dressed in strings of bananas.

Late 1936 brought perhaps the Winter Garden's best revue of all time—Vincente Minnelli's *The Show Is On,* a tribute to show business through the ages with Bea Lillie swinging out over the audience on a huge half-moon and dropping garters on bald-headed men, Bert Lahr immortalizing "Song of the Woodman," the Gershwins providing "By Strauss," and Hoagy Carmichael's "Little Old Lady."

In late 1937 Ed Wynn moved in with a marvelous antiwar musical *Hooray for What!* by Harold Arlen and E.Y. Harburg, Howard Lindsay, and Russel Crouse. Wynn played a zany inventor of gases who is pursued by nations that want his concoctions for their wars.

A phenomenon called *Hellzapoppin* opened at the Forty-sixth Street Theatre in 1938 and proved so successful that it was moved to the Winter Garden, where it became the longest-running Broadway musical up to that time (1,404 performances). Starring Olsen and Johnson, the revue was a lunatic uproar with all sorts of practical jokes played on the audience. It sparked two more Winter Garden revues—*Sons o' Fun* (1941) and *Laffing Room Only* (1944).

In between the last two Olsen and Johnson shows came two hits: Milton Berle, Ilona Massey, Arthur Treacher, and Jack Cole in the *Ziegfeld Follies of 1943,* and Cole Porter's *Mexican Hayride,* starring Bobby Clark and June Havoc, lavishly produced by Mike Todd.

In the summer of 1945, an operetta called *Marinka* opened at the Winter Garden and proved to be the last legitimate show to play there for several years. Once again, the theatre reverted to a movie house.

In November 1948 the rowdy Bobby Clark brought live theatre back to the Winter Garden in Michael Todd's funny *As the Girls Go,* a fast-paced musical in which Bobby played the husband of the first female president of the United States (Irene Rich). Todd's production was so lush and expensive that he charged a $7.20 top, a record price at that time. Todd continued his association with this theatre by presenting a high-class burlesque, *Michael Todd's Peep Show* (1950).

Phil Silvers, another raucous comic, scored at the Winter Garden in a noisy musical, *Top Banana* (1951), about television, with Silvers impersonating a TV comic said to be inspired by Milton Berle. Then, in 1953, Rosalind Russell triumphed in *Wonderful Town,* a brilliant musical by Leonard Bernstein, Betty Comden, and Adolph Green.

A rarely-performed classic, *Tamburlaine the Great,* by Christopher Marlowe, was given a spectacular production in 1956, with Anthony Quayle in the title role and a newcomer named Colleen Dewhurst listed in the cast as "A Virgin of Memphis" in Act One and "A Turkish Concubine" in Act Two. Her fall occurred during the intermission. During the same year, the Old Vic Company from England performed *Richard II, Romeo and Juliet, Macbeth,* and other plays.

Above: Fanny Brice, as Baby Snooks, pesters Bob Hope in the 1936 edition of the *Ziegfeld Follies. Right:* Barbra Streisand triumphs as Fanny Brice in *Funny Girl* (1964).

Top: Souvenir program for the musical *Follies* (1971). *Above:* Souvenir program for the 1974 revival of *Gypsy*, starring Angela Lansbury.

The last *Ziegfeld Follies* opened at the Winter Garden in 1957 and starred the illustrious Beatrice Lillie and Billy De Wolfe, but the critics were not enthusiastic and the show closed after 123 performances. In 1958, the landmark musical *West Side Story* blazed across the Winter Garden stage with its jazzy, violent treatment of *Romeo and Juliet* set in the rumble-ridden slums of Manhattan. The unusual musical was conceived, choreographed, and directed by Jerome Robbins, had a book by Arthur Laurents, music by Leonard Bernstein, and introduced Stephen Sondheim to Broadway as a lyricist.

The offbeat actress Tammy Grimes proved a sensation in *The Unsinkable Molly Brown* in 1960, playing an actual character from the early 1900s. Harve Presnell was her co-star in this popular Meredith Willson musical. Act II included a depiction of the sinking of the Titanic. It would not be the last musical to do so.

Fanny Brice, who had been a Winter Garden favorite for many decades, was memorably impersonated by Barbra Streisand in the 1964 bonanza *Funny Girl*, with a striking score by Jule Styne and Bob Merrill.

Another musical triumph was scored by Angela Lansbury in the title role of *Mame*, Jerry Herman's musical treatment of the popular play *Auntie Mame*. Ms. Lansbury won a Tony for her spirited performance. Beatrice Arthur and Jane Connell were her hilarious sidekicks. The hit show ran for 1,508 performances.

Hal Prince brought a most original musical to the Winter Garden in 1971: *Follies*. The title was meant to suggest both the glittering revues of the 1910s and 1920s, and the mistakes the main characters have made in their love lives. The musical focused on a reunion of a group of former *Follies* girls and their husbands on the stage of the theatre where they once performed. With an exciting score by Stephen Sondheim and a book by James Goldman, the surrealistic musical starred Alexis Smith, John McMartin, Dorothy Collins, Gene Nelson, and Yvonne De Carlo, and featured old-timers Ethel Shutta and Fifi D'Orsay. *Follies* won seven Tony Awards.

In 1972 and 1973 Neil Diamond and Liza Minnelli made highly successful personal appearances at the Winter Garden. Also praised was the New York Shakespeare Festival's revival of Shakespeare's *Much Ado About Nothing*, imaginatively set in Civil War times in the United

States by director A.J. Antoon. Sam Waterston played Benedick, and Kathleen Widdoes was a radiant Beatrice.

Angela Lansbury returned to the Winter Garden in 1974 in a dynamic revival of *Gypsy*. Hal Prince and Stephen Sondheim came back in 1976 with the original musical *Pacific Overtures*, about the opening of Japan by Commodore Perry. Boris Aronson won a Tony for his splendid settings, and Florence Klotz won another Tony Award for her colorful costumes. Prince's Tony-nominated staging incorporated many conventions of Japanese Kabuki theatre.

Zero Mostel, who won a Tony in 1965 for his portrayal of Tevye in the award-winning musical *Fiddler on the Roof,* recreated his performance in a 1976 revival of the famous musical. It played for 167 performances. In 1977 a multimedia show called *Beatlemania* vividly recreated the career of the Beatles in remarkable fashion. It stayed at the Winter Garden until 1979.

A series of shows and personal appearances filled the theatre during 1979 and 1980, including *Zoot Suit, Gilda Radner—Live from New York,* and *Twyla Tharp and Dancers*. In August of 1980 David Merrick returned from producing films in Hollywood to bring glamour and excitement to the Winter Garden with an opulent, tap-dancing musical based on the famous 1933 movie *42ⁿᵈ Street*. The brilliant opening night, Broadway's most exciting in years, was marred by Mr. Merrick's announcement, at the show's curtain calls, without prior knowledge of the cast, that the musical's choreographer and director, Gower Champion, had died that afternoon.

In 1981 Richard Harris starred in a revival of *Camelot,* and in 1982 Christopher Plummer played a memorable Iago to James Earl Jones's powerful Othello.

In the summer of 1982 the Shuberts renovated the Winter Garden extensively, indoors and out. One feature that was retained was the block-long billboard over the marquee, which has carried enormous advertisements for each show playing the theatre.

In preparation for the arrival of Andrew Lloyd Webber's British hit *Cats,* set designer John Napier and a battery of workmen transformed the theatre into a "cosmic garbage dump." The effort paid off. Not only did the unique *Cats* win seven Tony Awards, but by the time it closed on September 10, 2000, it had run for 7,485

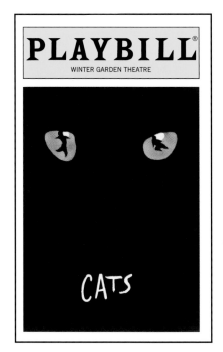

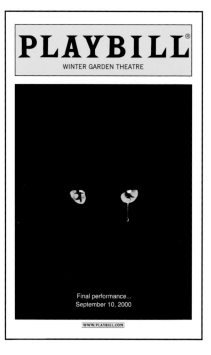

Left: The *Cats* PLAYBILL was handed out more times on Broadway than any other (1982). *Middle:* Terrence V. Mann as Rum Tum Tugger with fellow Jellicle Cats in the spectacular success *Cats* (1982). *Right:* Special PLAYBILL for the final performance of *Cats*.

performances, making it the longest running show in Broadway history. For eighteen years the yellow eyes of the logo (with tiny dancers as pupils) kept watch over Broadway.

Based on T.S. Eliot's book *Old Possum's Book of Practical Cats*, about a tribe of anthropomorphized felines calling themselves Jellicle Cats, the musical used spectacular choreography by Gillian Lynne to tell the stories of Rum Tum Tugger, Skimbleshanks, Mungojerrie, Rumpleteazer, Bustopher Jones, Mister Mistoffolees, Grizabella and the rest of the nimble band. The song "Memory" became one of the few showtunes to achieve pop standard status in the rock age. The show proved to be such a durable favorite with children and grownups

alike that it advertised for more than a decade with the slogan "Now and Forever." For a generation of youngsters, *Cats*—and the Winter Garden—formed their introduction to Broadway.

In constant use for nearly two decades, the Winter Garden closed following *Cats* for a yearlong refurbishment. It reopened in fall 2001 with *Mamma Mia!*, the latest in the theatre's long and colorful parade of hits. In spring 2002 the Shubert Organization announced that the Winter Garden would be rechristened the Cadillac Winter Garden, joining the Ford Center and the American Airlines Theatre in being renamed for a corporate sponsor.

Opening night PLAYBILL for *Mamma Mia!* (2001).

HELEN HAYES THEATRE

In July 1983, the former Little Theatre at 240 West Forty-fourth Street was officially renamed the Helen Hayes Theatre in honor of one of America's most beloved actresses. The tribute was deemed fitting by the theatrical community since the first theatre bearing the name of Helen Hayes, on West Forty-sixth Street, was torn down in 1982 to make way for the Marriott Marquis Hotel.

The Little was built by producer Winthrop Ames and opened on March 12, 1912. Ames, an aristocratic New Englander, rebelled against Broadway commercialism and built the Little, with only 299 seats, as an intimate house for the production of noncommercial plays that were too risky to stage in large Broadway theatres.

The New York Times admired the theatre's red-brick, green-shuttered exterior, its Colonial-style lobby with a fireplace, the auditorium that had no balcony or boxes and was built on an incline that afforded an unobstructed view of the stage.

The opening play was John Galsworthy's *The Pigeon*, which critic Ward Morehouse described as "a thoughtfully written comedy that brought forth human and delightful characterizations from Frank Reicher and Russ Whytal."

Ames's policy—to produce "the clever, the unusual drama that had a chance of becoming a library classic"—continued to be reflected in the Little Theatre's fare. Among the early productions, all financed solely by Ames, were George Bernard Shaw's *The Philanderer*

(1913); *Prunella*, a fantasy by Laurence Houseman and Harley Granville-Barker, starring Marguerite Clark and Ernest Glendinning (1913); and Cyril Harcourt's comedy *A Pair of Stockings* (1914).

By 1915 Ames was having financial problems with the Little. Because of his theatre's small seating capacity, the impresario was losing money, even with hits. On March 11, 1915, *The New York Times* reported that Ames was in danger of losing his house. To prevent this, Ames planned to increase the seating capacity to 1,000, add a balcony, and make the stage larger. In 1920 Burns Mantle reported that the Little had been remodeled and the seating capacity was now 450 seats.

Ames, whose money came from his family's manufacturing interests, began leasing the Little to outside producers such as the highly respected John Golden and Oliver Morosco.

During the 1918-19 season, Rachel Crothers directed her own comedy, *A Little Journey,* at the Little. It ran for 252 performances. This was followed by another hit, *Please Get Married,* a farce starring Ernest Truex.

The true purpose of the Little Theatre, to present new playwrights and experimental dramas, was fulfilled by its next two bookings. In January 1920 Oliver Morosco presented *Mamma's Affair*, a first play by Rachel Barton Butler that won a prize as the best drama written by a student of Professor George Baker's famous "English 47" class at Harvard. Morosco presented a cash award to

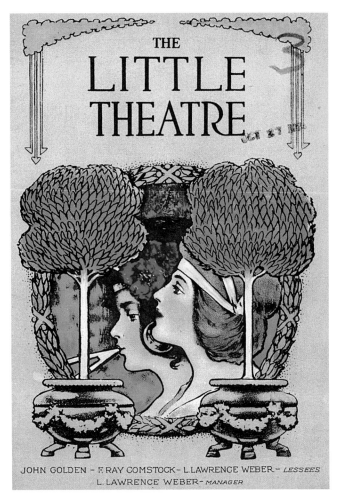

Left: Program cover for the 1924 hit, *Pigs. Right:* Program cover for Rachel Crothers's 1929 comedy, *Let Us Be Gay.*

the author and mounted her play successfully with Effie Shannon. The other drama was Eugene O'Neill's first full-length play, *Beyond the Horizon,* which had been playing matinees at other theatres before it was moved to the Little. It starred Richard Bennett and won the Pulitzer Prize.

The Little next housed one of its gold mines. *The First Year,* by actor Frank Craven, who starred in it with Roberta Arnold, proved to be a sensation. It opened on October 20, 1920, was produced by John Golden, and ran for 760 performances.

Producer Golden and playwright Craven thought that lightning might strike twice. In 1922 they tried again with Craven's *Spite Corner,* a small-town play about feuding families and lovers, but the comedy lasted only three months.

Guy Bolton, the prolific playwright who wrote many hit musicals and plays in his long career, had two comedies produced at the Little in 1923. The first, *Polly Preferred,* starring the vivacious blonde Genevieve Tobin and William Harrigan, was a daffy hit about a chorus girl who is sold to promoters like a product in a store window; the other, *Chicken Feed,* subtitled "Wages for Wives," was really ahead of its time. It would have delighted women's lib a half-century later. It was about the right of wives to share in their husbands's income.

At this time, Ames still owned the Little, but he leased it to John Golden, F. Ray Comstock, and L. Lawrence Weber, with Weber also managing the theatre.

Brooks Atkinson reported in his book *Broadway* that by 1922 Ames had lost $504,372 on the Little Theatre. His other theatre, the Booth, which he built with Lee

Shubert in 1913, was a commercial house and it is still successful today. When Ames died in 1937, his estate had dwindled to $77,000 and his widow was forced to move from the sprawling Ames mansion to a small cottage on their estate.

In 1924 a play oddly titled *Pigs* turned out to be one of the year's best. Produced by John Golden, it starred Wallace Ford as a speculator who bought fifty sick pigs, cured them, and sold them at an enormous profit. He was greatly helped by his girlfriend, played by the refreshing Nydia Westman, who garnered love letters from the critics. The hit ran for 347 performances.

Thomas Mitchell proved popular in a 1926 comedy, *The Wisdom Tooth,* by Marc Connelly; *2 Girls Wanted* was a smash in 1926; *The Grand Street Follies,* a popular annual revue that spoofed the season's plays and players, moved here from the Neighborhood Playhouse in 1927; and Rachel Crothers returned to the Little with *Let Us Be Gay,* a 1929 hit starring Francine Larrimore and Warren William.

In 1930 Edward G. Robinson was praised for his acting in *Mr. Samuel,* and Elmer Rice's *The Left Bank* (1931), about Americans in Paris, entertained patrons for 241 performances. A spate of plays with "Honeymoon" in their titles moved in. *Honeymoon* and *One More Honeymoon* were short-lived, but *Pre-Honeymoon,* by Alford Van Ronkel and Anne Nichols (author of *Abie's Irish Rose*), was a big enough hit to move from the Lyceum to the Little and to cause the theatre's name to be changed to Anne Nichols' Little Theatre.

In 1936 Sir Cedric Hardwicke made his U.S. debut in *Promise.* In 1937, when Cornelia Otis Skinner opened her one-woman show, *Edna His Wife,* the house reverted to being called the Little. A sparkling revue, *Reunion in New York,* opened in 1940 and reunited a group of talented performers from Vienna who had been introduced to New Yorkers previously in another revue, *From Vienna* (1939).

The Little Theatre ceased being a legitimate Broadway theatre for the next two decades. During this hiatus, the house, located adjacent to the headquarters of *The New York Times,* was known as The New York Times Hall from 1942 until 1959, when it became an ABC Television studio.

The Little returned to the legitimate fold in 1963 with *Tambourines to Glory,* a gospel music play by

Langston Hughes and Jobe Huntley. The Paul Taylor Dance Company appeared there in the same year. In 1964 Habimah, the national theatre of Israel, staged *The Dybbuk, Children of the Shadows,* and *Each Had Six Wings.* Later that year Paul Newman, Joanne Woodward, and James Costigan appeared in the Actors Studio production of Mr. Costigan's comedy *Baby Want a Kiss.* The critics gave it the kiss of death. In 1964, when the Pulitzer Prize-winning play *The Subject Was Roses* moved to this theatre from the Royale, the theatre's name was changed to the Winthrop Ames.

In March 1965 the name went back to the Little, which it retained until 1983. From late 1964 to

Aline MacMahon and Thomas Chalmers in Eugene O'Neill's Pulitzer Prize-winning play, *Beyond the Horizon* (1920).

Above: Danny Aiello, Barbara Coggin, and Kathleen Turner in *Gemini* (1977). *Right:* Harvey Fierstein gives a Tony Award-winning performance in his Tony-winning play, *Torch Song Trilogy* (1982).

mid-1974 the theatre was leased to Westinghouse Broadcasting and hosted the Merv Griffin and David Frost TV shows.

In 1974 the Little went legit again and housed Ray Aranha's play, *My Sister, My Sister.* *The Runner Stumbles* (1976) was a success, but *Unexpected Guests* (1977) was a failure. *Lamppost Reunion,* Louis LaRusso II's much heralded play about a Frank Sinatra-like singer returning to his old haunts in Hoboken, New Jersey, managed a run of only 77 performances.

In June 1977 Albert Innaurato's comedy *Gemini* moved in, and it epitomized the kind of show Winthrop Ames wanted in his theatre. The play was first done at Playwrights Horizons, then at the PAF Playhouse in Huntington, Long Island, followed by a production at the Circle Repertory Company. Finally, this production was moved to the Little, where it ran for an amazing 1,788 performances, making it the Little's longest-running show and the fifth-longest running straight play in Broadway history.

The Little's next three shows did not fare well. They were *Ned and Jack* (1981); William Alfred's *Curse of the Aching Heart* (1982), starring Faye Dunaway; and *Solomon's Child* (1982), an expose of fanatical religious cults.

In June 1982 another ideal Little Theatre play came to the house. It was *Torch Song Trilogy* by Harvey Fierstein, who starred in his trio of bittersweet comedies about gay life, all with the same central character. The triptych originated at LaMama E.T.C., was next done at the Richard Allen Center for Culture, and then at the Actors' Playhouse before it moved to the Little. *Torch Song Trilogy* won the 1983 Tony Award for Best Play, and a Tony for Outstanding Actor in a Play went to Mr. Fierstein.

The Helen Hayes is currently owned by The Little Theatre Group—Martin Markinson and Donald Tick—with Ashton Springer serving as managing director. In 1981 this group spent a considerable amount to restore the house. Its interior was beautifully redesigned by ADCADESIGN: Wayne Adams, John Carlson, and Wolfgang H. Kurth.

Torch Song Trilogy was followed by such varied productions as *The News* (1985), a rock musical about sensational journalism; *Corpse!* (1985), a comedy thriller starring Keith Baxter and Milo O'Shea; *Oh Coward!* (1986) a revival of Roderick Cook's 1972 revue of Noël Coward songs and skits, starring Mr. Cook, Patrick Quinn, and Catherine Cox; *Mummenschanz/The New Show* (1986), a new edition of the popular mime show; *The Nerd* (1987), the late Larry Shue's amusing comedy about a man posing as a jerk to help out a friend; Scott Bakula and Alison Fraser in *Romance/Romance* (1988), two charming one-act musicals that moved here from Off Broadway; *Mandy Patinkin in Concert: Dress Casual* (1989), the singing actor in a diverting program; *Artist Descending a Staircase* (1989), Tom Stoppard's complex comedy about the art world; *Miss Margarida's Way* (1990), Estelle Parsons in a return engagement of her acclaimed one-woman show about an explosive teacher and her unruly pupils.

Prelude to a Kiss (1990), Craig Lucas's fantasy which originally starred Alec Baldwin Off-Broadway, moved here with Timothy Hutton in Baldwin's role, plus Mary-Louise Parker, Barnard Hughes, and Debra Monk. The 1990s saw *The High Rollers Social and Pleasure Club* (1992) a musical revue set in New Orleans; *3 From Brooklyn* (1992) Rosalyn Kynd in a revue about Brooklyn; *Shakespeare For My Father* (1993), Lynn Redgrave in a highly praised one-woman show about her late father, actor Michael Redgrave; and Joan Rivers in *Sally Marr... and her escorts* (1994). Ms. Rivers not only starred in this play about Lenny Bruce's mother, but co-wrote it with Ernie Sanders and Lonny Price. She was nominated for a Tony Award for her performance. The voice of young Lenny Bruce was supplied by Jason Woliner.

In November, 1994, the popular Flying Karamazov Brothers juggling troupe opened here in their fourth Broadway appearance. They called their vaudeville show *The Flying Karamazov Brothers Do the Impossible*. They entertained for 50 performances.

The theatre's next tenant proved to be *Defending the Caveman*, a comic monologue on the differences between men and women. It had a prosperous run of 671 performances, a record for a non-musical solo show. It made way for another success: Alfred Uhry's *The Last Night of Ballyhoo* (1997) starring Paul Rudd and Dana Ivey, which ran for 557 performances. The play dealt with the conflicts within an Atlanta Jewish family at the time

of the 1939 premiere of the film *Gone With the Wind* in that city. The play won the Tony Award as Best Play of the season, making Mr. Uhry the only playwright to win a Tony Award, Pulitzer Prize (for *Driving Miss Daisy*), and an Academy Award (for the screenplay of *Driving Miss Daisy*). Tony Awards were also won by Dana Ivey and Terry Beaver for their performances in *The Last Night of Ballyhoo*.

This theatre's next two entries were not successful: *Getting and Spending* (1998), a play by Michael J. Chepiga, which originated at the Old Globe Theater in San Diego (41 performances); and *Band in Berlin*, a

Raphael Klackin (with balloons) and Aharon Meskin in *Children of the Shadows* (1964).

Above: Peter Michael Goetz and Kelly Bishop in the Tony-winning play *The Last Night of Ballyhoo* (1997). Photo by Carol Rosegg *Left:* Claudia Shear as Mae West in her play *Dirty Blonde* (2000). Photo by Joan Marcus.

musical about the Comedian Harmonists, a real-life troupe of singers popular in Germany in the 1920s, but banned by Hitler in the 1930s because it combined Jewish and non-Jewish performers.

In 1999, *Night Must Fall*, a revival of Emlyn Williams's 1936 thriller about a psychotic killer, moved here from the Lyceum Theater. It starred Matthew Broderick, Judy Parfitt and Pamela J. Gray and was produced by Tony Randall's National Arts Theater. It was based on an actual London murder case and it ran 96 performances.

Night Must Fall was followed by a comedy called *Epic Proportions,* by Larry Coen and David Crane, which spoofed the absurdities of filming a Hollywood Biblical spectacle with thousands of extras—all played by a cast of just eight. It starred Kristin Chenoweth and Richard B. Shull. Unfortunately, Mr. Shull died during the play's run. He was replaced by Lewis J. Stadlen. The play ran for 84 performances.

On May 1, 2000, *Dirty Blonde,* a hit Off-Broadway play, moved here from the New York Theatre Workshop. The comedy dealt with the famed actress/playwright Mae West. It was written by Claudia Shear, who also starred in a dual role as Ms. West and one of her fans. The play was conceived by Ms. Shear and James Lapine, who directed it. Kevin Chamberlin and Bob Stillman co-starred in a variety of roles. The play proved an instant hit and was nominated for five Tony Awards.

CORT THEATRE

Rarely has a Broadway legitimate theatre opened with as resounding a hit as the Cort had on the night of December 20, 1912. The play was *Peg o' My Heart* by J. Hartley Manners and it starred his illustrious wife, Laurette Taylor. The incandescent actress scored a triumph. As critic Brooks Atkinson reported years later: "J. Hartley Manners wrote a part for Laurette Taylor in 1912 that made her the most generally worshipped star of her time. She opened the new Cort Theatre on Forty-eighth Street as Peg and played it for 607 performances—the longest run of any dramatic play up to that time."

The critics also had praise for the new playhouse, located east of Broadway. Built by John Cort, a West Coast theatre impresario who came East, it was designed by architect Edward B. Corey in the style of Louis XVI. It had a marble façade with four Corinthian columns, a lobby of Pavanozza marble with panels of Marie Antoinette plaster work, and an auditorium with a seating capacity of 999 (later augmented to 1,084). According to *The New York Tribune*, "A distinctive feature of the interior is the proscenium arch, which is of perforated plaster work against a background of art glass capable of illumination during the performance. The sounding board has been decorated with a painting of a minuet during the period made famous in Watteau's drawings of French court life at Versailles."

The article added that instead of an orchestra (most

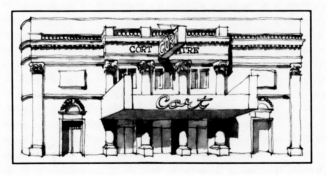

theatres had live orchestras to entertain the patrons) the Cort had a "Wurlitzer Hope-Jones unit orchestra, an electrical instrument capable of operation by one musician."

The Cort's luck continued with its next occupant, *Under Cover,* a play about an undercover customs agent, starring Harry Crosby, Ralph Morgan, and George Stevens. It opened in August 1914 and ran for 349 performances. In 1915 the Cort went musical with Victor Herbert's *The Princess Pat,* which had a hit tune: "Neapolitan Love Song." It ran for 158 performances.

Other successes during this period were a Chinese play called *The Yellow Jacket* (1916); *Flo-Flo* (1917), a musical with some vaudeville headliners; and John Drinkwater's masterly *Abraham Lincoln,* starring Frank McGlyn in the title role. It ran for 244 performances.

The Cort housed a wide variety of fare during the 1920s. A musical comedy called *Jim Jam Jems* featured an incredible collection of comics: Joe E. Brown, Frank Fay, Harry Langdon, Ned Sparks, and Mr. Jokes himself, Joe E. Miller. They provided solid yucks for 105 performances in 1920. The following year brought a farcical comedy, *Captain Applejack,* produced by the estimable Sam H. Harris, and it was funny enough to continue for 366 performances. Then, in 1922, came a classic American comedy: George S. Kaufman and Marc Connelly's *Merton of the Movies.* The critics were unanimous in their praise of this satire in which a shy, movie-crazy grocery

Above: A program cover for the Cort Theatre 1915. *Right:* The magnificent Laurette Taylor in the Cort's famed opening show, *Peg o' My Heart* (1912).

clerk, splendidly played by Glenn Hunter, went to Hollywood and became a success because he was such a terrible actor. It was on Burns Mantle's ten-best list and ran for 398 performances.

In contrast to *Merton of the Movies* was the genteel high comedy of Ferenc Molnar's *The Swan* (1923), starring the lovely Eva Le Gallienne as a princess sought by a prince (Philip Merivale) and a humble tutor (Basil Rathbone). The Hungarian romance charmed audiences for 253 performances.

After a number of failures in 1924, the Cort presented Ethel Barrymore, who was praised for her performance in a revival of Sir Arthur Wing Pinero's *The Second Mrs. Tanqueray,* staged by Arthur Hopkins. A comedy called *White Collars* with Cornelia Otis Skinner also found favor in 1925. Six shows followed, none of them successful, then came *The Jazz Singer*, starring George Jessel, which moved here from the Fulton Theatre and ran for 315 performances. This Samson Raphaelson play later became the first talking picture, starring Al Jolson.

A comedy called *The Little Spitfire* played for 201 performances in 1926. A strange drama came to the Cort later that year. It was called *The Ladder*, and before it had run its course (789 performances) it had played in five different Broadway theatres—including two engagements at the Cort. The play was about reincarnation and had Antoinette Perry and Ross Alexander in the cast. The critics called it hokum, and the producer, Brock Pemberton, sometimes let people in for nothing.

George Kelly's *Behold the Bridegroom* (1927), starring Judith Anderson, Mary Servoss, and Lester Vail, was admired, but lasted for only 88 performances. On November 12, 1928, a drama called *These Days* opened with a large cast of young girls playing rich young students in a finishing school. Among them was an actress making her Broadway debut—her name was Katharine Hepburn. The play ran for only 8 performances, but launched a spectacular career.

Alice Brady appeared at the Cort in *A Most Immoral Lady* in late 1928 and helped the play to run for 160 performances. The Cort's last show of the 1920s was *Your Uncle Dudley*, a homespun comedy by Howard Lindsay and Bertrand Robinson, starring Walter Connolly. It rang out the Roaring Twenties with 96 performances.

In April 1930 producer Jed Harris, known as the boy wonder, returned from London and produced and directed an acclaimed revival of Chekhov's *Uncle Vanya*, adapted by Mrs. Ben Hecht (Rose Caylor). Harris's direction and the acting of his sterling cast, Lillian Gish, Osgood Perkins, Walter Connolly, Eduardo Ciannelli Joanna Roos, and others, made the occasion a theatrical event.

The end of 1930 brought a taut, cynical expose of scandalmongering newspapers called *Five-Star Final*. It starred Arthur Byron, Frances Fuller, and Berton Churchill, and featured Allen Jenkins. Theatregoers supported it for 176 showings.

Two enterprising producers—Alfred de Liagre, Jr., and Richard Aldrich—brought a screwball family to the Cort in 1933 in a comedy called *Three-Cornered Moon*, making an auspicious producing debut. The excellent

Lillian Gish in the acclaimed Jed Harris production of *Uncle Vanya* (1930).

cast included Ruth Gordon, Richard Whorf, Brian Donlevy, and Cecilia Loftus.

Later in 1933 a sensational drama arrived from Britain. It was Mordaunt Shairp's *The Green Bay Tree* and it starred Laurence Olivier, James Dale, Jill Esmond (Mrs. Olivier at that time), O.P. Heggie, and Leo G. Carroll. Jed Harris's direction was highly praised for its subtlety in depicting a questionable relationship between a wealthy male hedonist and a poor, handsome young boy, played by Olivier.

From October 1935 to July 1938 the Cort had only two bookings, but they were both George Abbott smashes. The first one, the riotous *Boy Meets Girl*, by Bella and Samuel Spewack, was an hysterical spoof of Hollywood said to be inspired by the West Coast shenanigans of Ben Hecht and Charles MacArthur when they toiled there as scriptwriters. With Jerome Cowan and Allyn Joslyn as the madcap writers, Joyce Arling as an unwed mother,

Laurence Olivier and Jill Esmond in the British shocker *The Green Bay Tree* (1933).

and Abbott's famous "touch" in direction, *Boy Meets Girl* had Cort audiences in stitches for 669 performances.

On May 19, 1937, Abbott ushered in his production of another raucous farce, *Room Service*, by John P. Murray and Allen Boretz. With such expert farceurs as Sam Levene, Teddy Hart, Philip Loeb, Eddie Albert, and Betty Field, the comedy chronicled the plight of a group of hungry actors and some shoestring producers living in a seedy hotel while trying to get backing for the play they wish to put on. It was a Cort favorite for 500 performances, and later made into a film with the Marx Brothers.

The year 1939 witnessed memorable performances by Jessica Tandy and Barry Fitzgerald in Paul Vincent Carroll's *The White Steed*.

The 1940s brought exciting theatre to the Cort. Among the highlights: *The Male Animal* (1940), an intelligent comedy by James Thurber and Elliott Nugent,

starring Nugent, Gene Tierney, Ruth Matteson, and Don DeFore; a lively revival of *Charley's Aunt* (1940), staged by Joshua Logan, with José Ferrer and Mrs. Logan (Nedda Harrigan); the warmhearted *Café Crown* (1942), starring Sam Jaffe and Morris Carnovsky as leading actors of the Yiddish Theatre who gather each evening in a popular Second Avenue cafe; Maxwell Anderson's moving war drama *The Eve of St. Mark* (1942), with William Prince as a farm boy who goes to war and Aline MacMahon as his mother.

Next came *A Bell for Adano* (1944), Paul Osborn's faithful adaptation of John Hersey's novel about the American occupation of Italy at war's end, starring Fredric March as an army major; The Theatre Guild Shakespearean Company in *The Winter's Tale* (1946); Katharine Cornell and Cedric Hardwicke in Anouilh's version of *Antigone* (1946), alternating with Shaw's *Candida*, in which Marlon Brando played a rather prissy Marchbanks; Canada Lee in *On Whitman Avenue* (1946), a play about a black family moving into a white neighborhood; Cornelia Otis Skinner, Estelle Winwood, and Cecil Beaton in Wilde's *Lady Windermere's Fan* (1946-47), with sets, costumes, and lighting by Beaton; Meg Mundy's powerful performance in Sartre's *The Respectful Prostitute* (1948), which moved to the Cort from the New Stages Theatre on Bleecker Street; Melvyn Douglas and Jan Sterling in Sam Spewack's, political satire *Two Blind Mice* (1949); and a revival of Strindberg's *The Father* (1949), with Raymond Massey, Mady Christians, and, making her Broadway debut, Grace Kelly.

The Cort continued to house hits in the 1950s, beginning with Katharine Hepburn in an engaging revival of *As You Like It*, with William Prince as Orlando and Cloris Leachman as Celia. Wolcott Gibbs, drama critic for *The New Yorker*, came up with a hit comedy, *Season in the Sun*, about the (straight) denizens of Fire Island (1950). Uta Hagen drew praise for her Joan in Shaw's *Saint Joan* (1951). Joseph Kramm won a Pulitzer Prize for his harrowing drama *The Shrike* (1952), about a husband (José Ferrer) who is committed to a mental institution by his odious wife (Judith Evelyn).

The decade continued with Menasha Skulnik entertaining in a garment district spoof, *The Fifth Season* (1953). Geraldine Page, Albert Salmi, and Darren

Top: PLAYBILL covers for *The Male Animal* (1940), José Ferrer in *Charley's Aunt* (1940), and Wolcott Gibbs's comedy *Season in the Sun* (1950). *Above:* Katharine Hepburn and William Prince in the 1950 revival of *As You Like It.* *Left:* Grace Kelly, making her Broadway debut, with Mady Christians in *The Father* (1949).

McGavin enhanced *The Rainmaker* (1954). Frances Goodrich and Albert Hackett won a Pulitzer Prize, New York Drama Critics Circle Award, and Tony Award for

their moving play *The Diary of Anne Frank* (1955), starring Susan Strasberg as Anne, Joseph Schildkraut and Gusti Huber as her parents, and Lou Jacobi and Jack Gilford as other hideouts in the doomed Frank attic. Siobhan McKenna, Art Carney, and Joan Blondell scored in the tragic drama *The Rope Dancers* (1957); and *Sunrise*

Katharine Cornell in Anouilh's treatment of *Antigone* (1946).

at Campobello, Dore Schary's study of President Franklin Delano Roosevelt's early years, won four Tony Awards, including Best Play and Best Actor (Ralph Bellamy as Roosevelt) in 1958.

The 1960s brought Brendan Behan's rowdy play *The Hostage* (1960), with a cast largely drawn from Joan Littlewood's Theatre Workshop in London. Next came a dramatization of Allen Drury's popular political novel *Advise and Consent,* with a cast that included Richard Kiley, Ed Begley, Kevin McCarthy, and Barnard Hughes. It lasted for 212 performances. This was followed by the engaging *Purlie Victorious,* written by and starring Ossie Davis, with Ruby Dee, Alan Alda, and Godfrey Cambridge. In November 1961 a young Robert Redford held forth on the Cort stage in Norman Krasna's thin comedy *Sunday in New York,* produced by David Merrick, directed by Garson Kanin—and not very successful.

From mid-1962 until mid-1969 the Cort booked many shows, but few successes. Some of the more interesting exhibits were a brief visit by the Royal Dramatic

Theatre of Sweden acting in *The Father, Long Day's Journey into Night,* and *Miss Julie* (1962); Kirk Douglas in an unsuccessful adaptation of *One Flew Over the Cuckoo's Nest* (1963), which later proved a major hit Off-Broadway; and Louis Gossett and Menasha Skulnik in *The Zulu and the Zayda* (1965).

The marquee of the Cort can be seen momentarily in the classic film spoof of Broadway, *The Producers* (1968), which was shot at the since-demolished Playhouse Theatre directly across Forty-eighth Street.

In 1969, the Cort was leased to television for several years and served as the theatre from which "The Merv Griffin Show" emanated for a time.

On May 28, 1974, the Cort made a dazzling comeback. Owned for many years by the Shubert Organization, the theatre was beautifully restored for its return to the legitimate fold. It reopened with *The Magic Show,* a musical that would have died on its opening night if it had not had Doug Henning in the lead. Mr. Henning, one of the world's best and most amiable magicians, created such incredible magic on the Cort's stage that the show ran for 1,920 performances.

Al Pacino starred in a disastrous Brooklynese version of Shakespeare's *Richard III* (1979), and Tennessee Williams suffered critical arrows for his play about F. Scott and Zelda Fitzgerald, *Clothes for a Summer Hotel* (1980). An engaging black-themed play, *Home,* won favor that spring; and Glenda Jackson and Jessica Tandy acted grandly in the unsuccessful British play *Rose* (1981). In 1982 there was an engrossing revival of *Medea* starring Zoe Caldwell, whose passionate performance won her a Tony Award, and Judith Anderson, who put her stamp on the title role in 1947, playing the Nurse this time.

In 1983, Murray Schisgal's *Twice Around the Park,* two one-act plays, starred Eli Wallach and Anne Jackson, which was followed by August Wilson's first Broadway drama, *Ma Rainey's Black Bottom* (1984); a revival of O'Neill's *A Moon for the Misbegotten* (1984) starred Kate Nelligan and Ian Bannen.

Sarafina! (1988), the South African drama with music, played here for over a year. The Steppenwolf Theatre's production of John Steinbeck's classic *The Grapes of Wrath* won a Tony Award as the season's Best Play (1990). *Two Shakespearean Actors* by Richard Nelson

starred Victor Garber as Edwin Forrest and Brian Bedford as William Charles Macready, master thespians whose bitter rivalry caused the tragic Astor Place riots in 1847 in which 22 people were killed and 36 wounded. The play was presented by the Lincoln Center Theater in 1992, but it ran for only 29 performances.

On April 17, 1994, *Twilight: Los Angeles, 1992,* a new play conceived, written and performed by the remarkable Anna Deavere Smith (who played more than 40 characters with amazing skill) moved here from the New York Shakespeare Festival. Ms. Smith received a Tony nomination for her dazzling work embodying the people in and around a Los Angeles race riot.

In March 1995, Lincoln Center Theater presented a prestigious revival of *The Heiress,* the 1947 play by Ruth and Augustus Goetz, based on Henry James novel, *Washington Square.* The play received seven Tony Award nominations and won the following: Best Revival of a Play, Best Director of a Play (Gerald Gutierrez), Best Actress in a Play (Cherry Jones), and Best Featured Actress in a Play (Frances Sternhagen). It ran for 340 performances.

Lincoln Center Theater booked the Cort for new plays by two major playwrights, Christopher Durang and Wendy Wasserstein, in the 1996-97 season. They got very different responses. Mr. Durang's vulgar 1996 comedy, *Sex and Longing* repelled 13 critics (and audiences), and lasted only 45 performances. The cast included

Top left: Caricatures of José Ferrer and Judith Evelyn in *The Shrike* (1952). *Top Right:* Ralph Bellamy as FDR in *Sunrise at Campobello* (1958). *Above:* Susan Strasberg and Joseph Schildkraut in *The Diary of Anne Frank* (1955).

Left: Zöe Caldwell and Dame Judith Anderson in the 1982 revival of *Medea. Right:* The company in the spectacular fantasy, *The Green Bird* (2000). Photo by Joan Marcus.

Sigourney Weaver, Dana Ivey, and Peter Michael Goetz. Ms. Wasserstein's 1997 play, *An American Daughter,* garnered three favorable reviews, three mixed and four negative. It starred Kate Nelligan, Hal Holbrook, Peter Riegert, and Lynne Thigpen, the latter of whom won a Tony Award as Best Featured Actress in a Play. Ms. Nelligan played a candidate for U.S. Attorney General whose appointment runs into political trouble. The play ran for 88 performances.

John Leguizamo brought his amusing one-man show (which he wrote and starred in) to the Cort in 1998. He called it *Freak* and he outrageously spoofed his racy upbringing. Both his play and performance were nominated for Tonys and he entertained audiences for 145 performances. Late that same year, there was much publicity about the nude appearance of Nicole Kidman in David Hare's play *The Blue Room* freely adapted from Arthur Schnitzler's *La Ronde.* The two-character play, co-starring Ms. Kidman and Iain Glen, was a huge financial success (although Ms. Kidman was bare only briefly) but it was not a critical success. It ran for 81 performances.

On August 19, 1999, an entertainment called *Kat and the Kings* brought an exuberant vocal/dancing group from South Africa (via London) in a musical about the rise and fall of a doo-wop group in 1950s Capetown. The critics were impressed by the youthful cast's energy, but found the show's book weak. However, audiences were enthusiastic enough to attend the show for 157 performances.

On April 18, 2000, *The Lion King* director Julie Taymor returned to Broadway with *The Green Bird,* a spectacular satirical fable, featuring music by Elliot Goldenthal and a translation by Albert Bermel and Ted Emery from an Italian tale by Carlo Gozzi. Ms. Taymor directed the show and designed its masks and puppet designs, as she had done for *The Lion King.* The production originated with Theatre for a New Audience in 1996 at the New Victory Theatre on Forty-second Street. This production had sets by Christine Jones, costumes by Constance Hoffman and lighting by Donald Holder. Ms. Hoffman was nominated for a Tony Award for her dazzling costumes and Derek Smith for Best Featured Actor in a Play. The critics were more enchanted by the fable's visual splendors than with the play's foolish Venetian tale. The show closed after 55 performances.

PALACE THEATRE

"Playing the Palace"—it was the dream of every vaudeville performer. In its heyday, from 1913 until the 1930s, the "mecca of migrating minstrels" at Forty-seventh Street and Times Square booked everyone who was anyone—from Sarah Bernhardt to Trixie Friganza and her bag of Trix, from Ethel Barrymore to Dr. Rockwell ("Quack! Quack! Quack!").

The Palace was the dream house of impresario Martin Beck, but by the time it opened, he held only 25 percent interest in the theatre. By complex wheeling and dealing, vaudeville circuit mogul B.F. Keith and E.F. Albee (playwright Edward Albee's adoptive grandfather) stormed the Palace and gained control.

In her book *The Palace,* Marian Spitzer describes the opening of the theatre on Easter Monday, March 24, 1913: "The theatre itself, living up to advance publicity, was spacious, handsome and lavishly decorated in crimson and gold. But nothing happened that afternoon to suggest the birth of a great theatrical tradition."

On the Palace's opening vaudeville bill, presented twice daily with a $1.50 top at matinees and $2.00 at night, were such acts as Ota Gygi ("the court violinist of Spain"), McIntyre and Harty ("a comedy team"), La Napierkowska ("pantomimist and interpretive dancer"), *The Eternal Walk* ("a condensed Viennese operetta with a cast of 30"), and Ed Wynn ("The King's Jester"). It was the hope of the Palace Theatre management to give competition to its chief

rival, Oscar Hammerstein's Victoria Theatre at Broadway and Forty-second Street, but it did not achieve this goal during its opening week. The show was negatively received especially by *Variety,* the show business Bible, which lamented the poor quality of the acts and the outrageous $2.00 top.

It took the prestige of two major legitimate theatre actresses to put the Palace on the map. In its sixth week, the theatre presented the First Lady of the American Theatre—Ethel Barrymore—in a one-act play by Richard Harding Davis, *Miss Civilization,* and business began to improve. But the turning point came on May 5, when the Divine Sarah Bernhardt brought her French company of actors and her repertoire to the Palace and caused a sensation for almost a month. It was her first appearance in vaudeville in New York. She saved the Palace from disaster and helped turn it into the foremost vaudeville theatre in the world.

In the golden era of vaudeville, the Palace stage saw the likes of such great headliners as Harry Houdini, Will Rogers, W.C. Fields, Fanny Brice, Sophie Tucker, Ethel Merman, William Gaxton, Eddie Cantor, Jack Benny, Milton Berle, Smith and Dale, the Marx Brothers, Kate Smith, and countless others. Burns and Allen arrived with a new act every season. And then there were other acts like Fink's Mules and Power's Elephants.

The Palace was the queen of Broadway in 1927 when a talking picture called *The Jazz Singer* opened a few

Top Left: Palace program cover for week of May 8, 1922. *Top Right:* Program for Ethel Barrymore's appearance in 1923. *Below:* The Palace as it looked in 1942.

Left: Portrait of Judy Garland on the cover of the program for her 1951 concert. *Right:* Palace engagement; program sketch of Danny Kaye for his smash appearance in 1953.

blocks uptown. Once the silver screen began to talk, vaudeville was on its way out.

From the 1930s on, it was a constant struggle for survival. The Palace tried a little of everything—combination bills of movies and vaudeville shows, then just movies, and finally, in the 1950s, personal appearances by select superstars. The first arrived on the night of October 16, 1951, and her name was Judy Garland. She scored a triumph and played the Palace for nineteen weeks. Next came Betty Hutton, then Danny Kaye (fourteen weeks), followed by return engagements of Betty Hutton and Judy Garland. Jerry Lewis was a hit with his personal appearance show, but Liberace failed to draw crowds.

On August 13, 1957, the Palace reverted to showing movies, with no vaudeville, and interrupted this policy only once, starting December 15, 1959, when Harry Belafonte made a sensational appearance for more than three months.

On August 19, 1965, a miracle happened. James Nederlander, acting for the Nederlander family, who owned legitimate theatres in Detroit and Chicago, bought the Palace. At great expense, he had it beautifully restored to its original crimson and gold. Crystal chandeliers were removed from storage and rehung in the theatre, stage boxes that had been concealed for decades by false fronts were restored, and the lobby was refurbished and embellished with portraits of Palace greats, loaned by the Museum of the City of New York. The restoration of the Palace was achieved by the famed scene designer Ralph Alswang. When he and his workers were through, the Palace was ready for its first legitimate show.

The reopening of the Palace as a legitimate theatre on January 29, 1966, was a major news event and was covered by television cameras and the print media. Fortunately, the opening show was *Sweet Charity,* starring the great Gwen Verdon. Both the musical and the restored Palace were huge hits. With a book by Neil Simon, a jaunty score by Cy Coleman and Dorothy Fields, and spectacular choreography by Ms. Verdon's husband, Bob Fosse, the musical, based on Fellini's film *Nights of Cabiria,* brightened the Messrs. Nederlander's Palace for 608 performances.

In July 1967 Judy Garland returned in a production

Left to Right: Joel Grey as song-and-dance man George M. Cohan in the musical *George M!* (1968); Gwen Verdon in her hit *Sweet Charity*, which made the Palace "legitimate" (1966); Lauren Bacall played a Tony Award recipient in *Applause* (1970).

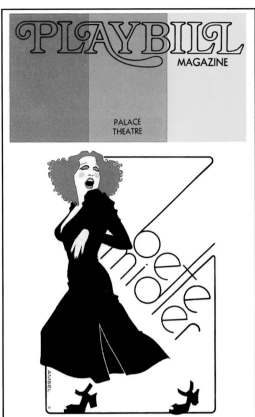

Left: PLAYBILL covers for Christopher Plummer in the musical *Cyrano* (1973) and Bette Midler in concert (1973).

called *At Home at the Palace,* followed later that summer by a double bill of Eddie Fisher and Buddy Hackett.

Don Ameche and Carol Bruce, aided by three talented young girls—Alice Playten, Neva Small, and Robin Wilson—were engaging in a musical called *Henry, Sweet Henry* (1967), but the show lasted only 80 performances. The Grand Music Hall of Israel paid a visit in the early months of 1968. Then, on April 10, *George M!* took over. It is ironic that George M. Cohan was one of the few headliners who never played the Palace. (Al Jolson was another.) But Cohan was skillfully impersonated by Joel Grey in *George M!* He strutted the Palace stage for 433 performances.

Lauren Bacall gave such a cyclonic performance in *Applause* (1970), her first Broadway musical, that she was awarded a Tony for her tour de force. The musical, with a book by Betty Comden and Adolph Green and a score by Charles Strouse and Lee Adams, was based on the celebrated Bette Davis film *All About Eve.* Supported by Len Cariou, Bonnie Franklin, Penny Fuller, and Lee Roy

Reams, Bacall flourished at the Palace for eighteen months, and the show continued for eight months more.

During the 1970s, superstars such as Bette Midler, Josephine Baker, Shirley MacLaine, and Diana Ross made splashy Palace appearances. Legitimate attractions included Christopher Plummer in his Tony Award winning performance in the title role of the musical *Cyrano* (1973); Carol Channing in a revised version of *Gentlemen Prefer Blondes,* called *Lorelei* (1974); Richard Kiley in a return engagement of *Man of La Mancha* (1977); Joel Grey in *The Grand Tour* (1979), a musical version of *Jacobowsky and the Colonel;* a lively revival of *Oklahoma!* (1979); and a colossal production of *Frankenstein* (1981), starring John Carradine, that closed on its opening night.

Lauren Bacall returned to the Palace in *Woman of the Year,* a musical version of the popular 1942 film of the same name starring Spencer Tracy and Katharine Hepburn. Bacall's co-star in the musical was Harry Guardino. The show won four Tonys: Outstanding

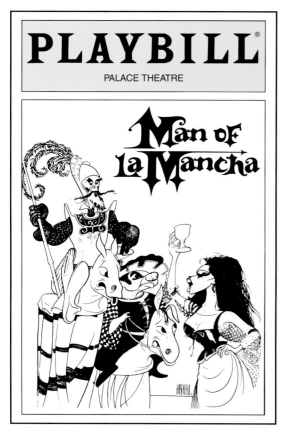

PLAYBILL covers for the 1977 revival of *Man of La Mancha* and the huge success *La Cage aux Folles* (1983).

Actress in a Musical (Bacall), Outstanding Featured Actress in a Musical (Marilyn Cooper), Best Musical Book (Peter Stone), and Best Musical Score (John Kander and Fred Ebb).

On August 21, 1983, the Palace welcomed *La Cage aux Folles*, with a score by Jerry Herman and a book by Harvey Fierstein. A musical version of the popular French film of the same name, it starred George Hearn and Gene Barry as gay lovers, and ran for 1,761 performances. It won the following Tony Awards: Best Musical, Best Score, Best Book, Best Direction of a Musical (Arthur Laurents), Best Actor in a Musical (Hearn), and Best Costume Designer (Theoni V. Aldredge).

After being closed for four years for extensive renovations, this historic theatre was beautifully restored for the opening of the Tony Award-winning musical *The Will Rogers Follies,* starring Keith Carradine as the Hoosier Philosopher and featuring Tony-winning staging by Tommy Tune; a Tony-winning score by Coleman, Comden and Green; and a Tony Award-winning book by Peter Stone. The show used the format of the *Ziegfeld Follies* (Ziegfeld himself was a character) to tell the story of Rogers's marriage, career, and dramatic demise in a plane crash. The musical ran for 983 performances.

This was followed by the spectacular musical *Beauty and the Beast* (1994), which broke box office records at this theatre and introduced children of all ages to the wonders of live Broadway entertainment. Adapted from the animated Disney film of the same title, the show marked composer Alan Menken's Broadway debut, and the inaugural presentation of Walt Disney Theatrical Productions, soon to become a powerhouse producer on Broadway. The show transferred in 1999 to the Lunt-Fontanne Theatre.

From December 1, 1999 to January 2, 2000, Liza Minnelli returned to the scene of her mother, Judy Garland's, triumph. However, her show, *Minnelli On*

Minnelli, paid tribute to her father, Vincente Minnelli, the celebrated Broadway and Hollywood director. Supported by six male singer/dancers, Ms. Minnelli performed memorable songs from her father's famed film musicals—*Meet Me In St. Louis, An American in Paris, The Bandwagon, Gigi,* and others. The revue was directed by her friend, the lyricist Fred Ebb, and had costumes by Bob Mackie and musical arrangements by Marvin Hamlisch.

On March 23, 2000, Hyperion Theatricals (a division of Walt Disney Theatrical Productions) presented a lavish new musical, *Aida,* with music by Elton John and lyrics by Tim Rice. Suggested by Verdi's classic opera about a fatal love triangle involving two princesses and a handsome army general in ancient Egypt, the spectacle starred Heather Headley, Adam Pascal, Sherie René Scott, John Hickok, Damian Perkins, Tyrees Allen and

Above: Susan Egan, as Belle, begins to tame the Beast (Terrence Mann) in *Beauty and the Beast.* Photo by Joan Marcus. *Below:* PLAYBILL covers for *The Will Rogers Follies* (1992) and *Beauty and the Beast* (1994).

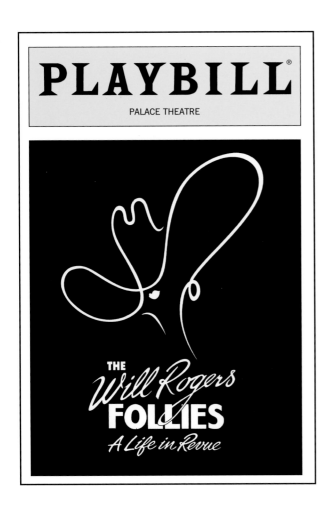

Left: Adam Pascal and Heather Headley (Tony Award) in *Aida* (2000). Photo by Joan Marcus. *Right:* Special PLAYBILL cover for George Abbott's centennial celebration in June 1987.

Daniel Oreskes. The musical received five Tony Award nominations and won the following four: Best Original Score (Elton John, Tim Rice); Best Scenic Design (Bob Crowley); Best Lighting Design (Natasha Katz); Best Leading Actress in a Musical (Headley). It quickly settled in for a long run.

LONGACRE THEATRE

A colorful character named H.H. Frazee built the Longacre Theatre at 220 West Forty-eighth Street, between Broadway and Eighth Avenue. It was named after nearby Longacre Square, the crossroads long since rechristened as Times Square. Frazee hired architect Henry Herts to create a theatre that would specialize in the staging of musical comedies. Herts, who designed some of Broadway's finest theatres, turned out a lovely playhouse that managed to look intimate while having two balconies and seating more than 1,400 patrons (currently reduced to 1,096).

The Longacre opened on the night of May 1, 1913, with an unfunny farce called *Are You a Crook?*, starring Marguerite Clark. It perished after a dozen showings. Frazee did much better with a musical show. On August 28 of that year, his theatre housed a French entertainment called *Adele* and it was the most successful import of the season. It delighted theatregoers for 196 performances.

A.H. Woods, a producer who thrived on melodramas, presented a play called *Kick In* in 1914. The interesting cast included John Barrymore, Katherine Harris (who became the first Mrs. Barrymore), Jane Gray, and Forrest Winant. The "crook" melodrama stole its way into playgoers' hearts for 188 performances. That year a farce called *A Pair of Sixes* also won favor and ran for 207 mirthful performances.

A number of shows played in 1915, including Lewis Stone in *Inside the Lines*, and May Vokes in *A Full House*.

But the most successful was a comedy called *The Great Lover*, starring Leo Ditrichstein, which focused on love among the egocentric temperaments of the opera world.

The Longacre welcomed its biggest hit to that date when *Nothing but the Truth* opened on September 14, 1916. Written by James Montgomery, the comedy starred the deadpan William Collier, who convulsed audiences as a man who vowed not to tell lies for one day. He managed to do this for 332 performances.

The kind of intimate, charming musical that Frazee envisioned for his house came to the Longacre in 1917. It was the Jerome Kern/ P.G. Wodehouse/Guy Bolton winner *Leave It to Jane*, about a football-crazy college campus. Among the Kern gems were: "The Siren's Song," "The Crickets Are Calling," "Cleopatterer," and the lilting title song. The Longacre had full houses for 167 performances.

Guy Bolton and George Middleton provided a palpable hit for the house with *Adam and Eva*, starring Otto Kruger and Ruth Shepley, in 1919.

Some highlights of the 1920s included a musical called *Pitter Patter* (1920), starring William Kent; *The Champion* (1920), with Grant Mitchell; and *Little Jesse James* (1923), an intimate musical with only one set, eight chorus girls, a modest cast that included future movie star Miriam Hopkins, one hit song—"I Love You"—and a smash run of 385 performances. This was followed by *Moonlight* (1924), another intimate musical

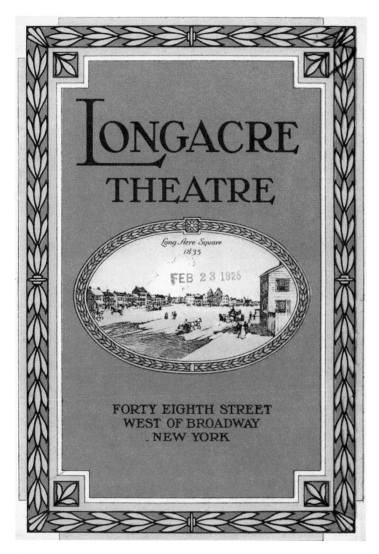

Above: Standard Longacre program cover in the 1920s. *Top Right:* The Longacre's first show, *Are You A Crook?,* with Marguerite Clark and Elizabeth Nelson (1913). *Right:* Dudley Diggs, Peter Holden, and Dorothy Stickney in *On Borrowed Time* (1938).

with tuneful Con Conrad music; *The Dark Angel* (1925), a poignant drama about a woman whose lover returns blind from World War I and pretends that he is dead; *Mercenary Mary* (1925), another Con Conrad musical with a jazz band and a star-and-garter chorus; George S. Kaufman's *The Butter and Egg Man* (1925), a hit "inside" comedy about a hick (memorably played by Gregory Kelly) who comes to Broadway with $20,000 to invest in a show and, after many tribulations, succeeds; a thrilling adaptation of Theodore Dreiser's novel *An American Tragedy* (1926), starring Morgan Farley as the murderer, Katherine Wilson as his victim, and Miriam Hopkins as his rich girlfriend; *The Command to Love* (1927), a surprisingly delightful German high comedy starring Basil Rathbone, Mary Nash, Violet Kemble Cooper, and Anthony Kemble Cooper that lasted for 236 performances; Richard Bennett and his attractive daughter Joan

The Group Theatre's stirring production of Clifford Odets's *Waiting for Lefty* (1935).

in a shocker about Hollywood low life called *Jarnegan* (1928); Clark Gable in an interesting murder mystery, *Hawk Island* (1929), that only ran for three weeks; and the final play of the 1920s, *A Primer for Lovers,* a sex farce with the delightful Alison Skipworth.

After a series of unsuccessful plays in 1930 and 1931, the Longacre finally had a hit in *Blessed Event* (1932), starring Roger Pryor in a thinly disguised impersonation of the egotistical Broadway columnist Walter Winchell, with Isabel Jewell and Allen Jenkins in support. A dramatization of the infamous Lizzie Borden ax murders, *Nine Pine Street*, had a fine performance by Lillian Gish as the neurotic killer, but it only ran a few weeks in 1933. The same fate was accorded *Wednesday's Child* (1934), a study of a young boy (Frank M. Thomas, Jr.) whose life is ruined when his parents divorce.

During the height of the Depression, the Longacre was dark for months on end. Most of the shows that played there were quick flops. A bright spot in 1935, however, was the arrival of the revolutionary Group Theatre company with two of Clifford Odets's inflammatory plays, *Waiting for Lefty* and *Till the Day I Die*. Mr. Odets appeared in *Waiting for Lefty,* and both plays had such Group stalwarts as Elia Kazan, Lee J. Cobb, Roman Bohnen, Russell Collins, and Alexander Kirkland. Later in 1935 another Odets play, *Paradise Lost,* with many of

the same actors, played the theatre.

Late in 1936 the great actress Nazimova played Ibsen's *Hedda Gabler* for a month; and Vincent Price and the beautiful Elissa Landi starred in a romantic Hungarian play about royal affairs, *The Lady Has a Heart* (1937).

Things took a better turn on February 3, 1938, when an enchanting play came to the Longacre: Paul Osborn's loving adaptation of a novel called *On Borrowed Time.* Said Brooks Atkinson in the Times: "Nothing so original and jovial has turned up on our stages for a long time." The fantasy concerned a grandfather (Dudley Digges) who chases Death (called Mr. Brink) up a tree so that he can have some more time to spend with his lovable grandson (Peter Holden). Grandma was played by Dorothy Stickney. Directed by Joshua Logan, the play brought bittersweet magic to the Longacre for 321 performances.

In late 1939 Paul Osborn returned to this theatre with another endearing play about small-town people—*Morning's at Seven.* Despite Joshua Logan's direction and a superb cast that included Dorothy Gish, Russell Collins, Enid Markey, Effie Shannon, and Jean Adair, this gentle comedy about life among the elderly lasted only 44 performances. It was clearly ahead of its time. When it was revived on Broadway in 1980, it ran for 564 performances, was hailed as an American classic, and

Jo Mielziner's enchanting setting for Paul Osborn's *Morning's at Seven* (1939).

won a Tony Award as the season's best revival.

The critics may have turned up their noses at a comedy called *Three's a Family* (1943), but audiences loved this play about the raising of babies and the care of expectant mothers. It was perfect escapist comedy for World War II theatregoers and it amused them for close to 500 performances. It was to be the Longacre's last legitimate show for a decade. From the spring of 1944 to the fall of 1953 the theatre was leased as a radio and television studio.

In November 1953 the Longacre reopened as a legitimate theatre with a promising play, *The Ladies of the Corridor*, by Dorothy Parker and Arnaud d'Usseau. Harold Clurman directed a cast that featured Edna Best, Betty Field, June Walker, Walter Matthau, and Shepperd Strudwick. Unfortunately, its depressing plot about lonely old women who live in hotels did not find a public.

The Longacre's best plays in the 1950s were Lillian Hellman's adaptation of Jean Anouilh's *The Lark* (1955), with Julie Harris as a radiant Saint Joan, also starring Boris Karloff and Christopher Plummer; and a silken comedy of manners, *The Pleasure of His Company* (1958), by Samuel Taylor, starring Cornelia Otis Skinner, Walter Abel, Cyril Ritchard, George Peppard, Charlie Ruggles, and Dolores Hart. In between these two hits there was an amiable comedy about the Seventh Avenue garment district, *Fair Game* (1957), starring the expert comic Sam

Levene and a new actress named Ellen McRae, who later changed her name to Ellen Burstyn and became a star.

In 1961 Zero Mostel's powerful performance in *Rhinoceros,* the antic play by Ionesco, won him a Tony Award. The excellent cast also included Eli Wallach, Anne Jackson, Morris Carnovsky, and Jean Stapleton. At the end of the year the popular *Purlie Victorious* moved to the Longacre from the Cort and stayed for six months.

Highlights of the 1960s included Henry Denker's courtroom drama A *Case of Libel* (1963), based on Quentin Reynolds's suit against Westbrook Pegler and starring Van Heflin, Sidney Blackmer, and Larry Gates; Gabriel Dell and Rita Moreno in Lorraine Hansberry's *The Sign in Sidney Brustein's Window* (1964); Margaret Leighton, Zoe Caldwell, and Kate Reid in Tennessee Williams's lunatic *Slapstick Tragedy* (1966); Hal Holbrook in his dazzling one-man show *Mark Twain Tonight* (1966); Holbrook again in Robert Anderson's somber autobiographical drama *I Never Sang for My Father* (1968), also starring Teresa Wright (then Mrs. Robert Anderson) and Lillian Gish; and a visit by the National Theatre of the Deaf (1969).

It was during this period that William Goldman, in his landmark 1969 survey of Broadway, *The Season,* used the Longacre as an example of a "bad" theatre—i.e. one avoided by producers for a variety of reasons. Goldman took readers through the "doublethink" and circular logic of producers who refused to put likely hits into the Longacre, leading to few hits opening there, in turn reinforcing the notion that no hits open there.

Breaking the cycle in 1975 was a rollicking hit, *The Ritz*, by Terrence McNally, with Rita Moreno and Jack Weston, which caused hysterics for a year, followed by a Tony Award winning performance by Julie Harris in her one-woman show *The Belle of Amherst*, in which she impersonated the poet Emily Dickinson. John Gielgud and Ralph Richardson were hypnotic in Pinter's *No Man's Land* (1976); Al Pacino garnered raves in a revival of David Rabe's *The Basic Training of Pavlo Hummel* (1977).

On May 9, 1978, *Ain't Misbehavin'* moved in and proved to be this theatre's biggest hit, eventually running 1,604 performances. This revue of Thomas "Fats" Waller's music was named Best Musical of the season by the Tony Awards, the New York Drama Critics Circle Awards, Drama Desk Awards, and Outer Critics Circle Awards. The brilliant performers were Ken Page, Nell Carter, Charlayne Woodard, Andre De Shields, Armelia McQueen, and pianist Luther Henderson. Director Richard Maltby, Jr. won a Tony.

The Longacre's longest-running non-musical, *Children of a Lesser God,* came to the theatre from the Mark Taper Forum in Los Angeles in 1980. A sensitive study of a woman with impaired speech and hearing, it won Tony Awards for Best Play (by Mark Medoff) and Outstanding Performances by a Lead Actress (Phyllis Frelich) and Actor (John Rubinstein). It ran for 887 performances.

The 1980s saw Lanford Wilson's fascinating *Angels Fall* (1983), followed by Peter Nichols's British play *Passion,* starring Frank Langella, Cathryn Damon, Bob Gunton, E. Katherine Kerr, Roxanne Hart, and Stephanie Gordon. The decade continued with *Play Memory* (1984); the musical *Harrigan 'n Hart* (1985); a splendid revival of *Joe Egg* starring Jim Dale and Stockard Channing, for which Ms. Channing won a Tony Award (1985); *Precious Sons*, George Furth's play starring Ed Harris and Judith Ivey (1986); the hilarious *Musical Comedy Murders of 1940* transferred here from Off-Broadway (1987); *Don't Get God Started*, a gospel musical (1987); *Hizzoner*, a solo show about New York Mayor

Sam Jaffe and Julie Harris in Lillian Hellman's adaptation of Anouilh's *The Lark* (1955).

Fiorello H. LaGuardia, transferred here from Off-Broadway (1989); *Truly Blessed* (1990), a musical celebration of Mahalia Jackson; and the dance musical *Tango Pasión* (1993).

That same year *Any Given Day,* a play by Frank D. Gilroy starring Sada Thompson, lasted only 32 performances. In 1994, Diana Rigg scored a personal triumph in a new adaptation of the classic *Medea* and won a Tony Award for her performance. The following year, Avery Brooks starred in the title role of *Paul Robeson*, a revival of Philip Hayes Dean's 1978 play with music about the life of the controversial actor/singer. The play included songs made famous by Mr. Robeson, including "Old Man River." Ernie Scott played Lawrence Brown. The play had a short run of 11 performances. Another revival came to the Longacre in 1996: Horton Foote's 1995 Off-Off-Broadway play, *The Young Man From Atlanta,* which had won the Pulitzer Prize. Rip Torn and Shirley Knight starred in the Broadway production which ran for 79 performances.

A revised version of David Henry Hwang's play *Golden Child,* opened in 1998, directed by James Lapine. The story of a Chinese man who must choose which of his three wives to keep when he embraces Christianity, *Golden Child* received the following Tony Award nominations: Featured Actress in a Play (Julyana Soelistyo), Best Play, and Costume Designer (Martin Pakledinaz). The play ran for 69 performances.

In April, 1999, *The Gershwin's Fascinating Rhythm,* a revue with ten singers and dancers, presented 27 songs by the Gershwin brothers in 90 minutes, without an intermission. Most of the critics loathed it, objecting to the incongruous musical arrangements and the vulgarity of some of the staging. The show was gone after 17 performances.

In August, 1999, a thriller called *Voices in the Dark* by John Pielmeier opened here. It starred Judith Ivey as a popular radio talk show host who finds herself menaced by a sinister caller. The suspense play won the Edgar Award (Best Play) from the Mystery Writers of America, but New York's drama critics were less kind. Critic John Simon called it worthless garbage and reported that the cottage set's walls displayed enough antlered heads to staff a revival of *Moose Murders* (see Eugene O'Neill Theatre).

The Longacre booked a promising play in March, 2000: Elaine May's comedy *Taller Than A Dwarf* with Matthew Broderick, Parker Posey, Joyce Van Patten, and others, directed by Alan Arkin. Unfortunately this power team was defeated by a script that was called tasteless, unfunny, and derivative. It had a short run.

Above: Armelia McQueen. Nell Carter. and Charlayne Woodard in *Ain't Misbehavin'* (1978). *Below:* John Rubinstein and Phyllis Frelich in *Children of a Lesser God* (1980).

SHUBERT THEATRE

The Shubert Theatre occupies a special niche in theatrical history. It was built by the Shubert brothers (Lee and J.J.) in tribute to their brother Sam S. Shubert, who got them started in the theatrical business before he died in a railroad accident when he was just twenty-nine years old.

Occupying a choice location in the heart of the theatre district, on West Forty-fourth Street between Broadway and Eighth Avenue, the Shubert Theatre opened on October 2, 1913. It was enhanced by an alleyway that separated it from the Hotel Astor and served as a private thoroughfare for the Shuberts. But because it also provided a shortcut to Forty-fifth Street for Broadway crowds, the passage later became famous as Shubert Alley. It was notable for being lined with posters of current Broadway shows, and by Shubert limousines parked between its gates, which were locked at night.

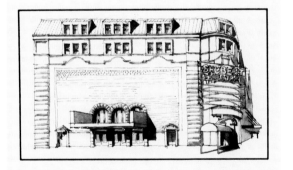

During the Depression years, a fence divided the alley in two. One side was used as the terminal for a New Jersey bus line; the other half served as the alley where the Shubert and Booth theatres had their stage doors. To improve the view, show posters were hung on the fence. This happy tradition soon became a fixture of Shubert Alley, and remained even after the bus terminal was removed and the fence came down. Room for the posters was provided on the common side wall of the Shubert and Booth. During intermissions, the casts of shows playing at these two theatres would congregate in that part of Shubert Alley for fresh air (theatres were not air conditioned yet), and the audiences could see them buying popsicles and soda pop.

Above the auditorium were the offices of the Shubert empire and an apartment where Lee Shubert lived. According to the *New York Tribune* for September 28, 1913, the new theatre had 1,400 seats, making it ideal for housing musicals. (The total has since been increased to 1,521.) The architect was Henry B. Harris, and the elaborate interiors, in a Venetian Renaissance style, were by O.H. Bauer, with mural paintings by Lichtenauer. A portrait of Sam S. Shubert adorned the attractive lobby, overseeing the new house.

The opening attraction, surprisingly, was not a Shubert operetta nor musical but the eminent British actor Johnston Forbes-Robertson in his farewell performance as Hamlet. He and his company also acted in other Shakespearean plays.

The Shubert's first musical, *The Belle of Bond Street,* opened on March 18, 1914, starring the stunning Gaby Deslys and the popular Sam Bernard. But it was not a success. Several other musical failures followed. Then there was a well-received revival of George Du Maurier's haunting play *Trilby* (1915), about the hypnotic influence of the sinister Svengali over the singer Trilby O'Farrell. Even the acerbic critic Alexander Woollcott, who had been barred from Shubert theatres for panning a Shubert show called *Taking Chances*, praised *Trilby*.

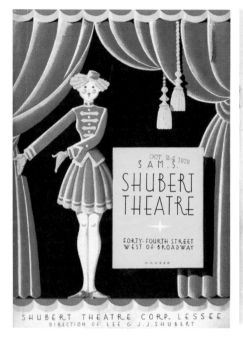

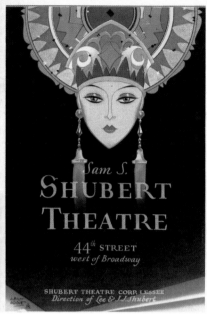

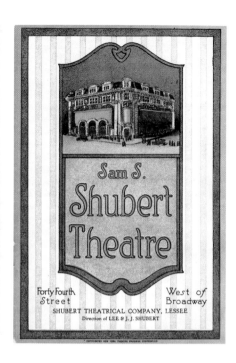

Top: (From left): Shubert program covers for 1927, 1928, 1929. *Left:* Lionel Barrymore in the stirring Civil War drama *The Copperhead* (1918). *Above:* Peggy Wood in the beloved Sigmund Romberg operetta *Maytime* (1917).

The Shubert's first musical success was *Alone at Last* (1915), a Franz Lehar show starring John Charles Thomas. Jerome Kern had a hit in *Love O' Mike* (1917), with Clifton Webb dancing suavely with Gloria Goodwin. But both these shows were topped by Sigmund Romberg's lushly romantic operetta *Maytime*, which was so successful that the Shuberts had to open a second company of it right across the street from the Shubert Theatre at the (now vanished) Forty-fourth Street Theatre. The stars at the Shubert were Peggy Wood, Charles Purcell, and Douglas J. Ward, who sang their hearts out for almost 500 performances (1917).

On February 18, 1918, Lionel Barrymore scored one of his greatest successes in *The Copperhead*, a Civil War drama in which Barrymore had to pretend to be a Dixie sympathizer while supplying military secrets to the Yanks. Despised by his family and friends, he could not reveal his true sympathies until twenty years later.

On October 4, 1918, Mae West and Ed Wynn convulsed Shubert audiences in Rudolf Friml's musical *Sometime*. Mae played a vamp who compromised Ed Wynn and caused his fiancée (Francine Larrimore) to drop him for five years in protest. The musical played only a month at the Shubert, then was transferred to another house where it completed its run of 283 performances.

Two 1919 musicals were moderately successful. *Good Morning, Judge*, a British import, wisely interpolated two George Gershwin numbers: "There's More to the Kiss Than XXX" and "I Was So Young." Sigmund Romberg's *The Magic Melody* was too reminiscent of his *Maytime* plot, even to the employment of its same leading man, Charles Purcell.

Some class returned to the Shubert in the fall of 1919 when E.H. Sothern and Julia Marlowe played their classical repertory at the theatre.

Highlights of the 1920s at this theatre included an appearance by the silent screen siren Theda Bara in a preposterous drama called *The Blue Flame* (1920), in which her dead body is brought back to life by a mad scientist; Margaret Anglin in *The Trial of Joan of Arc* (1921), translated from the French play by Emil Moreau; the luxurious *Greenwich Village Follies* revues, staged by John Murray Anderson, and the *Artists and Models* revues

Top: Al Jolson in his last Broadway show, *Hold On To Your Hats* (1940).
Above: Fay Bainter and Walter Huston squabble in the 1933 hit *Dodsworth*.

81

(1921-26), notorious for their nudity, starring period favorites such as Joe E. Brown, female impersonator Bert Savoy and Jay Brennan (his partner), Ted Lewis, Moran

Top: Ray Heatherton, Mitzi Green, and Alfred Drake in *Babes in Arms* (1937). *Above:* Alfred Lunt and Lynn Fontanne in the heavenly comedy *Amphitryon 38* (1937).

and Mack, and Vincent Lopez and his orchestra. Expert comics Jimmy Savo and Fred Allen starred in a revue called *Vogues of 1924*. An interesting failure, *The Magnolia Lady*, starred Ruth Chatterton and Ralph Forbes, performers usually associated with dramas and comedies rather than musicals.

For a change of pace, the Shubert presented Walter Hampden in *Othello* in January 1925, and the actor set a record for that time by playing the role for eight consecutive weeks. In 1943, at the same theatre, Paul Robeson would also break records with his magnificent portrayal of Shakespeare's tragic Moor.

The homespun comic Chic Sale had a hit with a revue called *Gay Paree* (1925) that had nothing to do with Paris; *Countess Maritza* (1926), an operetta by Emmerich Kálmán, with the popular song "Play Gypsies—Dance Gypsies," was an enormous success; "rubber legs" Leon Errol had some hilarious drunk scenes in the hit musical *Yours Truly* (1927); the noisy nightclub hostess Texas Guinan, who coined the phrase "Hello, suckers," attracted customers in a revue called *Padlocks of 1927,* supported by Lillian Roth and J.C. Flippen singing some clever lyrics by Billy Rose; not even Laurette Taylor could save Zoe Akins's murder mystery *The Furies* (1928) from rigor mortis; *Ups-a-Daisy* (1928) is a musical worth mentioning only because its cast included a comic butler played by a young man named Bob Hope; *A Night in Venice*, starring Ted Healy and His Stooges (later The Three Stooges), was a minor musical that brought the 1920s to a close at the Shubert.

The 1930s began with sobriety. The Chicago Civic Shakespeare Society, headed by Fritz Leiber, staged nine of Shakespeare's greatest plays in repertory. Nonsense returned with Walter Slezak making his debut in a musical, *Meet My Sister* (1930). Ann Pennington, Oscar Shaw, Frances Williams, and a newcomer named Harriette Lake (later, Ann Sothern of the films) played for 127 performances in a musical called *Everybody's Welcome* (1931), which boasted an immortal song by Herman Hupfeld: "As Time Goes By." Another celebrated song, the theme song of the Depression—"Brother, Can You Spare a Dime?"—was first heard in *Americana*, a revue that played the Shubert in 1932.

In January 1933 Fred Astaire's last Broadway musical,

The Gay Divorce, moved from the Barrymore to the Shubert and Fred danced "Night and Day" with Claire Luce for six more months. Walter Huston, Fay Bainter, Maria Ouspenskaya, and Nan Sunderland (Mrs. Huston) were the hit of the season in Sidney Howard's *Dodsworth,* a skillful adaptation of the Sinclair Lewis novel of the same name.

The Shubert housed its first Pulitzer Prize play in March 1936. Robert E. Sherwood's antiwar drama *Idiot's Delight,* with glittering performances by Alfred Lunt as a seedy hoofer and Lynn Fontanne as the mysterious mistress of a munitions maker, took Broadway by storm and was one of the finest plays that the prestigious Theatre Guild produced in its distinguished history.

In 1937 Maxwell Anderson's *The Masque of Kings,* a retelling of the Mayerling tragedy, ran only 89 performances despite the brilliant acting of Dudley Digges (Emperor Franz Joseph) and Margo, Henry Hull, and Leo G. Carroll in other roles. The gloom of this drama was dispelled in April of that year when Rodgers and Hart's *Babes in Arms* opened with a young, largely unknown cast singing such gems as "Where or When," "The Lady Is a Tramp," "My Funny Valentine," "I Wish I Were in Love Again," and "Johnny One Note." George Balanchine supplied the fantastic choreography.

The Lunts returned to the Shubert in S.N. Behrman's elegant adaptation of Jean Giraudoux's *Amphitryon 38* (1937), in which Lunt impersonated Jupiter, who in turn masquerades as Amphitryon in order to woo Amphitryon's wife, Alkmena, blissfully played by Lynn Fontanne. They were excellently supported by Richard Whorf and Sydney Greenstreet. This Olympian frolic was followed by a heavenly musical, *I Married An Angel* (1938), with felicitous Rodgers and Hart songs, angelic dancing by Vera Zorina to Balanchine choreography, glorious singing by Dennis King and Vivienne Segal, clowning by Walter Slezak and Audrey Christie, and lovely Jo Mielziner sets that were whisked on and off on treadmills.

On March 28, 1939, a landmark event occurred at the Shubert: Philip Barry's enchanting high comedy *The Philadelphia Story* opened. It proved a life-saver for Katharine Hepburn (who had been branded "box office poison" in Hollywood); for Mr. Barry, who hadn't had a

Katharine Hepburn in her greatest hit, *The Philadelphia Story* (1939).

hit in years; and for the Theatre Guild, which was on the verge of bankruptcy. Hepburn's company included Shirley Booth, Joseph Cotten, and Van Heflin, and their

Above: Uta Hagen and Paul Robeson in the lauded 1943 revival of *Othello.*
Right: Judy Holliday and Sydney Chaplin in the popular *Bells Are Ringing* (1956).

Webster and designed by Robert Edmond Jones.

Mae West wiggled her hips in Mike Todd's production of her play *Catherine Was Great* (1944), with Gene Barry as one of Mae's lovers; Celeste Holm clinched her star status as a suffragette in the tuneful musical *Bloomer Girl* (1944); Bobby Clark enlivened Victor Herbert's *Sweethearts* (1947) with Marjorie Gateson for 288 performances.

High Button Shoes (1947), a charming musical with Jerome Robbins's dances, Nanette Fabray's singing, and Phil Silvers's comedy, moved to the Shubert from the Century Theatre and stayed for almost a year; Maxwell Anderson's *Anne of the Thousand Days* (1948) won Rex Harrison a Tony Award as outstanding lead actor; the Lunts celebrated their twenty-fifth anniversary as America's foremost acting couple in S.N. Behrman's family chronicle play *I Know My Love* (1949); Cole Porter's phenomenal *Kiss Me, Kate* moved from the Century Theatre to the Shubert in 1950 and thrilled musical comedy buffs for a full year.

During the 1950s the Shubert continued its policy of alternating between musicals and straight fare. The

radiant acting kept the show selling out for most of its 417 performances.

During the 1940s, Rodgers and Hart suffered one of their rare flops, *Higher and Higher* (1940), at the Shubert; Al Jolson and Martha Raye drew raves in the musical *Hold On to Your Hats* (1940), with an entrancing score by Burton Lane and E.Y. Harburg; Katharine Cornell was hailed in her revival of Shaw's *The Doctor's Dilemma* (1941), with Raymond Massey, Bramwell Fletcher, Ralph Forbes, and Clarence Derwent; Mary Boland, Bobby Clark, Walter Hampden, and Helen Ford romped through a revival of Sheridan's *The Rivals* (1942); Rodgers and Hart provided Ray Bolger with one of his best musicals, *By Jupiter* (1942), based on the play *The Warrior's Husband;* Paul Robeson, Uta Hagen, and José Ferrer were cheered in *Othello* (1943), brilliantly directed by Margaret

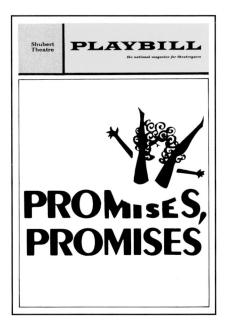

Lerner and Loewe show *Paint Your Wagon* (1951), starring James Barton, stayed for 289 performances; Katharine Hepburn and Cyril Ritchard sparkled in Shaw's *The Millionairess* (1952); Rex Harrison and Lili Palmer were their usual urbane selves in Peter Ustinov's *The Love of Four Colonels* (1953).

Cole Porter's *Can-Can* was a huge hit for two years (1953-55); Rodgers and Hammerstein's *Pipe Dream* (1955), based on John Steinbeck's novel *Sweet Thursday*, was one of their lesser efforts; Judy Holliday scored one of her major coups in the Comden/Green/Jule Styne musical *Bells Are Ringing* (1956), with Sydney Chaplin; Gertrude Berg and Cedric Hardwicke had a hit in *A Majority of One* (1959).

The last hit of the 1950s at this theatre was *Take Me Along* (1959), a musical adaptation of Eugene O'Neill's comedy *Ah, Wilderness!* starring Jackie Gleason (who feuded with the show's producer, David Merrick, all through the run), Walter Pidgeon, Eileen Herlie, Robert Morse, and Una Merkel.

Highlights of the 1960s included Barbra Streisand's Broadway debut in a small but noticeable part in the musical *I Can Get It for You Wholesale* (1962), starring her future husband, Elliott Gould; Anthony Newley starring

Top: PLAYBILL covers for three musical hits at the Shubert. *Above:* Alan Alda and Barbara Harris as Adam and Eve in *The Apple Tree* (1966).

in *Stop the World—I Want to Get Off* (1962), which he wrote with Leslie Bricusse; and its follow-up, *The Roar of the Greasepaint—The Smell of the Crowd* (1965), from the same team.

Craig Stevens and Janis Paige starred in Meredith Willson's *Here's Love* (1963), adapted from the popular movie *Miracle on 34th Street*, but it did not enjoy the success of his *The Music Man* or *The Unsinkable Molly Brown*, and proved to be his final Broadway musical.

On Oct. 2, 1963, the Shuberts celebrated the fiftieth anniversary of their eponymous theatre by unveiling a plaque dedicating Shubert Alley to "all those who glorify the theatre" and use the short thoroughfare. It confirmed Shubert Alley's place as the heart of the Broadway theatre district.

The Shubert Theatre hosted Barbara Harris, Alan Alda, Larry Blyden, and Robert Klein in an offbeat three-part musical, *The Apple Tree* (1966), by Jerry Bock and Sheldon Harnick. Steve Lawrence, Eydie Gorme, and

Top: The original cast of *A Chorus Line*, Broadway's longest-running musical until *Cats* came along. *Center:* PLAYBILL for the final performance of *A Chorus Line. Above:* The chorus asks "Who am I anyway? Am I my resumé?"

Harry Groener sings "I Can't Be Bothered Now" in *Crazy for You* (1992).

Marilyn Cooper starred in *Golden Rainbow* (1968), a musical version of the play *A Hole in the Head*. The last show of the decade was the smash musical *Promises, Promises,* Neil Simon's adaptation of the film *The Apartment,* with a jaunty score by Burt Bacharach and Hal David, starring Jerry Orbach.

The demolition of the Astor Hotel on the east side of Shubert Alley and its replacement by an office tower with a windowed restaurant at ground level changed the ambience of the alley.

Some of the shows that played the Shubert Theatre in the 1970s were Hal Prince's production of *A Little Night Music* (1973), with a book by Hugh Wheeler and score by Stephen Sondheim, based on the Ingmar Bergman film *Smiles of a Summer Night,* starring Glynis Johns, Len Cariou, and Hermione Gingold; and *Over Here!* (1974), a nostalgic World War II musical with two of the Andrews Sisters—Maxene and Patty—and, in smaller roles, John Travolta and Treat Williams.

The Shubert's second Pulitzer-winning play, Edward Albee's *Seascape* (1975), starred Deborah Kerr and Barry Nelson, and won a Tony Award for supporting actor Frank Langella in the unlikely role of a giant, talking sea lizard. Ingrid Bergman made her last Broadway appearance in a revival of Maugham's *The Constant Wife* in April 1975.

On July 25, 1975, Joseph Papp and the New York Shakespeare Festival hosted the Broadway opening of their sensational Off-Broadway hit, *A Chorus Line.* Directed by Michael Bennett, with choreography by Mr. Bennett and Bob Avian, the musical introduced 24 dancers auditioning for an unnamed Broadway show, then took audiences inside their hearts and heads to learn their secret dreams and desires as the moment approached when all but eight of them would be eliminated. In September 1983 this Pulitzer Prize-winning musical, with a book by James Kirkwood and Nicholas Dante, score by Marvin Hamlisch and Edward Kleban, became Broadway's longest-running musical to that date, and the Shubert Theatre, still owned by the Shubert Organization, celebrated the longest-running show ever to play in the 70-year-old house.

The record-setting 6,137-performance run of *A Chorus Line* ended April 28, 1990. After a summer-long renovation, the Shubert reopened in November 1990 with *Buddy: The Buddy Holly Story,* a musical about the late rock star who died in a 1959 plane crash. The show was an enormous success in London—where it opened in 1989 and was still running in 2000—but it failed to repeat its success on Broadway, running for only 225 performances.

Jon Cypher and Dan Jenkins perform the number "Fun" while dancing on a giant keyboard in the musical in *Big* (1996).

Next, on February 19, 1992, the Shubert welcomed another big hit, *Crazy For You,* a revised version of the 1930 Gershwin musical *Girl Crazy,* with interpolated songs from many of the George and Ira Gershwin Broadway and film musicals. Starring Jodi Benson and Harry Groener, the show had a hilarious new book by Ken Ludwig and brilliant direction by Mike Ockrent. It won three Tony Awards: Best Musical, Best Choreography (Susan Stroman), and Best Costume Design (William Ivey Long). It closed in 1996 after 1,622 performances.

The husband/wife team of director Ockrent and choreographer Stroman returned to the Shubert on April 28, 1996 with *Big,* a musical version of the hit 1988 film of the same name about a boy who is magically granted his wish to become "big"—that is, a grown-up. The stage adaptation, with a book by John Weidman, music by David Shire and lyrics by Richard Maltby, Jr., lacked the charm of the movie and ran for only 192 performances.

In 1996, the City Center's "Encores! Great American Musicals in Concert" series produced a sensational concert version of the 1975 musical *Chicago,* with music by John Kander, lyrics by Fred Ebb, and a book by Mr. Ebb and Bob Fosse. It was so successful (despite the virtual absence of sets; the buff dancers providing the only needed visual element) that it transferred to Broadway, first to the Richard Rodgers Theatre (November 14, 1996) and then to the Shubert Theatre (February 12, 1997). The concert cast was retained: Bebe Neuwirth, Ann Reinking, James Naughton, Joel Grey, Marcia Lewis, and many others. The megahit won the following 1997 Tony Awards: Best Revival of a Musical, Best Leading Actor in a Musical (Naughton), Best Leading Actress in a Musical (Neuwirth), Best Direction of a Musical (Walter Bobbie), Best Choreography (Reinking), and Best Lighting (Ken Billington). It stayed at the Shubert for a very long run.

BOOTH THEATRE

This warm, intimate theatre was a joint venture of the aristocratic producer Winthrop Ames, owner of the even smaller Little Theatre, and impresario Lee Shubert. Their aim was to offer theatregoers a cozy house for the viewing of dramas and comedies. It was named the Booth in remembrance of another Booth Theatre in Manhattan (named for actor Edwin Booth), in which Mr. Ames's father had held financial interest.

The 668-seat (later augmented to 785) Booth Theatre on West Forty-fifth Street was built back-to-back with the Shubert Theatre and shared Shubert Alley with it. According to newspapers at the time of the Booth's opening, the theatre was designed by architect Henry B. Herts in early Italian Renaissance style "with designs in agrafitto in brown and ivory, colors which harmonize with the exterior of the theatre, which is yellow brick and ivory terra cotta." An unusual feature of the Booth was a wall that partitioned the entrance from the auditorium, preventing street and lobby noises and drafts from coming to the interior of the house. Woodwork and walls were in neutral tints of driftwood gray; draperies, upholstery, carpeting, and the house curtain were in various shades of mulberry. Chandeliers and appliqués along the wall gave the impression of candlelight. The theatre contained many Booth souvenirs, including the actor's favorite armchair, a statue of him, and many handbills and posters of Booth's appearances.

The Booth opened with fanfare on October 16, 1913, with the first American production of Arnold Bennett's play *The Great Adventure*, dramatized by him from his novel *Buried Alive*. The stars were Janet Beecher and Lyn Harding and the fascinating plot dealt with a famous artist who is pronounced dead and who decides to go along with the erroneous obituary. Unfortunately, the play lasted only 52 performances.

The Booth's first hit was *Experience*, an allegorical play with music, in which William Elliott played a character who symbolized Youth. It ran for 255 performances in 1914-15. This was followed by another success, *The Bubble*, starring Louis Mann, which had a run of 176 showings. On February 5, 1917, the distinguished producer/director Arthur Hopkins piloted a hit called *A Successful Calamity*, by Clare Kummer, starring William Gillette, Estelle Winwood, Roland Young, and William Devereaux. Later that year, *DeLuxe Annie*, with Jane Grey and Vincent Serrano, proved to be another good show.

The year 1918 started out with a huge hit for the Booth. Ruth Gordon, Gregory Kelly, Paul Kelly, and Neil Martin appeared in a delightful adaptation of Booth Tarkington's *Seventeen*. There were two hits the following year: Janet Beecher and Lowell Sherman in a mystery called *The Woman in Room 13*, and a comedy called *Too Many Husbands*.

Program-cover motif for a 1921 Booth Theatre production.

and the Pauper, with actress Ruth Findlay playing the dual roles of the title, and with William Faversham and Clare Eames in other choice parts.

Highlights of the 1920s at the Booth included George Arliss as the Raja of Ruka in a lush adventure play, *The Green Goddess* (1921), set in the Himalayas, which ran for 440 performances. A.A. Milne's engrossing play, *The Truth About Blayds* (1922), starred O.P. Heggie as Blayds, a famed poet who reveals that someone else wrote all his poems, with Leslie Howard, Frieda Inescort, and Ferdinand Gottschalk helping to keep his secret. Austin Strong's unforgettable *Seventh Heaven* (1922) featured Helen Menken and George Gaul as the poor lovers in a Parisian garret. They moved in for 683 performances.

Next came *Dancing Mothers* (1924), a daring play in which a mother (played by Mary Young) rebels against her flapper daughter (Helen Hayes) and philandering husband (Henry Stephenson) by going wild herself and walking out on them. Edna Ferber and George S. Kaufman's *Minick* (1924) provided a gentle portrait of an old man going to live with his son and daughter-in-law.

Alfred Lunt and Lynn Fontanne appeared at the Booth in their fourth play together, Molnar's *The Guardsman* (1924), which was so successful that it moved from the Garrick Theatre to the Booth and delighted Theatre Guild audiences.

The 1920s continued with publisher Horace Liveright's startling modern-dress production of *Hamlet* (1925), which depicted Basil Sydney as the Melancholy Dane in a dinner suit, King Claudius (Charles Waldron) in flannels, and Ophelia (Helen Chandler) in flapper frocks; *The Patsy* (1925), a winning comedy starring Claiborne Foster; Winthrop Ames's 1926 production of a fanciful Philip Barry comedy, *White Wings* (a fancy term for street cleaners), which should have lasted longer than 27 performances; Ruth Gordon, Roger Pryor, and Beulah Bondi in Maxwell Anderson's timely comedy about youth, *Saturday's Children* (1927); and Leslie Howard and Frieda Inescort in John Galsworthy's excellent drama *Escape* (1927), brilliantly produced and staged by Winthrop Ames.

The Grand Street Follies of 1928, an annual topical revue that spoofed current plays and players, featured

The Roaring Twenties at the Booth began rousingly with a lively melodrama, *The Purple Mask*, with Leo Ditrichstein, Brandon Tynan, and Lily Cahill in a cloak-and-dagger masquerade set in Napoleon's time. Alexander Woollcott loved it and wrote in *The New York Times* that Tom Sawyer and Penrod would have, too. This swashbuckler was followed by a charming play, *Not So Long Ago*, a nostalgic Cinderella tale set in early New York, with Eva Le Gallienne giving an enchanting performance as a poor girl who marries a rich boy. She was supported by Sidney Blackmer and Thomas Mitchell. The Booth went back to melodrama in November 1920 with a rousing adaptation of Mark Twain's *The Prince*

James Cagney tapping and Dorothy Sands stopping the show with her impression of Mae West playing Shakespeare; Cagney, Sands and others returned to do parodies for *The Grand Street Follies of 1929*. The last show of the 1920s at the Booth was a contemporary comedy of ill manners called *Jenny* (1929), starring Jane Cowl as an actress who tries to straighten out a wayward family but ends up running off with the father of the house, capitally played by Guy Standing.

During the 1930s some fifty shows played the Booth, many of them quick failures, and a number of them transferred from other theatres. Among the most noteworthy tenants were: Margaret Sullavan in her Broadway debut, in a shabby play called *A Modern Virgin* (1931); Rose Franken's drama about family tyranny, *Another Language* (1932), splendidly acted by Margaret Wycherly, Margaret Hamilton, Glenn Anders, Dorothy Stickney, and John Beal; *No More Ladies* (1934), an intelligent comedy about infidelity, by A.E. Thomas, starring Lucile Watson and Melvyn Douglas; Gladys

Left: Alfred Lunt and Lynn Fontanne in their joyous hit *The Guardsman* (1924). *Above:* Leslie Howard in John Galsworthy's engrossing drama *Escape* (1927).

Cooper making her Broadway debut with Raymond Massey and Adrianne Allen in Keith Winter's *The Shining Hour* (1934), another play about infidelity.

Also: John Van Druten's "comedy of women," called *The Distaff Side* (1934), superbly acted by Sybil Thorndike, Mildred Natwick, Estelle Winwood, and Viola Roache; J.B. Priestley's *Laburnum Grove* (1935), in which Edmund Glenn pretended to be a counterfeiter in order to get rid of sponging relatives who wished to borrow money from him; Melvyn Douglas, Cora Witherspoon, Claudia Morgan, Violet Heming, Elsa Maxwell, Blanche Ring, and Tom Ewell—a million-dollar cast—all wasted in a maudlin play called *De Luxe* (1935), by novelist Louis Bromfield and John Gearon.

The radiant Grace George starred in a chilling drama, *Kind Lady* (1935), about a rich old lady held captive in her own home by a gang of clever thieves headed by Henry Daniell. The 1930s continued with *Blind Alley* (1935), another thriller, with Roy Hargrave as a gangster who is destroyed when a psychologist (George Coulouris) he is holding captive delves into his mind; a classical Chinese drama, *Lady Precious Stream* (1936), starring Helen Chandler, Bramwell Fletcher, and Clarence Derwent; *Sweet Aloes* (1936), a British play by Joyce Carey, with Miss Carey, Evelyn Laye, and Rex Harrison making his Broadway debut; and a rowdy farce about wrestling, *Swing Your Lady* (1936).

Henry Travers and Josephine Hull headed an insane family of lovable eccentrics in Kaufman and Hart's Pulitzer Prize comedy *You Can't Take It with You* (1936), which ran almost two years at the Booth. There followed Montgomery Clift, Jessie Royce Landis, Morgan James, and Onslow Stevens in *Dame Nature* (1938), a sexual drama adapted from the French by actress Patricia Collinge; Philip Barry's arresting drama *Here Come the Clowns* (1938), with Eddie Dowling, Madge Evans, Doris Dudley, and Russell Collins; and a bright, richly designed revue, *One for the Money* (1939), by Nancy Hamilton and Morgan Lewis, with future stars Alfred Drake and Gene Kelly, along with Keenan Wynn, Grace McDonald and Brenda Forbes.

Another Pulitzer Prize-winning play brought the 1930s to a close at the Booth: William Saroyan's daffy comedy *The Time of Your Life,* with Eddie Dowling, Julie Haydon, Gene Kelly, William Bendix, Edward Andrews, and Celeste Holm.

In the 1940s, the Booth had fewer productions than in the preceding decade, but more long-running hits. The decade started out with a sequel to the revue *One for the Money* called, aptly, *Two for the Show,* by the same authors. This edition boasted a memorable song, "How High the Moon," and comic and tuneful performances by *One for the Money* veterans Drake and Wynn, along with Betty Hutton, Eve Arden, Richard Haydn, Brenda Forbes, Tommy Wonder, Eunice Healey, and Nadine Gae. On February 12, 1941, a genuine hit called *Claudia* came to the Booth and stayed for a little over a year. Written by Rose Franken, the touching play about a childlike wife made a star out of Dorothy McGuire and brought back to the stage the famed Belasco actress Frances Starr to play Claudia's mother, with Donald Cook as her husband.

Noël Coward's blissful comedy *Blithe Spirit* moved from the Morosco to the Booth in 1942, with Clifton Webb, Peggy Wood, Leonora Corbett, and Mildred Natwick, and the merry spooks stayed for a year. Another

Kaufman and Hart's 1936 Pulitzer Prize-winning comedy, *You Can't Take It with You.*

huge hit, *The Two Mrs. Carrolls* (1943), starring Elisabeth Bergner, Victor Jory, Vera Allen, and Irene Worth, thrilled Booth audiences with its homicidal plot and stayed for 585 performances.

A war drama, *The Wind Is Ninety,* had a remarkable cast (Kirk Douglas, Wendell Corey, Joyce Van Patten and her brother "Dickie," Blanche Yurka, and Bert Lytell) and played for more than 100 performances in 1945. *You Touched Me!* (1945), by Tennessee Williams and Donald Windham, had fine performances by Montgomery Clift and Edmund Glenn, but was a lesser Williams work. Bobby Clark added burlesque touches to Molière's *The Would-Be Gentleman*, with June Knight and Gene Barry; Ben Hecht and Charles MacArthur's psychological murder mystery *Swan Song* played for 158 performances; and a revival of Synge's *The Playboy of the Western World* (1946) had Burgess Meredith, Mildred Natwick, J.C. Nugent, Julie Harris, and, making her Broadway debut, Maureen Stapleton.

Additional 1940s hits included: Norman Krasna's farce-comedy *John Loves Mary* (1947), with Nina Foch, Tom Ewell, and William Prince; Gilbert Miller's revival of Molnar's bubbly comedy *The Play's the Thing* (1948), with Louis Calhern, Ernest Cossart, Arthur Margetson, and Faye Emerson making her Broadway debut; James B. Allardice's comedy, *At War with the Army* (1949), staged by Ezra Stone, with Gary Merrill giving an excellent performance; and Grace George, Walter Hampden, Jean Dixon, and John Williams in a pleasant religious drama, *The Velvet Glove* (1949).

The 1950s began auspiciously with William Inge's first Broadway play, *Come Back, Little Sheba,* with Shirley Booth and Sidney Blackmer winning Tony Awards for their powerful performances. Beatrice Lillie was the toast of the town in the hilarious revue *An Evening with Beatrice Lillie* (1952), in which she sang some of her most celebrated songs and acted in some of her most outlandish sketches with Reginald Gardiner for 278 performances. A popular comedy called *Anniversary Waltz* (1954), directed by Moss Hart and starring his wife, Kitty Carlisle, and Macdonald Carey, moved from the Broadhurst to the Booth and stayed for ten months; *Time Limit* (1956), a taut drama about the Korean War by Henry Denker and Ralph Berkey, starred Richard Kiley,

Souvenir program for Noël Coward's enchanting comedy, *Blithe Spirit* (1942).

Arthur Kennedy, Allyn McLerie, and Thomas Carlin, and played for 127 performances.

Gore Vidal's science fiction delight, *Visit to a Small Planet* (1957), starring Cyril Ritchard as a comic extraterrestrial and Eddie Mayehoff as an imbecilic general, ran for a year. William Gibson's *Two for the Seesaw* (1958), an enchanting two-character love story starring Henry Fonda and Anne Bancroft, ran for almost two years; and Paddy Chayefsky's *The Tenth Man,* about the exorcism of a dybbuk in suburban Mineola, with Gene Saks as a rabbi and Jack Gilford, George Voskovec, Jacob Ben-Ami, and Lou Jacobi giving sublime performances, played 623 times.

Highlights of the 1960s included Julie Harris, Walter Matthau, William Shatner, Gene Saks, and Diana van der Vlis in the continental comedy *A Shot in the Dark* (1961); Murray Schisgal's outré comedy, *Luv* (1964),

Top: Shirley Booth and Sidney Blackmer in William Inge's poignant play, *Come Back, Little Sheba* (1950). *Above:* Souvenir program for Beatrice Lillie's hit (1952).

directed by Mike Nichols, with Eli Wallach, Anne Jackson, and Alan Arkin as three miserable creatures who cavort on a bridge, which lasted for 901 performances; Flanders and Swann, the British comedy team, in *At the Drop of Another Hat* (1966), a follow-up to their popular two-man revue *At the Drop of a Hat*; and Harold Pinter's sinister play *The Birthday Party* (1967), his first full-length work on Broadway.

Next came one of the Booth's most popular tenants, Leonard Gershe's *Butterflies Are Free*, the story of a blind man, his kooky neighbor, and his overprotective mother, which stayed for 1,128 performances. The cast featured Keir Dullea, Blythe Danner (who made her Broadway debut and won a Tony Award for her luminous acting), and Eileen Heckart (later replaced by Gloria Swanson).

In 1972 the Booth housed another Pulitzer-winning play, Joseph Papp's production of *That Championship Season* (1972), by actor Jason Miller, which moved from the downtown New York Shakespeare Festival and played for almost two years at the Booth. Other attractions of the decade included Terrence McNally's zany *Bad Habits* (1974), two playlets about therapy, which moved uptown from the Astor Place Theatre; Cleavon Little in Murray Schisgal's *All Over Town* (1974), directed by Dustin Hoffman; a revival of Jerome Kern's 1915 musical *Very Good Eddie* (1975), from the Goodspeed Opera House in Connecticut; and Ntozake Shange's *For Colored Girls Who Have Considered Suicide/When the Rainbow Is Enuf* (1976), an exalted program of poetry acted by an extraordinary cast of black artists for 742 performances.

The Elephant Man (1979), Bernard Pomerance's enthralling study of a disfigured man who strives to keep his humanity though he is displayed in a carnival freak show, was enhanced by memorable performances from Philip Anglim, Kevin Conway, and Carole Shelley. The drama moved from Off-Broadway's Theatre at Saint Peter's Church to the Booth and won the New York Drama Critics Circle Award for best play and three Tony Awards.

In 1975 the Booth was home to a unique, though failed, experiment on the part of New York Shakespeare Festival's Joseph Papp, who was then flush from the phenomenal success of *A Chorus Line* at the neighboring Shubert Theatre. Advertising "Broadway for bupkes"

Left: Alan Arkin, Anne Jackson, and Eli Wallach in *Luv* (1964). *Right:* Keir Dullea, Eileen Heckart, and Blythe Danner in the long-running *Butterflies Are Free* (1969).

(Yiddish for very little money), he booked the Booth for what was to have been a subscription series of Broadway dramas at a cost of just $10. The series did not survive the failure of its first offering, Dennis J. Reardon's *The Leaf People,* which closed after 8 performances.

In 1979 the famed interior designer Melanie Kahane, who had redone four of other Shubert Organization theatres, was hired to restore the Booth to its original elegance and grandeur. "What I've tried to do with these old houses is get back to the beginning and then modernize them in some way," she told PLAYBILL at the time. "The Booth was a sad old sack. All in brown. I kept the brown below—to anchor—then put light beige on top. The light color brings your eye up, so you notice the detail." Ms. Kahane characterized the Booth as "very Jacobean." She got rid of the delicate French chandeliers, which she felt didn't belong in that house, and restored the elegant old theatre in the short space of three weeks.

Most of the thousands of theatre fans who visit the One Shubert Alley memorabilia store in Shubert Alley don't realize it is actually one of the Booth's converted former dressing rooms.

In November 1981, *Mass Appeal,* by Bill C. Davis,

directed by Geraldine Fitzgerald, made another successful transfer from Off-Broadway to the Booth. This religious drama, first presented at the Circle Repertory Theatre and the Manhattan Theatre Club, featured excellent performances by Milo O'Shea as a luxury-loving priest and Michael O'Keefe as his rebellious protégé.

The Booth's 1980s tenants included the Royal Shakespeare Company's production of *Good,* by the British playwright C. P. Taylor, starring Alan Howard as an intellectual German in Frankfurt in 1933 who turns into a rabid Nazi; *Total Abandon,* a short-lived play by Larry Atlas, starring Richard Dreyfuss as a parent who is guilty of child abuse and murder; and *Sunday in the Park With George,* a unique musical by Stephen Sondheim and James Lapine, in which an Impressionist painting comes to life. Mandy Patinkin and Bernadette Peters starred.

Herb Gardner's *I'm Not Rappaport* (1985) brought the Best Play Tony Award to the Booth, with its story of a feisty old codger who tries to hold onto life and dignity in his relationships with his friend, his daughter, and a young woman he meets in Central Park. It played for 890 performances. Judd Hirsch won the Tony as Best Actor in a Play.

Above: Risë Collins and Trazana Beverley in *For Colored Girls Who Have Considered Suicide/When the Rainbow Is Enuf* (1976). *Opposite:* Graphic PLAYBILL covers for three Booth Theatre hits.

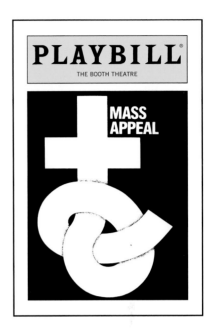

The London hit *Shirley Valentine* (1989) struck a chord with its story of a working class woman who grows tired of being taken for granted by her family and takes the bold step of abandoning then to pursue her dream of going to Greece. Pauline Collins won a Tony Award for her performance in Willy Russell's solo play, which occupied the Booth for 324 performances.

The year 1990 brought *Once on This Island*, the Broadway debut of the songwriting team Lynn Ahrens and Stephen Flaherty, later to create *My Favorite Year, Ragtime* and *Seussical*. Their first Broadway production retold a Caribbean tale about a peasant girl whose romance with a handsome aristocrat is aided by spirits of the land, air and water. The fairytale musical lasted 469 performances and earned the team a Tony nomination for Best Score.

In 1992, a British play, *Someone Who'll Watch Over Me* by Frank McGuinness, was splendidly acted by Stephen Rea, Alec McCowen, and James McDaniel, and ran for 216 performances. It was nominated for two Tony Awards: Best Play and Best Actor in a Play (Mr. Rea). The following year, *The Twilight of the Golds* by Jonathan Tolins had an interesting premise: a pregnant woman learns, via genetic testing, that her future son will be gay, but the critics dismissed the theme as shallow. It closed after 29 performances. On April 24, 1994, Arthur Miller's *Broken Glass,* starring Amy Irving, Ron Rifkin, and David Dukes, explored the theme of American Jews during the Holocaust. But the play drew mixed reviews with several critics finding the work "unfinished." It closed after 73 performances.

In December of that year, *A Tuna Christmas* arrived for a limited engagement. A sequel to the 1982 hit, *Greater Tuna,* the show was once again performed by two actors—Jaston Williams and Joe Sears (who co-wrote it with Ed Howard). They portrayed a variety of characters in the small town of Tuna, Texas. Mr. Sears was nominated for a Best Actor Tony for his versatile performance.

Having Our Say arrived at the Booth on April 6, 1995. Mary Alice and Gloria Foster starred as the Delany sisters, the daughters of a former slave, whose lives encompassed a century of African-American history. Both of the play's real-life subjects were more than 100 years old when the play opened, and attended one of the performances. The play was adapted by Emily Mann from the sisters' autobiography. The play achieved 308 performances and received the following Tony Award nominations: Best Play (Emily Mann), Best Director of a Play (Ms. Mann), and Best Actress (Mary Alice).

The Booth was filled with laughter when Jackie Mason brought his one-man comedy show, *Love Thy Neighbor,* there in 1996. With his hilarious barbs at contemporary society, the comic kept audiences happy for 236 performances. Another one-man comedy show moved to the Booth from the Helen Hayes Theatre on January 29, 1997. It was the popular hit, *Defending the Caveman,* written and performed by Rob Becker. During the run at the Booth Mr. Becker was succeeded by Michael Chiklis. The comedy closed June 21, 1997 after 645 performances (at the Hayes and the Booth combined).

David Mamet's *The Old Neighborhood* opened on November 19, 1997, offering a collection of three memory plays about the Chicago neighborhood where the author grew up. Performed without intermission, the plays starred Peter Riegert, Patti LuPone, Vincent Guastaferro, and Rebecca Pidgeon (Mrs. Mamet). The production received mixed reviews and ran for 197 performances.

An Evening With Jerry Herman, a revue of Mr. Herman's songs, opened on July 28, 1998 with the composer/lyricist at the piano, assisted by actor Lee Roy Reams, singer Florence Lacey, and Jered Egan on bass. The entertainment had a lukewarm reception and departed after 28 performances.

Caustic comic Sandra Bernhardt insulted show biz celebrities in her one-woman show, *I'm Still Here... Dammit!,* to the delight of some theatregoers and the chagrin of others. Her profane barbs ceased after 51 airings.

David Hare's provocative one-man show, *Via Dolorosa,* showcased his vivid recollections of Jews and Arabs he met on a visit to the West Bank. Opening on March 18, 1999, as a production of the Lincoln Center Theater, it enthralled audiences for 85 performances.

On October 17, 1999, the Booth enjoyed a riotous explosion with the opening of *Dame Edna: The Royal Tour.* Australian actor Barry Humphries, who for years had delighted audiences with his impersonation of a flamboyant, eccentric "housewife superstar" called Dame Edna, captivated critics and audiences with this entertainment that involved much audience participation. Mr. Humphries won a special Tony Award for his brilliant impersonation and threw gladiolas at audiences until July 2, 2000.

In November 2000 Lily Tomlin brought her celebrated 1985 one-woman show, *The Search for Signs of Intelligent Life in the Universe,* back to Broadway for a

Top: Patti LuPone and Peter Riegert reminisce in Mamet's *The Old Neighborhood* (1997). *Above:* Barry Humphries in one of his flamboyant creations for *Dame Edna: The Royal Tour* (1999).

limited engagement. Written and directed by Jane Wagner, the tour de force had earned Ms. Tomlin the 1986 Tony Award for Best Leading Actress in a Play.

The Booth has always been—and still is today—an ideal house for dramas, comedies, and intimate musical shows.

BROADHURST THEATRE

George H. Broadhurst, the Anglo-American dramatist (1866-1952), came to America in 1886. In addition to writing popular plays, he managed theatres in Milwaukee, Baltimore, and San Francisco before he opened his own self-named New York theatre in association with the Shubert brothers.

Located at 235 West Forty-fourth Street, right next door to the Shubert Theatre, the Broadhurst was designed by architect Herbert J. Krapp, one of the major theatre designers of that era. With a seating capacity of 1,155 (later augmented to 1,186) and a wide auditorium that offered unobstructed views of the stage, the theatre was constructed to house both musicals and straight fare, which it has done successfully for more than eighty years.

The Broadhurst's opening show was George Bernard Shaw's *Misalliance* on September 27, 1917, starring Maclyn Arbuckle. This was the first New York production of Shaw's philosophical 1910 comedy and it ran for only 52 performances. It was not performed again on Broadway until a City Center revival in 1953.

In 1918 the Broadhurst had a hit musical in *Ladies First,* starring Nora Bayes and comic William Kent. This suffragette show centered on a woman (Bayes) who dares to run for mayor against her boyfriend. She loses the election but wins the boy. The show had a score by A. Baldwin Sloane. During the run at the Broadhurst, one

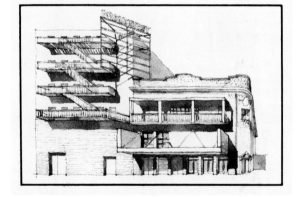

George Gershwin song, "Some Wonderful Sort of Someone," was interpolated.

The Broadhurst had two hits in 1919. Rachel Crothers's *39 East* was a comedy of manners that starred Alison Skipworth, Henry Hull, and Constance Binney. Later in the run Hull was replaced by Sidney Blackmer and Binney by a striking young actress named Tallulah Bankhead. On December 30 Jane Cowl scored one of her early successes in a romantic drama called *Smilin' Through,* which she coauthored with Allan Langdon Martin. Ms. Cowl played a ghost in some scenes and the ghost's niece in others, serving to confuse critic Alexander Woollcott, who complained that these quick-change tricks belonged more to vaudeville than to the legitimate theatre. But audiences loved *Smilin' Through* for 175 performances.

In September 1921 George Broadhurst brought his American version of the British play *Tarzan of the Apes* to his theatre. *The New York Times*'s critic labeled the show "rather astonishing." A British actor, Ronald Adair, played Tarzan, and there were real lions and monkeys onstage, but the Ape Man managed to swing from tree to tree for only 13 performances.

In November 1921 Lionel Barrymore won plaudits for his acting in a French play called *The Claw,* in which he played a politician who is ruined by a conniving woman. Critic Alexander Woollcott reported in

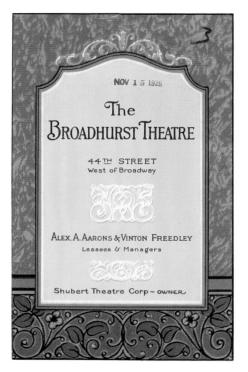

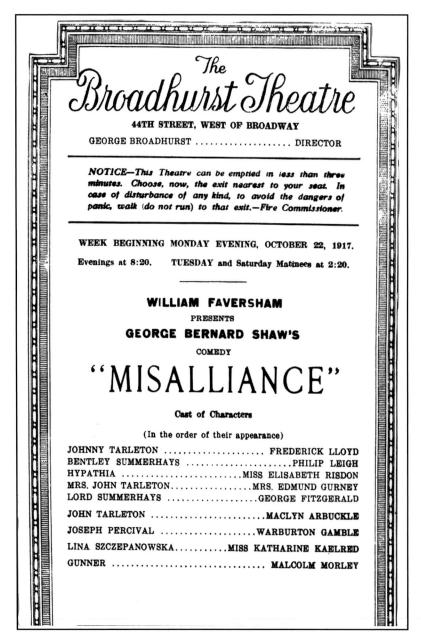

The
Broadhurst Theatre
44TH STREET, WEST OF BROADWAY
GEORGE BROADHURST .... DIRECTOR

NOTICE—This Theatre can be emptied in less than three minutes. Choose, now, the exit nearest to your seat. In case of disturbance of any kind, to avoid the dangers of panic, walk (do not run) to that exit.—Fire Commissioner.

WEEK BEGINNING MONDAY EVENING, OCTOBER 22, 1917.

Evenings at 8:20.   TUESDAY and Saturday Matinees at 2:20.

WILLIAM FAVERSHAM
PRESENTS
GEORGE BERNARD SHAW'S
COMEDY

"MISALLIANCE"

Cast of Characters

(In the order of their appearance)

JOHNNY TARLETON .... FREDERICK LLOYD
BENTLEY SUMMERHAYS ....PHILIP LEIGH
HYPATHIA ....MISS ELISABETH RISDON
MRS. JOHN TARLETON..................MRS. EDMUND GURNEY
LORD SUMMERHAYS ....GEORGE FITZGERALD

JOHN TARLETON ....MACLYN ARBUCKLE

JOSEPH PERCIVAL ....WARBURTON GAMBLE

LINA SZCZEPANOWSKA..........MISS KATHARINE KAELRED

GUNNER .... MALCOLM MORLEY

Above: Program for the first production at the Broadhurst, in 1917. *Right:* Program covers for the theatre in 1926.

The New York Times that the play was attended by "the most bronchial audience of the season that coughed competitively through each scene and applauded with vehemence at its conclusion."

One of the most popular themes of this era—that of two generations of lovers from the same family—cropped up again in the musical *Marjolaine,* starring Peggy Wood. It ran for 136 performances in 1922. In 1923 *The Dancers,* the London play by Sir Gerald Du Maurier in which Tallulah Bankhead had made her dazzling British debut, came to the Broadhurst with Richard Bennett and Florence Eldridge. It was a hit. Later in the year a revue called *Topics of 1923,* with Alice Delysia, frolicked for 143 performances.

On February 12, 1924 (the same day that George Gershwin's famous *Rhapsody in Blue* had its Manhattan premiere), the Broadhurst celebrated Lincoln's birthday with a distinguished hit, *Beggar on Horseback,* by George S. Kaufman and Marc Connelly. This expressionistic play focused on a composer (Roland Young) who almost marries into a stuffy rich family but is saved from this fate by an extended surrealistic dream about how life would be with them. It caused a sensation, ran for 224 performances, and is still regarded as a classic of its genre.

Another sensation was caused by Katharine Cornell in *The Green Hat* (1925), by Michael Arlen. Based on Mr. Arlen's shocking novel of the same name, the play was considered extremely daring. It dealt with a bride (Cornell) whose husband commits suicide on their honeymoon. The audience learns later that the husband threw himself out of a hotel window because he had a venereal disease. The excellent cast included Leslie Howard, Margalo Gillmore, Eugene Powers, and Paul Guilfoyle. The play was staged by Ms. Cornell's husband, Guthrie McClintic.

One of the Broadhurst's greatest entertainments opened on September 16, 1926. Jed Harris, the boy wonder, brought his production of *Broadway* to the Broadhurst and it hit Times Square like a thunderbolt. Written by Philip Dunning and George Abbott, it mesmerized first-nighters and subsequent audiences with its kaleidoscopic view of life in a New York nightspot called the Paradise Club. A jazz band, dancing girls, a fast-talking hoofer perfectly played by Lee Tracy, gangsters,

Katharine Cornell as Iris March in the sensational Michael Arlen play, *The Green Hat* (1925).

bootleggers, murderers, and nightclub habitués thronged the Broadhurst stage and electrified theatregoers for 603 performances. Winston Churchill once declared that this was his favorite show of all time.

Winthrop Ames brought his production of *The Merchant of Venice* to the theatre in 1928. With George Arliss as Shylock and Peggy Wood as Portia, it managed to run for a respectable 72 performances.

On October 10, 1928, Bert Lahr achieved immortality in a raucous musical, *Hold Everything,* by DeSylva, Brown, and Henderson. Lahr played a punch-drunk boxer named Gink Schiner who was given to making strange sounds like "gnong, gnong, gnong"; these utterances later became his trademark. The cast also included the beloved Victor Moore, Jack Whiting, Ona Munson, and Betty Compton, but it was Lahr who got the raves and who kept the musical running for 413 performances. The hit song was "You're the Cream in My Coffee."

The Broadhurst had another winner in 1929, *June Moon.* A satire on Tin Pan Alley's song writers, the play was written by George S. Kaufman and Ring Lardner, and it kept the Broadhurst shaking with laughter for 272 performances. Norman Foster played a lyricist who writes an imbecilic hit tune, "June Moon." The tart Jean Dixon, Philip Loeb, and Linda Watkins gave comic support to this tuneful cartoon.

Rodgers and Hart came back from Hollywood in 1931 with a new musical, *America's Sweetheart,* that naturally spoofed the movie capital. The two young hopefuls who go to Hollywood were played by beautiful Harriette Lake (who subsequently went to Hollywood for real and became Ann Sothern) and Jack Whiting. There was one hit song, the infectious Depression lament "I've Got Five Dollars," and acerbic performances by Jeanne Aubert and Inez Courtney, but the book by Herbert Fields was proclaimed dull and dirty, and the show ran for only 135 performances.

Norman Bel Geddes, set designer extraordinaire, tackled Shakespeare's *Hamlet* at the Broadhurst in 1931. He adapted the play, designed its sets, costumes, and lighting, and directed it. Raymond Massey was the Melancholy Dane, Mary Servoss was Gertrude, Celia Johnson was Ophelia, and Colin Keith-Johnston was Laertes. Wrote Brooks Atkinson in *The New York Times,*

Lee Tracy and Sylvia Field in the classic Jed Harris production, *Broadway* (1926).

"Mr. Bel Geddes has hacked and transposed until no idle philosophy is left to trip up his scenery. What he has left is, to this department, an incoherent, flat and unprofitable narrative." The production expired after 28 performances.

Philip Barry restored art to the Broadhurst with his finely written high comedy *The Animal Kingdom* in 1932.

Leslie Howard gave one of his most ingratiating performances as a man who marries the wrong woman. The blue-chip cast included Frances Fuller, Ilka Chase, and William Gargan. It was Barry at his best.

Claude Rains and the fetching Jean Arthur could not save a drama called *The Man Who Reclaimed His Head* in 1932. Also in the cast, as a maid, was Lucille Lortel, who later became a patroness of the Off-Broadway movement and renamed the Theatre de Lys in Greenwich Village after herself.

The *Broadway* team of George Abbott and Philip Dunning produced another hit in 1932, but not of their authorship. They presented Hecht and MacArthur's rambunctious farce *Twentieth Century,* which took place on board the Twentieth-Century Limited luxury train en route from Chicago to New York. Moffat Johnston played an egomaniacal Broadway producer (said to be inspired by Jed Harris) trying to get a famous actress (Eugenie Leontovich) to sign a contract with him. Directed with express-train speed by Abbott, the comedy delighted for 154 performances and later became the basis for the musical *On the Twentieth Century.*

Another highlight of the 1930s included the Group Theatre's realistic production of Sidney Kingsley's hospital drama *Men in White*, which won the Pulitzer Prize for the 1933-34 season. Starring Alexander Kirkland, Luther Adler, J. Edward Bromberg, Morris Carnovsky, and Russell Collins, it also featured such Group luminaries as Clifford Odets and Elia Kazan. Staged by Lee Strasberg, the play contained an operation scene that held audiences spellbound with its chilling realism.

Eva Le Gallienne brought her Civic Repertory Company to the Broadhurst in 1934 and performed with Ethel Barrymore (and Barrymore's children, Ethel and Samuel Colt) in Rostand's costume play *L'Aiglon.* Without Ethel, Ms. Le Gallienne also presented and acted in *Hedda Gabler* and *The Cradle Song.*

On January 7, 1935, Leslie Howard returned to the Broadhurst in Robert E. Sherwood's *The Petrified Forest.* He enthralled audiences with his portrayal of an intellectual wanderer who allows a gangster to kill him so that he may leave his insurance money to a lovely young woman who wishes to study art in Paris. The gangster was played so vividly by Humphrey Bogart that Leslie Howard

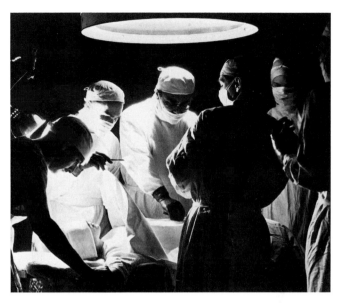

The tense operating scene in Sidney Kingsley's Pulitzer Prize-winning play, *Men in White* (1933).

brought him to Hollywood to repeat his performance in the film version, which made him a star.

Helen Hayes scored perhaps her greatest triumph in *Victoria Regina* in 1935, playing the queen from a young girl to an aged monarch with remarkable physical changes. Gilbert Miller's lavish production and staging, and the enormous cast, including Vincent Price as Prince Albert, made this one of the Broadhurst's most memorable events.

The remainder of the 1930s included Ruth Gordon's brilliant Nora in *A Doll's House,* which moved from the Morosco in 1938; Dodie Smith's charming family-reunion play *Dear Octopus* (1939); the great Bill Robinson in Mike Todd's splashy production of *The Hot Mikado* (1939); and Carmen Miranda's cyclonic Broadway debut in *The Streets of Paris* (1939), a lusty revue also starring Bobby Clark, Abbott and Costello, Luella Gear, Gower (Champion) and Jeanne, and Jean Sablon.

During the 1940s, musicals, revues, and comedies brightened the Broadhurst. Ed Wynn convulsed his fans in *Boys and Girls Together* (1940), with Jane Pickens and the dancing DeMarcos. George Jessel, Bert Kalmar, and Harry Ruby created a lively musical about a burlesque troupe, *High Kickers* (1941). Jessel, Sophie Tucker, Betty Bruce, and a cast of burlesque comics turned it into a hit.

Above: Helen Hayes in her triumphant *Victoria Regina* (1935). *Below Right:* Humphrey Bogart achieves fame as the killer in *The Petrified Forest* (1935).

Eva Le Gallienne and Joseph Schildkraut sent shivers down the spine in the mystery melodrama *Uncle Harry* (1942). Dorothy Kilgallen's husband, Richard Kollmar, produced and starred in *Early to Bed* (1943), a Fats Waller musical about a track team that mistakes a bordello for a hotel. It ran for 380 performances despite bad reviews.

Agatha Christie's *Ten Little Indians,* with practically the entire cast ending as stiffs, enjoyed success in 1944. *Follow the Girls* (1945), a noisy musical with Jackie Gleason and Gertrude Niesen, moved from the New Century to the Broadhurst and stayed for almost a year. *Three to Make Ready* (1946), the third and last of the revue series by Nancy Hamilton and Morgan Lewis, starred Ray Bolger, Gordon MacRae, Brenda Forbes, Arthur Godfrey, Harold Lang, and Carleton Carpenter, and ran five months after it moved to the Broadhurst

from the Adelphi. Helen Hayes returned in *Happy Birthday* (1946), a comedy by Anita Loos about a shy Newark, New Jersey, librarian, and the sentimental play ran for 564 performances.

From 1948 to 1950, four revues played the Broadhurst. They were *Make Mine Manhattan*, with Sid Caesar, David Burns, Sheila Bond, Joshua Shelley, and Kyle MacDonnell; Nancy Walker, Jackie Gleason, Hank Ladd, and Carol Bruce in *Along Fifth Avenue*; Charles Gaynor's delirious *Lend an Ear* (which moved from the National Theatre), with Carol Channing, Yvonne Adair, William Eythe, Gene Nelson, and Jenny Lou Law; and Jean and Walter Kerr's *Touch and Go*, with Nancy Andrews, Peggy Cass, Dick Sykes, Kyle MacDonnell, Helen Gallagher, and Jonathan Lucas.

The 1950s brought some long-running hits to the Broadhurst, but *Romeo and Juliet,* with Olivia de Havilland and Douglas Watson, was not one of them. It achieved only 49 performances in 1951. An interesting musical, *Flahooley,* with Barbara Cook, Ernest Truex, Jerome Courtland, Irwin Corey, Yma Sumac, and the Bill Baird Marionettes, managed only 40 performances in 1951 but later attracted a small cult following. A musical version of *Seventeen* (1951) fared much better, playing for 180 performances. A revival of the 1940 Rodgers and Hart musical *Pal Joey* (1952), with Vivienne Segal repeating her

Harold Lang and Vivienne Segal in the superlative 1952 revival of *Pal Joey*, which ran longer than the original production.

role as the lusty Vera, who keeps the young Joey (Harold Lang) in a luxurious love nest, was even more successful than the original production, running for 540 performances.

Katharine Cornell starred in a fair melodrama, *The Prescott Proposals* (1953), by Howard Lindsay and Russel Crouse. Kitty Carlisle and Macdonald Carey had a comparatively long run in a vapid comedy, *Anniversary Waltz* (1954). Sidney Kingsley turned comic with a madcap play, *Lunatics and Lovers* (1954), starring Buddy Hackett, Dennis King, Sheila Bond, and Vicki Cummings, which had a healthy run.

Also in the 1950s, Shirley Booth found a suitable vehicle in William Marchant's *The Desk Set* (1955); Rosalind Russell made *Auntie Mame* immortal (1956); *The World of Suzie Wong* (1958), a bit of pseudo-Oriental romantic claptrap starring William Shatner and France

Nuyen, managed to last for 508 performances.

The last show of the 1950s—the musical *Fiorello!* by Jerome Weidman, George Abbott, Sheldon Harnick, and Jerry Bock—brought another Pulitzer Prize to this theatre. Tom Bosley played the beloved Mayor Fiorello H. La Guardia and won a Tony for his performance. The show also won Tony Awards for Best Musical, Best Direction (Abbott), Best Book (Weidman and Abbott), Best Music (Bock), Best Lyrics (Harnick), and Best Producers of a Musical (Robert Griffith and Harold Prince).

In 1962 Noël Coward's musical *Sail Away* sailed into the Broadhurst, with Elaine Stritch as a hostess on a luxury liner, but it was all too dated and chichi for 1960s audiences and it departed for London after 167 performances. Richard Rodgers fared better with *No Strings*, the first musical for which he wrote both music and lyrics, with a book by Samuel Taylor. The show moved here from the Fifty-fourth Street Theatre and starred Richard Kiley and Diahann Carroll. They made beautiful music together for 580 performances.

Above: Colleen Dewhurst, Arthur Hill, and Ingrid Bergman in O'Neill's *More Stately Mansions* (1967). *Above:* Ellen March and cast members of the record-breaking musical *Grease* (1972).

Other interesting Broadhurst bookings in the 1960s included the Tom Jones and Harvey Schmidt musical *110 in the Shade* (1963); the British import *Oh What a Lovely War* (1964); another British musical, *Half a Sixpence* (1965) starring Tommy Steele.

On November 20, 1966, a cherished musical came to this theatre: *Cabaret*, a musical version of John Van Druten's play, *I Am a Camera*, which, in turn was adapted from Christopher Isherwood's stories about his youthful days in Berlin, dazzled audiences with its innovative direction by Harold Prince and Joel Grey's mesmerizing performance as the leering nightclub Emcee. The brilliant show won the following Tony Awards: Best Musical, Best Musical Director (Prince), Best Music and Lyrics (Fred Ebb and John Kander), Best Supporting Actor (Grey), Best Supporting Actress (Peg Murray), Best Set Designer (Boris Aronson), and Best Costumes (Patricia Zipprodt). It ran for 1,166 performances, but not all at the Broadhurst.

Next at this theatre was Eugene O'Neill's *More Stately Mansions*, starring Ingrid Bergman, Colleen Dewhurst, and Arthur Hill, directed by José Quintero; and Woody Allen's *Play It Again, Sam*, starring Mr. Allen, Tony Roberts, and Diane Keaton.

By the 1970s the revue genre was dead and the Broadhurst fare veered from dramas and comedies to musicals. Highlights included Sada Thompson's brilliant portrayal of three sisters and their mother in *Twigs* (1971), by George Furth; *Grease*, a rock musical about the after-effects of "summer love" on high school students in the 1950s, which moved from the downtown Eden Theatre to the Broadhurst and became (briefly) the longest-running musical in Broadway history (after a move to the Royale); Neil Simon's uproarious comedy about two veteran comics, *The Sunshine Boys* (1972); John Wood in a marvelous revival of William Gillette's *Sherlock Holmes* (1974); Katharine Hepburn and Christopher Reeve in Enid Bagnold's curious comedy *A Matter of Gravity* (1976); the wonderful musical *Godspell* (1976), based on the *Gospel According to St. Matthew*, which moved from Off Broadway to the Broadhurst.

Preston Jones's ambitious work, *A Texas Trilogy* (1976), was not as successful in New York as it had been in Washington, D.C. Larry Gelbart's *Sly Fox*, a wild

adaptation of Ben Johnson's *Volpone* (1976), featured George C. Scott and Bob Dishy giving bravura performances. Bob Fosse's dance explosion, *Dancin'* (1978), a revue spotlighting Fosse's flashy choreography and Broadway's best dancers, ran at the Broadhurst for almost three years (becoming the theatre's longest-running show) before moving to the Ambassador Theatre.

Dancin' was followed by another triumph. On December 17, 1980, Peter Shaffer's acclaimed London play *Amadeus* opened at the theatre, with Ian McKellen as Salieri, Tim Curry as a comic Mozart, and Jane Seymour as the composer's wife. The season's most distinguished offering, it won the Tony Award for Best Play and Mr. McKellen won as Best Actor. This drama was followed by the musical *The Tap Dance Kid* about a talented youngster who is driven by the need to dance.

In 1984, Dustin Hoffman starred in a new production of Arthur Miller's *Death of a Salesman;* this was followed by a gender-switched revised version of Neil Simon's *The Odd Couple* starring Sally Struthers and Rita Moreno as the mismatched roommates; a new production of O'Neill's *Long Day's Journey Into Night* starring Jack Lemmon and Bethel Leslie; a return engagement of *The Life and Adventures of Nicholas Nickleby*; Neil Simon's popular *Broadway Bound*, which won a Tony Award for Linda Lavin; Andrew Lloyd Webber's musical *Aspects of*

Top: One of the dazzling numbers from Bob Fosse's *Dancin'* (1978). *Above:* Dan Stone as Jesus in *Godspell*, the long-running musical that moved from Off Broadway to the Broadhurst (1976).

107

Love; Joan Collins in a revival of Noël Coward's *Private Lives;* the short-lived *Shimada*; and Andre Heller's strange vaudeville evening, *Wonderhouse.*

The Broadhurst next served as home for Harold Prince's multi-Tony Award-winning musical *Kiss of the Spider Woman* with a score by Kander and Ebb and a book by Terrence McNally, starring Chita Rivera, Brent Carver, and Anthony Crivello, all of whom won Tony Awards for their performances. The musical, about prisoners in a Brazilian jail who escape into fantasies culled from movie musicals, had a long run of 906 performances.

The New York Shakespeare Festival brought George C. Wolfe's production of *The Tempest* to the Broadhurst on November 1, 1995. Patrick Stewart was praised for his performance as Prospero. The revival thrived for 71 performances. The next tenant at this theatre in March, 1996 was an unsuccessful comedy thriller called *Getting Away With Murder* by Stephen Sondheim and George Furth. In the cast were John Rubinstein, Christine Ebersol, Terrence Mann, and others, but the critics found the play neither thrilling nor funny. It expired after 17 performances.

Just in time for Christmas in 1996, a new production of the musical *Once Upon A Mattress* arrived, but it did not enjoy the success of the 1959 production which brought stardom to Carol Burnett. Sarah Jessica Parker, Jane Krakowski, Lewis Cleale, and David Aaron Baker headed the cast of the new version and the show, despite mostly negative reviews, managed to run for 187 performances.

On April 29, 1998, David Hare's *Judas Kiss* opened for a limited engagement. It starred Liam Neeson as Oscar Wilde and Tom Hollander as his lover, Lord Alfred Douglas. The play received mixed reviews with some critics feeling that Mr. Neeson was miscast. It ran for 38 performances.

A blockbuster came to the Broadhurst on January 14, 1999: *Fosse*, an exuberant dance revue spotlighting the choreography of Bob Fosse from his Broadway and Hollywood musicals. The razzle-dazzle spectacle found immediate favor with audiences, and went on to win the 1999 Tony Award as Best Musical. Some of the numbers were repeats from the earlier Fosse revue—*Dancin'*—but were brilliantly recreated by Ann Reinking, Chet Walker, and Gwen Verdon, and explosively performed by thirty-two dancers. It ran more than 1,100 performances.

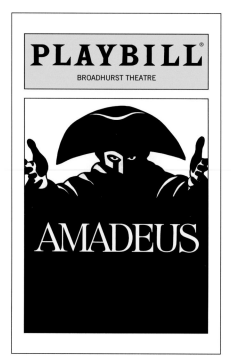

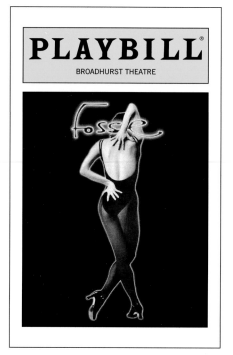

Left: PLAYBILL cover for *Amadeus* (1980). Peter Shaffer's prize-winning play. *Center:* Illustration of Sarah Jessica Parker cavorting as Princess Winnifred in the musical *Once Upon A Mattress* (1996). *Right:* PLAYBILL cover for *Fosse.*

PLYMOUTH THEATRE

By the time the Shuberts built the Plymouth Theatre in 1917, *The New York Times* reported: "It is a dull week when no new theatre opens." The Shuberts now had a block of theatres—the Plymouth and Booth on West Forty-fifth Street and the Shubert and Broadhurst, back-to-back with these, on West Forty-fourth Street.

The Shuberts leased their new Plymouth Theatre to the distinguished producer/director Arthur Hopkins. It was designed by architect Herbert J. Krapp, and *The Times* reported that it was simple in decor, was decorated in shades of brown, blue, and gold, and had a seating capacity of about 1,000 (since increased to 1,079), with only one balcony.

An unusual aspect of the opening bill on the night of October 10, 1917, was that it was not a new show. Clare Kummer's comedy *A Successful Calamity,* starring William Gillette, had been a hit the previous year at the Booth next door and it was revived with virtually the same cast at the Plymouth when it opened.

Producer Hopkins brought John Barrymore to the Plymouth in 1918 to play one of his most successful parts—Fedya in a dramatization of Tolstoy's *Redemption.* Hopkins directed the play, and Robert Edmond Jones designed a sumptuous production. Barrymore and the huge cast gave splendid performances. The producer even invited Tolstoy's son to attend a dress rehearsal, but the Russian's only comment afterward was "Where's Fedya's beard?"

Later in 1918 Walter Hampden played Hamlet at the Plymouth in a revival of Shakespeare's tragedy. On April 9, 1919, Hopkins jolted the town with his superlative production of *The Jest,* an Italian play by Sem Benelli starring John Barrymore as an effete painter and Lionel Barrymore as an odious Captain of the Mercenaries. The brilliant acting of the Barrymore brothers as deadly enemies, Robert Edmond Jones's magnificent Renaissance sets, and Hopkins's direction made this one of the early milestones in American theatre.

On December 22, 1919, Hopkins tried again with a Russian classic—Maxim Gorki's *The Lower Depths,* retitled *Night Lodging.* But despite excellent performances by Edward G. Robinson and Pauline Lord, it lasted only 14 performances.

The Roaring Twenties started auspiciously at the Plymouth with *Little Old New York,* a hit comedy by Rida Johnson Young that took place in New York of 1910, when, as Burns Mantle noted, "John Jacob Astor spoke with a German accent and Cornelius Vanderbilt ran a ferry." The play concerned an Irish girl, played by Genevieve Tobin, who masquerades as a boy in order to inherit a vast fortune. But she falls in love with the boy

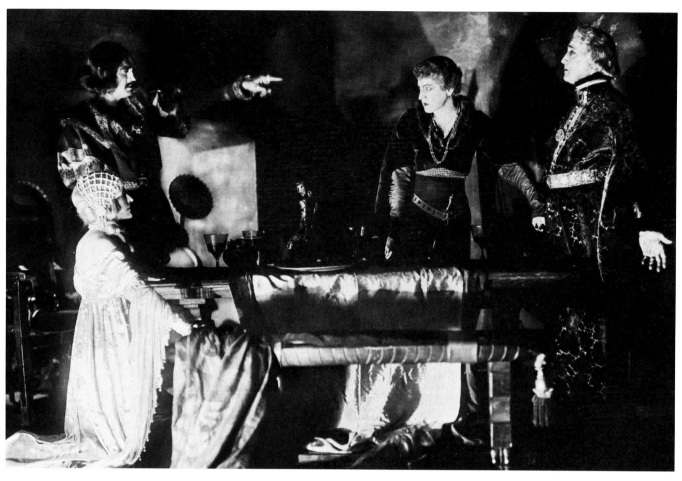

Maude Hanaford, Lionel Barrymore, John Barrymore, and Arthur Forrest in *The Jest* (1919).

who is the rightful heir and gives up her inheritance to win him (and his inheritance). This bit of Irish blarney was good for 311 performances.

Other highlights of the 1920s included Zoe Akins's serious study of a marriage gone wrong, *Daddy's Gone A-Hunting* (1921), with fine acting by Marjorie Rambeau, Frank Conroy, and Lee Baker; Arthur Hopkins's production of *The Old Soak* (1922), a lovable comedy about an alcoholic (Harry Beresford) and his wife, Matilda (Minnie Dupree), that was named one of the ten best plays of the season by Burns Mantle. Another family comedy, *The Potters,* by J.P. McEvoy, starred Donald Meek as Pa Potter, Catharine Calhoun Doucet as Ma, Raymond Guion (later Gene Raymond of the movies) as Bill Potter, and Mary Carroll as Mamie Potter. *The Potters* amused for 245 performances.

One of the American theatre's most significant plays,

What Price Glory?, by Maxwell Anderson and Laurence Stallings, detonated at the Plymouth on September 5, 1924. The drama, produced and directed by Arthur Hopkins, was the first war play to use the profane speech of soldiers. The program carried this puzzling note by Mr. Hopkins: "I am presenting *What Price Glory?* exactly as it has been given at the Plymouth Theatre for every performance, except for the elimination of three expressions that are used in the best families and by our noblest public officials." The play focused on battling army buddies, First Sergeant Quirt (William Boyd) and Captain Flagg (Louis Wolheim), and the characters became so memorable that a number of films were made about them. *What Price Glory?* ran for 435 performances.

Laurette Taylor, Frank Conroy, and Louis Calhern tried to make a success of Philip Barry's metaphysical play *In a Garden* (1925), but it was a bit too murky for

Above: In the foreground, Leyla Georgie, Louis Wolheim, and William Boyd in the rousing *What Price Glory?* (1924). *Below Right:* Zita Johann and Clark Gable as illicit lovers in the surrealistic *Machinal* (1928).

theatregoers. Winthrop Ames presented several Gilbert and Sullivan operettas during 1927. On September 1 of that year, another huge hit came to this theatre: a lively comedy called *Burlesque*, by Arthur Hopkins and George Manker Watters. It starred Hal Skelly as a burlesque comic and Barbara Stanwyck as his wife who performs in a seedy act with him. Burns Mantle named it one of the year's ten best plays and it had a healthy run of 372 performances.

The sensational Snyder-Gray murder case (Ruth Snyder was the first woman in America put to death by electrocution, for plotting to murder her husband) inspired an interesting surrealistic play, *Machinal* (1928), by Sophie Treadwell. Arthur Hopkins staged the drama, which was superbly played by Zita Johann in the Snyder role and by a young actor named Clark Gable as the lover who murders Snyder's husband.

On November 26, 1928, playwright Philip Barry returned to the Plymouth, this time in triumph. Arthur Hopkins produced and staged his felicitous comedy *Holiday,* and it became one of the theatre's most prized high comedies. Written specifically for Hope Williams, the socialite turned actress, the play dealt with a young man, Johnny Case (Ben Smith), who has made some money and wants to take a holiday and enjoy it while he

is still young. His socialite fiancée and her stuffy father oppose this, so he takes his joyous holiday with his fiancée's rebellious sister, played by Miss Williams. The star was understudied by Katharine Hepburn, who never got to play the role on Broadway but starred in the excellent movie version.

Hope Williams returned to the Plymouth in 1930 in *Rebound,* a comedy about divorce written especially for her by Donald Ogden Stewart, who had appeared with her at the Plymouth in *Holiday.* Burns Mantle selected it for his best-plays volume.

Highlights of the 1930s at the Plymouth included: Paul Muni at his finest in Elmer Rice's *Counselor-at-Law* (1931); Roland Young, Laura Hope Crews, and Frances Fuller in Clare Kummer's hilarious comedy *Her Master's Voice* (1933), voted one of the year's ten best plays by Burns Mantle; Tallulah Bankhead suffering a brain tumor in *Dark Victory* (1934); and Constance Cummings giving a memorable performance in Samson Raphaelson's comedy *Accent on Youth* (1934). Sidney Howard's *Paths of Glory* (1935), an impassioned play about a true, unjust incident in World War I, should have run longer than its 24 performances.

The second half of the 1930s saw Helen Jerome's

Top: Donald Ogden Stewart, Hope Williams, Ben Smith, and Barbara White in the charming Philip Barry comedy, *Holiday* (1928). *Above:* Paul Muni in Elmer Rice's *Counselor-at-Law* (1931).

faithful adaptation of Jane Austen's *Pride and Prejudice* (1935), which moved to the Plymouth from the Music Box and made the year's ten-best list; Robert E. Sherwood's deft adaptation of the French play *Tovarich*

(1936), with the famed Italian actress Marta Abba making her Broadway debut, co-starring with the suave John Halliday, another on Mantle's best-plays-of-the-year list; Gertrude Lawrence in one of her greatest roles, as a sappy society woman who finds God in the Oxford movement, in Rachel Crothers's scintillating *Susan and God* (1937), another best play of the year.

Robert E. Sherwood's *Abe Lincoln in Illinois* (1938), winner of the Pulitzer Prize and the first production of the new Playwrights Company, starred Raymond Massey as an incredibly convincing Abe. Clare Boothe's anti-Nazi play *Margin for Error* (1939), directed by Otto Preminger, featured Sam Levene as a comic police officer and Mr. Preminger as an odious German consul.

The Plymouth was constantly operating during the 1940s, with new hits, transfers from other theatres, and a few revivals. William Saroyan's *Love's Old Sweet Song* (1940), a screwball comedy about the plight of mankind, with Walter Huston, Jessie Royce Landis, and Alan Hewitt, was not as successful as his earlier plays. Alan Dinehart, Glenda Farrell, and Lyle Talbot ran seemingly forever in a sleazy comedy, *Separate Rooms* (1940); Mary Anderson was so nasty in *Guest in the House* (1942) that audiences hissed her, while critics raved.

Thornton Wilder won another Pulitzer Prize and rattled theatregoers with *The Skin of Our Teeth* (1942), a lunatic cartoon about the human race, starring Tallulah Bankhead as the eternal temptress; Fredric March as the inventor of the alphabet, the wheel, and adultery; Florence Eldridge as his homespun wife; and Montgomery Clift and Frances Heflin as his children.

Katharine Cornell, Raymond Massey, and Henry Daniell had a moderate success at the Plymouth in Dodie Smith's *Lovers and Friends* (1943). *Chicken Every Sunday* (1944), a homey comedy by Julius J. and Philip G. Epstein, was a wartime hit. Spencer Tracy returned to Broadway after many years in Hollywood to star in Robert E. Sherwood's drama *The Rugged Path* (1945), but the idealistic play, directed by Garson Kanin, ran for only 81 performances.

Mary Martin went Asian in a charming musical, *Lute Song* (1946), adapted from a Chinese classic by Sidney Howard and Will Irwin, with a score by Raymond Scott and two unknowns in the cast (Yul Brynner and Nancy Davis—later Mrs. Ronald Reagan). Clifton Webb returned to Broadway in Noël Coward's light comedy *Present Laughter* (1946), but it was too thin for critics and audiences. Tallulah Bankhead arrived in a dusty drama, *The Eagle Has Two Heads* (1947), by Jean Cocteau, with Helmut Dantine replacing Marlon Brando out of town because Ms. Bankhead claimed Brando was picking his nose and scratching his behind onstage, which would have helped this turkey considerably.

Alfred Drake and Marsha Hunt brought *Joy to the World* (1948), a play about the dangers of liberalism in Hollywood. Tallulah Bankhead and Donald Cook turned Noël Coward's *Private Lives* (1948) into a roughhouse wrestling match, and they succeeded for 248 performances.

The 1950s started out with a huge hit for this theatre. Samuel Taylor's *The Happy Time*, a sentimental comedy about a French Canadian family, starred Claude Dauphin, Kurt Kasznar, Johnny Stewart, and Eva Gabor. The Rodgers and Hammerstein production ran for 614 performances. In April 1952 Paul Gregory's production of Shaw's *Don Juan in Hell*, which had previously played at Carnegie Hall and the Century Theatre, moved to the Plymouth for a two-month run. It starred Charles Boyer, Charles Laughton (who staged it), Cedric Hardwicke, and Agnes Moorehead. On October 29 of the same year, one of the Plymouth's biggest hits opened. It was Frederick Knott's *Dial 'M' for Murder*, a thriller about a husband hiring a hit man to kill his wife. It starred Maurice Evans, Gusti Huber, Richard Derr, and John Williams as an impeccable inspector, and it ran for 552 performances.

Above: Gertrude Lawrence and Paul McGrath embrace the Oxford movement in *Susan and God* (1937). *Below:* PLAYBILL cover for the Pulitzer Prize-winning play *Abe Lincoln in Illinois* (1938).

Above Left: Tallulah Bankhead and baby dinosaurs in Thornton Wilder's *The Skin of Our Teeth* (1942). *Above Right:* Florence Eldridge and Fredric March in Wilder's Pulitzer Prize-winning play. *Below:* Donald Cook and Tallulah Bankhead during the calm before the storm in *Private Lives* (1948).

Highlights of the remainder of the 1950s included *The Caine Mutiny Court-Martial* (1954), staged by Charles Laughton, starring Henry Fonda, Lloyd Nolan, and John Hodiak in Herman Wouk's powerful adapta-tion of his novel *The Caine Mutiny;* Marge and Gower Champion and Harry Belafonte in *3 For Tonight* (1955), a "diversion in song and dance;" Margaret Sullavan in her last Broadway appearance, Carolyn Green's bubbly comedy *Janus* (1955), with Robert Preston and Claude Dauphin; Maurice Evans, Claudia Morgan, and Signe Hasso in a revival of Shaw's *The Apple Cart* (1956); Arnold Schulman's amusing *A Hole in the Head* (1957), with an expert cast including Paul Douglas, David Burns, Kay Medford, Joyce Van Patten, Lee Grant, and Tom Pedi; Peter Ustinov's satiric *Romanoff and Juliet* (1957), starring Ustinov as a general who plays cupid to a Russian boy and an American girl; Leslie Stevens's sexy comedy *The Marriage-Go-Round* (1958), starring Claudette Colbert, Charles Boyer, Julie Newmar, and Edmond Ryan, which ran into 1960.

The Plymouth greeted the 1960s with a smash musical, *Irma La Douce* (1960), that came by way of France and England. Directed by Peter Brook, it starred Elizabeth Seal who won a Tony for her performance as a French hooker, and Keith Michell as her boyfriend who disguises himself as her only patron to keep her to himself. Paddy Chayefsky's *Gideon* (1961) starred Fredric March as a debating angel, who is really God. Margaret Leighton and Anthony Quinn brought sparkle to a French/English play, *Tchin-Tchin* (1962).

Lillian Hellman had one of her rare failures with a satiric comedy about American materialism, *My Mother, My Father and Me* (1963), directed by Gower Champion, and starring Ruth Gordon and Walter Matthau. Arnold Wesker's British hit, *Chips with Everything* (1963), amused with the adventures of young recruits in an RAF training unit. Alec Guinness won a Tony Award for his memorable portrayal of the title role in *Dylan* (1964), with Kate Reid as his wife. William Hanley's *Slow Dance on the Killing Ground* (1964) was named one of the best plays of the year, but audiences avoided it.

In 1965, Neil Simon came up with his best and most immortal comedy, *The Odd Couple*, starring Walter Matthau as a sloppy sports announcer who rooms with an incredibly neat divorced man, played to perfection by Art Carney. It achieved a run of 965 performances. In 1966, however, Anthony Perkins, Connie Stevens, and Richard Benjamin starred in Mr. Simon's most insipid comedy, *The Star-Spangled Girl* (1966), a stultifying evening of vapidity; Edward Albee also came a cropper with his play *Everything in the Garden* (1967), based on a true incident involving Long Island wives who made

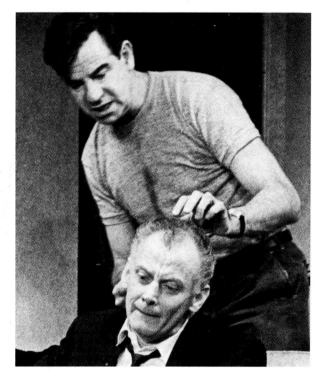

Top: The PLAYBILL cover had to change weekly to satisfy stars' egos (1958). *Above:* Walter Matthau and Art Carney in *The Odd Couple* (1965).

extra money as hookers. Mr. Simon redeemed himself with a deft trio of playlets called *Plaza Suite* (1968), starring Maureen Stapleton and George C. Scott in vignettes set at New York's celebrated Plaza Hotel. It ran for 1,097 performances.

During the 1970s, the Plymouth continued to reign as one of Broadway's top legitimate theatres. On December 13, 1970, Mr. Simon attempted his first serious drama with *The Gingerbread Lady*, a play supposedly inspired by Judy Garland's erratic career. It

Left: Clive Reville, Elizabeth Seal, and Keith Michell in *Irma La Douce* (1960). *Above:* George C. Scott and Maureen Stapleton in Neil Simon's *Plaza Suite* (1968).

starred Maureen Stapleton, who won a Tony as the alcohol-drenched singer, but it ran only 193 performances. In 1973 Jean Kerr came up with *Finishing Touches,* a comedy about a college professor's middle-age problems, but even with Barbara Bel Geddes and James Woods in the leads the play lingered for only five months.

Peter Cook and Dudley Moore assembled a sequel to their highly successful revue *Beyond the Fringe,* and they called the show *Good Evening* (1973), which ran for 228 performances. The Plymouth then had another British invader, which turned out to be one of its most illustrious tenants: Peter Shaffer's *Equus,* a London hit based on a true, bizarre case about a young boy who blinds a stable full of horses. It starred Anthony Hopkins as a psychiatrist and Peter Firth as the disturbed youth. Later in the run, Mr. Hopkins was succeeded by Anthony Perkins and Richard Burton. *Equus,* which ran for 1,209 performances in New York, won the Tony Award as best play of the season and won another Tony for its director, John Dexter.

Another British import, *Otherwise Engaged* (1977), by Simon Gray, starred Tom Courtenay as a British intellectual who tries to play a classical record and keeps getting interrupted by his scabrous friends; Elizabeth Swados's *Runaways* (1978) moved from the downtown New York Shakespeare Festival for 267 performances; *Ain't Misbehavin'* (1979), the Tony Award winning revue based on Fats Waller's music, moved from the Longacre and played for two more years. Jane Lapotaire, repeating her triumph from Britain as Edith Piaf in *Piaf,* won a Tony for her interpretation of the famous street singer.

In the fall of 1981, the Royal Shakespeare Company brought its acclaimed production of Dickens's *The Life and Adventures of Nicholas Nickleby* (1981), and the Plymouth Theatre had to accommodate its complex scenic design by constructing catwalks all over the house. The eight-hour play (performed over two nights, or on matinee day with a dinner intermission) caused a sensation for its staging (and $100 ticket price) and won a Tony for Best Play and for Best Performance by an Actor—Roger Rees. Directors Trevor Nunn and John Caird were also honored with a Tony for their inspired direction of this extremely complex production.

In 1982 the Circle in the Square offered Colleen Dewhurst in a revival of Ugo Betti's *The Queen and the*

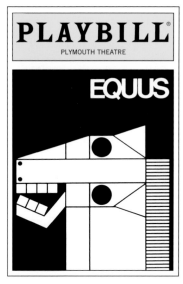

Far Left: Jane Lapotaire gives a Tony Award performance in *Piaf* (1981). *Left:* PLAYBILL cover for the award-winning *Equus* (1974). *Below:* Roger Rees and Emily Richard in the epic *The Life and Adventures of Nicholas Nickleby* (1981).

Rebels. In 1983, the New York Shakespeare Festival's production of the British play *Plenty* garnered raves. Written by David Hare, it offered memorable performances by Canadian actress Kate Nelligan and by American actor Edward Herrmann.

In 1983, this theatre housed an all-star revival of Kaufman and Hart's Pulitzer Prize-winning comedy, *You Can't Take It With You* with Jason Robards, Elizabeth Wilson, Colleen Dewhurst, Maureen Anderman, James Coco, Meg Mundy, Bill McCutcheon, and many others. This was followed by Tom Stoppard's Tony Award-winning play, *The Real Thing*, which also won Tony Awards for its stars, Jeremy Irons, Glenn Close, and Christine Baranski, and for its director, Mike Nichols. The play ran for 566 performances.

Another bonanza opened here in 1985: Lily Tomlin in her virtuoso one-woman show, *The Search For Signs of Intelligent Life in the Universe* by Jane Wagner, which won Ms. Tomlin a Tony Award for her dazzling performance. Next came a revival of Shaw's *Pygmalion* starring Peter O'Toole and Amanda Plummer; and Lanford Wilson's *Burn This,* with an explosive performance by John Malkovich and a Tony Award-winning performance by Joan Allen. Wendy Wasserstein's play, *The Heidi Chronicles,* won the Pulitzer Prize for its story of art historian Heidi Holland, whose life reflects the evolution of the feminist movement over 25 years. The play moved to the Plymouth from Off Broadway's Playwrights Horizons.

The Plymouth's next tenants were Tracey Ullman in *The Big Love* (1991); and Brian Friel's Tony Award-

winning play, *Dancing at Lughnasa,* a portrait of small-town Irish life, with Dublin's famed Abbey Theatre players. The drama won Tony Awards for Best Play

Donna Murphy plays a homely young woman smitten with a handsome soldier (Jere Shea) in Stephen Sondheim's *Passion* (1994).

(Brian Friel), Best Featured Actress (Brid Brennan) and Best Direction of a Play (Patrick Manson); and ran for 421 performances.

Gypsy Passion, the Flamenco musical that had been a success at Town Hall, played a return engagement in 1992 at this theatre. The following year *The Song of Jacob Zulu*, a Steppenwolf Theatre Company production, played here, followed by another Friel drama, *Wonderful Kentucky*, also from the Abbey Theatre. But this one received mixed reviews and closed after 9 performances.

The next Plymouth tenant fared better: *Passion* with music and lyrics by Stephen Sondheim, book and direction by James Lapine. The rather depressing tale of an odd romance between an ugly Italian woman and a handsome Italian officer was performed without inter-

mission. Although the musical received mixed reviews, reflecting the strongly mixed audience reaction, it ran for 280 performances and won the following Tony Awards: Best Musical, Best Book of a Musical (Lapine), Best Original Musical Score (Sondheim), Best Actress in a Musical (Donna Murphy). It was additionally nominated for these Tony Awards: Best Actor in a Musical (Jere Shea), Best Featured Actor in a Musical (Tom Aldredge), Best Featured Actress in a Musical (Marin Mazzie), Best Director of a Musical (Lapine), Best Costume Designer (Jane Greenwood), and Best Lighting Designer (Beverly Emmons).

Brian Friel had his third opening at the Plymouth in four years on March 19, 1995, when Brian Dennehy and Donal Donnelly starred in a revival of his 1981 play, *Translations*. It lasted only 25 performances.

The Lincoln Center Theater produced a splendid revival of Edward Albee's 1966 play *A Delicate Balance* on April 21, 1996 with Rosemary Harris, George Grizzard, Elaine Stritch, Elizabeth Wilson, Mary Beth Hurt, and John Carter. Highly praised by critics, the revival ran for 186 performances and won the following Tony Awards: Best Revival of a Play, Best Direction of a Play (Gerald Gutierrez), Best Actor (Grizzard). Rosemary Harris and Elaine Stritch earned Tony nominations for Best Actress in a Play.

April 28, 1997, brought a long-running musical to this theatre: *Jekyll & Hyde* with music by Frank Wildhorn and book and lyrics by Leslie Bricusse. It starred Robert Cuccioli as Jekyll/Hyde, Christiane Noll, and Linda Eder. The show received the following Tony Award nominations: Actor in a Musical (Cuccioli), Musical Book (Bricusse), Costume Designer (Ann Curtis), and Lighting Designer (Beverly Emmons), but won none. Despite very mixed reviews, the musical found its audience (many of whom christened themselves "Jekkies" and tracked the show through the Internet) and ran for 1,543 performances.

AMERICAN AIRLINES THEATRE

The American Airlines Theatre was originally the Selwyn Theatre, built by brothers Arch and Edgar Selwyn, celebrated producers of the 1910s. George Keister was the architect and the intimate theatre (1,051 seats) with one balcony was designed in Italian Renaissance style.

The October 3, 1918, opening night program boasted of the Selwyn as the most modern theatre in New York. But this was the height of World War I, and the program also had this startling message on the back cover: "BUY LIBERTY BONDS. Every German or Austrian in the United States, unless known by years of association to be absolutely loyal, should be treated as a potential spy. Keep your eyes and ears open. Whenever any suspicious act or disloyal word comes to your notice, communicate at once with the Bureau of Investigation of the Department of Justice, 15 Park Row, New York. We are at war with the most merciless and inhumane nation in the world."

Unfortunately, the opening production at the Selwyn was not memorable. The acclaimed actress and playwright Jane Cowl starred in *Information Please*, written by her and Jane Murfin. It was a flop. However, Ms. Cowl (famed for her portrayal of Juliet in Shakespeare's tragedy) redeemed herself in the next play, *The Crowded Hour*.

In 1919, two popular actors, Holbrook Blinn and Alan Dinehart, starred in a socialist drama called *The Challenge* by Eugene Walter. It ran for 72 performances.

The Selwyn's first hit was a World War I musical *Buddies*, by George V. Hobart, music and lyrics by B.C. Hilliam. According to Gerald Bordman in his excellent volume *American Musical Theatre*, one song was partially written by Cole Porter. The musical took place in Normandy shortly after the Armistice. A shy Yank (Roland Young) is in love with a French girl named Julie (Peggy Wood) but is too bashful to woo her. She's in love with him, but to arouse his interest, she flirts with his best buddy Sonny (Donald Brian). It works. Critics raved about the three leads and the musical ran for 259 performances although the score was considered mediocre.

On August 17, 1920, a musical called *Tickle Me* opened at this theatre. It had book and lyrics by Otto Harbach, Oscar Hammerstein II, and Frank Mandel, and music by Herbert Stothart. The popular comic Frank Tinney starred in it and employed his usual bit about talking to the audience during the show. The plot revolved around a company of actors who travel to Tibet to shoot a film. The show ran for six months, which in those days was considered substantial.

The Circle, Somerset Maugham's brilliant high comedy, proved popular at the Selwyn in 1921. Its distinguished cast included Leslie Carter, in her comeback; John Drew, who had also been away from the stage for several years; Estelle Winwood; and John Halliday. The circle of the plot involves a titled Englishwoman who had abandoned her husband and daughter and eloped with

Cover and billboard page from the program distributed on the opening night of the Selwyn Theatre in 1918. The play was *Information, Please*.

her lover. When the two elopers return to her estate years later, they discover that their son's wife is about to abandon him and run off with her lover. The circle is completed when the young elopers borrow the old elopers' car to take them to London. This high society fluff ran for 175 performances.

In 1921 a tragic incident occurred involving this theatre. At the time, several of the theatres on Forty-second Street supplanted their income by showing silent movies. In May 1921, the theatre was featuring the silent film of *A Connecticut Yankee in King Arthur's Court*. Katharine Hepburn was visiting her aunt in New York with her young brother Tom and took him to see the film. In the movie there was a scene in which a man devised a way to hang himself without dying. The next morning, when Hepburn went to wake her brother, she found him hanging dead in his upstairs bedroom. Hepburn's father told the press that his son was merely trying to emulate the false hanging, but to this day there is belief that he committed suicide, having had a history of depression.

A modest musical hit called *The Blue Kitten*, by Otto Harbach and William Clay Duncan, opened on January 13, 1922. It starred two old-timers—Joseph Cawthorn and Lillian Lorraine—and told of a headwaiter who tries to conceal his station in life so his daughter can marry a socialite. Although the score was pronounced inferior, the musical ran for 140 performances.

The famous actress Alla Nazimova appeared here in 1923 in a turgid drama called *Dagmar*, by Louis Anspacher, adapted from a French play. The sexually promiscuous heroine (Nazimova) promises her latest lover that he can kill her if she is ever unfaithful to him. Sure enough, she winds up with her throat slit. This turkey played 56 times.

An improbable drama called *The Guilty One* opened on March 20, 1923. Written by Michael Morton and Peter Traill, it told of a married woman who gets involved in the murder of her lover. It lasted only 31 performances.

A short-lived drama (15 performances) opened here on April 17, 1923. Called *Within Four Walls* by Glen Macdonough, it depicted a man who returns to Greenwich Village the day before his family home is to be demolished, which leads to a lot of nostalgic flashback scenes.

A whimsical musical titled *Helen of Troy, New York* arrived here on June 19, 1923. Written by two of the century's greatest wits, George S. Kaufman and Marc Connelly, with a score by Bert Kalmar and Harry Ruby,

Helen told of a woman (Helen Ford) who works in a collar factory in Troy, New York, but loses her job because she falls in love with the boss's son. She later invents the semi-soft style of collar which becomes highly commercial and wins back her lover. Paul Frawley and Queenie Smith also glowed in this frolic. It ran for 191 performances. As a promotional stunt, the producers sent out cardboard shirt collars with the name of the show and theatre on them.

A musical comedy called *Battling Butler*, starring the popular actor Charles Ruggles, arrived on October 8, 1923. Written by Ballard MacDonald, adapted from a British musical, *Battling Butler* had music by Walter L. Rosemont. The plot told of Alfred Butler, who resembles a boxer called Battling Butler so much that he's able to pass himself off as the pugilist. The real Battling Butler then urges him to take his place in the ring. *The New York Times* proclaimed that "musical comedies are getting better" and the show prospered for 288 performances.

Three plays of short duration next appeared. *Puppets*, a melodrama by Frances Lightner, had two actors in it who would become popular movie stars: Fredric March and Miriam Hopkins. Their play about a puppeteer lasted only 54 performances in 1925. *The Sapphire Ring* by

Laszlo Lakatos starred Helen Gahagan and Frank Conroy. This play about fidelity in marriage disappeared after 13 performances. A comedy thriller called *The Gorilla* by Ralph Spence featured two comic detectives and a gorilla in a spooky house. This one departed after 15 performances, although it was made into several films.

On November 10, 1925, the second edition of the famed *Charlot's Revue* returned with three of its original stars: Beatrice Lillie, Gertrude Lawrence, and Jack Buchanan. Ms. Lillie repeated her hilarious routine called "March With Me" that had fractured Broadway in 1924, and a new song, "A Cup of Coffee, A Sandwich and You," proved a hit. Although not as sensational as the 1924 edition, the 1926 *Charlot's* still managed to amuse audiences for 138 performances.

On May 25, 1926, something different opened at this theatre. Fakir Rahman Bey, in his first visit to the U.S., demonstrated practices of Fakirism including Body Rigidity, Thought Reading, Hypnotism, Burial Alive, and Talismans. He cavorted for three weeks.

A minor comedy called *The Man From Toronto*, by Douglas Murray, opened late in the season and tarried for only 28 performances. It concerned a woman who is

Fred Allen (front, in parka) and Fred MacMurray (second from left) in a takeoff on polar explorer Admiral Byrd from the revue *Three's a Crowd* (1930).
Right: Libby Holman sings "Something To Remember You By" to MacMurray in the same show.

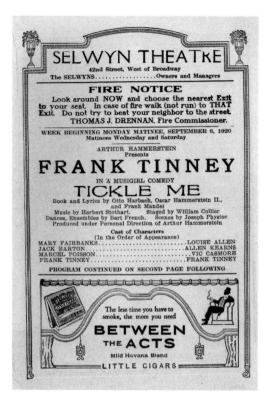

Program for *Tickle Me* (1926), the hit musical by Otto Harbach, Oscar Hammerstein II, and Frank Mandel.

forced by a will to marry a man she's never met, so she pretends to be the maid of the house to see if she likes him. She does.

A fun musical, *Castles In The Air*, came to the Selwyn via Chicago in September, 1926. Starring Vivienne Segal, J. Harold Murray, Bernard Granville, and Gregory Ratoff, it concerned two college cutups who mistakenly enter an exclusive club, thinking it's a hotel. In order to stay, one of them pretends to be a Latvian prince, and Ms. Segal is smitten. Her wealthy uncle sees through the ruse and to cure his niece, rents a Latvian castle where he intends to expose the fake prince. As usual in 1920s musicals—the prince turns out to be real and he and the niece live happily ever after. The book and lyrics were by Raymond W. Peck and the music by Percy Wenrich. It played for 160 performances.

In 1927-28, the Broadway season that witnessed the production of 270 shows, the Selwyn had its ups and downs. *The Mating Season*, a farce by William A. Grew, started things badly. It expired after 24 showings. A revue called *The Manhatters* fared a bit better, running for 68

performances. Three future movie stars—Alison Skipworth, Miriam Hopkins, and Douglas Montgomery—couldn't save Avery Hopwood's *The Garden of Eden*, which was cast out after 23 performances.

Nightstick, a melodrama by John Wray, the Nugents, and Elaine Stern Carrington, ran for 52 performances, then returned for 32 more. In the cast were Thomas Mitchell, Lee Patrick, and the author, John Wray. Ms. Patrick played a woman who has two love interests: a prisoner (Wray) and a detective (Mitchell). Of course, the detective wins out.

The Selwyn's biggest hit arrived on December 28, 1927. *The Royal Family* by George S. Kaufman and Edna Ferber was a thinly disguised farce about two royal families of the theatre, the Barrymores and the Drews, although the authors denied this. Suffice to say that Ethel Barrymore took great umbrage at the play and stopped speaking to Mr. Kaufman. The family in the play was called Cavendish and, certainly, the madcap Anthony Cavendish, actor, philanderer, alcoholic, and outrageous charlatan, could be no one but John Barrymore. The role was played to the hilt by Otto Kruger. The erratic Jed Harris produced this huge success, which filled the Selwyn for 345 performances. The comedy is still revived today and a musical version of it was in preparation for Broadway at this writing—in an age when Drew and Barrymore descendant Drew Barrymore is continuing her family's tradition of acting (and cutting up).

Producer Arch Selwyn was instrumental in bringing some of Britain's greatest revues to Broadway. In November 1928 he imported Noël Coward's triumphant *This Year of Grace*, the first revue in which Coward supplied all the music, lyrics, and sketches. He and Beatrice Lillie headed the show and it was pronounced the acme of wit and melody. Three Coward classics were sung: "A Room With a View," "Dance, Little Lady," and "World Weary," which Ms. Lillie sang sitting on a stool while biting an apple. Under the personal direction of C.B. Cochran, the stylish revue had dances by Tilly Losch and Max Rivers, sets and costumes by Oliver Messel, G.E. Calthrop, Norman Hartness, and Doris Zinkeisen. Beatrice Lillie's sketches—at a bus stop and on the Lido—were hilarious. The sophisticated romp ran for 158 performances.

This gem was followed by a dreadful revue called *Keep It Clean* in 1929. The tasteless material included a risque song about the marriage of Charles Lindbergh to Anne Morrow, and a hapless imitation of the great Beatrice Lillie. After 16 performances, this mess expired.

The Selwyn was graced with another stylish London revue, *Wake Up and Dream*, in 1929. The show starred Jack Buchanan, Jessie Matthews, and the ethereal dancer Tilly Losch who beautifully interpreted Cole Porter's song "What Is This Thing Called Love?" This was another C.B. Cochran revue and it was applauded for 138 performances.

By now, the Selwyn had become a prime house to showcase splendid revues. The next offering, *Three's A Crowd*, starring the great trio of Clifton Webb, Fred Allen, and Libby Holman (who had glittered in *The Little Show* on Broadway), proved that. The skilled cast also included Tamara Geva, Portland Hoffa (Mrs. Fred Allen), and Fred MacMurray. Howard Dietz and Arthur Schwartz wrote most of the music, but a squad of composers and lyricists contributed such gems as "Body and Soul" (danced by Mr. Webb and Ms. Geva in a strikingly lighted set by Hassard Short), and "Something To

Programs from *Shooting Star* (1933), *The Devil Passes* (1932), and *Three's a Crowd* (1930).

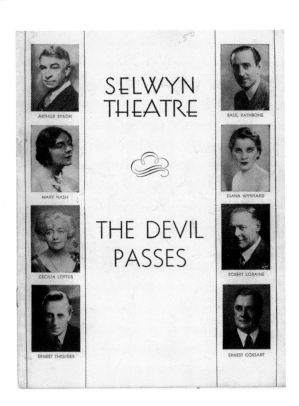

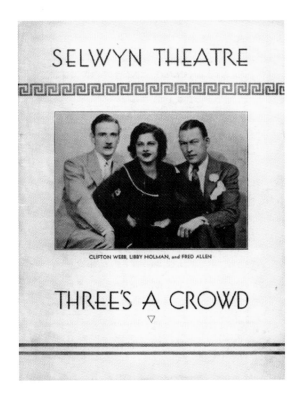

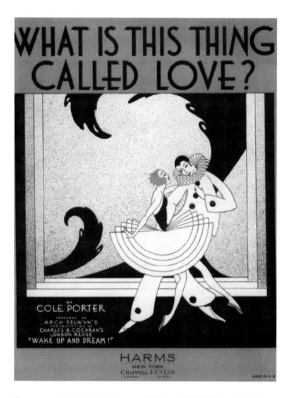

Sheet music for Cole Porter's "What Is This Thing Called Love?" from *Wake Up and Dream!* (1930).

Also at this time, Roundabout announced that it would rechristen the Selwyn the American Airlines Theatre, as part of a deal for the patron company to donate $8.5 million over ten years toward the project's expected $21 million cost.

The Selwyn was magnificently restored and reduced to a more intimate capacity of 750 seats. *The Daily News* reported that the restoration wound up costing $25 million, but extolled the theatre's wider seats and expanded leg room, the restored Renaissance-style murals, and the reddish-brown interior with a huge domed ceiling in blue, and little blue domes at the back. Most of all, critic Howard Kissel of *The News* praised the theatre's acoustics.

The American Airlines Theatre opened on July 27, 2000 with a revival of Kaufman and Hart's 1939 comedy *The Man Who Came To Dinner*, starring Nathan Lane as Sheridan Whiteside, a thinly disguised, acerbic portrait of critic Alexander Woollcott. Both the comedy and the new theatre on 42nd Street were warmly welcomed back.

Remember You By." The sketches were mostly by Mr. Dietz. Mr. Allen was riotous in a scene ribbing Admiral Byrd at the North Pole. Albertina Rasch staged the memorable dances and Hassard Short received an award from General Electric for his dazzling lighting. The revue ran for 272 performances.

The Selwyn had serious troubles in the Depression years. It housed eleven consecutive flops and, under new ownership, started showing films in 1934. In the 1950s it tried an experiment, attempting to combine films with live drama, but audiences weren't interested.

The Selwyn continued showing films into the 1990s. But late in that decade, as part of the Forty-second Street renaissance, the Roundabout Theatre Company, the 30-year-old, not-for-profit troupe that had been operating out of temporary quarters at the Criterion Center in Times Square, announced that it would restore the Selwyn and make it the company's permanent home. The project proceeded despite the collapse of the building housing the Selwyn's lobby. A new building, complete with magnificent rehearsal space, was built in its place.

Nathan Lane (in a wheelchair) as Sheridan Whiteside in Roundabout Theatre Company's revival of *The Man Who Came To Dinner* (2000) at the rechristened American Airlines Theatre.

AMBASSADOR THEATRE

The Ambassador was the first of six new theatres that the Shuberts built on West Forty-eighth and West Forty-ninth streets in the early 1920s. The plot at 215 West Forty-ninth Street presented a challenge to veteran theatre architect Herbert J. Krapp, being too narrow for a conventional theatre layout. The resourceful Mr. Krapp responded with an unorthodox configuration, placing the auditorium diagonally on the site. Its auditorium is wide rather than deep, offering an excellent view of the stage from all seats.

There have been some erroneous reports that this theatre opened with the Shuberts' famous operetta *Blossom Time*. Not so. The Ambassador welcomed a musical called *The Rose Girl* as its inaugural production on February 11, 1921, starring Marjorie Gateson. It was a success.

In May of 1921, a soldier revue called *Biff! Bing! Bang!* amused theatregoers. Later that year *Blossom Time* did open at the Ambassador and it was this theatre's first smash hit. A musical biography of composer Franz Schubert, it featured melodies adapted by fellow composer Sigmund Romberg from Schubert's themes. The showstopper was "Serenade." The operetta, which ran for 576 performances, became a perennial Shubert revival.

Operettas were the rage in the 1920s, and the Ambassador had its share of them. After *Blossom Time* came *The Lady in Ermine* (1922), a European import with added numbers by Al Goodman, who conducted pit orchestras for many Broadway shows, and by Mr. Romberg, whose "When Hearts Are Young" was the hit of the show. This success was followed by *Caroline* (1923), an American adaptation of a German operetta by Edward Kunneke, starring Tessa Kosta. Next came Victor Herbert's last show, *The Dream Girl* (1924), a fantasy that involved Fay Bainter and Walter Woolf in one of those "dream" plots which takes them back to the fifteenth century. There were some Sigmund Romberg interpolations in this operetta too, which was produced after Mr. Herbert's death.

A change of fare came to the Ambassador in 1925 when a highly successful revival of Shaw's *Candida*, starring Katharine Cornell, who became famed for her interpretation of the leading role, moved from the Eltinge Theatre to this house. More drama arrived when William A. Brady brought in his production of F. Scott Fitzgerald's *The Great Gatsby* (1926), adapted by Owen Davis and starring James Rennie as Gatsby, Florence Eldridge as Daisy, and Elliott Cabot as Tom Buchanan. Directed by George Cukor, the future great film director, the play ran for 113 performances.

The Ambassador returned to musicals with a solid hit, *Queen High,* which ran for almost 400 performances in 1926-27. It starred Charles Ruggles. From September 1927 until December 1929, the Ambassador had a string

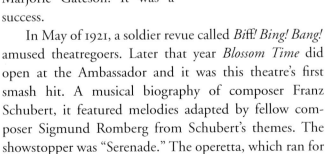

Above: James Bell and Spencer Tracy in the taut prison drama, *The Last Mile* (1930). *Right:* Olga Cook and Bertram Peacock in the popular operetta, *Blossom Time* (1921).

of quick flops. The few exceptions were an exciting police drama, *The Racket* (1927), starring Edward G. Robinson, Norman Foster, and John Cromwell, which ran for 120 performances and was named one of the year's ten best plays; and *Little Accident,* a play by Floyd Dell and Thomas Mitchell, with Mitchell starring as a man about to marry one woman when he discovers he is the father of another woman's child. This hit comedy moved from the Morosco Theatre and played for six months at the Ambassador.

In December 1929 *Street Scene*, Elmer Rice's Pulitzer Prize-winning play that took place in front of a Manhattan tenement house, moved from the Playhouse and completed its run of 601 performances at the Ambassador. *The Last Mile,* a prison drama by John Wexley, starring Spencer Tracy, Joseph Spurin-Calleia, and Henry O'Neill, moved from the Sam H. Harris Theatre to the Ambassador in October 1930. This lauded drama, one of the year's ten best, served as the springboard for Spencer Tracy's career in Hollywood.

Highlights of the 1930s at this theatre included *Are You Decent?* (1934), a comedy by Crane Wilbur in which Claudia Morgan announced to two suitors that she wished to have a baby without bothering with matrimony; *Kill That Story* (1934), a George Abbott/Philip Dunning production about a newspaperman whose wife unjustly divorces him because she believes he's having an affair with a stenographer at the newspaper; and Lucile Watson and Percy Kilbride in *Post Road* (1935), a comedy

about kidnapping that moved here from the Masque Theatre.

Ayn Rand's fascinating courtroom drama, *The Night of January 16* (1935), starring Doris Nolan and Walter Pidgeon, featured a jury selected from the audience at each performance to decide if Ms. Nolan was guilty of murder.

Other 1930s highlights: The Abbey Theatre Players from Dublin in a season of repertory, including *Katie*

Above: Sketch of actor David Garrick on the Ambassador PLAYBILL cover (1934). Right: Pixie Imogene Coca in The Straw Hat Revue (1939).

Roche, The Plough and the Stars, The Playboy of the Western World, and Juno and the Paycock (1937); Danny Kaye making his Broadway debut in The Straw Hat Revue (1939), with Imogene Coca, Alfred Drake, and Jerome Robbins in the cast, spoofing Broadway shows and current trends.

In 1935, the Shuberts sold their interest in this theatre; they did not buy it back until 1956. During those two decades, the Ambassador did not always function as a legitimate theatre. It was, on different occasions, leased as a movie theatre and as a studio for radio and TV.

The Ambassador returned to legitimacy on November 16, 1941, with Cuckoos on the Hearth, an insane comedy that moved here from the Mansfield Theatre, with Percy Kilbride, Janet Fox, and Howard St. John. Then two years elapsed before the theatre again housed a play. The Messrs. Shubert brought in a revival of Blossom Time in 1943, but it lasted for only 47 performances. Edward Chodorov's successful drama Decision moved here from the Belasco in 1944; the critically disdained but popular comedy School for Brides, starring Roscoe Karns, moved here from the Royale in 1944.

For the next twelve years, the Ambassador was leased to radio and television networks. In 1956 the Shuberts once again became the owners and reopened the refurbished house with a comedy, The Loud Red Patrick, starring

David Wayne and Arthur Kennedy. It was not successful and neither was the next tenant, Tallulah Bankhead in Eugenia, adapted from Henry James's The Europeans.

In 1957 Meyer Levin's adaptation of his book Compulsion, about the famous Leopold/Loeb murder trial in Chicago, played for 140 performances with Dean Stockwell and Roddy McDowall as the murderers and Ina Balin as one of their college classmates. In March 1958 Tyrone Power and Faye Emerson played Adam and Eve in George Bernard Shaw's Back to Methuselah for 29 performances. George C. Scott made his Broadway debut at the Ambassador with Judith Anderson in the 1958 drama, Comes a Day, and caused an immediate sensation by strangling a bird onstage (a prop, we hope). In 1959, Melvyn Douglas, E.G. Marshall, and Jean Dixon appeared in The Gang's All Here, a play about the scandalous

Top: Percy Kilbride (far left) and cast members of *Cuckoos on the Hearth* (1941). *Above:* Roddy McDowall and Dean Stockwell in *Compulsion* (1957).

Harding administration in Washington, D.C.

The 1960s at the Ambassador brought Paddy Chayefsky's *The Tenth Man* (1961) from the Booth Theatre; Gladys Cooper in an interesting adaptation of E.M. Forster's *A Passage to India* (1962); Joseph Cotten, Patricia Medina (his wife), Russell Collins, and John Beal in Joseph Hayes's drama about corruption in big business, *Calculated Risk* (1962); *Stop the World—I Want to Get Off* (1963), the celebrated Anthony Newley/Leslie Bricusse musical, transferred from the Shubert Theatre; Ira Wallach's *Absence of a Cello* (1964), with Fred Clark giving a comic performance; and appearances by the Paul Taylor Dance Company and Charles Aznavour (1965).

The second half of the decade brought Robert Preston and Rosemary Harris in James Goldman's witty play *The Lion in Winter* (1966), about Henry II and Eleanor of Aquitaine; Robert Anderson's captivating playlets under the collective title *You Know I Can't Hear You When the Water's Running* (1967), starring Martin Balsam, Eileen Heckart, and George Grizzard; and *We Bombed in New Haven* (1968), the unsuccessful Joseph Heller play about men at war, starring Jason Robards, Jr.

On January 22, 1969, the Ambassador hosted an experimental musical, *Celebration*, from the writers of *The Fantasticks*, Tom Jones and Harvey Schmidt. Called by Jones a "ritual experience. With laughs. And a few naked girls," *Celebration* enacted a battle between winter and summer in the persons of an old rich man and an orphan lad who vie for the love of a young woman named Angel. Starring Keith Charles, Susan Watson, and Ted Thurston, it stayed for 109 performances.

The 1970s brought unusual and varied fare to this theatre. A revival of Sandy Wilson's parody of 1920s musicals, *The Boy Friend* (1970), starring Sandy Duncan and Judy Carne, did not fare as well as the original. *Paul Sills' Story Theatre* (1970) turned out to be a delightful entertainment that presented children's classic stories with dance, song, narration, and pantomime. Melvin Van Peebles's *Ain't Supposed to Die a Natural Death* (1971) offered an original look at the black experience. Subsequent productions included Jim Dale in a lively revival of *Scapino* (1974) that featured the startling stunt of Dale dashing out into the audience balancing on the backs of seats; Estelle Parsons in a one-woman tour de

Robert Preston and Rosemary Harris in *The Lion in Winter* (1966). Can you spot the error on this 1967 PLAYBILL cover?

force, *Miss Margarida's Way* (1977) which treated the audience as a classroom of misbehaving children; a marvelous revue of Eubie Blake songs called *Eubie!* (1978); a revival of the gospel musical *Your Arms Too Short to Box with God* (1980); *Dancin'* (1980), the Bob Fosse dance triumph that moved here from the Broadhurst; and a 1983 revival of Arthur Miller's revised version of *A View from the Bridge,* with potent performances by Tony Lo Bianco, Rose Gregorio, James Hayden, Alan Feinstein, and Robert Prosky.

In 1985, this theatre housed *Leader of the Pack,* a revue of bouncy, early 1960s pop songs by Ellie Greenwich. In 1987, *Barbara Cook: A Concert for the Theatre* opened here, followed by a revival of the musical *Dreamgirls.* A revival of *Ain't Misbehavin'* in 1988 (with a reunion of the 1978 musical's original cast) proved popular, staying for nearly six months, though the Brazilian revue *Oba Oba '90* managed only 45 performances.

In 1989, Rex Harrison, Glynis Johns, and Stewart Granger starred in a revival of Somerset Maugham's witty comedy, *The Circle.* Mr. Granger made his Broadway debut in this play. Unfortunately, it was his only appearance on Broadway, as well as Harrison's last. Both were deceased a short time afterwards. The play ran for 208 performances.

Red Buttons On Broadway, a solo show featuring the comedian, played a short engagement at the Ambassador, then was followed by a big hit: the Off-Broadway musical *Bring in 'da Noise, Bring in 'da Funk,* which transferred to Broadway on April 25, 1996. Described as a "performance piece," the unique entertainment was based on an idea by Savion Glover (who choreographed and starred in it) and George C. Wolfe. Produced by the New York Shakespeare Festival, it thrilled critics and audiences with its vivid sketches of African-American history as expressed through dynamic dancing and singing. The musical earned nine Tony Award nominations and won the following: Best Director of Musical (Wolfe),

Top Left: Maurice Hines, Gregory Hines, and Lonnie McNeill in *Eubie* (1978). *Top Right:* Frances Conroy and Patrick Stewart in Arthur Miller's *Ride Down Mt. Morgan* (2000). *Above:* Saundra Santiago, Tony Lo Bianco, and James Hayden in the 1983 revival of *A View from the Bridge.*

Best Choreography (Glover), Best Featured Actress in a Musical (Ann Duquesnay) and Best Lighting (Jules Fisher). The hit ran for 1,130 performances.

In February 1999, a new production of Clark Gesner's 1967 Off-Broadway musical, *You're a Good Man, Charlie Brown* opened and won Tony Awards for its two featured performers, Kristin Chenoweth and Roger Bart. Chenoweth's performance of the interpolated song "My New Philosophy" by Andrew Lippa made her a star. The production was also nominated for Best Musical Revival and Best Direction of a Musical (Michael Mayer).

Arthur Miller's drama *Ride Down Mt. Morgan* opened here on April 9, 2000, to mixed reviews. Critics felt that it was an unfinished work. The play, about a charismatic bigamist whose two families meet after he's injured in a car accident, starred Patrick Stewart and Frances Conroy. Mr. Stewart caused controversy after one performance by making a curtain speech and accusing the play's producers of not properly publicizing the production. He was censured by Actors Equity and ordered to apologize. The drama earned a Best Play Tony nomination and a Best Featured Actress nomination for Ms. Conroy, and played for 120 performances.

WALTER KERR THEATRE

Formerly the Ritz, this theatre at 219 West Forty-eighth Street was renamed the Walter Kerr in 1990, in honor of the Pulitzer-winning drama critic for *The New York Times* and *The Herald Tribune.*

Jujamcyn Theatres, which acquired this intimate house in 1981, has spent millions to restore the theatre to its original splendor. A 1983 refurbishment returned the house to legitimacy after years as a cinema. A fuller refurbishment in 1990, the work of the Roger Morgan Studio, Inc., has made this one of Broadway's most impressive smaller playhouses.

The Ritz was built by the Shuberts as a sister theatre to their Ambassador Theatre on West Forty-ninth Street. It was built in a record sixty-six days in 1921. The architect was Herbert J. Krapp, the eminent theatre designer of that era, and the interior was done in Italian Renaissance with much gold leaf and Italian scrollwork.

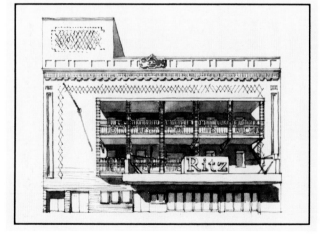

On March 21, 1921, the intimate (under 1,000 seats) new house opened with Clare Eames in John Drinkwater's *Mary Stuart,* preceded by a pantomime called *A Man About Town* that included in its cast the future opera composer Deems Taylor.

The Ritz flourished in the 1920s with some distinguished plays and players. A 1921 highlight was an ebullient performance by Ina Claire in *Bluebeard's Eighth Wife.* Roland Young appeared in *Madame Pierre* the following year, and in 1923, Katharine Cornell was admired in *The Enchanted Cottage,* as was Lynn Fontanne in *In Love with Love.* Audiences in 1924 were spellbound by Sutton Vane's eerie *Outward Bound,* starring Alfred Lunt, Leslie Howard, and Margalo Gillmore as dead passengers on a boat that is sailing to the "other world." The same year unveiled Hassard Short's *Ritz Revue,* hailed for its scenic splendors, and John Galsworthy's *Old English,* starring the noted character actor George Arliss.

A saucy Claudette Colbert graced *The Kiss in the Taxi* in 1925, followed by Helen Hayes in *Young Blood,* and Frank Morgan, Ralph Morgan, and Estelle Winwood in *A Weak Woman.* The next year found a young Ruby Keeler tapping in *Bye, Bye, Bonnie;* the beautiful Grace George in *The Legend of Leonora;* and Alice Brady and Lionel Atwill in *The Thief.*

On the day after Christmas 1927, bubbly Miriam Hopkins and Frank McHugh cheered first-nighters in *Excess Baggage,* followed by another winner, Janet Beecher in *Courage,* which ran until May 1929. The decade came to an end with the successful *Broken Dishes,* with Donald Meek and a young actress named Bette Davis, who was immediately snapped up by Hollywood.

Highlights of the 1930s at the Ritz included the famed comedy team of Smith and Dale in a hit play called *Mendel, Inc.;* noted monologist Ruth Draper in

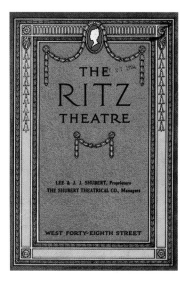

Top: Pixie children in *The Enchanted Cottage* peer out of a window seat (1923). *Above Right:* Standard Ritz program cover in the 1920s. "Herald" for Sutton Vane's mystical play *Outward Bound* (1924). *Right:* Bette Davis and Duncan Penwarden in *Broken Dishes* (1929). *Above:* Claudette Colbert vamps John Williams in *The Kiss in the Taxi* (1925).

some of her celebrated character sketches; the thriller *Double Door*; Frank Lawton and Mildred Natwick in *The Wind and the Rain*; Dennis King and Leo G. Carroll in Mark Reed's delightful *Petticoat Fever*; Ilka Chase and Peggy Conklin in *Co-Respondent Unknown*; the Surry Players (including Shepperd Strudwick, Anne Revere, and Katherine Emery) in a revival of *As You Like It*; and Jessica Tandy and Dame Sybil Thorndike in J.B. Priestly's *Time and the Conways*.

During the late 1930s the Federal Theatre Project (also known as the WPA Theatre) staged some exciting productions at the Ritz. Among them were T.S. Eliot's verse drama *Murder in the Cathedral;* the stirring *Power*, staged by the WPA's Living Newspaper unit, which ran for five months; and a lavish production of *Pinocchio* that ran for 197 performances.

In 1939 the Ritz became the CBS Theatre No. 4, from which live radio shows were broadcast, including the programs of the Town Crier, drama critic Alexander Woollcott. On December 22, 1942, the theatre went legit again with Leonard Sillman's *New Faces of 1943*, with the producer onstage to introduce fresh talent, including John Lund and Alice Pearce. After that, the long-running *Tobacco Road* moved in from the Forrest Theatre. Toward the end of 1943, NBC took the theatre over for use as a radio and TV studio; later, so did ABC.

It was not until December 1970 that the Ritz returned to legitimacy, with previews for a new rock

Top: (from left): Frank Lawton in *The Wind and the Rain* (1934). Standard Ritz program-cover sketch in the 1930s of British actors Mr. and Mrs. John Wood in *As You Like It*. Program art of Ruth Draper in her character sketches (1932). Above: The cast of *New Faces of 1943*.

opera called *Soon*. The show, which opened on January 12, 1971, marked the Broadway debuts of Peter Allen, Nell Carter, and Richard Gere. Also featured in the cast were Barry Bostwick, Marta Heflin, and Leata Galloway. Unfortunately, it closed after 3 performances. Later that year, Rip Torn and Viveca Lindfors played a brief run in Strindberg's *Dance of Death*.

Following a renovation in late 1971, the Ritz reopened on March 7, 1972, with the short-lived thriller *Children, Children*, starring Gwen Verdon in a rare non-

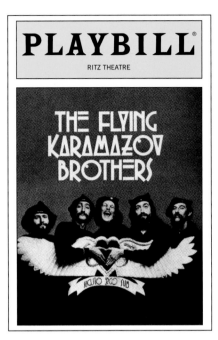

Above (from left): PLAYBILL cover for the rock musical *Soon* (1971). Program for *The Flying Karamazov Brothers*, which restored the Ritz to legitimacy in 1983. Program cover for *I Hate Hamlet* (1991).

musical role. In 1973 it housed a brief run of the English farce *No Sex, Please, We're British.* Shortly thereafter, the theatre was christened the Robert F. Kennedy Children's Theatre and, for a while, showed films.

The Ritz reopened under Jujamcyn ownership on May 10, 1983, with an entertaining troupe of New Vaudeville jugglers who named their show after themselves: *The Flying Karamazov Brothers.*

This was followed by the acclaimed *Ian McKellen Acting Shakespeare,* a one-man show of brilliance (1984); *Dancing in the End Zone,* a play with Pat Carroll and Laurence Luckinbill (1984); *Doubles,* the hit comedy about four tennis players, starring John Cullum, Ron Leibman, Austin Pendleton, and Tony Roberts (1985); *Jerome Kern Goes to Hollywood,* a revue of Kern melodies which brought back Elizabeth Welch, an American singer of fame in the 1930s who scored a huge success in London musicals (1986); a new play called *A Month of Sundays* (1987); the musical *Late Nite Comic* with music and lyrics by Brian Gari and a book by Allan Knee (1987); the comedy team of Penn & Teller (1987); and a revival of the musical *Chu Chem* (1989).

In 1990, Jujamcyn spent $1.5 million to restore the

Ritz to its original legitimate splendour. According to *Interior Design* magazine, the total interior renovation of the Ritz was achieved by Karen Rosen of KMR Designs, Ltd., Manhattan. Her client, Richard Wolff, then president of the Jujamcyn Theatre Corp., requested that the Ritz be made elegant by restoring its classical feeling of the 1920s. Ms. Rosen chose a color scheme of pink/mauve/gray touched with black to reflect the '20s look while appealing to current tastes. She restored ceiling decorations and murals and designed Art Deco-type sconces, chandeliers, balcony, and ceiling lights to achieve illumination without jarring glare.

When the refurbished 947-seat Ritz Theatre was rechristened the Walter Kerr in 1990, the inaugural production was August Wilson's *The Piano Lesson,* which won both the Pulitzer Prize and the New York Drama Critics Awards for the season's best play. After that came Paul Rudnick's amusing *I Hate Hamlet,* with Nicol Williamson playing the ghost of John Barrymore and sparkling performances by Celeste Holm, Adam Arkin, Jane Adams, and Evan Handler. *Crazy He Calls Me* ran briefly in 1991, and then came *Two Trains Running,* another chapter in August Wilson's cycle of plays about black life in twentieth-century America, which won a Tony Award for Larry Fishburne as Best Featured Actor in a Play.

Tony Kushner's *Angels in America: Millennium Approaches* caused a sensation here in 1993. The first half of this epic drama about AIDS, loyalty, and war in heaven during the Reagan era won the Pulitzer Prize, the Tony Award, and the New York Drama Critics Circle Award for the best play of the season. Additional Tony Awards went to Ron Leibman (Best Leading Actor), Stephen Spinella (Best Featured Actor), and George C. Wolfe (Best Direction of a Play). The play continued for 367 performances.

In 1994, Part II of the play, *Angels in America: Perestroika*, joined it in repertory, and was critically acclaimed. *Perestroika* again won the Tony Award as Best Play, and Mr. Spinella won a second Tony for his acting in the role of Prior Walter, this time Best Leading Actor. The Best Featured Actor award went to Jeffrey Wright. *Perestroika* continued for 216 performances, closing Dec. 4, 1994, just two weeks after *Millennium Approaches* ended its run.

In February, 1995, Terrence McNally's play *Love! Valour! Compassion!* moved here from its successful Off-Broadway run at the Manhattan Theatre Club. The play dealt with three weekends spent by a group of gay friends in Dutchess County, New York and it received glowing reviews. It won Tony Awards for Best Play (Terrence McNally) and Best Featured Actor (John Glover). The play ran for 249 performances.

Patti LuPone On Broadway starred the popular diva backed by four men. Act I featured a variety of show tunes; Act II offered songs from Ms. LuPone's Broadway career. The entertainment ran for 46 performances.

On March 28, 1996, the August Wilson play cycle added another chapter at the Walter Kerr with the opening of *Seven Guitars*, which received a dozen favorable reviews. The play, about a Pittsburgh musician who dreams of going to Chicago to record a hit song, won the 1996 New York Drama Critics Circle Award for Best Play, and a Tony Award for Featured Actor in a Play (Reuben Santiago-Hudson), Other Tony Award nominations included Featured Actor (Roger Robinson), Featured Actresses (Viola Davis and Michele Shay), Best Play (August Wilson), Best Director (Lloyd Richards), Best

Top: Program cover for *Angels in America: Millennium Approaches* (1993). *Above:* Stephen Spinella is transported by the supernatural Ellen McLaughlin in Tony Kushner's *Angels in America: Millennium Approaches*, which won the Pulitzer Prize and Tony Award. Photo by Joan Marcus.

Scenic Designer (Scott Bradley), and Best Lighting (Christopher Akerlind). It had 187 performances.

A new production of Noël Coward's comedy *Present Laughter* (first seen on Broadway in 1946 with Clifton Webb) arrived on November 18, 1996. This time Frank Langella acted the role of Garry Essendine, said to be patterned on Mr. Coward himself. The new production included full frontal male nudity, which some critics and theatregoers found gratuitous. The comedy ran for 175 performances and was nominated for the Tony Award as Best Revival of a Play.

The Beauty Queen of Leenane, an Irish play by Martin McDonagh, transferred from Off Broadway to the Walter Kerr on April 23, 1998, to much acclaim. Concerning the thorny relationship between a repressed Irish woman and her manipulative mother with whom she lives, the drama was hailed for its writing and acting and won the following Tony Awards: Best Actress (Marie Mullen), Best Featured Actress (Anna Manahan), Best Featured Actor (Tom Murphy), and Best Director (Garry Hynes). It was also nominated for Best Featured Actor (Brian F. O'Byrne) and Best Play (Martin McDonagh). It played for 372 performances.

April 1, 1999, brought another Irish play to this theatre—*The Weir* by Conor McPherson. The play took place in an Irish pub where several local men and a female visitor exchange increasingly chilling ghost stories. The play was moderately successful and ran until the end of November.

The next tenant was *Waiting in the Wings,* a 1960 play by Noël Coward that had never been produced on Broadway. Timed to the centenary of Coward's birth, the play starred Lauren Bacall and Rosemary Harris as rival actresses in an English retirement home, with many vintage stars in supporting roles. The play was updated by Jeremy Sams. It received two Tony Award nominations: Rosemary Harris (Best Actress) and Helen Stenborg (Best Supporting Actress). It ran at the Walter Kerr Theatre for three months starting in December 1999, then moved to the Eugene O'Neill Theatre. Sadly, it was the last Broadway show produced by Alexander H. Cohen, who passed away in spring 2000.

Fall 2000 saw Mary Louise Parker starring in David Auburn's *Proof,* which won the Pulitzer Prize.

Left: PLAYBILL cover for *The Weir* (1999). *Center:* Brian O'Byrne and Marie Mullen in *The Beauty Queen of Leenane* by Martin McDonagh (1998). Photo by Carol Rosegg. *Right:* PLAYBILL cover for Pulitzer Prize-winner *Proof* (2000).

NEDERLANDER THEATRE

The Nederlander Theatre has had a long and distinguished history under several different names: the National, the Billy Rose, and the Trafalgar.

Walter C. Jordan, a theatrical agent of note, built the National Theatre at 208 West Forty-first Street. When it opened on September 1, 1921, *The New York Times* reported that the new house cost $950,000 to build, was designed by architect William Neil Smith, and contained 1,200 seats, making it capable of housing both dramatic productions and musicals.

At the time of its opening, there were still plenty of other full-size theatres on the downtown side of Times Square. But with the demolition of the Casino, the Comedy, the Empire, the old Broadway, and other vintage playhouses over the years, the National eventually became the southern outpost of the Broadway theatre district, a distinction it has held for nearly half a century.

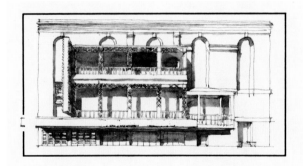

The theatre's original interior was done in burnished Italian walnut with gold embellishments. "The style is early Renaissance and the carved figures are of lyric and epic subjects, unobtrusive but attractive, and emerging in the half round from wood like Flemish carvings," wrote *The New York Times*. The paper went on to praise Mr. Jordan for providing actors with luxurious dressing rooms with baths and the audience with the latest in rest rooms and lounges, making a trip to the new theatre a comfortable and pleasurable experience.

Unfortunately, the National's opening show was *Swords*, Sidney Howard's first play, which ran for only 36 performances. Mr. Howard, however, benefitted from the experience. He married Clare Eames, who played the leading role.

In February 1922 the theatre had a stroke of luck in booking a thriller that would become a classic of its genre: *The Cat and the Canary*, written by actor John Willard. Critic Alexander Woollcott wrote in *The Times*, "He has turned out a creepy young thriller, nicely calculated to make every hair on your head rise and remain standing from 8:30 till nearly 11." The play, which took place in a spooky mansion on the Hudson, required an heiress (Florence Eldridge) to remain sane, while people were being snuffed out all around her, in order to win her inheritance. Henry Hull was the costar.

In 1923 Walter Hampden revived the Rostand classic *Cyrano de Bergerac* and was rewarded with great notices and a run of 250 performances. The blank verse adaptation of the play was by Brian Hooker. Another hit followed in 1924 when H.B. Warner starred in *Silence,* a melodrama in which a crook (Warner) takes the rap for a crime that his daughter has committed.

The popular movie actress Lila Lee appeared at the National in 1925 in one of those French farces about young people who are forced to marry by their parents and then discover that they really love each other. Movie fans bought it for 146 performances. Later in the year *The*

Top: Florence Eldridge as the menaced heiress in *The Cat and the Canary* (1922). *Above:* Walter Hampden in the classic *Cyrano de Bergerac* (1923).

Gorilla, a popular spoof of mystery plays, transferred here from the Selwyn Theatre. Walter Hampden next moved in from his own house, the Hampden Theatre, with his production of *Hamlet,* and this classic was followed early in 1926 by the great magician Houdini in a spectacular personal appearance.

Fredric March came to the National in 1926 in *The Half-Caste,* subtitled "A story of love and sacrifice in a Land of Forgotten Men," but *The Times* labeled it "a trite and loquacious drama." The National's next offering fared better. It was George M. Cohan's production of a play called *Yellow,* in which Chester Morris played a rotter. (There was a young actor in the supporting cast named Spencer Tracy.) Some first-nighters felt that the play's author, Margaret Vernon, was a pseudonym for Mr. Cohan. It ran for 132 performances.

John Willard, who had given the National the smash *The Cat and the Canary,* tried again with a melodrama called *Fog* in 1927, but the critics found it murky and it evaporated after 97 performances. Next came a huge hit and one of the National's most fondly remembered shows. It was A.H. Woods's production of Bayard Veiller's *The Trial of Mary Dugan* and it starred Ann Harding as the Mary who was accused of murdering one Edgar Rice. The court remained in session for 437 times.

The 1920s came to a dramatic close at the National with the opening of Martin Flavin's *The Criminal Code,* which jolted theatregoers with its realistic view of life in the big house. Arthur Byron gave a powerful performance as an inmate who witnessed a murder in the warden's office but chose not to reveal which of his prison mates committed the crime. It thrilled audiences for 174 performances.

Peking's most illustrious actor, Mei Lan-Fang, played a highly successful Broadway engagement with his Chinese company of actors, singers, and musicians in 1930. He opened first at the Forty-ninth Street Theatre, then moved to the National for an additional three weeks. On November 13, 1930, a landmark theatrical event occurred at the National: Herman Shumlin opened his production of *Grand Hotel,* a swirling drama based on a play by Vicki Baum, translated from the German by William A. Drake. The opulent production was the first dramatic play on Broadway to use a revolving stage, and

Top Left: Henry Hull and Eugenie Leontovich in *Grand Hotel* (1930). *Top Right:* Lillian Gish, Moffat Johnston, and Kathryn Collier in *Within the Gates* (1934).

it captivated audiences with its portrayal of life in a luxury hotel in Berlin. Eugenie Leontovich played a weary Russian ballerina, Sam Jaffe played a clerk with only a few weeks to live, Henry Hull was a baron who gets murdered in the hotel, and the rest of the enormous cast played employees and guests of the Grand Hotel, with myriad problems. It ran for 459 performances, and was adapted as a hit musical in 1988.

The National had a series of failures and quick bookings during 1932 and 1933 and was dark for more than a year during those gray Depression days. But on October 22, 1934, a distinguished drama opened at this theatre. It was Sean O'Casey's *Within the Gates,* directed by Melvyn Douglas and starring Lillian Gish as a prostitute, Bramwell Fletcher as a poet, and Moffat Johnston as a bishop. The play took place in London's Hyde Park, and the very large cast represented the great variety of humanity who spent their days in the park. There was music, dancing, and philosophizing, and Brooks Atkinson in *The Times* pronounced: "Nothing so grand has risen in our impoverished theatre since this reporter first began writing of plays."

A charming, nostalgic play, *Remember the Day,* by Philip Dunning and Philo Higley, came to the National on September 25, 1935. It starred Frankie Thomas as a schoolboy who has a crush on his teacher (Francesca Bruning) until he sees her kissing the school's athletic coach (Russell Hardie). A novelty of the well-received play was that Frank M. Thomas, Sr., played the father of Frankie Thomas.

Another fine drama, *Ethan Frome,* adapted by Owen and Donald Davis from the novel of the same name by Edith Wharton, opened in January 1936. Staged by Guthrie McClintic, the play had magnificent performances by Raymond Massey, Ruth Gordon, and Pauline Lord, but its depressing story and somber atmosphere resulted in a run of only 119 performances.

On November 24, 1936, New York's elite descended upon the National in their finest evening wear and jewels to welcome Noël Coward and Gertrude Lawrence back to the Broadway stage in Coward's collection of one-act plays under the umbrella title *Tonight at 8:30.* The nine playlets were performed in groups of three at three different performances. Coward and Lawrence had not been seen on Broadway together since 1931, when they triumphed in Coward's *Private Lives,* and their return was the social event of the 1936-37 season. On opening night, during the first intermission, a lady had her chinchilla coat stolen. At openings in those days, there was always a gray-haired detective stationed in the theatre to keep an eye on the audience. This supersleuth apprehended the thieves and the lady had her coat back by the time the final curtain fell.

In 1938 Orson Welles and John Houseman's celebrated Mercury Theatre had such success with its revivals of Shakespeare's *Julius Caesar* and Thomas Dekker's *The Shoemaker's Holiday* that they moved these productions from the small Mercury Theatre to the larger National. The group was the sensation of the season. They played *Julius Caesar* in black shirts as an indictment of fascism;

Top: Program-cover art of British actress Elizabeth Simpson Inchbald.
Above: Gertrude Lawrence and Noël Coward in *Tonight at 8:30*.

and *The Shoemaker's Holiday* was turned into a rowdy, lusty prank without an intermission. The Mercury Theatre company for these two productions included such actors as Mr. Welles, Joseph Cotten, Martin Gabel, Hiram Sherman, John Hoysradt, George Coulouris, Stefan Schnabel, Vincent Price, Ruth Ford, Edith Barrett, Elliott Reid, and Whitford Kane.

On February 15, 1939, the National housed one of its finest tenants. Lillian Hellman's vitriolic play about greed, *The Little Foxes,* starred Tallulah Bankhead as Regina Giddens. It was Tallulah's first superior role in the American theatre. Herman Shumlin's direction was praised and so was the supporting cast: Patricia Collinge, Frank Conroy, Dan Duryea, Carl Benton Reid, Charles Dingle, and Florence Williams. It ran for 410 performances.

During the 1940s the National housed some memorable productions. Ethel Barrymore had one of her greatest triumphs in Emlyn Williams's drama *The Corn Is Green,* in which she played a determined schoolteacher in Wales who discovers literary talent in one of the local miners and exerts all her power to make a success of him. The New York Drama Critics Circle named it the best foreign play of the year, and it ran for 477 performances during the 1940-41 season.

Another notable production came to this theatre in November 1941: Maurice Evans and Judith Anderson in Shakespeare's *Macbeth.* Staged by Margaret Webster, the revival was acclaimed as one of the finest productions of this classic ever mounted in the United States. It ran for 131 performances. In 1943 Sidney Kingsley's *The Patriots* opened and won the New York Drama Critics Award as best play of the season. The cast included Raymond E. Johnson as Thomas Jefferson, House Jameson as Alexander Hamilton, and Cecil Humphreys as George Washington. Mrs. Sidney Kingsley, Madge Evans, played a romantic role.

A failure of note was a musical called *What's Up?,* which happened to be Alan Jay Lerner and Frederick Loewe's first Broadway musical. Jimmy Savo had the lead, and the staging and choreography were by George Balanchine, but the critics declared that nothing was up and the show closed after 63 performances in 1943. Early in 1944, Eva Le Gallienne and Joseph Schildkraut acted brilliantly in a revival of Chekhov's *The Cherry Orchard,*

Top Left: Ethel Barrymore and Richard Waring in *The Corn is Green* (1940). *Top Right:* Tallulah Bankhead in her biggest hit, *The Little Foxes* (1939).

staged by Ms. Le Gallienne and Margaret Webster. Later that year Ethel Barrymore returned to this theatre in an adaptation of the Franz Werfel novel *Embezzled Heaven*, but the play was not a success. Lerner and Loewe returned to the National in November 1945 with a delightful musical called *The Day Before Spring,* about a college reunion. Anthony Tudor created the ballets and the cast included Irene Manning, John Archer, Bill Johnson, Estelle Loring, and dancer Hugh Laing. The pleasant musical lasted for 165 performances. This was followed by one of the most entertaining revues ever produced on Broadway—*Call Me Mister*—satirizing the plight of the returning servicemen and servicewomen from World War II. Produced by Melvyn Douglas and Herman Levin, the revue had a beguiling score by Harold Rome and sharp performances by Betty Garrett, Jules Munshin, Danny Scholl, Bill Callahan, Maria Karnilova, and many others, and had a gratifying run of 734 performances.

Judith Anderson returned to the National in her shattering performance as Medea in 1947. Assisted by John Gielgud as Jason and Florence Reed as the Nurse, she brought Robinson Jeffers's adaptation of Euripides' tragedy to painful life. It had a run of 214 performances, still a Broadway record for the 2,400-year-old classic. Mr. Gielgud was in the National's next production as well,

Crime and Punishment, costarring Lillian Gish, but the adaptation of Dostoyevsky's novel was not a success. Another failure followed in 1948: Gertrude Lawrence attempted to revive Noël Coward's *Tonight at 8:30,* with young Graham Payn, but it did not come off. That spring Michael Redgrave and Flora Robeson revived *Macbeth,* but that, too, failed.

The string of flops was broken in December 1948, when a delirious revue, *Lend an Ear,* written entirely by Charles Gaynor, which became an audience favorite. Carol Channing was an overnight success as a loony, wide-eyed blonde in such numbers as "The Gladiola Girl" and "Opera Without Music"; and Yvonne Adair, William Eythe, Gene Nelson, and the rest of the cast made this one of the theatre's most fondly remembered revues.

John Garfield and Nancy Kelly starred in Clifford Odets's *The Big Knife,* an expose of Hollywood, in 1949, but despite excellent performances and expert direction by Lee Strasberg the play was only a moderate success. The 1940s came to a scintillating end at the National with Sir Cedric Hardwicke and Lilli Palmer in a shimmering revival of Shaw's *Caesar and Cleopatra,* staged by Hardwicke.

Highlights of the 1950s included an appearance by Les Ballets de Paris and Louis Calhern in *King Lear,* both in 1950; Katharine Cornell, Grace George, and Brian

Above: Souvenir program for Judith Anderson in *Medea* (1947). *Below:* The happy military revue, *Call Me Mister* (1946).

Aherne in a highly successful revival of Somerset Maugham's *The Constant Wife* (1951); Tennessee Williams's fascinating but obscure play, *Camino Real* (1953), with Eli Wallach as Kilroy; and Margaret Sullavan, Luella Gear, John Cromwell, and Scott McKay in Samuel Taylor's sterling comedy of manners *Sabrina Fair* (1953).

In 1955 Paul Muni returned to the Broadway stage in one of his finest roles, in *Inherit the Wind,* the Jerome Lawrence/Robert E. Lee play about the sensational Scopes "Monkey Trial." Mr. Muni and his costar, Ed Begley, both won Tony Awards for their powerful performances in parts inspired by the great trial lawyer Clarence Darrow (Muni) and William Jennings Bryan (Begley). The enormous cast also included Bethel Leslie, Muriel Kirkland, Staats Cotsworth, and Tony Randall (who, as artistic director of his own National Actors Theatre, gave the play a major Broadway revival in 1996). Directed by Herman Shumlin, it ran for 806 performances, the longest running non-musical in this theatre's history. Mr. Muni was succeeded by Melvyn Douglas during the run.

In 1958, Arlene Francis, Joseph Cotten, and Walter Matthau amused audiences for 263 performances in Harry Kurnitz's *Once More with Feeling.* This comedy was the last show to play the National Theatre before it was bought by Billy Rose, who renamed it after himself. A songwriter, producer, and millionaire art collector, Mr. Rose spent a fortune refurbishing his new theatre in lush red and gold and reopened it on October 18, 1959, with Maurice Evans, Sam Levene, Diane Cilento, Pamela Brown, Diane Wynyard, and Alan Webb in Shaw's *Heartbreak House.* The revival ran for 112 performances.

The Billy Rose greeted the 1960s with Katharine Cornell in her final play on Broadway before retirement. It was *Dear Liar,* Jerome Kilty's comedy, with Ms. Cornell and Brian Aherne reading letters adapted for the stage

from the correspondence of Mrs. Patrick Campbell and George Bernard Shaw. The play ran for only 52 performances.

In October 1960 *The Wall,* an adaptation of John Hersey's novel, presented a harrowing story about the Warsaw Ghetto. The cast included George C. Scott, Joseph Buloff, David Opatoshu, and Marian Seldes, and the drama ran for 167 performances.

Edward Albee's first full-length play, *Who's Afraid of Virginia Woolf?,* opened at the Billy Rose on October 14, 1962, and sent shockwaves through Times Square. The stinging drama about a self-destructive married couple, brilliantly played by Uta Hagen and Arthur Hill, and their unfortunate guests—George Grizzard and Melinda Dillon—was the sensation of the season and won Tony Awards for its author, director (Alan Schneider), stars (Ms. Hagen and Mr. Hill), and producers (Richard Barr and Clinton Wilder). It ran for 664 performances. Two years later, Mr. Albee tried again at this theatre with a play called *Tiny Alice,* starring John Gielgud and Irene Worth, but not even the actors seemed to understand what this pretentious play was all about. A series of short plays by Albee and Samuel Beckett was presented at the Billy Rose by the Playwrights Repertory Theatre in 1968, followed by the Minnesota Theatre Company's revivals of *The House of Atreus* and *The Resistible Rise of Arturo Ui.* The decade came to an end with a sleek revival of Noël Coward's *Private Lives,* costarring Brian Bedford and Tammy Grimes, who won a Tony Award for her hoydenish performance as Amanda.

In 1971, the Royal Shakespeare Company's production of *A Midsummer Night's Dream,* directed by Peter Brook, provided great fun; and later that year, Harold Pinter's *Old Times* was hailed. In 1974 Brian Bedford and Jill Clayburgh were delightful in Tom Stoppard's buoyant comedy, *Jumpers.*

The theatre closed for a year in 1978, but then was bought by James and Joseph Nederlander and the British firm of Cooney-Marsh. It was beautifully refurbished and renamed the Trafalgar. It housed two British hits: *Whose Life Is It Anyway?,* starring Tom Conti, who won a Tony Award for his performance, and Pinter's *Betrayal,* starring Raul Julia, Blythe Danner, and Roy Scheider.

In late 1980 the Trafalgar became the Nederlander Theatre, named in honor of the late theatre owner David

Top: PLAYBILL covers for two British hits, *Whose Life Is It Anyway?* (1979) and *Betrayal* (1980). *Above:* Uta Hagen, Arthur Hill, and George Grizzard trade insults in *Who's Afraid of Virginia Woolf?* (1962).

Tobias Nederlander, whose sons now operate the Nederlander Organization.

On May 12, 1981, this theatre housed one of its most distinguished attractions. The incomparable Lena Horne opened in a spectacular personal appearance called *Lena Horne: The Lady and Her Music.* The unforgettable concert program won her a special Tony Award

Top: Peter Brook's production of *A Midsummer Night's Dream* (1971). *Below*: PLAYBILL cover portrait of Lena Horne in her sensational musical autobiography, *Lena Horne: The Lady and Her Music* (1981). *Opposite*: PLAYBILL covers for *Sherlock's Last Case* (1987) and *Our Country's Good* (1990).

and a special citation from the New York Drama Critics Circle for her singing and the way she recounted the highlights of her brilliant career as the top black star in 1940s Hollywood.

The Nederlander Theatre's subsequent tenants included the charming British import, *84 Charing Cross Road*, by Helene Hanff, starring Ellen Burstyn and Joseph Maher; and a musical version of the James Baldwin play *The Amen Corner*.

In 1984 this theatre housed Peter Ustinov's *Beethoven's Tenth*, followed by Glenda Jackson in a revival of Eugene O'Neill's *Strange Interlude* (1985); the musical *Wind in the Willows* (1985) with Nathan Lane and David Carroll; another musical, *Raggedy Ann*; Frank Langella and Donal Donnelly in *Sherlock's Last Case* (1987); Graciela Daniele's dance production *Dangerous Games* (1989); the Hartford Stage Company's production of

Our Country's Good, under the auspices of The Broadway Alliance; and Stacy Keach in a dazzling one-man performance in *Solitary Confinement*, a thriller by Rupert Holmes.

On April 29, 1996 a spectacular musical success with a tragic history opened at this theatre. *Rent*, a rock opera inspired by Puccini's *La Bohème*, with music, lyrics, and book by young Jonathan Larson, transferred here from its successful Off-Broadway engagement at New York Theatre Workshop, and received a tumultuous reception. Unfortunately, Mr. Larson was not alive to enjoy the theatrical triumph of his musical about the preciousness of life and friendship in the face of AIDS and greed. Larson had died January 25, 1996, of an aortic aneurysm after attending the final Off-Broadway dress rehearsal of the show. He was 35 years old.

The Nederlander was a good choice for the anti-establishment *Rent*. Standing geographically apart from the rest of the Broadway theatre district on the far side of the pre-Disney Forty-second Street abutting the (then) seedy Port Authority neighborhood, the site reflected a modicum of the grungy East Village atmosphere that the musical sought to capture on stage. To enhance the environmental staging, the inside of the theatre was redecorated to resemble a downtown club, and the marquee used only the outline of the word "Rent" on bare fluorescent bulbs.

Rent immediately became the hottest ticket in town and won the Pulitzer Prize, the Tony Award, and New York Drama Critics Circle Award for Best Musical. It also won Tony Awards for Best Original Score, Best Book of a Musical, and Featured Actor in a Musical (Wilson Jermaine Heredia).

The producers's policy of setting aside the first two rows of the orchestra as the cheapest seats (not the last row of the mezzanine or balcony as had been the usual case), made the daily lineup of students and workers on Forty-first Street into a signature Broadway experience of the late 1990s.

Rent settled in for years at the Nederlander Theatre, becoming its longest-running production.

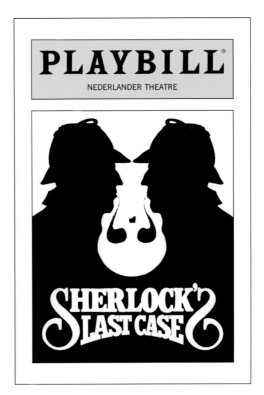

Left: The cast of *Rent* (1996) delivers one of Jonathan Larson's exuberant songs. Photo by Carol Rosegg. *Right:* PLAYBILL cover for *Rent.*

MUSIC BOX THEATRE

This lovely playhouse on West Forty-fifth Street, which Moss Hart described as everyone's dream of a theatre, celebrated its seventy-fifth birthday on September 22, 1996. Never once in its many decades was its elegant limestone facade marred by a movie or burlesque marquee.

The Music Box was built by the late producer Sam H. Harris and composer Irving Berlin to house a series of lavish revues to be composed by Mr. Berlin. The composer's estate now co-owns the theatre with the Shubert Organization.

On September 22, 1921, the resplendent theatre, designed by C. Howard Crane, opened with the first *Music Box Revue,* starring Mr. Berlin, Sam Bernard, Florence Moore, Joseph Santley, and—in the chorus—young Miriam Hopkins. The critics raved about the show and the new theatre, but it was the show's comic, Sam Bernard, who best described the opulent new house: "It stinks from class."

Four editions of the *Music Box Revue,* starring such luminaries as Fanny Brice, Grace Moore, Bobby Clark, Robert Benchley, and Charlotte Greenwood, brought fame to Berlin and the Music Box. In 1925 the theatre departed from its revues-only policy to present a smash hit comedy called *Cradle Snatchers,* starring Mary Boland, Humphrey Bogart, Edna May Oliver, and Raymond Guion (later Gene Raymond of the movies).

Other big Music Box hits in the 1920s include *Chicago* (1926), later made into a successful musical; *The Spider* (1927), a clever thriller that moved here from the 46th Street Theatre; Philip Barry's charming comedy, *Paris Bound* (1927); Cole Porter's *Paris* (1928); and the last Music Box show of the 1920s, the historic intimate revue *The Little Show* (1929), starring Clifton Webb, Fred Allen, and Libby Holman.

The Music Box faced the Depression with élan. *Topaze,* a French comedy starring Frank Morgan, was a hit in early 1930, followed by the famed satire *Once in a Lifetime,* the first collaboration of George S. Kaufman and Moss Hart. In 1931, Beatrice Lillie graced the Music Box in *The Third Little Show,* in which she introduced Noël Coward's celebrated song "Mad Dogs and Englishmen" to American audiences.

On December 26, 1931, *Of Thee I Sing* marched into the Music Box and became the first musical comedy to win a Pulitzer Prize. The musical had a biting book by George S. Kaufman and Morrie Ryskind, memorable music by George Gershwin, and stinging lyrics by his brother Ira. William Gaxton played President John P. Wintergreen, Victor Moore was mousy Vice President Alexander Throttlebottom, and George Murphy played a featured role. At 441 performances, the show became the longest-running book musical of the 1930s.

Souvenir book for the second *Music Box Revue* (1922).

Mr. Kaufman (with Edna Ferber) brought another hit to the Music Box in 1932. *Dinner at Eight* was a fascinating comedy about a socialite's problems in arranging a dinner for British royalty, who cancel their appearance at the last moment. The play examined the lives of all those invited to the dinner. During its run, the rising star Margaret Sullavan joined the cast as a replacement. The comedy ran for 232 performances and was later made into a hit MGM classic film with an all-star cast.

The Music Box really struck it rich with its next tenant. Irving Berlin and Moss Hart teamed to create a topical revue that would use newspaper headlines to satirize celebrities of that era. The show was called *As Thousands Cheer* and it starred Marilyn Miller, Clifton Webb, Helen Broderick, and Ethel Waters, who stopped the show at every performance with "Heat Wave," "Harlem on My Mind," and "Supper Time." The revue ran for 400 performances at the Music Box and was one of the biggest hits of Depression-era Broadway.

Kaufman and Hart once again joined forces to write the next Music Box show: *Merrily We Roll Along* (1934).

This unusual comedy started in the present and went backwards in time. It served as the basis for a 1981 musical of the same title by Stephen Sondheim and George Furth.

Five shows played the Music Box in 1935: Tallulah Bankhead in a revival of *Rain*; a hit melodrama about pilots, *Ceiling Zero*, starring Osgood Perkins (Anthony's illustrious father); a prophetic drama, *If This Be Treason*, in which the United States and Japan almost engage in war; a successful adaptation of Jane Austen's *Pride and Prejudice*; and George S. Kaufman and Katherine Dayton's political comedy *First Lady*, starring the noted actress Jane Cowl playing a role said to be inspired by Alice Longworth Roosevelt.

Margaret Sullavan, now a big Hollywood star, returned to the Music Box in 1936 in *Stage Door*, by Kaufman and Ferber. Set in the Foot-Lights Club (modeled on the actual Rehearsal Club in Manhattan), the play presented a group of aspiring actresses who live in a popular boarding house for young theatricals. One of the characters—a radical playwright named Keith Burgess—was said to be based on the Group Theatre's Clifford Odets.

Young Madam Conti (1937), starring Constance Cummings, was one of the theatre's lesser tenants, but this melodrama was followed by John Steinbeck's *Of Mice and Men* in 1937, starring Wallace Ford and Broderick Crawford, and directed by George S. Kaufman. It won the New York Drama Critics Circle Award as best play of the season.

George M. Cohan played President Franklin D. Roosevelt in *I'd Rather Be Right*, which opened at the Alvin Theatre in 1937, but ended its successful run at the Music Box. The satirical political musical by Kaufman and Hart, with a score by Richard Rodgers and Lorenz Hart, dared to portray a living president who was still in

the White House when the show opened. Mr. Cohan garnered raves for his good-natured performance, and the show was one of the season's top tickets.

In September 1938 Kaufman and Hart came to the Music Box in a new guise. In association with Max Gordon, they presented a topical musical revue called *Sing Out the News,* by Harold Rome and Charles Friedman. The revue perfectly suited the Music Box tradition of topical satire, but was only moderately successful.

In 1939 two more revues graced the house. One of them, *Set to Music,* by Noël Coward and starring Beatrice Lillie, was the type of sophisticated revue for which the Music Box was built—and a genre of entertainment that

Lois Moran and William Gaxton sing the Gershwins's title song on election night in the Pulitzer Prize-winning musical, *Of Thee I Sing* (1931).

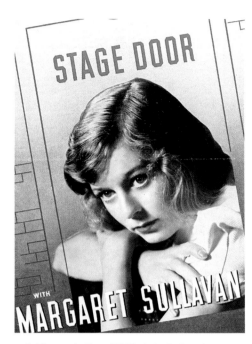

Left: Marilyn Miller, Clifton Webb, and Helen Broderick in the "Easter Parade" finale of the famed revue, *As Thousands Cheer* (1933). *Right:* Radiant Margaret Sullavan returns from Hollywood stardom to appear in the theatrical comedy *Stage Door* (1936).

would become almost obsolete after World War II. The celebrity-studded opening was the kind of glittering first night that would become rare in years to come. *Set to Music* was followed by a charming entertainment called *From Vienna* (1939), a revue featuring performers who were Viennese refugees.

It is fitting that the last show to play the Music Box in the 1930s was another satire by Kaufman and Hart. Both were close friends of the obese, waspish, self-promoting critic, author, and radio celebrity Alexander Woollcott, and they wrote a classic comedy about what would happen if someone like him (called Sheridan Whiteside in the play) slipped on the ice while visiting a middle-class Midwestern family and had to stay with them while recovering from a fractured hip. Called *The Man Who Came to Dinner*, this comedy of outrages and insults starred Monty Woolley as Whiteside and also caricatured such luminaries as Noël Coward, Gertrude Lawrence, and Harpo Marx. The comedy proved to be the Music Box's longest-running show to that time, playing for 739 performances.

World War II brought a change in audience tastes on Broadway. The revue form and plays that satirized celebrities soon began to vanish. The last revue to play

the Music Box for many years to come was Mike Todd's rowdy *Star and Garter*, starring strippers Gypsy Rose Lee and Georgia Southern and low comics Bobby Clark, Pat Harrington, and Professor Lamberti. The critics were not overjoyed with the burlesque, but audiences loved the show and it ran for 609 performances.

After *Star and Garter* closed at the Music Box, there was a definite change in the house's fare. For the next four decades, only three musicals were housed there: *Lost in the Stars* (1949), *Rainbow Jones* (1974), and *Side by Side by Sondheim* (1977). One of the reasons for the lack of musical bookings was that the theatre's 1,010-seat capacity was no longer considered adequate to support an expensive musical show.

During the ensuring four decades, the Music Box thrived on romantic comedies, usually with small casts, and dramas. *I Remember Mama* (1944) starred Mady Christians and Oscar Homolka, with a young Marlon Brando making his Broadway debut. This was followed by Tennessee Williams's *Summer and Smoke* (1948); *Lost in the Stars,* by Kurt Weill and Maxwell Anderson (1949); and *Affairs of State,* a light comedy starring Celeste Holm that moved from the Royale to the Music Box.

Playwright William Inge inaugurated his happy association with this theatre in 1953. Over the next five years, he was to have three solid hits in the house: *Picnic* (1953) (Pulitzer Prize, New York Drama Critics Circle Award); *Bus Stop* (1955); and *The Dark at the Top of the Stairs* (1957).

Other 1950s hits included a revival of *The Male Animal;* Josephine Hull in *The Solid Gold Cadillac* (moved from the Belasco); *Separate Tables* (1956), starring Margaret Leighton and Eric Portman; Rod Steiger and Claire Bloom in *Rashomon* (1959); Cornelia Otis Skinner, Cyril Ritchard, Walter Abel, Charlie Ruggles, and George Peppard in *The Pleasure of His Company* (from the Longacre Theatre); and *Five Finger Exercise* (1959), with Jessica Tandy and Brian Bedford.

In 1961, *A Far Country* presented Steven Hill as Sigmund Freud and Kim Stanley as his patient in Henry Denker's case study. In 1962, Bert Lahr convulsed theatregoers playing numerous roles in S.J. Perelman's *The Beauty Part.* More laughter followed in 1963 when Gertrude Berg starred in *Dear Me, The Sky is Falling.* Sandy Dennis, Gene Hackman, Rosemary Murphy, and Don Porter came to the Music Box in February 1964 in *Any Wednesday,* and the comedy stayed for 983 performances, a new record holder for this theatre.

Harold Pinter's *The Homecoming* chilled patrons in 1967, followed by Gig Young in the warm British comedy *There's a Girl in My Soup.* On November 12, 1970, Anthony Shaffer's *Sleuth* opened with Anthony Quayle and Keith Baxter and played for a record-breaking 1,222 performances. The following year, the Music Box celebrated its fiftieth anniversary, and Irving Berlin was photographed by *The New York Times* proudly standing before the theatre. Mr. Berlin stated that he and the Shubert Organization were constantly refurbishing the theatre.

Absurd Person Singular, a British import, amused capacity audiences in 1974 with stars Geraldine Page, Richard Kiley, Larry Blyden, Carole Shelley, Sandy Dennis, and Tony Roberts. Ben Gazzara's revival of *Who's Afraid of Virginia Woolf?* arrived in 1976, followed by the British play *Comedians,* and the delightful portfolio of Sondheim songs *Side by Side by Sondheim* (1977). Then, in 1978, came John Wood and Marian Seldes in Ira Levin's thriller *Deathtrap.* The comedy murder mystery had such an original plot that theatregoers attended it for 1,793 performances, making it the Music Box's champion

Irene Bordoni glitters in Cole Porter's 1928 musical, *Paris.*

attraction, and the longest-running such thriller in Broadway history. In 1982, stark drama returned to the Music Box with *Agnes of God,* starring Geraldine Page, Elizabeth Ashley, and Amanda Plummer, who won a

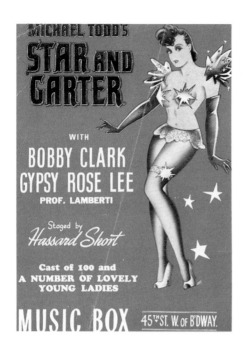

Top left: Herald for Mike Todd's rowdy burlesque revue, *Star and Garter* (1942). *Right:* Beatrice Lillie sings "I Went to a Marvelous Party" in Noël Coward's revue *Set to Music* (1939). *Above:* Monty Woolley needles Edith Atwater, Carol Goodner, and Theodore Newton in the classic comedy of insults, *The Man Who Came to Dinner* (1939).

Mady Christians (far left) and a young Marlon Brando with members of the cast of *I Remember Mama* (1944).

Tony Award for her performance. The religious drama played for 599 performances.

In 1985, a delightful revival of Noël Coward's amusing trifle *Hay Fever* won approval for its sterling cast headed by Rosemary Harris, Roy Dotrice, Mia Dillon, and Charles Kimbrough. The following year, another revival, *Loot*, by Joe Orton, also gained applause for hilarious performances by Joseph Maher, Zeljko Ivanek, Zoe Caldwell, and Alec Baldwin in his Broadway debut. Mary Tyler Moore starred here in A.R. Gurney, Jr.'s comedy *Sweet Sue* (1987). This was followed by a British hit, *Les Liaisons Dangereuses* by Christopher Hampton, given a stunning production by the Royal Shakespeare Company. In 1988, this theatre housed an offbeat musical, *Mail*, followed by Kate Nelligan in a play by Michael Weller, *Spoils of War*. Cy Coleman's musical *Welcome to the Club* came here in 1989 and later that year, *A Few Good Men*, an explosive military drama by Aaron Sorkin (later to write TV's "West Wing"), enjoyed a long run. Julie Harris starred in *Lucifer's Child*, a one-woman show about the Danish author Isak Dinesen (1991); Jason Robards and Judith Ivey starred in *Park Your Car in*

Harvard Yard (1991), followed by Alan Ayckbourn's *A Small Family Business* (1992).

The British musical *Blood Brothers* (1993) told of fraternal twins who are separated at birth. One is raised in wealth, the other in poverty, and they meet later in life to become violent rivals, neither realizing the other is his brother until the final moments of the play. A long-running hit in London, *Blood Brothers* received mostly negative reviews on Broadway, but caught on with playgoers and ran for 839 performances.

Swinging on a Star, a songbook revue of the lyrics of Johnny Burke, came to Broadway in October 1995 from its production at the Goodspeed-at-Chester/Norma Terris Theatre in Connecticut, with virtually the same cast. It received mixed reviews but managed to run for 97 performances and earn a Tony nomination as Best Musical.

Master impresario David Merrick's last Broadway production opened at this theatre on March 27, 1996. The musical was a stage adaptation of Rodgers and Hammerstein's film *State Fair*—both the 1945 and 1962 versions—including some previously unused Rodgers and Hammerstein songs. The show had a glittering cast:

Top left: Ralph Meeker and Janice Rule smolder in William Inge's *Picnic* (1953). *Top right:* Paul Rogers and Vivien Merchant (in foreground) under family scrutiny in Harold Pinter's sinister puzzle, *The Homecoming* (1967).

Andrea McArdle, Kathryn Crosby, John Davidson, Scott Wise, Donna McKechnie, and others. It received mixed reviews and played for 118 performances. Mr. Merrick's final publicity stunt, suing the Tony Awards when it nominated only part of the score for Best Score, ended in dismissal.

Christopher Plummer scored a triumph in the play *Barrymore* in March, 1997. His splendid portrayal of actor John Barrymore, one month before his death in 1942, won him a Tony Award for Leading Actor in a Play. The play, which starred Mr. Plummer onstage and Michael Mastro as an off-stage voice, received rave reviews and ran for 238 performances.

December 4, 1997, brought a new production of Frances Goodrich and Albert Hackett's play, *The Diary of Anne Frank,* newly adapted by Wendy Kesselman. It starred Natalie Portman as Anne Frank, and the cast included George Hearn (Otto Frank), Sophie Hayden (Edith Frank), Linda Lavin (Mrs. Van Daan), and Austin Pendleton (Mr. Dussel). Some critics objected to some of the changes made in this revised version, which made it more sexually explicit, among other changes, but the play

ran for more than six months. The production received two Tony Award nominations: Best Revival of a Play and Best Featured Actress (Lavin).

The next play to open at the Music Box was a controversial London drama, *Closer,* by Patrick Marber. It starred Natasha Richardson, Ciaran Hinds, Rupert Graves, and Anna Friel and it followed the sexual shenanigans of two couples. The language and situations were graphic and offended some playgoers, but the play won the season's Best Foreign Play Award bestowed by the New York Drama Critics Circle, and was nominated for the Best Play Tony Award. It ran for 173 performances.

October 19, 2000 brought Neil Simon's *The Dinner Party* with a stellar cast: Len Cariou, John Ritter, Henry Winkler, Jan Maxwell, Veanne Cox, and Penny Fuller. Performed without intermission, the play proved trying for audiences and some critics. The scene was a chic restaurant in Paris, but, as some critics complained, the characters sounded more like people from the Bronx. Nevertheless, it proved a solid hit for the 73-year-old Simon, the first in nearly a decade for one of the most durable comedy writers in Broadway history.

Clockwise from top left: Keith Baxter (in disguise) and Anthony Quayle play Anthony Shaffer's complex games in *Sleuth* (1970). Geraldine Page and Amanda Plummer anguish over a baby's murder in the tense drama, *Agnes of God* (1982). Millicent Martin and Julie McKenzie in the song book *Side by Side by Sondheim* (1977). Stephen Lang and Tom Hulce in Aaron Sorkin's military courtroom drama, *A Few Good Men*. Photo by Joan Marcus.

Left: PLAYBILL from *State Fair*. *Right:* John Ritter and Henry Winkler in *The Dinner Party* (2000). Photo by Carol Rosegg.

IMPERIAL THEATRE

In 1923 *The New York Times* reported that the new theatre being built at 249 West Forty-fifth Street by the Shuberts was the fiftieth playhouse that the theatrical brothers from Syracuse had built in the New York City area. Herbert J. Krapp designed the Imperial obviously as a musical comedy house, with a large seating capacity of 1,650 (since reduced to 1,421). The main body of the playhouse is situated on the Forty-sixth Street side of the block, but is reached by a long, opulent gallery from its entrance on Forty-fifth Street. The Imperial has been the Shuberts's pride since it opened, housing some of Broadway's most notable and successful musicals.

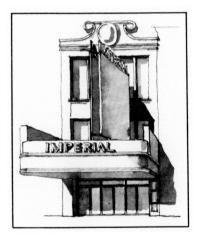

The theatre's first show set the pace: a hit musical called *Mary Jane McKane*, with Mary Hay in the title role and a jaunty score by Vincent Youmans. It opened on Christmas night 1923 and it ran for a then-impressive 151 performances. In September 1924 this theatre housed one of its most celebrated shows, the Rudolf Friml operetta *Rose-Marie*, with a book by Otto Harbach and Oscar Hammerstein II. According to Gerald Bordman in *American Musical Theatre*, this musical was "not only the biggest hit of the season, but the biggest grosser of the decade." Mary Ellis played Rose-Marie, a singer in a hotel located in the Canadian Rockies, and Dennis King was Jim Kenyon, the man she loved, who was unjustly accused of murder. The score included the lilting title song, the sonorous "Indian Love Call" ("I'll be calling you-oo-oo-oooh-oo-oo-ooh") and "The Song of the Mounties." *Rose-Marie* ran for 557 performances on Broadway and there were four road companies touring America at the same time.

The Imperial's next show was a musical called *Sweetheart Time*, with Eddie Buzzell and Mary Milburn, but it was only a moderate hit. The theatre's next bonanza occurred on November 8, 1926, with the opening of *Oh, Kay!* a musical with a score by George and Ira Gershwin and a book by Guy Bolton and P.G. Wodehouse. Gertrude Lawrence was the star, and her singing of "Someone to Watch Over Me" to a rag doll is one of the musical theatre's most cherished moments. Victor Moore and Oscar Shaw were Lawrence's costars in this merry musical about Long Island bootleggers. Other hit tunes from the score were "Maybe," "Do Do Do," and "Clap Yo' Hands." When Ira Gershwin became ill during the creation of this hit, Howard Dietz wrote some of the lyrics for the show.

On September 19, 1928, another blockbuster came to this house: Sigmund Romberg's glorious operetta *The New Moon*, with a libretto by Oscar Hammerstein II, Frank Mandel, and Laurence Schwab. Set in New Orleans at the time of the French Revolution, the operetta was studded with such gems as "Wanting You," "Lover, Come Back to Me," "Softly As in a Morning Sunrise," "Stouthearted Men," and "One Kiss." It was the only show of that otherwise bountiful season to run for more than 500 performances.

A snappy World War I musical, *Sons o' Guns*, starring

Jack Donahue, Lily Damita, and William Frawley, exploded at the Imperial in November 1929 and, despite the stock market crash, spread mirth for 297 performances. Two hit songs—"Why?" and "Cross Your Fingers"—emerged from the lively score by J. Fred Coots, Arthur Swanstrom, and Benny Davis.

Highlights of the 1930s at the Imperial included Ed Wynn in his joyous vaudeville-type show, *The Laugh Parade* (1931), in which he introduced some of his latest zany inventions and interrupted other people's acts with lisping comments. An elaborate revue, *Flying Colors* (1932) boasted modernistic sets by Norman Bel Geddes, hit songs by Howard Dietz and Arthur Schwartz ("Louisiana Hayride," "Alone Together," "A Shine on Your Shoes"), and a dream cast consisting of Clifton Webb, Tamara Geva, Patsy Kelly, Charles Butterworth, Imogene Coca, Larry Adler, and Vilma and Buddy

Ebsen. *Let 'Em Eat Cake* (1933), a sequel to *Of Thee I Sing* (by the same creators), reunited William Gaxton, Victor Moore, and Lois Moran, the stars of the first show, but was not successful. Bob Hope, Harry Richman, Lillian Emerson, and "Prince" Michael Romanoff starred in a saucy musical, *Say When* (1934).

Despite the Depression, some 1930s opening nights on Broadway were the pinnacles of glamour, and such was the case at the glittery opening of the Cole Porter/Moss Hart musical *Jubilee* on October 12, 1935. An opulent satire about the royal holiday of the king and queen of a mythical country (splendidly played by Mary Boland and Melville Cooper), the show drew a bejeweled audience who had heard that some of the characters depicted were really spoofs of Noël Coward, Johnny Weissmuller, Elsa Maxwell, and Britain's Royal Family. Burns Mantle of the *Daily News* gave the musical his rare

Left: Oscar Shaw and Gertrude Lawrence in this 1926 delight, *Oh, Kay!* *Above:* Ed Wynn in his sappy revue *The Laugh Parade* (1931). *Opposite:* (clockwise from top left): Imperial program cover for 1926. Sheet music for the title song of the operetta *Rose Marie* (1924). PLAYBILL cover sketch of Mrs. Hartley of Covent Garden during run of *Jubilee* (1935). Souvenir program for Sigmund Romberg's *The New Moon* (1928). Imperial program cover for 1930.

four-star rating, and years afterward, two of its Porter songs became classics: "Begin the Beguine" and "Just One of Those Things."

Another memorable musical followed *Jubilee* into the Imperial: *On Your Toes*, the Rodgers/Hart/George Abbott spoof of the Russian ballet craze. It starred Ray Bolger, Tamara Geva, Luella Gear, and Monty Woolley, and it broke the mold of American musical comedies by using two extended George Balanchine ballets as an integral part of the plot. One of these, *Slaughter on Tenth Avenue*, is the only ballet score from a musical to become popular, and the ballet itself has joined the repertoire of the New York City Ballet.

The battle of the *Hamlet*s raged on Broadway in the fall of 1936. John Gielgud opened first as the Melancholy Dane at the Empire Theatre in October and triumphed. Leslie Howard played the same part at the Imperial in November and came in a poor second. Howard's last Broadway play had been *The Petrified Forest*. When reviewing Howard's Hamlet, critic Robert Benchley wrote in *The New Yorker* that it was "the petrified Hamlet." Gielgud's production ran for 132 performances; Howard's only 39.

The Shuberts brought an elaborate operetta,

Desi Arnaz pounds the conga as the chorus sings in Rodgers and Hart's college musical, *Too Many Girls* (1939).

Frederika, to the Imperial in February 1937, but despite lilting music by Franz Lehar, it ran for only 94 performances. The excellent cast included Dennis King, Ernest Truex, Helen Gleason, and Edith King, but as Brooks Atkinson noted in the *Times*, operetta had become passé on Broadway. At the end of 1937, Dietz and Schwartz returned with a glossy musical about a bigamist who had one wife in London and another in Paris. *Between the Devil* showcased three bright British stars, Jack Buchanan, Evelyn Laye, and Adele Dixon, and featured dancers Vilma Ebsen and Charles Walters. But the bigamy theme was distasteful to some and the musical called it quits after 93 performances.

The Cole Porter show *Leave It to Me*, which sailed smartly into the Imperial in the fall of 1938, starred Victor Moore, William Gaxton, Sophie Tucker, and Tamara, but it made Broadway history by introducing a Texas singer named Mary Martin doing a polite striptease in a Siberian railway station while singing "My Heart Belongs To Daddy." The musical, based on Sam and Bella Spewack's play *Clear All Wires*, was a huge hit and featured some Porter winners, such as "Get Out of Town" and "Most Gentlemen Don't Like Love." One of the chorus boys was future film star Gene Kelly.

The last musical of the 1930s at this theatre was also a hit. Rodgers and Hart and George Marion, Jr., collaborated on a college campus show, *Too Many Girls*, which took place at Pottawatomie College in Stop Gap, New Mexico, where the female students wore "beanies" if they were virgins. The only hatless female onstage was Mary Jane Walsh, who played a divorcee. George Abbott directed the show with lightning speed; Robert Alton was highly praised for his swirling dances. Eddie

Bracken, Richard Kollmar, Marcy Wescott, Hal Le Roy, Desi Arnaz (pre-*I Love Lucy*), and Ms. Walsh sang and danced such Rodgers and Hart delights as "I Didn't Know What Time It Was," "I'd Like to Recognize the Tune," and "Give It Back to the Indians." One of the chorus boys with a few spoken lines was a newcomer named Van Johnson.

Smash hit musicals continued to populate the Imperial in the 1940s. Irving Berlin and Morrie Ryskind rang the bell with *Louisiana Purchase*, a political musical set in New Orleans, starring Victor Moore, William Gaxton, Vera Zorina, and Irene Bordoni. Mr. Balanchine provided the choreography and Mr. Berlin some fetching songs, such as "It's a Lovely Day Tomorrow," the title song, and some spirited numbers for Carol Bruce. It ran for 444 performances.

Cole Porter returned to the Imperial in 1941 with a rousing wartime musical, *Let's Face It*. Based on the hit 1920s comedy *Cradle Snatchers*, the show focused on three married women (Eve Arden, Edith Meiser, and Vivian Vance) who took up with young soldiers to get even with their philandering husbands. One of the soldiers was Danny Kaye, who stopped the show with specialty numbers, some written by his wife, Sylvia Fine. Porter provided such hits as "Everything I Love," "Farming," "Let's Not Talk About Love," "Ace in the Hole," and "I Hate You Darling."

The enormous success of the operetta *Rosalinda* (1943), Max Reinhardt's version of *Die Fledermaus*, caused it to be moved to the Imperial from the Forty-fourth Street Theatre. Starring Dorothy Sarnoff and Oscar Karlweis, the comic show also featured Shelley Winters and ran for 521 performances.

Mary Martin, who made her debut as an unknown

at the Imperial in *Leave It to Me*, returned as a star in *One Touch of Venus* (1943), a musical fantasy with a haunting score by Kurt Weill and a witty book by S.J. Perelman and Ogden Nash. Ms. Martin played a statue of Venus that comes to life and is pursued by an art gallery owner (John Boles) and a barber (Kenny Baker). Ms. Martin scored a triumph singing "Speak Low," "I'm a Stranger Here Myself," and "That's Him." Paula Lawrence sang the amusing title song and "Very, Very, Very." The show had a smashing run of 567 performances, but not all at the Imperial.

Another successful musical that moved to the Imperial from the Winter Garden was the *Ziegfeld Follies of 1943* and it starred Milton Berle (who stuck his two cents into everybody's act), the film beauty Ilona Massey, Arthur Treacher, and Jack Cole. The critics praised Berle's highjinks, and this *Follies* still holds the record—553 performances—for the longest run of any *Ziegfeld Follies*.

On May 16, 1946, one of the Imperial's hallmark shows arrived. Ethel Merman opened in Irving Berlin's *Annie Get Your Gun* and made it one of her most memorable portraits. Jerome Kern was slated to write the score for this show, but he died before he could start it. His successor, Berlin, wrote what many consider his greatest score, with such hits as "They Say It's Wonderful," "There's No Business Like Show Business," "The Girl That I Marry," "Doin' What Comes Natur'lly," "I Got the Sun in the Morning," and many others. Few Broadway musicals have produced as many song hits as this one. It was Merman's longest-running show: 1,147 performances.

The last two shows at the Imperial during the 1940s were minor successes. A revue called *Along Fifth Avenue* moved from the Broadhurst and starred Nancy Walker, Jackie Gleason, Carol Bruce, and Hank Ladd, but it lasted only seven months. Irving Berlin's *Miss Liberty* had a book by Robert E. Sherwood and starred Eddie Albert, Mary McCarty, and Allyn McLerie, but the critics felt that the project fell flat. It managed to run for 308 performances.

During the 1950s, musicals continued to be the major fare at this theatre. In 1950 there was a successful adaptation of *Peter Pan*, with new music by Leonard Bernstein. Jean Arthur made a perfect Peter, and Boris Karloff doubled as Mr. Darling and the evil Captain

Left: Melville Cooper and Mary Boland in *Jubilee* (1935). *Right:* Mary Martin and behind her, at left, Gene Kelly in Cole Porter's *Leave It to Me* (1938).

Top: Ethel Merman in Irving Berlin's galvanic *Annie Get Your Gun* (1946). Above: Jerry Orbach, Pierre Olaf, and Anna Maria Alberghetti in the musical, *Carnival* (1961).

Hook. This was followed by Ethel Merman in another Irving Berlin winner, *Call Me Madam*, in which she played a Pearl Mesta-type Washington, D.C. hostess. Howard Lindsay and Russel Crouse wrote the amusing book, Paul Lukas was Ms. Merman's romantic costar; and Merman and a newcomer, Russell Nype, stopped the show with their singing of the contrapuntal melody "You're Just in Love." It ran for 644 performances. In June 1952 *Wish You Were Here*, a fair musical version of Arthur Kober's delightful play *Having Wonderful Time*, opened and managed to run for 598 performances, mainly because Eddie Fisher (who was not in the show) recorded the title song and it became a Hit Parade favorite. The show also had a real pool onstage, which garnered much publicity. In December 1953 one of Broadway's last opulent revues—*John Murray Anderson's Almanac*—arrived, with Hermione Gingold, Billy De Wolfe, Harry Belafonte, Polly Bergen, Orson Bean, Kay Medford, and Carleton Carpenter, but despite some funny sketches and good songs it was a financial failure, proving that TV was killing the revue form on Broadway.

Cole Porter's last musical, *Silk Stockings*, an adaptation of Garbo's famous film *Ninotchka*, was a hit in 1955, with Don Ameche, Hildegarde Neff, and Gretchen Wyler. Frank Loesser was acclaimed for his opera *The Most Happy Fella* (1956), based on Sidney Howard's play *They Knew What They Wanted*. Lena Horne was a popular success in the Harold Arlen/E.Y. Harburg musical *Jamaica* (1957), with Ricardo Montalban. Dolores Gray and Andy Griffith had a hit in *Destry Rides Again* (1959), a musical version of the James Stewart/Marlene Dietrich film, aided by dazzling Michael Kidd choreography, although a feud between Ms. Gray and Mr. Kidd made all the newspapers.

During the 1960s, the Imperial housed some very long-running musicals. Ethel Merman in her triumphant *Gypsy* moved here from the Broadway Theatre in 1960 and was followed by David Merrick's smash *Carnival* (1961), a musical adapted from the film *Lili*, starring Jerry Orbach (fresh from his Off-Broadway success in *The Fantasticks*) and Anna Maria Alberghetti, with excellent choreography and staging by Gower Champion. The British import, Lionel Bart's *Oliver!*, based on Dickens's *Oliver Twist*, starred Clive Revill and Georgia Brown, and had two song hits: "As Long As He Needs Me" and "Consider Yourself." It played at the Imperial for eighteen months.

On September 22, 1964, *Fiddler on the Roof* opened and stayed at this theatre for more than two years before moving to the Majestic. The multi-award-winning musical, written by Joseph Stein, Jerry Bock, and Sheldon Harnick, was based on Sholem Aleichem's tales. Zero Mostel gave the greatest performance of his career as the Russian-Jewish milkman who talks to God and tries to find good husbands for his daughters in tumultuous times. Directed and choreographed by Jerome Robbins, the musical filled the Imperial with tunes that became part of people's lives: "Sunrise, Sunset," "If I Were a Rich

Above: PLAYBILL cover for the British hit *Oliver!* (1961). *Right:* Zero Mostel talks to God in the multi-award-winning musical *Fiddler on the Roof* (1964).

Ben Vereen and chorus have "Magic To Do" in the long running *Pippin* (1972).

Man," "Tradition." The show won numerous Tony Awards, including Best Musical. It eventually became, for a time, the longest-running musical in Broadway history, and was produced around the world.

Another landmark musical, *Cabaret*, came to the Imperial from the Broadhurst Theatre and continued for a year and half in 1967-68. Kander and Ebb, who wrote the memorable score for *Cabaret*, also wrote the score for the next Imperial tenant, *Zorba* (1968), a musical based on the film *Zorba the Greek*. But the stage version did not have the distinction of the film and it ran for a moderately successful nine months. *Minnie's Boys*, a musical about the Marx Brothers, had a short run in 1970. Richard Rodgers and Martin Charnin also had a minor success with their musical *Two by Two* (1970), a biblical story about Noah and his family based on Clifford Odets's play *The Flowering Peach*. It starred Danny Kaye as Noah, and the comic took to ad-libbing during the

show's run, which some in the audience found unprofessional. Two revivals—*On the Town* (1971) and *Lost in the Stars* (1972)—struck out before the next home run was hit from this theatre.

On October 23, 1972, *Pippin* opened, and it stayed for 1,944 performances, making it the longest-running show to open at the Imperial. With a score by Stephen Schwartz, this unorthodox musical about Charlemagne's irresolute son was boosted to success by Bob Fosse's inventive choreography, by Ben Vereen's animated dancing, and by one of the most successful TV commercials ever produced for a Broadway show, "One Minute From *Pippin*."

Drama returned to the Imperial with a revival of Eugene O'Neill's *Anna Christie* (1977), starring Liv Ullmann, and Victor Borge returned in a short run of his show *Comedy with Music* (1977). Two Neil Simon shows next occupied the Imperial and both were long-running hits. *Chapter Two* (1977), a drama about Mr. Simon's

Above: Jennifer Holliday, Sheryl Lee Ralph, and Loretta Devine in *Dreamgirls* (1981). *Below:* PLAYBILL covers for two Neil Simon hits (1977, 1979).

personal experience losing his first wife to cancer, starred Judd Hirsch, Anita Gillette, and Cliff Gorman and ran for 857 performances, the longest-running non-musical in this theatre's history. The other Simon show, *They're Playing Our Song* (1979), was a musical with a score by Marvin Hamlisch and Carole Bayer Sager, about a songwriter (Robert Klein) and his kooky romance with his lyricist (Lucie Arnaz). This ran for a hefty 1,082 performances.

In 1981, Michael Bennett's blockbuster musical *Dreamgirls* opened here and stayed until 1985. With a score by Henry Krieger and Tom Eyen and a book by Eyen, the musical about a singing trio patterned after The Supremes won six Tony Awards, including Best Actor and Actress in a Musical: Ben Harney and Jennifer Holliday.

In 1985, *The Mystery of Edwin Drood* (a title later shortened to *Drood*) by Rupert Holmes, a musical first done by the New York Shakespeare Festival at Central Park's Delacorte Theatre, transferred here and promptly

won Five Tony Awards, including Best Musical, Best Book of a Musical (Holmes), Best Original Score (Holmes), Best Leading Actor in a Musical (George Rose) and Best Direction of a Musical (Wilford Leach). Based on an unfinished mystery novel by Charles Dickens, the show was notable for allowing the audience to vote on which of several endings would be played that night. Actors (in character) would "campaign" during intermission to be chosen as the murderer. It played here until May, 1987.

The British hit *Chess* opened in 1988 in a revised version, but the Tim Rice musical did not repeat its London success in New York. *Jerome Robbins' Broadway* came next, a compilation of musical numbers from Robbins's musicals and won Tony Awards for Best Musical, Best Actor in a Musical (Jason Alexander), Best Featured Actor in a Musical (Scott Wise), Best Featured Actress in a Musical (Debbie Shapiro), Best Direction of a Musical (Robbins), and Best Lighting Designer (Jennifer Tipton).

In 1990, *Les Misérables* moved from the Broadway Theatre and continued its epic run here, eventually breaking the Imperial record.

The Imperial, which was completely refurbished by the Shubert Organization, is one of the finest musical comedy houses ever built, and has been one of Broadway's most consistently successful houses.

Opening night PLAYBILLs from musicals *Chess* (1988) and *Jerome Robbins' Broadway* (1989).

MARTIN BECK THEATRE

The Martin Beck Theatre serves as the western outpost of the Times Square theatre district, being located just west of Eighth Avenue at 302 West Forty-fifth Street.

At the time of its opening in 1924, the Martin Beck was described by *The New York Times* as the only theatre in America designed in the Byzantine style. Martin Beck, the vaudeville mogul who built the house, conceived the building's style and entrusted its design and execution to San Francisco architect G. Albert Lansburgh. The theatre is distinguished by its unusually large foyer and promenade, and its details of wrought iron and stained glass. With a seating capacity of 1,200 (today 1,437) and dressing rooms for 200 actors, the house was ideal for musicals and spectacular productions. Curiously, it has in its nearly eighty years of operation housed many distinguished dramatic plays, some of which were definitely not spectacular.

The Martin Beck opened on November 11, 1924, with a Viennese operetta, *Mme. Pompadour*, adapted by playwright Clare Kummer, but the public was wearying of schmaltzy operettas at this time and the show ran for a moderate 80 performances.

The theatre had better luck in 1925 when *Captain Jinks* arrived. This was a musical version of Clyde Fitch's play *Captain Jinks of the Horse Marines*, which had made a star of Ethel Barrymore. In this version the marine captain (J. Harold Murray) is in love with a world-famous dancer, Trentoni (Louise Brown). Also in the cast was comedian Joe E. Brown as a hack driver. Five collaborators worked on the musical, and it ran for 167 performances.

One of the most sensational plays ever produced on Broadway, John Colton's *The Shanghai Gesture,* made waves on February 1, 1926. It starred Florence Reed as Mother Goddam, the owner of a notorious Shanghai whorehouse. It was her most famous role. Seeking revenge on a Britisher who once dumped her to marry an English woman, she lures him to her brothel, then sells his own daughter off as a prostitute. Then, discovering that the daughter she had by the Britisher has turned into a dope fiend, she strangles her to death. The critics scoffed at this purple melodrama, but audiences loved it and kept the Martin Beck full for 210 performances.

Next, the Martin Beck booked a comedy that turned out to be its biggest hit to that time: *The Shannons of Broadway,* written by actor James Gleason, who also starred in it. Playing a vaudevillian, he and his wife (Lucile Webster) have comic adventures when they buy and operate a hotel in New England. The popular comedy ran for 288 performances.

Beginning in December 1928 the prestigious Theatre Guild began producing a number of fascinating plays at

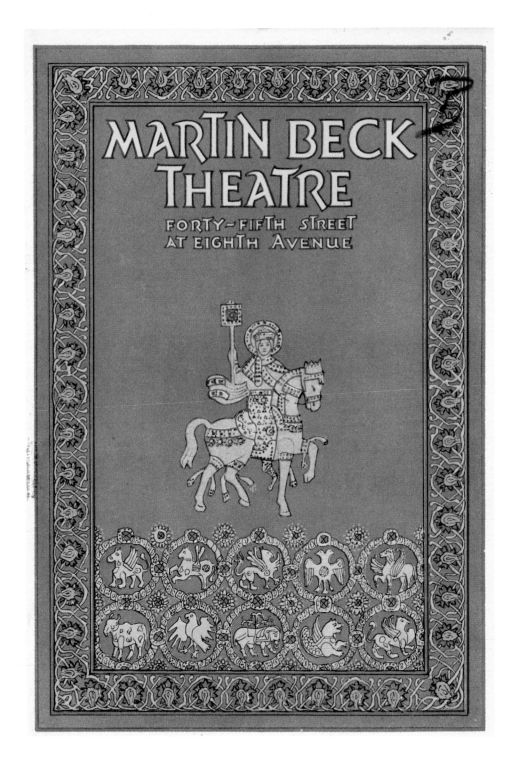

Standard program cover for the Martin Beck Theatre in the 1920s.

Above: Eva Clark, Wilda Bennett, and Leeta Corder in *Mme. Pompadour,* the Martin Beck's first show (1924). *Below:* Florence Reed as the sinister Mother Goddam in *The Shanghai Gesture* (1926).

the Martin Beck, featuring the famed Theatre Guild Acting Company. Their first production, an anti-war play called *Wings Over Europe,* was chosen by Burns Mantle as one of the year's ten best. Next, in February 1929, they presented Eugene O'Neill's unusual play, *Dynamo,* which pitted religion against science, and starred Claudette Colbert, Dudley Digges, Glenn Anders, and Helen Westley. Despite its offbeat attraction, the play lasted only 66 performances.

More successful was *The Camel Though the Needle's Eye* (1929), a play about an illegitimate girl (Miriam Hopkins) who meets a rich man (Claude Rains) and makes a success out of him by going into the dairy business with him. The excellent cast also included Henry Travers, Helen Westley, and Morris Carnovsky. The play ran for 195 performances.

Theatre Guild productions included a Russian play, *Red Rust* (1929), with Lee Strasberg, Luther Adler, and Franchot Tone, who would soon be prominent in the Group Theatre; Philip Barry's metaphysical play *Hotel Universe* (1930), in which guests at a French villa recall incidents from their youth that had a profound influence on their lives, brilliantly acted by Franchot Tone, Ruth Gordon, Glenn Anders, Katherine Alexander, Morris Carnovsky, and others; and *Roar China!* (1930), a play about a Chinese rebellion in which an enormous British warship occupied the vast reaches of the Martin Beck stage.

In 1931 the Theatre Guild moved its successful production of Maxwell Anderson's *Elizabeth the Queen,* starring the Lunts, from the Guild Theatre to the Martin Beck. The Lunts next appeared at this theatre in one of their acting triumphs, Robert E. Sherwood's romantic comedy, *Reunion in Vienna* (1931).

Just before the Lunts' triumph in *Reunion in Vienna,* the Martin Beck housed the first production of the Group Theatre, made up of younger members of the Theatre Guild who had been responsible for the presentation of *Roar China!* The play was Paul Green's *The House of Connelly* and it was produced under the auspices of the Theatre Guild. Chosen as one of the year's ten best, it was staged by Lee Strasberg and Cheryl Crawford and dealt with the clash of generations in an aristocratic Southern family. The critics were very receptive to the production.

In 1932 the Abbey Irish Theatre Players (including Barry Fitzgerald) played a season of repertory, including such Irish classics as *The Far-off Hills, Juno and the Paycock, Playboy of the Western World,* and *The Shadow of a Gunman.*

In December 1933 Broadway waited with great anticipation for the return of Katharine Hepburn to the stage. Her chosen vehicle was a British play, *The Lake,* directed by Jed Harris. Miss Hepburn had gone to Hollywood and become a superstar in a very short time and so eminent was she that Mr. Harris forbade the rest of the cast (including many distinguished actors) to speak to her offstage. The play opened, and Hepburn's nervous performance inspired the famed Dorothy Parker crack, "She ran the gamut of emotions—from A to B." The general opinion was that Miss Hepburn flopped in *The Lake.*

Sidney Howard's documentary play *Yellow Jack* (1934), written with Paul de Kruif and adapted from de Kruif's book *The Microbe Hunters,* opened next. It was

Above: Glenn Anders and Claudette Colbert in Eugene O'Neill's *Dynamo* (1930). *Bottom:* A giant battleship and sampans were the highlights of Lee Simonson's epic set for the Theatre Guild's *Roar China!* (1930).

Katharine Hepburn flops in *The Lake* (1933).

based on the true record of Walter Reed and the researchers who discovered that the killer Yellow Fever was propagated by mosquitos. The large cast included James Stewart, Edward Acuff, Myron McCormick, and Sam Levene as Marine privates who volunteered to be bitten by the deadly insects. The play ran only 79 performances but was admired by the critics.

The D'Oyly Carte Opera Company played a four-month season at the Martin Beck in 1934, followed by Katharine Cornell as a radiant Juliet in *Romeo and Juliet*, with Basil Rathbone as Romeo, Brian Aherne as Mercutio, Orson Welles as Tybalt, and Edith Evans as the Nurse. Miss Cornell was hailed for her luminous performance, and the sumptuous production, with magical sets by Jo Mielziner and dances by Martha Graham, ran for 78 performances. Miss Cornell followed her Juliet with two other productions at the Martin Beck: a revival of her beloved gem *The Barretts of Wimpole Street* (1935), with Brian Aherne, Burgess Meredith, and Brenda Forbes; and John Van Druten's anti-war play *Flowers of the Forest* (1935), with Miss Cornell, Mr. Meredith, and Margalo Gillmore.

A major dramatic event occurred at the Martin Beck on September 25, 1935. Maxwell Anderson's *Winterset* opened and proved to be a fascinating and controversial blank-verse drama. Starring Burgess Meredith, Margo, Richard Bennett, and Eduardo Ciannelli, the tragedy dealt with a son's quest for his father's murderer. The action took place beneath the Brooklyn Bridge, and Jo Mielziner's majestic set was one of his greatest designs. The play won the first award as best drama of the season conferred by the newly formed New York Drama Critics Circle. It ran for 195 performances.

On March 9, 1936, Katharine Cornell returned in glory to this theatre in her acclaimed revival of Shaw's *Saint Joan*. Brilliantly directed by her husband, Guthrie McClintic, who piloted all her plays, the production was hailed as a work of art. Maurice Evans was the Dauphin, and the large cast also included Brian Aherne, Arthur Byron, Eduardo Ciannelli, Kent Smith, George Coulouris, and the future film idol Tyrone Power, Jr..

The D'Oyly Carte Opera Company paid a return visit with their repertory in 1936, followed by another Maxwell Anderson play, a fantasy called *High Tor*, which won the second Best Play award conferred by the New York Drama Critics Circle. The fanciful play starred Burgess Meredith, and British actress Peggy Ashcroft, and featured young Hume Cronyn. It was set on top of an actual mountain on the Hudson called High Tor and involved the young man who owned it and who refused to sell it. Ghosts of ancient Dutch sailors waiting for the return of Henry Hudson's boat added comic relief, and the refreshing play ran for 171 performances.

The remainder of the 1930s found the Martin Beck occupied by Ina Claire in an unsuccessful adaptation of Trollope's *Barchester Towers* (1937); a revival of *Victoria Regina*, with Helen Hayes repeating her celebrated role (1938); another engagement of the D'Oyly Carte Opera Company (1939); and Helen Hayes again, this time in a modern, murder trial play, *Ladies and Gentlemen* (1939), adapted by her husband, Charles MacArthur, and Ben Hecht from a Hungarian play. It was a moderate success, running for 105 performances.

In 1940, *Lady in Waiting*, a dramatization of Margery Sharp's popular novel *The Nutmeg Tree*, boasted a sterling comic performance by Gladys George, but ran for only

Above Left: Alfred Lunt, Lynn Fontanne, and Henry Travers in *Reunion in Vienna* (1931). *Right:* Maurice Evans and Katharine Cornell in *Saint Joan* (1936). *Left:* Katharine Cornell and Basil Rathbone in *Romeo and Juliet* (1934). *Above:* Burgess Meredith and Peggy Ashcroft in *High Tor* (1936).

87 performances. On April 1, 1941, Lillian Hellman's prophetic play, *Watch on the Rhine*, starring Paul Lukas, Lucile Watson, Mady Christians, and George Coulouris, stunned audiences with its anti-fascist theme. Directed by Herman Shumlin and brilliantly acted, the play won the Best American Play award conferred by the New York Drama Critics Circle, and ran for 378 performances. John Steinbeck's adaptation of his novel *The Moon Is Down* (1942) was next, but did not achieve great success. The popular comedy hit *My Sister Eileen* moved here from the Biltmore Theatre and stayed for four months. The Lunts arrived in November 1942 with *The Pirate*, S.N. Behrman's colorful adaptation of an idea in a play by Ludwig Fulda. It gave Lunt an opportunity to walk a tightrope and pretend he was a notorious pirate whom Fontanne idolizes. This bizarre burlesque ran for 176 performances.

One of the Martin Beck's biggest hits was Mr. Behrman's adaptation of Franz Werfel's play *Jacobowsky and the Colonel* (1944), starring Louis Calhern, Oscar Karlweis, Annabella, J. Edward Bromberg, and E.G. Marshall. The adventurous story involved a comical and enterprising refugee named Jacobowsky (Karlweis), an aristocratic Polish colonel (Calhern), and a beautiful blonde (Annabella) fleeing together in a car from Nazi-occupied France. The comedy ran for 417 performances.

In March 1945 Tallulah Bankhead and Donald Cook opened in *Foolish Notion*, Philip Barry's most foolish play. This misguided venture was followed by the rollicking Bernstein/Comden/Green musical *On the Town*, which moved in from the 44th Street Theatre for a stay of five months. Next came the melodious Harold Arlen/Johnny Mercer musical *St. Louis Woman* (1946), with Pearl Bailey, Rex Ingram, Juanita Hall, and the Nicholas Brothers, directed by Rouben Mamoulian: Eugene O'Neill's *The Iceman Cometh* (1946), with James Barton, Dudley Digges, E.G. Marshall, Nicholas Joy, Tom Pedi, and Jeanne Cagney; Nancy Walker in a musical, *Barefoot Boy with Cheek* (1947), adapted from his humorous book of the same name by Max Shulman; Katharine Cornell, Godfrey Tearle, Kent Smith, Eli Wallach, Maureen Stapleton, Charlton Heston, Lenore Ulric, and Douglass Watson in a revival of Shakespeare's *Antony and Cleopatra* (1949); unsuccessful revivals of

Carl Benton Reid, James Barton, Dudley Digges, and Nicholas Joy toast to their pipe dreams in Eugene O'Neill's *The Iceman Cometh* (1946).

Shaw's *You Never Can Tell* and Jerome Kern's *Sally* (1948); and Katharine Cornell in one of her poorest productions, *That Lady* (1949), in which she performed with a black patch over her eye.

During the 1950s at the Martin Beck, Helen Hayes appeared in *The Wisteria Trees* (1950), Joshua Logan's adaptation of *The Cherry Orchard* set in America's deep South. Gilbert Miller unveiled his sumptuous production of *Ring Round the Moon* (1950), Christopher Fry's translation of Jean Anouilh's charade with music. Maureen Stapleton, Eli Wallach, Don Murray, and Phyllis Love gleamed in Tennessee Williams's *The Rose Tattoo* (1951), with Stapleton and Wallach winning Tony Awards for their performances and the play winning a Tony as the best drama of the season.

Maxwell Anderson's *Barefoot in Athens* was a failure in 1951, and Truman Capote's *The Grass Harp* flopped in 1952. Arthur Miller's *The Crucible* (1953), with Arthur Kennedy, Beatrice Straight, E.G. Marshall, Walter Hampden, and Madeleine Sherwood, focused on the

Left: John Forsythe (in striped robe) is harassed in *Teahouse of the August Moon* (1953). *Right:* Geraldine Page and Paul Newman in *Sweet Bird of Youth* (1959).

Salem witch hunts as a metaphor for anti-Communist hysteria in then-contemporary America, but was more successful when it was later revived Off Broadway.

On October 15, 1953, one of the Martin Beck's most memorable productions opened: John Patrick's enchanting comedy, *Teahouse of the August Moon.* The production won five Tony Awards, including Best Actor (David Wayne) and Best Play, and stayed at the Martin Beck for 1,027 performances. Also starring John Forsythe and Paul Ford, *Teahouse* delighted with its comical depiction of the American occupation of Okinawa island.

On October 30, 1956, Shaw's *Major Barbara* was successfully revived. The production, directed by Charles Laughton, also starred Mr. Laughton and Cornelia Otis Skinner, Burgess Meredith, Glynis Johns, and Eli Wallach. It moved to the Morosco to make way for the Beck's next tenant, *Candide,* a musical version of the Voltaire classic with music by Leonard Bernstein, book by Lillian Hellman, lyrics by Richard Wilbur, John Latouche, Leonard Bernstein, and Dorothy Parker. With these geniuses at the helm, the production (directed by Tyrone Guthrie) should have been a triumph, but it was not. However, the cast album captured the brilliance of the score, and the show has had two (drastically revised) revivals on Broadway.

A minor Tennessee Williams's play, *Orpheus Descending,* with Maureen Stapleton, Cliff Robertson, and Lois Smith, lasted only 68 performances in 1957; but a flimsy comedy, *Who Was That Lady I Saw You With?,* with Mary Healy, Peter Lind Hayes, and Ray Walston, managed to last 208 times. The final show of the 1950s at the Beck was a Tennessee Williams winner, *Sweet Bird of Youth,* with Geraldine Page giving an unforgettable performance as a fading movie star who is living with a young hustler (Paul Newman). It ran for 375 performances.

On April 14, 1960, a jubilant hit came to the Martin Beck. *Bye Bye Birdie,* an exuberant musical parody of early rock 'n' roll and the gyrating Elvis Presley, was an instant hit and won the following Tony Awards: Best Musical, Best Book (Michael Stewart); Best Score (Charles Strouse and Lee Adams); Best Direction and Best Choreography (Gower Champion); Best Supporting Actor (Dick Van Dyke). The gifted cast also included Chita Rivera, Paul Lynde, Dick Gautier (as a Presley clone), Kay Medford, and Michael Pollard. It ran for 607 performances.

During the 1960s, the Martin Beck housed a number of shows that moved there from other houses. Some highlights that originated at the Beck during this decade included Jerry Herman's *Milk and Honey* (1961), about the new Israel; Anne Bancroft, Barbara Harris, Gene Wilder, and Zohra Lampert in a revival of Brecht's *Mother Courage and Her Children* (1963), staged by Jerome Robbins; Colleen Dewhurst and Michael Dunn in Edward Albee's adaptation of Carson McCullers's *The Ballad of the Sad Cafe* (1963); Jessica Tandy, Hume Cronyn, and Robert Shaw in Friedrich Dürrenmatt's *The Physicists* (1964), directed by Peter Brook; and Buddy Hackett and Richard Kiley in the rowdy musical *I Had a Ball* (1964).

The Royal Shakespeare Company's mesmerizing production of *The Persecution and Assassination of Marat As Performed by the Inmates of the Asylum of Charenton Under the Direction of the Marquis de Sade* brought nudity—and a startling sense of the stage's possibilities—to Broadway in 1965.

Highlights of the late 1960s included Jessica Tandy, Hume Cronyn, Rosemary Murphy, and Marian Seldes in Edward Albee's *A Delicate Balance* (1966); Leslie Uggams, Robert Hooks, Lillian Hayman, and Allen Case in the Tony Award winning musical *Hallelujah, Baby!* (1967), by Betty Comden, Adolph Green, and Jule Styne; the long-running musical *Man of La Mancha*, which moved here from the downtown ANTA Theatre (1968).

The Martin Beck Theatre remained in the Beck family until 1966. The theatre is currently owned and operated by Jujamcyn Theatres, which has kept the house in the finest condition.

During the early 1970s the Martin Beck had a run of plays and musicals that did not last very long. The most notable were Edward Albee's *All Over* (1971), with Jessica Tandy, Colleen Dewhurst, Betty Field, and George Voskovec; a musical version of *The Grass Harp* (1971), starring Barbara Cook; and a British import, *Habeas Corpus* (1975), with June Havoc, Rachel Roberts, Richard Gere, Celeste Holm, Jean Marsh, and Paxton Whitehead.

The streak of flops ended on October 20, 1977, when Frank Langella opened in the title role of *Dracula*, and the Martin Beck became a happy haven for thrill-seekers for 925 performances. Mr. Langella was succeeded by Raul Julia and David Dukes. The much publicized

Frank Langella as the Count in *Dracula* (1977).

Broadway debut of Elizabeth Taylor in *The Little Foxes* had a sellout run in 1981.

The Martin Beck's 1980s tenants included a baseball musical, *The First* (1981); Robert Altman's *Come Back to the Five and Dime Jimmy Dean, Jimmy Dean* (1981), with Cher making her Broadway debut; Angela Lansbury in *A Little Family Business* (1982); and the Royal Shakespeare Company's splendid revival of Shakespeare's *All's Well That Ends Well* (1983).

In 1984, Liza Minnelli and Chita Rivera opened here in *The Rink*, a musical by Terrence McNally, John Kander and Fred Ebb. Ms. Rivera won a Tony Award for her performance. The following year, John Lithgow starred in a stage adaptation of Rod Serling's successful TV and movie story, *Requiem for a Heavyweight*, but it was short-lived. Also doomed was a revival of the musical *Take Me Along* (based on Eugene O'Neill's nostalgic comedy, *Ah, Wilderness!*), which closed on its opening night in 1985.

The Stephen Sondheim/James Lapine musical *Into*

book by Luther Davis, songs by Robert Wright, George Forrest, and Maury Yeston, direction and choreography by Tommy Tune. Performed without intermission, the musical detailed the lives and intrigues of guests at the Grand Hotel in Berlin in 1928. This atmospheric musical was nominated for 11 Tony Awards and won the following: Best Featured Actor in a Musical (Michael Jeter), Best Costume Design (Santo Loquasto), Best Musical Director (Tommy Tune), Best Choreography (Mr. Tune), Best Lighting Design (Jules Fisher). During rehearsals, Mr. Yeston (*Nine, Titanic*) was brought in to supply additional music and lyrics to a project Wright and Forrest had been developing for more than two decades. The musical ran for 1,077 performances and ended its long run in 1992 at the Gershwin Theatre.

Another huge hit played at this theatre when the

Above: Elizabeth Taylor makes her Broadway debut in *The Little Foxes*, with Ann Talman (1981). *Right:* PLAYBILL for *The Sound of Music* (1998).

the *Woods* fared better in 1987 and ran for 765 performances. The interweaving of classic fairy tales (e.g. "Cinderella," "Rapunzel," "Little Red Riding Hood," "Jack and Beanstalk") won Tony Awards for Best Book of a Musical (Lapine), Best Original Score (Sondheim) and Leading Actress in a Musical (Joanna Gleason). The producers advertised the production by attaching a huge inflatable leg and spiked boots to the front of the theatre, to make it appear that the Giant of the beanstalk was sitting atop the Martin Beck!

On November 12, 1989, the musical *Grand Hotel* opened, based on the popular Vicki Baum novel, with a

PLAYBILL

MARTIN BECK THEATRE

THE SOUND OF MUSIC

Above: Philip Bosco and Carol Burnett ham it up in *Moon Over Buffalo* (1995). *Below Right:* PLAYBILL for *Guys and Dolls* (1992).

classic 1950 musical *Guys and Dolls*, by Frank Loesser, Jo Swerling, and Abe Burrows, was revived in 1992. The stars this time included Nathan Lane, Faith Prince, Peter Gallagher, Josie de Guzman, Scott Wise, and Walter Bobbie, and the revival received a rapturous reception. It ran for 1,143 performances—nearly as long as the original—and won the following Tony Awards: Best Musical Revival, Best Actress in a Musical (Prince), Best Musical Director (Jerry Zaks), and Best Scenic Design (Tony Walton).

My Thing of Love, a play about a broken marriage, opened on May 3, 1995 starring Laurie Metcalf, but lasted for only 13 performances.

On October 1, 1995, Carol Burnett and Philip Bosco brought convulsive slapstick to the Martin Beck in Ken Ludwig's farce, *Moon Over Buffalo.* Not all critics were amused. Some found that the comedy about a hammy theatrical troupe appearing at a Buffalo theatre strained too hard to be funny. Nevertheless both Ms. Burnett (in her first Broadway appearance since 1964) and Mr. Bosco received Tony Award nominations for their performances. They were ably supported by Jane Connell, Randy Graff, and others, and ran for 308 performances. Later in the run, the two leads were succeeded by Lynn Redgrave and Robert Goulet. An unusual aspect of the production was that a fascinating documentary called *Moon Over Broadway* was filmed by D.A. Pennebaker backstage during the creation and rehearsals of this

comedy, which vividly detailed the bickering and problems that ensue when "the show must go on."

The famed magician David Copperfield brightened the 1996 holiday season at this theatre with his lavish magic show, *Dreams & Nightmares.* Described as "an intimate evening of grand illusion," the spectacle was created and performed by Mr. Copperfield with startling special effects. Francis Ford Coppola served as the creative advisor. The sold-out extravaganza ran for 54 performances.

A new production of the 1977 musical *Annie* received a very mixed reception in March 1997. Nell Carter played Miss Hannigan and Brittny Kissinger was Annie, but they did not enjoy the success of Dorothy Loudon or Andrea McArdle of the original production.

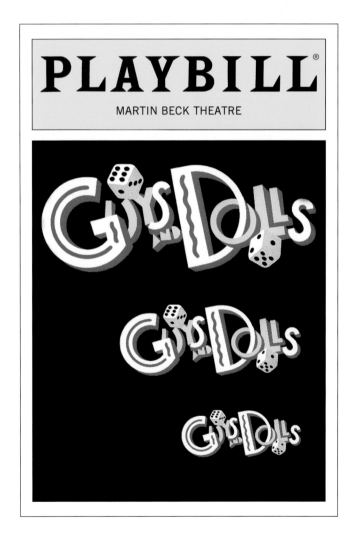

It received a Tony Award nomination for Best Revival, but didn't win. It ran for 238 performances.

Rebecca Luker starred as Maria in a beautifully mounted 1998 revival of *The Sound of Music*. During the run, TV star Richard Chamberlain stepped into the role of Captain von Trapp, with 18-year-old Laura Benanti at his side to sing "Do Re Mi."

A nostalgic event occurred at this theatre on November 18, 1999. A new production of Cole Porter's classic 1948 *Kiss Me, Kate* (the first musical to win a Tony Award) opened to vociferous cheers. The splendid book by Sam and Bella Spewak deftly combined Shakespeare's *The Taming of the Shrew* with the backstage antics of a theatrical troupe performing a musical version of the comedy in Baltimore. Porter's score is considered to be his best. In the new production the leads were played by Brian Stokes Mitchell, Marin Mazzie, Amy Spanger, and Michael Berresse. A nostalgic note: the original leads in 1948 were Alfred Drake, Patricia Morison, Lisa Kirk, and Harold Lang. Ms. Morison, the only surviving member of this quartet, attended the 1999 opening night and looked radiant.

Kiss Me, Kate received 12 Tony Award nominations and won the following: Best Musical Revival; Best Orchestrations (Don Sebesky); Best Costumes (Martin Pakledinaz); Best Musical Direction (Michael Blakemore), Best Leading Actor in a Musical (Brian Stokes Mitchell). The musical enjoyed a lengthy run at the Martin Beck.

In response to the box office plunge that followed the September 11, 2001 terrorist attack on the World Trade Center, the cast made a memorable eleventh-hour effort to save the show. In a dramatic curtain speech at what was to have been the final performance September 23, it was announced that in addition to taking a twenty-five percent pay cut, the company volunteered to allocate an additional quarter of their salaries to buy tickets to the show and donate them to the rescue workers who have had a hand in the recovery effort. The gesture helped keep *Kate* running until the box office recovered.

RICHARD RODGERS THEATRE

Through the efforts of producer Alexander H. Cohen and the Nederlander Organization, the former 46th Street Theatre was renamed the Richard Rodgers in 1990, in honor of the late composer whose music brightened more than three dozen Broadway musicals.

During the 1920s, brothers Irwin S. and Harry I. Chanin, who had a lucrative construction business, became interested in show business. They built six legitimate theatres in the short span of five years. One of these was called Chanin's 46th Street Theatre, located at 226 West Forty-sixth Street, and spent many years known simply as the 46th Street Theatre.

The architect was the very busy Herbert J. Krapp, and this time he came up with a novel notion. Instead of building the orchestra level in the style of other theatres, he had the seats—from Row "L" on—slope upward so that theatregoers in the rear of the orchestra had an excellent view of the stage. The rear section of the orchestra was really as high as a mezzanine, and patrons in that section had to climb stairs to reach their orchestra seats.

According to Brooks Atkinson in his book *Broadway*, the Chanins made critics feel welcome by putting nameplates on the seats they occupied on opening nights. For their opening attraction on Christmas Eve, 1924, the brothers chose the 1924 edition of the *Greenwich Village Follies,* which was not new. It had already played at the

Shubert and Winter Garden Theatres and it stayed only briefly at the new house.

This theatre was to have a curious history in its early years. It had a policy of booking shows that had played in other theatres first, and, on occasion, these shows had interrupted runs. This was the case with the 46th Street Theatre's second booking. *Is Zat So?*, the long-running comedy about boxing, moved in from the 39th Street Theatre in February 1925 and played until mid December. On Christmas Eve, the latest edition of the *Greenwich Village Follies* opened, and ran until March. Then, on March 15, 1926, *Is Zat So?* reopened at the theatre and stayed until the end of July.

In September 1926 the lurid melodrama *The Shanghai Gesture* moved here from the Shubert and stayed for three months. This was followed by the eminent French team of Sacha Guitry and his wife, Yvonne Printemps, in two plays by Mr. Guitry: *Mozart* and a short piece, *Deburau.* The stars alternated these plays with another comedy by Guitry, *L'illusioniste.* The French company of actors was highly praised.

In March 1927 a tingling thriller called *The Spider* excited audiences by a novel device. The scene of the play was a vaudeville house, and the murders took place in the audience, with policemen, detectives, and nurses running up and down the aisles during the performance. A theatregoer could attend this play with the wonderful appre-

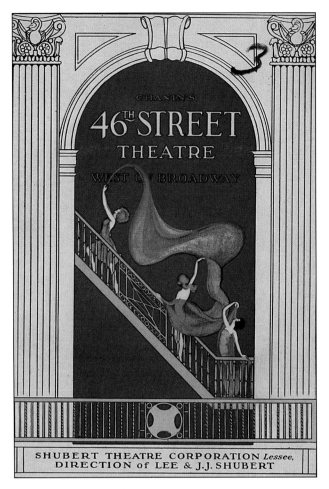

Two standard covers used for the 46th Street Theatre in the 1920s: The musical *Follow Thru* (1929); the revue *Greenwich Village Follies* (1926).

hension that he might be seated next to the murderer.

The 46th Street's next tenant, *Baby Mine* (1927), lasted only 12 performances, but it attracted publicity because it marked the return to the stage of Roscoe ("Fatty") Arbuckle, a famed movie comic whose film career was ruined by a notorious sex murder case. *The New York Times* reported that the actor was given "an extremely cordial reception."

September 6, 1927, saw the opening of this theatre's biggest hit to date—and one of the 1920s's most famous musicals. It was the spirited *Good News* by the rah-rah team of DeSylva, Brown, Henderson, and Laurence Schwab. To get the audience in the mood for this youthful football scrimmage, the ushers wore college jerseys and the musicians in George Olsen's nifty jazz orchestra delivered school cheers before the overture. The sappy

plot about a dumb football player who has to be tutored in order to pass an exam and be allowed to play in the season's biggest game was enlivened by such durable musical comedy songs as "The Best Things in Life Are Free," "Lucky in Love," "Just Imagine," and two rousing show-stoppers, "Good News" and "The Varsity Drag," both sung by a fabulous flapper named Zelma O'Neal.

The four creators of *Good News* scored again in 1929 when they brought *Follow Thru* to this theatre. This time the subject was golf, and they paired Zelma O'Neal with the likable comic Jack Haley, later to achieve immortality as the Tin Man in the film *The Wizard of Oz*. Their big number was the infectious "Button Up Your Overcoat." *Good News* ran for 551 performances; *Follow Thru* for 401. The latter show had a sensational tap dancer in the cast: the young Eleanor Powell.

Christmas night, 1929, brought a platinum gift to the 46th Street Theatre: the Broadway debut of Ginger Rogers as Babs Green, a wealthy young thing who stopped the show with a song called "Hot and Bothered." The musical was called *Top Speed* and it ran for 104 performances.

The enterprising songwriter Billy Rose became a producer in November 1930 by putting his illustrious wife, Fannie Brice, into a revue, *Sweet and Low*, to which he also contributed some excellent lyrics. Miss Brice was a standout, assisted by George Jessel and James Barton.

Another college musical, *You Said It*, breezed into the 46th Street Theatre on January 19, 1931, bringing Lou Holtz, Benny Baker, and the Polish sexpot Lyda Roberti. Ms. Roberti stopped the proceedings with her torrid singing of Harold Arlen's "Sweet and Hot."

The radiant Margaret Sullavan appeared briefly in 1932 in a drama called *Happy Landing* and was praised by critic Brooks Atkinson as having fine possibilities as an actress. Two shows from other theatres—*Of Thee I Sing* and *Autumn Crocus* (Richard Nixon's favorite play)—were next, followed by a hit comedy, *She Loves Me Not*, by Howard Lindsay, which took place at Princeton. The lunatic plot involved a nightclub singer (Polly Walters) who hides out in a Princeton dorm because she is wanted as a witness to a murder. Burgess Meredith and John Beal played two students, and the merry campus lark sang for 367 performances.

In October 1934 young actor Henry Fonda finally played a part that attracted attention—Dan Harrow in *The Farmer Takes a Wife*—and his performance got him whisked off to Hollywood to repeat his role in the film version of this play about the Erie Canal. Another future *Oz* star, Margaret Hamilton, went with him to repeat her performance as Lucy Gurget.

Cole Porter's smash musical *Anything Goes* moved here in the summer of 1935 from the Alvin (minus Ethel Merman). For several years after this, the 46th Street Theatre had a series of undistinguished plays.

In September 1938 Olsen and Johnson brought their insane show *Hellzapoppin* to this theatre. The critics hated this rowdy vaudeville revue, but Walter Winchell kept plugging it and turned it into a hit. It was quickly moved to the Winter Garden, where it became

Broadway's longest-running musical (1,404 performances) until its record was surpassed by *Oklahoma!*

The 1930s went out in style at this theatre with a ribald Cole Porter triumph called *DuBarry Was a Lady* (1939). The trumpet-voiced Ethel Merman and the baggy-pants clown Bert Lahr played dual roles in this royal fantasy: She was a nightclub singer, May Daly, and DuBarry in the dream sequences; Lahr was Louis Blore, a washroom attendant, and Louis XV, king of France, in the dream scenes. The cast also included Betty Grable, Benny Baker, Ronald Graham, and Charles Walters. Porter's hit songs were "Do I Love You?" and "Friendship."

Porter and Merman struck another lucky vein with their next musical, *Panama Hattie,* at this theatre. It opened in October 1940 and ran for 501 performances. For the first time in her fabulous career, Merman received solo star billing. Her supporting cast included Arthur Treacher, James Dunn, Betty Hutton, Rags Ragland, and little Joan Carroll, who stopped the show with Merman

Jack Haley and Zelma O'Neal in the golf musical *Follow Thru* (1929).

Henry Fonda and June Walker in *The Farmer Takes a Wife* (1934), the play that won Fonda a Hollywood contract.

in their charming duet "Let's Be Buddies." The chorus line for this musical featured such forthcoming talents as June Allyson, Betsy Blair, Lucille Bremer, Vera-Ellen, Constance Dowling, and Doris Dowling.

In March 1945 an unusual play, *Dark of the Moon,* called "a legend with music," opened to some negative reviews, but the public found this sexual drama about a witch boy (Richard Hart) who wants to be human so he can marry Barbara (Carol Stone) fascinating, and it ran for 318 performances.

In 1945 the successful revival of Victor Herbert's *The Red Mill* moved here from the Ziegfeld Theatre and

remained for a year. On January 10, 1947, the joyful *Finian's Rainbow* opened and played for 725 performances. This entrancing fantasy about a leprechaun (David Wayne), an Irishman (Albert Sharpe), and his daughter (Ella Logan) was the work of Burton Lane, E.Y. "Yip" Harburg, and Fred Saidy. The memorable score included such delights as "How Are Things in Glocca Morra?," "If This Isn't Love," "Old Devil Moon," "Look to the Rainbow," "When I'm Not Near the Girl I Love," and "Something Sort of Grandish."

Alan Jay Lerner and Kurt Weill supplied the next musical at this theatre, but *Love Life* (1948), starring Nanette Fabray and Ray Middleton, was only a moderate success. An opera version of Lillian Hellman's *The Little Foxes,* called *Regina,* by Marc Blitzstein, starring Jane Pickens, Brenda Lewis, William Warfield, and Priscilla Gillette, could muster only 56 performances in 1949. *Arms and the Girl* (1950), a musical version of the play *The Pursuit of Happiness,* was more successful, running for 134 performances. It had a score by Morton Gould and Dorothy Fields; book by Herbert and Dorothy Fields: and starred Nanette Fabray, Pearl Bailey, and Georges Guetary.

A landmark musical, *Guys and Dolls,* opened here on November 24, 1950, and stayed put for three years. Earning one of the most vociferous (and unanimous) set of raves in the history of Broadway, the show escorted audiences into Damon Runyon's urban Neverland of gamblers, gangsters, nightclub singers, and Salvation Army soul-savers who supplied the heartbeat of old Times Square. Based on a story and characters by Damon Runyon, with a book by Jo Swerling and Abe Burrows, a superb score by Frank Loesser, and direction by George S. Kaufman, the show won eight Tony Awards, was named Best Musical by the New York Drama Critics Circle, and ran for 1,200 performances.

In 1954 the lovely Audrey Hepburn illuminated the theatre as a water sprite in Giraudoux's *Ondine,* staged by Alfred Lunt and co-starring Ms. Hepburn's husband, Mel Ferrer. The play won four Tony Awards, including Best Actress (Hepburn), Best Director (Lunt), Best Costume Designer (Richard Whorf), and Best Set Designer (Peter Larkin).

A revival of the 1936 Rodgers and Hart musical *On*

Above Left: Ethel Merman and Bert Lahr in the raucous *DuBarry Was a Lady* (1939). *Above Right:* Merman, Rags Ragland, Frank Hyers, and Pat Harrington in Cole Porter's *Panama Hattie* (1940). *Below:* The whimsical hit *Finian's Rainbow* (1947).

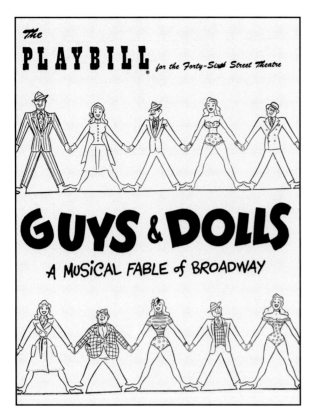

Program cover for Frank Loesser's award-winning musical *Guys and Dolls* (1950).

Your Toes, starring Vera Zorina, Bobby Van, and Elaine Stritch, did not wear well in 1954, but Maxwell Anderson's frightening play, *The Bad Seed,* fascinated audiences for 334 performances. Little Patty McCormack, as a sweet-as-taffy murderess, got rid of some of the cast. Nancy Kelly, who played her mother, won a Tony Award for her bravery.

From May 5, 1955, until mid-March 1960, this theatre could have been renamed the Gwen Verdon Theatre. The great singer/dancer reigned here in three successive musicals: *Damn Yankees, New Girl in Town,* and *Redhead.* Ms. Verdon was rewarded for her bravura talents by winning three Tony Awards as Best Actress in a Musical in all three shows. The hit musicals also won Tonys for the other creative talents involved.

Highlights of the 1960s at the 46th Street Theatre included Maurice Evans in the musical *Tenderloin* (1960); and the Pulitzer Prize-winning musical, *How To Succeed in Business Without Really Trying* (1961), by Frank Loesser, Abe Burrows, Jack Weinstock, and Willie Gilbert.

Starring Robert Morse and Rudy Vallee, the parody of corporate life played for 1,417 performances.

Do I Hear a Waltz? (1965), the moderately successful musical version of *The Time of the Cuckoo,* was the sole collaboration between legends of two generations: Richard Rodgers (music) and Stephen Sondheim (lyrics). Arthur Laurents supplied the book, and the musical starred Sergio Franchi, Elizabeth Allen, and Carol Bruce.

Mary Martin and Robert Preston teamed for the two-character musical *I Do! I Do!* (1966), based on the hit play *The Fourposter,* with libretto and score by Tom Jones and Harvey Schmidt. The last musical of the 1960s at this theatre, *1776,* the Sherman Edwards/Peter Stone depiction of events leading up to the signing of the Declaration of Independence, was awarded a Tony for Best Musical and ran for 1,217 performances.

The happy 1971 revival of the 1925 musical *No, No, Nanette* brought Ruby Keeler back to the stage in triumph. It ran for 861 performances, far surpassing its predecessor, which registered only 329 showings. Ms. Keeler sang and tapped and won many accolades for her comeback. Also in the cast was her old friend Patsy Kelly, plus Helen Gallagher, Bobby Van, Jack Gilford, and Susan Watson.

A 1973 revival of *The Women* did not win favor, but *Raisin,* a musical adaptation of Lorraine Hansberry's play *A Raisin in the Sun,* fared better, running for 847 performances and being named Best Musical in the Tony Awards. Virginia Capers also won a Tony for her performance. The 1975 revival of *Private Lives,* starring Maggie Smith and John Standing, directed by John Gielgud, won raves and stayed for three months.

A musical version of the 1920s play *Chicago* proved a solid hit in 1975 with dazzling choreography and staging by Bob Fosse and an evocative score by John Kander and Fred Ebb. Starring the sensational Gwen Verdon (in a return to the scene of her 1950s triumphs), Chita Rivera, and Jerry Orbach, it ran for 898 performances. It was nominated for eleven Tony Awards, but lost them all, mainly to that year's juggernaut, *A Chorus Line.*

The blockbuster *The Best Little Whorehouse in Texas* moved to this theatre in July 1978 from the Entermedia Theatre and stayed for three years and nine months, making it the 46th Street Theatre's longest-running show.

Carlin Glynn and Henderson Forsythe won Tony Awards for their performances.

On May 9, 1982, the offbeat musical *Nine* opened and promptly won Tony Awards for Best Musical, Best Score, Best Direction, Best Costumes, and Best Featured Actress (Liliane Montevecchi). An adaptation of the Fellini film *8½*, this unusual musical had an arresting score by Maury Yeston, adaptation from the Italian by Mario Fratti, book by Arthur Kopit, and direction by Tommy Tune. Raul Julia played the Italian film director and lover Guido Contini, a young boy played Guido as a child, and the rest of the cast was composed mainly of the many women in this Don Juan's life. Anita Morris stopped the show with her torrid dance, "A Call From the Vatican," and Karen Akers, Shelly Burch, Taina Elg, Camille Saviola, and Kathi Moss all had spectacular supporting roles.

From 1983 to 1986, *Brighton Beach Memoirs*, the first part of Neil Simon's planned trilogy about his own family, enjoyed a huge success here and won Tony Awards for Matthew Broderick (Best Featured Actor in a Play), and Gene Saks (Direction).

In June 1986, Jean Stapleton and an all-star cast brought hilarity in a revival of the celebrated homicidal comedy *Arsenic and Old Lace*. The following year, August

Wilson's powerful play *Fences* won the Pulitzer Prize and Tony Award for Best Play, along with additional Tonys for James Earl Jones (Best Actor in a Play), Mary Alice (Best Featured Actress), and Lloyd Richards (Best Director). In August 1988, *Checkmates* arrived with Denzel Washington, Marsh Jackson, Ruby Dee, and Paul Winfield. This was followed by a revival of Garson Kanin's classic comedy *Born Yesterday*, starring Madeline Kahn, Ed Asner, and Daniel Hugh Kelly. In the fall of 1989, Dustin Hoffman starred in a revival of *The Merchant of Venice* in which he played Shylock for a limited run of 81 performances.

When this theatre was rechristened the Richard Rodgers in 1990, the inaugural production was Rupert Holmes' short-lived thriller, *Accomplice*, produced by Alexander H. Cohen and his wife Hildy Parks. David Merrick returned to Broadway in 1990 with a revival of the Gershwins's musical *Oh, Kay!*, but it ran for only 77 performances. This theatre had an enormous success when Neil Simon's *Lost in Yonkers* opened in 1991 and won the Pulitzer Prize, plus the following Tony Awards: Best Play, Leading Actress (Mercedes Ruehl), Featured Actress (Irene Worth), and Featured Actor (Kevin Spacey).

In 1993, the Boys Choir of Harlem and Friends performed here; later that year, the delightful *Fool Moon*

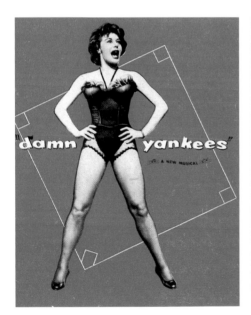
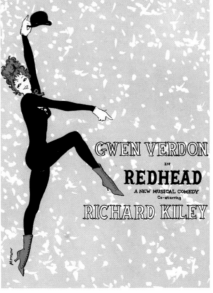
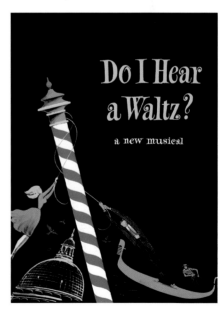

Souvenir programs for Gwen Verdon in *Damn Yankees* (1955); Verdon in *Redhead* (1959); and the Richard Rodgers/Stephen Sondheim musical, *Do I Hear A Waltz?* (1965).

Left: Ronald Holgate, Howard Da Silva, William Daniels in the historical musical *1776* (1969). *Above:* Saucy Anita Morris in her torrid dance number, "A Call From the Vatican," in *Nine* (1982).

starring pantomimists Bill Irwin and David Shiner amused for 109 performances. Additional hilarity was triggered by Neil Simon's *Laughter on the 23rd Floor,* a zany memoir of his early years as a comedy writer for Sid Caesar's memorable TV series, "Your Show of Shows." The stage comedy was brightened by the antics of Nathan Lane, Randy Graff, Mark Linn-Baker, Lewis J. Stadlen, John Slattery, Ron Orbach, J.K. Simmons, Stephen Mailer, and Bitty Schram. It ran for 320 performances.

On March 23, 1995, the 1961 Pulitzer Prize-winning musical *How To Succeed In Business Without Really Trying* returned to this theatre. The famed show was favorably received and won a Tony Award for its star, Matthew Broderick, his second at this theatre. This new *How To Succeed* ran for 548 performances, far less than the original, which ran for 1,417.

Another hit musical of the past returned to the 46th Street the following year, but with far greater success. The 1975 musical *Chicago,* with a score by John Kander and Fred Ebb and book by Mr. Ebb, Bob Fosse, and script adaptation by David Thompson, had been acclaimed as a staged concert presented by City Center's "Encores!" series in spring 1996 season. On November 14, 1996, it transferred to the Richard Rodgers Theatre with great success. It played here until May 1997, then continued its long run at the Shubert Theatre. It starred Bebe Neuwirth, Ann Reinking, Joel Grey, James Naughton, and Marcia Lewis, and won the following Tony Awards: Best Revival of a Musical, Best Actor in a Musical (Naughton), Best Actress in a Musical (Neuwirth), Best Director of a Musical (Walter Bobbie), Best Choreographer (Reinking), and Best Lighting (Ken Billington).

Another Kander/Ebb musical, *Steel Pier,* opened here in 1997, with a book by David Thompson, but it did not enjoy the success of *Chicago.* Depicting the dance marathon craze of the 1920s in Atlantic City, it starred Daniel McDonald, Karen Ziemba, Debra Monk, and Gregory Harrison, and closed after 76 performances. The following cast members were nominated for a Tony Award: Mr. McDonald, Ms. Ziemba, Ms. Monk, and Joel Blum. Other Tony nominations included Best

Musical Book (David Thompson), Best Musical, Best Musical Director (Scott Ellis), Best Scenic Designer (Tony Walton), Best Choreographer (Susan Stroman), Best Score (Kander and Ebb), and Best Orchestrations (Michael Gibson).

October 16, 1997, brought a most unusual musical to this theatre. Called *Side Show*, it depicted the show business careers of real-life Siamese twins Daisy and Violet Hilton, brilliantly acted by Emily Skinner and Alice Ripley. With book and lyrics by Bill Russell and music by Henry Krieger, the production had many admirers, but the public resisted attending a musical about sisters who were literally joined at the hip. It received the following Tony Award nominations: Best Musical Actress (shared by Ripley and Skinner), Best Musical Book (Russell), Best Musical, and Best Score (Krieger and Russell). It closed after only 91 performances, but became a pet show of disabled theatre fans. The cast chipped in to pay for a ticket so one especially devoted wheelchair-bound fan could see the show one last time on the final performance.

Footloose, a musical based on a popular film of the same name, arrived on October 22, 1998, and enjoyed a long run, despite several negative reviews. It dealt with a small-town minister battling the evils of rock 'n' roll on the town's young people. It received several Tony Award nominations, but did not win.

The characters of the whimsically rhymed Dr. Seuss children's books took to the stage in a musical called *Seussical* in 2000. With a score by the *Ragtime* team of Stephen Flaherty and Lynn Ahrens and a book by Ahrens (conceived by Monty Python alumnus Eric Idle), the show wove several of the Seuss stories into a single narrative, with the mischievous Cat in the Hat serving as emcee. After a difficult tryout in Boston, the show opened on Broadway in the fall, and tried to build an audience on the charm of songs like "Anything's Possible" and "Alone in the Universe," and on the appeal of leads David Shiner, Kevin Chamberlin, and Janine Lamanna.

In 1932 the Chanins lost the 46th Street Theatre and their name no longer graced the marquee. Today, the renamed Richard Rodgers Theatre is owned by the Messrs. Nederlander and it is still one of Broadway's prime musical comedy houses.

Left to Right: PLAYBILL covers from *Chicago* (1996), *Steel Pier* (1997), and *Footloose* (1998).

Left: PLAYBILL cover for the Siamese twins musical, *Side Show* (1997). *Right:* The Cat in the Hat arrives in New York in this poster image from *Seussical* (2000).

BROADWAY THEATRE

The Broadway Theatre at Broadway and Fifty-third Street is one of the few legitimate theatres that was built as a movie house. B.S. Moss, a mogul who operated a chain of movie houses that also featured vaudeville, built this theatre in 1924. Designed by architect Eugene DeRosa, the house had one of the largest seating capacities (1,765) of any theatre on Broadway, thus making it ideal, in later years, for the staging and performing of musical comedies.

It also served for many years as the northern outpost of the Times Square theatre district until a refurbished Studio 54 (formerly the Gallo Opera House) one block north returned to legitimacy in 1998.

When this movie/vaudeville palace opened on Christmas Eve, 1924, it was called B.F. Moss's Colony Theatre. By 1930 Moss realized that the talkies were killing vaudeville and he converted his house to a legitimate theatre called the Broadway. At this time, he placed an ad in PLAYBILL in which he stated that his new playhouse "embodies an ideal not only for the theatrical profession, but equally for the public it serves. This ideal combines the magnitude, luxury and courtesy of the theatre with the comforts and charm of the drawing room. Every modern device for the production of greater entertainment has been incorporated into the physical perfection of the New Broadway. This insures not only more pretentious [sic] productions, but a price scale that is within the reach of every man's pocketbook. It is the aim

of the management to make this theatre the last word in theatrical entertainment—the brightest spot on Broadway."

After that credo, Moss had to come up with something glittering for his first legitimate show. He chose *The New Yorkers,* a very sophisticated "sociological" musical by Cole Porter and Herbert Fields in which a Park Avenue woman (played by the true blueblood Hope Williams) dreams that she's in love with a bootlegger. The show opened on December 8, 1930, and the critics liked it, especially the outlandish clowning of Jimmy Durante. The gold-plated cast also included Fred Waring and his Pennsylvanians, Ann Pennington, Frances Williams, Charles King, and Rags Ragland, who sang a Porter song called "I Happen to Like New York" that Bobby Short popularized years later. Another song from this show, the sensuous "Love for Sale," was banned on the radio as obscene. Despite Moss's claim that his price scale would suit every man's pocketbook, he charged a $5.50 top, which was quite high in 1930. He soon had to lower his prices, but the Depression was on, and after twenty weeks *The New Yorkers* closed at a financial loss.

The Broadway's next show was a new edition of the *Earl Carroll Vanities* (1932), with the up and coming comic Milton Berle, deadpan comedienne Helen Broderick, and the beautiful ballerina Harriet Hoctor. Outstanding features of this revue were the spectacular neon effects by a young genius named Vincente Minnelli,

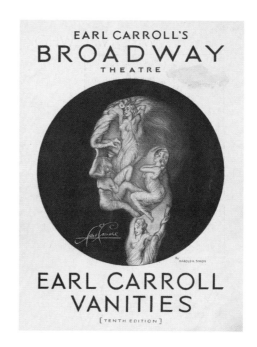

Far Left: Peter Arno's program sketch for the "sociological musical satire," *The New Yorkers* (1930). *Left*: Harold K. Simon's cover sketch of showman Earl Carroll for the tenth edition of *The Earl Carroll Vanities* (1932).

plus a hit tune, "I've Got a Right to Sing the Blues," by Harold Arlen and Ted Koehler. But times were bad and the show ran for only eleven weeks.

After a dud called *The O'Flynn* in 1934, the Broadway went back to showing talkies. Then, in 1940, it went legit again and began a policy that it was to pursue on and off during the rest of its history. It became the last stop for big hit Broadway musicals that were nearing the end of their runs. They would move to the huge Broadway Theatre and offer seats at lower prices until their runs came to an end. This began with the Rodgers and Hart musical *Too Many Girls,* which moved here from the Imperial in 1940.

A great theatrical event occurred at the Broadway on July 4, 1942. America was at war, and Irving Berlin, who had written a famed World War I soldier show called *Yip, Yip, Yaphank,* came up with another. It was *This Is the Army,* and its opening night at the Broadway was one of the greatest in the history of the theatre. All proceeds from the show went to Army Emergency Relief. Singer Kate Smith, who had immortalized Berlin's "God Bless America," paid $10,000 for two seats. Berlin himself appeared in the revue, repeating his world-famous number "Oh, How I Hate to Get Up in the Morning," from his earlier soldier show. The cast of *This Is the Army* consisted of professional actors who were in the armed serv-

ices, and their wives. Many of these performers later became famous on stage and screen. Berlin's score had such standout numbers as "I Left My Heart at the Stage Door Canteen," "I'm Getting Tired So I Can Sleep," and the rousing title tune.

Later in 1942, the hit comedy *My Sister Eileen* moved in from the Biltmore; and in 1943, Gertrude Lawrence returned from a tour in her psychological musical *Lady in the Dark,* and played for three months at the Broadway in this Moss Hart/Kurt Weill/Ira Gershwin classic. This was followed by a revival of *The Student Prince* and the San Carlo Opera Company in repertory.

On December 2, 1943, Billy Rose brought his production of *Carmen Jones* to this theatre and the critics flipped. Oscar Hammerstein II, who was back on top with *Oklahoma!,* conceived the offbeat notion of doing an all-black *Carmen* set in a parachute factory in America's South during World War II. The experiment worked and the jazz opera ran for 503 performances.

The policy of moving hit shows to the Broadway continued with Mike Todd's *Up in Central Park,* which moved from the Century Theatre in 1945 and stayed for nine months. The operetta *Song of Norway* moved from the Imperial in 1946, and the propaganda play *A Flag Is Born* transferred from the Music Box.

Late in 1946 Duke Ellington collaborated with John

LaTouche on a version of *The Beggar's Opera,* which he called *Beggar's Holiday.* It starred Alfred Drake and featured Avon Long and Zero Mostel (who got panned); it was not a success.

The year 1948 brought a revival of *The Cradle Will Rock,* also starring Alfred Drake, which moved from the Mansfield. Leonard Bernstein appeared in this as a clerk. The Habimah Players from Palestine (soon to be Israel) presented a repertory of *The Golem, The Dybbuk, Oedipus Rex,* and other plays in 1948.

In the summer of 1949 concert impresario Sol Hurok brought a dancing/singing show from Madrid called *Cabalgata* for a three-month engagement.

Olsen and Johnson of *Hellzapoppin* and other zany revues tried a new one out here called *Pardon Our French* in 1950, but even with French beauty Denise Darcel in the show it managed to run for only 100 performances. *Where's Charley?,* the Ray Bolger smash from the St. James Theatre, ended its run here; then a revival of Marc Connelly's Pulitzer Prize play *The Green Pastures* arrived in 1951, but lasted only 44 more performances. Mae West wiggled in with a revival of her play *Diamond Lil* (1951), which didn't fare too well; nor did revivals of the Gertrude Stein/Virgil Thompson opera *Four Saints in Three Acts* (1952) and the black revue *Shuffle Along* (1952). The Pulitzer Prize-winning musical *South Pacific* transferred from the Majestic and ended its run here, chalking up 1,925 performances.

Les Ballets de Paris and Spanish dancer Jose Greco played the Broadway in 1954, and there was the premiere engagement of Gian-Carlo Menotti's opera *The Saint of Bleeker Street,* a powerful religious work that ran for 92

Left: Ethel Merman doing "Rose's Turn" in the memorable musical *Gypsy* (1959). *Above:* Irving Berlin and Ezra Stone in Berlin's all-soldier revue, *This Is the Army* (1942).

performances. More dance companies paid visits—Katherine Dunham, Azuma Kabuki Dancers and Musicians—before Sammy Davis, Jr. opened in the popular musical *Mr. Wonderful* in 1956. With comic Jack Carter, Chita Rivera, and Pat Marshall in the cast, the musical recorded 383 performances.

Mel Brooks and Joe Darion made a musical of Don Marquis's *archy and mehitabel*, called *Shinbone Alley*, but Eartha Kitt, Eddie Bracken, and others could not turn it into gold. *The Most Happy Fella* dropped in from the Imperial to end its long run and stayed for three months. A new musical, *The Body Beautiful*, with a score by Jerry Bock and Sheldon Harnick, went nowhere, and closed to make room for Les Ballets de Paris, the Beryozka Russian Dance Company, and the Old Vic, imported by Sol Hurok, doing *Henry V, Twelfth Night,* and *Hamlet.*

In May 1959 one of the Broadway Theatre's milestones arrived. It was Ethel Merman in *Gypsy* and it offered the great singer her most memorable part—Rose, the pushy mother of Gypsy Rose Lee and June Havoc. With a book by Arthur Laurents, soaring score by Jule Styne and Stephen Sondheim, choreography and direction by Jerome Robbins, this tough show about show business has become a classic of the American musical theatre. Merman's eleven o'clock spot—"Rose's Turn"—was electrifying, as was her belting of "Everything's Coming Up Roses." The Broadway Theatre was extensively renovated for this engagement and the house had one of its most impressive bookings.

In 1963 *Tovarich* was notable for offering Vivien Leigh in her musical comedy debut with Jean Pierre Aumont as her co-star. Ms. Leigh won a Tony for her delightful performance, and the show ran for 264 performances. Noël Coward's musical *The Girl Who Came to Supper* (1963) was almost as boring as the play from which it was adapted (*The Sleeping Prince*). It starred Florence Henderson and José Ferrer, but it was music hall singer Tessie O'Shea who woke up the audience and was awarded with a Tony for her efforts.

The Obratsov Puppets, the *Folies-Bergère,* and dancer Zizi were booked in the early 1960s. Alexander H. Cohen opened his lavish musical *Baker Street* in 1965 with Fritz Weaver as Sherlock Holmes, Peter Sallis as Dr. Watson, Martin Gabel as the nefarious Professor Moriarty, and

Inga Swenson as the love interest. Hal Prince directed the show, which had a rare (for the time) four-color PLAYBILL cover, and ran for nine months.

The Devils, a dramatization of Aldous Huxley's nightmarish book about diabolism in seventeenth-century France, scared theatregoers away from the box office in 1966, although it starred Jason Robards, Jr. and Anne Bancroft. A musical version of Richard Llewellyn's famed novel *How Green Was My Valley,* retitled *A Time for Singing,* was also unsuccessful that year. The Lincoln Center revival of Irving Berlin's *Annie Get Your Gun,* with its original star, Ethel Merman, and a new Berlin showstopper, "Old Fashioned Wedding," was so popular that it moved here in 1966, to be followed by the Winter Garden hit *Funny Girl,* which ended its long run here.

After the Harkness Ballet played an engagement, Kander & Ebb's new musical version of the hit comedy *The Happy Time* (1968) opened and offered a Tony Award-winning performance by Robert Goulet. It was brilliantly directed by Gower Champion and attracted much publicity because of an incident that occurred on opening night. Clive Barnes, the critic for *The New York Times,* was delayed on a plane, and the first-night curtain was held until he arrived. His critical colleagues were highly critical of this excessive favoritism.

Cabaret and *Mame* moved in from other theatres to finish their long runs (1968-69), and a new musical, *Purlie,* based on the hit play *Purlie Victorious,* opened in 1970 and ran for 688 performances. Cleavon Little and Melba Moore won Tony Awards for their engaging performances. In 1972, *Fiddler on the Roof,* the multi-award-winning musical, moved here, and on the evening of June 17, 1972, it became the longest-running show in Broadway history up to that time (3,225 performances). By the time it ended its run shortly thereafter, it had reached 3,242 performances.

The creators of *Hair,* the enormously popular rock musical, opened their newest, *Dude* (1972), which required that the Broadway Theatre be drastically renovated, with tons and tons of dirt brought in to create a bare-earth playing area, and bleachers constructed to replace theatre seats. It was all for naught. The critics buried this disaster and the Broadway had to be restored to normalcy.

Left: Mark Baker in the title role of *Candide,* the musical that won five Tony Awards. *Above:* Patti LuPone in her Tony Award-winning performance as Eva Peron in *Evita* (1979).

In 1974, *Candide,* Leonard Bernstein's musical version of Voltaire's classic which had flopped on Broadway in 1956, came to the Broadway in a revised version. With additional lyrics by Stephen Sondheim and a new book by Hugh Wheeler, it was tried out first at the Chelsea Theatre Center of Brooklyn, with dynamic, arena-style staging by Harold Prince. It was so successful that it was transferred to the Broadway Theatre, where it triumphed for almost two years. The house was again renovated, this time into a labyrinth, with the audience seated on many levels and the action occurring all over the theatre. Mr. Prince won a Tony Award for his galvanic staging, but so many seats were removed for the experimental arrangement that the show struggled to turn a profit.

An all-black revival of *Guys and Dolls,* with new orchestrations, proved popular in 1976-77. This was followed by another hit black musical, *The Wiz,* which transferred here from the Majestic and stayed for more than a year and a half. A new musical, *Saravà,* which moved from the Mark Hellinger, played for four months

in early 1979 and was followed by the phenomenal *Evita,* by Andrew Lloyd Webber and Tim Rice, with revolutionary staging by Harold Prince. It won seven Tony Awards, including Best Musical.

After *Evita* ended its long run, a new production of the musical *Zorba* moved in, starring Anthony Quinn. Lila Kedrova, a featured actress in the show, won a Tony Award for her performance. In 1984, Yul Brynner made his last Broadway appearance, in a revival of *The King and I,* which had earned him a Tony Award in 1952. On this occasion, he was accorded a special Tony.

Another 1984 musical did not fare as well at this theatre. It was a new version of the old Ziegfeld show, *The Three Musketeers* (with a revised book by Mark Bramble). It lasted only 9 performances.

Also ill-fated was *Big Deal* in 1986, Bob Fosse's last Broadway show. He wrote the book, directed and choreographed the musical, which was based on the film *Big Deal on Madonna Street.* The score consisted of hit songs of the past by a battery of composer/lyricists. Although

Left: PLAYBILL for the Tony Award-winning musical *Les Misérables* (1987). *Right:* PLAYBILL for *Miss Saigon* (1991).

Fosse won a Tony Award for his choreography, the musical danced for only 62 performances.

In 1987, a blockbuster from London, *Les Misérables*, opened and won eight Tony Awards, including Best Musical of the season. The French songwriting team of Alain Boublil and Claude-Michel Schönberg (with Herbert Kretzmer) created this musical version of the Victor Hugo classic about a man, Jean Valjean, who steals a loaf of bread and spends the rest of his life on the run across a terrain of poverty and revolution from single-minded police inspector, Javert. This epic set the standard for the quasi-operatic "megamusicals" of the 1980s and '90s.

Boublil and Schönberg also provided the next block-buster at this theatre, *Miss Saigon* (with co-lyricist Richard Maltby, Jr.), which retold the story of *Madame Butterfly*, but set in the context of the Vietnam War. It

opened in April 1991 (*Les Misérables* moved to the Imperial Theatre and continued to flourish) and won Tony Awards for its leading actor (Jonathan Pryce), its leading actress (Lea Salonga), and its featured actor (Hinton Battle).

The north wall of the Broadway Theatre faces West Fifty-third street where, for most of the 1990s and into the 2000s, the CBS-TV program "The Late Show With David Letterman" frequently staged pranks. A wall of show posters soon appeared there, such as the ones in Shubert Alley. The Broadway's marquee was sometimes seen on the TV program, and the Broadway Theatre casts sometimes took part in the skits.

When *Miss Saigon* finally closed on January 28, 2001, after 4,095 performances, it had become the longest-running show in the history of this theatre, which is currently owned by the Shubert Organization.

VIRGINIA THEATRE

The Virginia Theatre at 245 West Fifty-second Street originated as the Guild Theatre, built by the Theatre Guild to be used as a home base for its own repertory company. The Guild, which began presenting plays on Broadway in 1919, had been using the Garrick Theatre for many of its shows. But after its fourth season its directors decided to build a theatre of their own so that the Guild's 15,000 subscribers and its acting company and school could prosper in comfort and luxury.

In his book *The Magic Curtain,* Lawrence Langner, the founder of the Guild, wrote that the theatre was built in the then popular "pseudo-Italian style." It was designed by C. Howard Crane, Kenneth Franzheim, and Charles Bettis, in consultation with set designers Norman Bel Geddes and the Guild's Lee Simonson. According to Langner, the

Guild Theatre was one of the company's greatest failures. The stage was made so large that there was little room left for dressing rooms or even audience space. "We made the ghastly mistake," he wrote, "of providing a theatre with all the stage space necessary for a repertory of plays without enough seating capacity to provide the income necessary to support the repertory." The theatre had 914 seats (later increased). Nevertheless, the Guild Theatre building was one of the most impressive legitimate houses in Manhattan, and a novel aspect of it was that the auditorium was not on street level but on the second story of the edifice.

The Guild Theatre debuted with great fanfare on the evening of April 13, 1925. President Calvin Coolidge officially opened the theatre by pushing an electric button in Washington, D.C., throwing the lights on a lush production of Shaw's *Caesar and Cleopatra,* starring Helen Hayes as the Egyptian queen and Lionel Atwill as Caesar. The critics were kind, and the revival managed to run for 128 performances.

The Guild Theatre's next production was also a Shaw revival—*Arms and the Man*—and this offering proved even more successful. It starred the Guild's foremost acting couple, Alfred Lunt and Lynn Fontanne, and it prospered for 181 performances.

Ferenc Molnar, one of the Guild's favorite playwrights, provided the theatre's next show, a romantic play called *The Glass Slipper,* starring June Walker, Lee Baker, and Helen Westley, but audiences attended it for only 65 performances. Since the Guild had 15,000 subscribers, each play it produced ran a few weeks for the subscribers. If the reviews were good and the show was a hit, it could be moved to a larger theatre, while the Guild continued with its repertory at its own house.

From the mid-1920s on, the Guild presented its company in a great variety of plays, many of them by foreign authors. Stars such as Lunt and Fontanne, Edward G. Robinson, Dudley Digges, Helen Westley, Philip Loeb, Armina Marshall (Mrs. Lawrence Langner), Henry Travers, Clare Eames, and many artists who would later establish the Group Theatre appeared at the Guild Theatre in plays that usually ran for 50 or more performances. The Lunts appeared together at the Guild Theatre in Franz Werfel's bizarre play *Goat Song* (1926), C.K. Munro's *At Mrs. Beam's* (1926), Werfel's *Juarez and Maximilian* (1926), a dramatization of Dostoevski's *The Brothers Karamazov* (1927), S.N. Behrman's witty comedy *The Second Man* (1927), Shaw's *The Doctor's Dilemma* (1927), Sil-Vara's *Caprice* (1928), and in another Behrman comedy, *Meteor* (1929).

The Lunts did not always appear as a team, however. At the Guild Theatre, Lunt appeared without Fontanne as Marco Polo in Eugene O'Neill's *Marco Millions* (1928); and Lynn appeared without Alfred in a revival of Shaw's *Pygmalion* (1926).

Other interesting productions presented at the Guild during the 1920s that did not star the Lunts were Edward G. Robinson in Pirandello's *Right You Are if You Think You Are* (1927); a straight version of *Faust* (1928), with Dudley Digges as Mephistopheles, Helen Chandler as Margaret, and George Gaul as Faust; Alice Brady, Otto Kruger, Frank Conroy, Gale Sondergaard, and Claude Rains in *Karl and Anna* (1929); and the same stars (except Sondergaard) in Romain Rolland's *The Game of Love and Death* (also 1929). During these years, the Theatre Guild practiced "Alternating Repertory," which meant that its actors would perform in one play for a week (perhaps at the John Golden or Martin Beck theatres), then report to the Guild Theatre the following week and appear in a different production. Lawrence Langner wrote in *The Magic Curtain* that this plan was highly successful and that the 1920s constituted the Guild's golden era.

The 1930s changed the Theatre Guild's operating system. The "Alternating Repertory" became too difficult to manage and the Depression did not help the Guild's economic situation. Although it continued to present fine actors in excellent plays, there were also many flops that drained the company's resources.

Helen Hayes as the Egyptian queen in the Guild's opening production of Shaw's *Caesar and Cleopatra* (1925).

In 1930 the Guild Theatre housed a revival of Turgenev's *A Month in the Country*, with Nazimova, Dudley Digges, and Henry Travers. It was successful, and during the run Katharine Hepburn joined the cast. It was her first role with the Guild and she was to play an important role in the Guild's survival in years to come.

Some highlights of the 1930s at this theatre included the third edition of the popular revue *The Garrick Gaieties* (1930), with Imogene Coca,

Alfred Lunt and Lynn Fontanne in *The Second Man* (1927) and *Elizabeth the Queen* (1930).

Cynthia Rodgers, Edith Meiser, and many others, who were joined during the run by the young Rosalind Russell, making her Broadway debut; the Lunts in Maxwell Anderson's verse play *Elizabeth the Queen* (1930), which moved from the Guild to the larger Martin Beck Theatre; Lynn Riggs's lovely *Green Grow the Lilacs* (1931), which would save the Guild in 1943 when it became the landmark musical *Oklahoma!*

On October 26, 1931, the Guild Theatre hosted one of its greatest triumphs: Eugene O'Neill's five-hour trilogy (with a dinner intermission) called *Mourning Becomes Electra.* O'Neill based his three plays on Aeschylus' *Oresteia,* but changed the locale to New England during the Civil War. The tragedy, which starred Nazimova, Alice Brady, Earle Larimore, and Lee Barker, was hailed by critics as a masterpiece. The eminent critic

Joseph Wood Krutch wrote: "It may turn out to be the only permanent contribution yet made by the twentieth century to dramatic literature." The play posed a fashion problem to first-nighters. The performance started at 5:00 PM. Should they wear evening clothes or afternoon wear? Critic George Jean Nathan wore afternoon clothes, but when he saw financier Otto Kahn arrive in evening clothes, Nathan ran home at intermission to change. Kahn also ran home and changed to afternoon wear.

Other 1930s highlights included Beatrice Lillie and Hope Williams in a revival of Shaw's *Too True to Be Good* (1932); Nazimova, Henry Travers, Claude Rains, Sydney Greenstreet, and Jessie Ralph in an adaptation of Pearl Buck's novel *The Good Earth* (1932); Ina Claire in one of her greatest high comedy performances in S.N. Behrman's *Biography* (1932); Judith Anderson, Humphrey

Bogart, Shirley Booth, and Leo G. Carroll in *The Mask and the Face* (1933), translated by Somerset Maugham from an Italian play; George M. Cohan and Gene Lockhart in Eugene O'Neill's only comedy, *Ah, Wilderness!* (1933); Maxwell Anderson's *Valley Forge* (1934), with Philip Merivale as General George Washington; Jimmy Savo, Eve Arden, Charles Walters, and Ezra Stone in a colorful revue, *Parade* (1935); the Lunts, Richard Whorf, and Sydney Greenstreet in an inspired revival of *The Taming of the Shrew* (1935); Ina Claire, Osgood Perkins, Van Heflin, Mildred Natwick, and Shepperd Strudwick in another Behrman gem, *End of Summer* (1936); and Sylvia Sidney, Leslie Banks, and Evelyn Varden in Ben Hecht's *To Quito and Back* (1937).

Despite brilliant acting, some of the above plays ran barely longer than 50 performances and there were many in between that ran fewer. By the end of 1938, the Guild found itself in such financial straits that it began renting the Guild Theatre to other producers. In October 1938,

Gilbert Miller presented J.B. Priestley's *I Have Been Here Before,* but it failed; and in December, Herman Shumlin presented Max Reinhardt's production of Thornton Wilder's *The Merchant of Yonkers,* starring Jane Cowl and featuring Percy Waram, June Walker, and Nydia Westman. This farce was a curious flop. Wilder later rewrote it as *The Matchmaker,* which was a hit; then it was turned into *Hello, Dolly!*

William Saroyan's first Broadway play, with a Group Theatre cast—*My Heart's in the Highlands*—played a brief but acclaimed run in 1939, followed in February 1940 by Saroyan's *The Time of Your Life,* which won both the Pulitzer Prize and the New York Drama Critics Circle Award, and moved to the Guild Theatre from the Booth. In the early 1940s, the Theatre Guild had a series of short-lived plays at their theatre—a revival of *Ah, Wilderness!,* with Harry Carey; Frederic March and Florence Eldridge in *Hope for a Harvest*; Celeste Holm and Jessie Royce Landis in *Papa Is All*; Paul Muni, Jessica

Left: Earle Larimore and Alice Brady in Eugene O'Neill's masterly *Mourning Becomes Electra* (1931). Right: Gene Lockhart and George M. Cohan in Eugene O'Neill's *Ah, Wilderness!* (1933).

Ina Claire and Van Heflin in S.N. Behrman's captivating comedy, *End of Summer* (1936).

Tandy, and Alfred Drake in *Yesterday's Magic;* Stuart Erwin and Lillian Gish in *Mr. Sycamore*; and finally, a Russian drama called *The Russian People.*

With all these disasters, the Theatre Guild decided to lease its theatre as a radio playhouse in 1943 and it remained so until 1950.

At this time, the federally chartered American National Theatre and Academy bought the theatre and renamed it the ANTA Playhouse. Lawrence Langner observed: "ANTA has now taken it over, and are operating it on a tax-free basis with subsidies and concessions from all the unions, which will make their burden far less than ours; and I wish them better luck with the building than we had." In 1944 the Theatre Guild moved out of the Guild Theatre to an imposing town house on West Fifty-third Street.

The beautifully renovated ANTA Playhouse opened auspiciously on November 26, 1950, with Judith Anderson, Marian Seldes, and Alfred Ryder in *The Tower Beyond Tragedy,* by Robinson Jeffers. The critics hailed Anderson's acting, but the verse tragedy based on the Electra theme played for only 32 performances. On Christmas Eve, 1950, Santa brought a gilt-edged gift to this beleaguered theatre: Gloria Swanson and José Ferrer in a revival of Hecht and MacArthur's comedy *Twentieth Century.* It was so successful that it was moved to the Fulton Theatre. The ANTA Play Series continued with revivals of *Mary Rose* (1951); Molière's *L'Ecole des Femmes,* performed in French by Louis Jouvet and company; *Desire Under the Elms* (1952), with Karl Malden, Douglas Watson, and Carol Stone, directed by Harold Clurman; and *Golden Boy* (1952), with John Garfield, Lee J. Cobb, and Jack Klugman. During this time, a genuine hit moved to the ANTA—Mary Chase's delightful fantasy, *Mrs. McThing* (1952), starring Helen Hayes, Ernest Borgnine, Jules Munshin, and Brandon de Wilde—but it tarried briefly before moving to the Morosco. In 1955 Katharine Cornell, Tyrone Power, and Christopher Plummer appeared in Christopher Fry's "winter comedy" *The Dark Is Light Enough.* The light burned out after 69 performances. A musical version of *Seventh Heaven,* with Chita Rivera, Beatrice Arthur, Gloria DeHaven, Ricardo Montalban, and Kurt Kasznar, had just 44 showings. ANTA's star-studded revival of *The Skin of Our Teeth* (1955) had Helen Hayes, Mary Martin, George Abbott, Florence Reed, and Don Murray in the cast. It played successful engagements in Paris, Washington, D.C., and Chicago before coming to the ANTA.

In 1956 the Lunts returned to the theatre where they had performed so often for the Guild. Their vehicle, *The Great Sebastians,* was one of their poorest. A melodramatic comedy by Howard Lindsay and Russel Crouse in which they played a mind-reading act, the play managed to last for 174 performances.

On February 8, 1956, the ANTA Theatre finally housed a play that enjoyed a relatively long run (477 performances). Edward G. Robinson returned to this theatre, where he had acted for the Guild many times, and garnered superlatives for his performance in Paddy Chayefsky's *Middle of the Night,* a love story about a fifty-

Helen Hayes as a wealthy-aristocrat-turned-scrubwoman in Mary Chase's comic fairy tale, *Mrs. McThing* (1952).

three-year-old man who falls in love with a twenty-four-year-old woman, played by Gena Rowlands. June Walker, Anne Jackson, and Martin Balsam were also in the cast. Joshua Logan produced and directed.

The success of the Chayefsky play at the ANTA turned the tide for this house. After engagement by the Dancers of Bali and Dancers of India, the house booked several hits that enjoyed substantial runs. *Say, Darling* (1958), a comedy about the troubles encountered when producing a Broadway musical, was satiric fact rather than fiction. It was plainly about the backstage shenanigans in getting *The Pajama Game* produced on Broadway. David Wayne, Vivian Blaine, Johnny Desmond, and Constance Ford were in the cast, but Robert Morse stole the show doing an outrageous

impersonation of a flamboyant producer/director said to be inspired by Hal Prince. The comedy ran for 332 performances.

The ANTA's next tenant won the Pulitzer Prize. It was *J.B.* (1958), a verse drama by Archibald MacLeish, with Pat Hingle as J.B. (Job), Raymond Massey as Mr. Zuss (God), and Christopher Plummer as Nickles (Satan). Elia Kazan directed the Biblical drama, which ran for 364 performances.

Critics praised Rex Harrison's acting in Anouilh's comedy *The Fighting Cock* (1959), but audiences supported it for only 87 performances. Next came a healthy hit, *A Thurber Carnival* (1960), described as "a new entertainment patterned after the revue form," by James Thurber, with music by Don Elliott. The show was a series of humorous sketches based on the *New Yorker* magazine wit's writings, and performed with charm by Tom Ewell, Peggy Cass, Paul Ford, John McGiver, Alice Ghostley, and others.

Highlights of the 1960s included Hugh Wheeler's *Big Fish, Little Fish* (1961), with Jason Robards, Jr., Hume Cronyn, Martin Gabel, Elizabeth Wilson, and George Grizzard, directed by Sir John Gielgud; Robert Bolt's distinguished historical play, *A Man for All Seasons* (1961), which won six Tony Awards, including Best Play, Best Actor (Paul Scofield), and Best Director (Noel Willman), later brought Faye Dunaway into the cast, and ran for 640 performances; and James Baldwin's *Blues for Mister Charlie* (1964), with Diana Sands, Al Freedman, Jr., John McCurry, Rosetta Le Noire, Pat Hingle, and Rip Torn, directed by Burgess Meredith.

Sands returned to the ANTA with Alan Alda in the comedy *The Owl and the Pussycat* (1964), which ran for 421 performances. Peter Shaffer's *The Royal Hunt of the Sun* (1965) starred Christopher Plummer as Spanish conqueror Pizarro and George Rose as Ruiz, with David Carradine as the leader of the Incas. Next came engagements by the National Repertory Theatre (1967) and the American Conservatory Theatre (1969); Len Cariou in the American Shakespeare Festival's production of *Henry V* (1969); and a revival of *Our Town* (1969) for the Plumstead Playhouse, with Henry Fonda, Ed Begley, Elizabeth Hartman, Harvey Evans, Mildred Natwick, John Beal, and Margaret Hamilton.

Top Left: Katharine Cornell and Tyrone Power as they appeared on the PLAYBILL cover for Christopher Fry's *The Dark Is Light Enough* (1955). *Above*: Raymond Massey and Christopher Plummer in the Pulitzer Prize-wining drama, *J.B.* (1958). *Left*: Mona Freeman (in touring cast) and Edward G. Robinson in *Middle of the Night* (1956).

Diana Sands and Alan Alda in the 1964 comedy *The Owl and the Pussycat.*

The 1970s brought Helen Hayes, James Stewart, and Jesse White in a revival of *Harvey* (1970), jointly produced by ANTA and the Phoenix Theatre; engagements of the dance companies of Alvin Ailey, Louis Falco, Pearl Lang, Paul Taylor, Nikolais, and the Dance Theatre of Harlem (all in 1971); the musical *Purlie* from the Broadway Theatre, which played for seven months in 1971; Julie Harris winning a Tony Award for her performance in *The Last of Mrs. Lincoln* (1972); Elizabeth Ashley, Keir Dullea, Fred Gwynne, and Kate Reid in a revival of *Cat on a Hot Tin Roof* (1974); the exuberant black musical *Bubbling Brown Sugar* (1976), which ran for 766 performances; Charles Repole in a revival of Eddie Cantor's 1920s hit *Whoopee* (1979), from the Goodspeed Opera House; and Maggie Smith in Tom Stoppard's *Night and Day* (1979).

Derek Jacobi starred in a Russian drama, *The Suicide*, in 1980, for 60 performances. A musical version of Dickens's *David Copperfield*, its title shortened to *Copperfield*, had a brief run of 13 performances in 1981. *Annie* moved in from the Alvin across the street for one month, followed by the campy musical *Oh, Brother!*, based on Shakespeare's *The Comedy of Errors*, with the action transferred to the contemporary Middle East. It had the misfortune to open while the memory of American hostages in Iranian captivity was still fresh in people's memories, and it lasted just 3 performances. It was followed by the Pilobolus Dance Theatre (1981).

In August 1981 the ANTA theatre was acquired by Jujamcyn Theatres and subsequently renamed the Virginia Theatre, in honor of Mrs. Virginia M. Binger, owner of Jujamcyn along with her husband, James Binger. Richard G. Wolff, then president of Jujamcyn Theatres, supervised the renovation of the theatre and announced the firm's intention of booking both legitimate attractions and dance companies at the Virginia.

In June, 1982, a musical called *Play Me A Country Song* had a very brief run here; and in December of that year, Eva Le Gallienne revived her adaptation of *Alice in Wonderland* (co-authored with Florida Friebus) for a brief run. This was followed by a superlative new production of the 1936 Rodgers and Hart musical *On Your Toes*, which won a Tony Award for Best Revival of the season and another Tony for its brilliant ballet star, Natalia Makarova. It ran 505 performances.

Emily Mann's *Execution of Justice*, a docudrama of the trial of Dan White, who murdered George Moscone, mayor of San Francisco, and City Supervisor Harvey Milk, had a short run in 1986, and was succeeded later that year by Ian McKellen in *Wild Honey*. The following year brought a Canadian production of *The Mikado* and a musical version of the macabre Stephen King novel, *Carrie*, which closed on its opening night, but inspired a small, devoted cult. Ray Cooney's British smash, *Run For Your Wife*, did not repeat its success in New York. A new production of the hit musical *Shenandoah* failed to run as long as the original, but it was followed by the successful musical *City of Angels*, which won six Tony Awards: Best Musical, Best Score (Cy Coleman, David Zippel), Best Book (Larry Gelbart), Best Actor in a Musical (James

(Standing L-R) David Zippel, Dee Hoty, Randy Graff, James Naughton, Kay McClelland, Cy Coleman, (Seated, L-R) Rene Auberjonois, Larry Gelbart, and Gregg Edelman at a rehearsal for *City of Angels* (1989).

Naughton), Best Featured Actress in a Musical (Randy Graff), and Best Scenic Designer (Robin Wagner). A film noir mystery about a troubled writer and the cool detective character he creates in his novels (the latter sections performed with black and white costumes and sets), *City of Angels* ran 878 performances here from 1989 to 1992, setting a new house record.

In the spring of '92, another hit musical arrived—*Jelly's Last Jam,* an impressionistic biography of jazz pioneer Jelly Roll Morton, which won a Tony Award for

its star, Gregory Hines, and one for featured actress Tonya Pinkins. A new production of the Lerner & Loewe classic *My Fair Lady* opened in 1993 and starred Richard Chamberlain as Henry Higgins, Melissa Errico as Eliza Doolittle and Julian Holloway as Alfred P. Doolittle (the role his father Stanley Holloway had originated in the original 1956 production). *The New York Times* stated that it was a touring show and looked it. It ran for only 165 performances and received no Tony nominations.

On March 2, 1995, a megahit musical arrived at the

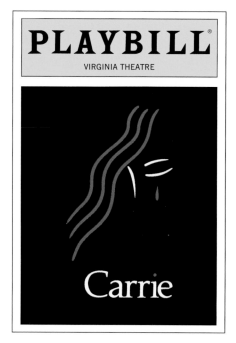

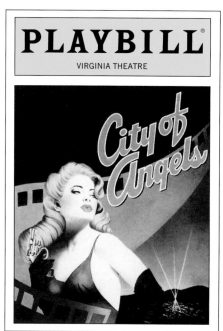

PLAYBILLs for *Carrie* (1987), *City of Angels* (1989), and *Smokey Joe's Cafe* (1995).

Virginia. *Smokey Joe's Cafe*, a revue featuring the hit 1950s-1960s songs of Jerry Leiber and Mike Stoller ("Stand By Me," "On Broadway," "Hound Dog," "Spanish Harlem" and many others) was praised for its brilliant performers and dancing. It dazzled for 2,036 performances, making it the longest-running musical revue in Broadway history and the Virginia Theatre's longest-running show. It received seven Tony Award nominations and its cast album won a Grammy Award.

The Virginia Theatre's next tenant was a theatrical oddity called *The Wild Party*, based on a 1928 poem by Joseph Moncure March, with music and lyrics by Michael John LaChiusa and a book by LaChiusa and George C. Wolfe (who also directed). It was produced in April 2000 by The New York Shakespeare Festival/Joseph Papp Public Theater and starred Mandy Patinkin, Toni Collette, and Eartha Kitt. The production will forever carry an asterisk next to its title owing to the fact that another musical with the same title, based on the same

poem, but with book, music and lyrics by Andrew Lippa, was produced Off-Broadway by the Manhattan Theatre Club at almost the same time, from February 24 to April 9, 2000. The Manhattan Theatre Club's production received better reviews, but the Broadway version had some wild admirers and received seven Tony Award nominations. It ran for just 68 performances, a costly flop for the New York Shakespeare Festival.

Later that year, the Virginia hosted a revival of *Gore Vidal's "The Best Man,"* with the author's name added to the original title to avoid confusion with a recent film of the same name. Examining the morality of a fictional 1950s presidential race, it opened in the midst of the 2000 campaign. Viewers found many parallels between life and art. The producers set up a voting booth in the lobby so ticket holders could cast non-binding votes on the outcome of the 2000 contest. Voters at the Virginia overwhelmingly went for Al Gore, but the general election had a surprise in store.

EUGENE O'NEILL THEATRE

The Eugene O'Neill Theatre at 230 West Forty-ninth Street originated as the Forrest Theatre in 1925. It was named after one of America's greatest classical actors, Edwin Forrest, whose bitter feud with the classical British actor William Charles Macready ignited the tragic 1849 riot at the Astor Place Opera House in New York City. In the course of that event twenty-two persons were killed and several hundred wounded.

The Forrest Theatre was built by the Shuberts and designed in the Georgian style by architect Herbert J. Krapp. The capacity was 1,200, making it flexible for the staging of dramas or musical comedies. Unfortunately, the new theatre began with a string of flops. The theatre opened officially on November 25, 1925, with a musical comedy called *May-flowers*, starring Ivy Sawyer, Joseph Santley, and a newcomer named Nancy Carroll, who would later become a movie star. *The New York Times* labeled the show "attractive," but it lasted for only 81 performances.

After *Mayflowers*, it housed such short-lived shows as *The Matinee Girl, Mama Loves Papa, Rainbow Rose,* and *My Country.*

After six more very short-lived plays in 1927, the Forrest finally had a hit with a drama called *Women Go on Forever.* Produced by William A. Brady, Jr., and Dwight Deere Wiman, the play featured this impressive cast: Mary Boland, Osgood Perkins, Douglass Montgomery, and James Cagney. A seamy, realistic play

that *The Times* found "cheap and malodorous," the show attracted the public for 118 performances.

After that, the Forrest reverted to potboilers whose very titles denoted their doom: *Bless You, Sister; Mirrors; It Is to Laugh; The Skull; Fast Life; The Common Sin; The Squealer;* and *Cafe de Danse,* all from December of 1927 to December of 1928. Ruth St. Denis and Ted Shawn brought some class to the house with their dancing in 1929 and things brightened a bit when the popular comedy, *Bird in Hand* by John Drinkwater, transferred here from the Masque Theatre in 1930.

The Blue Ghost, a mystery play, managed to run for 112 performances in 1930, possibly because it was the only creepy show in town. Ushers at the Forrest Theatre wore blue hoods over their heads to get the audience in the proper shivery mood, but *The New York Times* declared that after that device they expected the worst—and got it.

A farce, *Stepping Sisters*, about three ex-queens of burlesque, moved to the Forrest from the Royale Theatre in August 1930 and stayed for two months. In October of that year, the theatre suddenly became Edgar Wallace's Forrest Theatre when Mr. Wallace's play *On the Spot* opened there. This gangster play, with Anna May Wong and Glenda Farrell, was the theatre's biggest hit thus far, running for 167 performances.

A terrible farce called *In the Best of Families* was pronounced dull and dirty by Brooks Atkinson of *The Times*, so it ran for 141 performances, moving to the

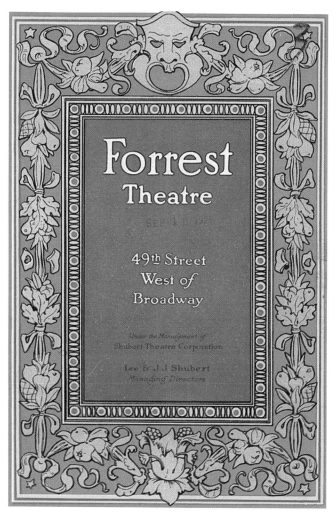

Above: Standard program cover for the Forrest Theatre in the 1920s. *Opposite:* A formal portrait of the turnip-eating Jeeter Lester family in *Tobacco Road.* From left: Reneice Rehan, Margaret Wycherly, Sam Byrd, James Barton (as Jeeter), and Ruth Hunter.

From January through August 1934 the Forrest had seven flops, including a lavish musical romance, *Caviar,* with dancer Jack Cole in the cast, and a musical revue, *Keep Moving,* starring Tom Howard. Then, in September 1934, a bonanza finally arrived at this theatre. It was *Tobacco Road,* Jack Kirkland's shocking dramatization of Erskine Caldwell's novel of the same name, which had opened at the Masque Theatre on December 5, 1933. Starring Henry Hull as Jeeter Lester, Margaret Wycherly as Ada, and Dean Jagger as Lou, this seamy play, which many critics disliked, stayed at the Forrest from September 1934 until the week of May 25, 1941. When it ended its marathon run at the Forrest, it had played for 3,182 performances, making it the longest-running play in the history of the American theatre. Today, it is second only to *Life with Father,* which ran for 3,224 performances. Henry Hull was succeeded by the following actors during *Tobacco Road's* record run: James Barton, James Bell, Eddie Garr, and Will Geer. *Tobacco Road* came back to the Forrest in 1942, after a long road tour, and then John Barton, son of James, was playing Jeeter Lester. But the return engagement lasted only 34 performances. Audiences had had enough of squalor, sex, and turnips in this drama about Georgia "crackers." Meanwhile, the mayor of Chicago had deemed the play too dirty to be staged there, and Rhode Island and the American South had made the same decision.

The 1940s at the Forrest reverted to the unfortunate booking of a series of flop shows. Occasionally, hits from another theatre, such as *Three Men on a Horse* and *Claudia,* played there, but usually they were clinkers like *Bright Lights of 1944; Manhattan Nocturne; Topical Revue; Listen Professor; Dark Hammock,* and *Hand in Glove.* The last show to play the Forrest before it changed its name was a comedy called *The Overtons* (1945), which moved in from the Booth. It played for three months at the Forrest before the theatre closed for extensive renovations.

In 1945 City Playhouses Inc., with Louis A. Lotito as managing director, bought the Forrest from the Select Operating Corporation, which was controlled by the Shuberts. The new owners completely renovated this theatre, turning it into a stunning playhouse covered with silken gray fabrics. Renamed the Coronet, it became one of the handsomest playhouses in Manhattan. And

Forrest from the Bijou in March 1931. From October of that year until November of 1932, this theatre housed seven plays of such mediocrity that none of them ran for more than 36 performances and four ran for fewer than 12 performances.

Things picked up a bit in 1932 when the Helen Hayes/Walter Connolly hit *The Good Fairy* moved here from Henry Miller's Theatre and stayed for two months. A revival of Rachel Crothers's comedy *As Husbands Go* chalked up 144 performances in 1933. The Ballets Jooss played a gratifying engagement from October to December of 1933.

with this new dressing and new management, its luck changed—though not immediately. The first show to play the Coronet, *Beggars Are Coming to Town,* opened on October 27, 1945. It had an impressive cast: Paul Kelly, Luther Adler, Dorothy Comingore, Herbert Berghof, E.G. Marshall, George Mathews, and Adrienne Ames. Despite excellent acting and expert direction by Harold Clurman, it ran for only 25 performances.

But the Coronet's second show turned out to be a winner. Elmer Rice's enchanting fantasy, *Dream Girl,* was written for his wife, Betty Field, and she gave a captivating performance as a woman who enlivened her dull life with vivid daydreams. She was ably supported by Wendell Corey, Evelyn Varden, and Edmon Ryan, and the cheerful comedy ran for 348 performances.

In January 1947 Arthur Miller's first successful play, *All My Sons,* opened here and stayed for 328 performances. The cast featured Ed Begley, Arthur Kennedy, Karl Malden, and Lois Wheeler, and Brooks Atkinson in *The New York Times* wrote: "With the production of *All My Sons* at the Coronet... the theatre has acquired a new talent... Arthur Miller."

For a change of the pace, the Coronet next booked a revue, *Angel in the Wings* (1947), and it was one of the

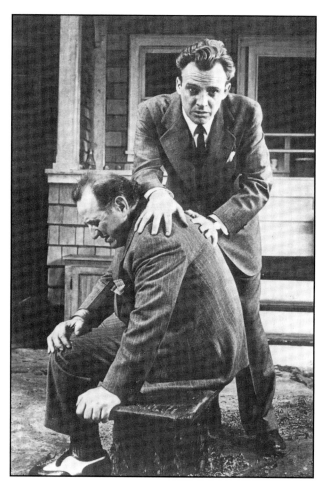

Left: Betty Field and Wendell Corey in Elmer Rice's bewitching comedy *Dream Girl* (1945). *Right:* Ed Begley (seated) and Arthur Kennedy in Arthur Miller's first success, *All My Sons* (1947).

season's big hits. Starring the infectious dance satirists, Paul and Grace Hartman, assisted by Hank Ladd, Elaine Stritch, Nadine Gae, Johnny Barnes, and others, the revue cheered audiences for 308 performances. Another bright revue, *Small Wonder* (1948), followed this, and its scintillating cast included Tom Ewell, Alice Pearce, Mary McCarthy, Jack Cassidy, Joan Diener, Jonathan Lucas, and many others. Staged by Burt Shevelove and choreographed by Gower Champion, it pleased revue lovers for 134 performances.

The indestructible Mae West revived her play *Diamond Lil* with sumptuous sets and gaudy costumes in February 1949, and the public flocked to it for 181 performances.

Maurice Evans was featured in Terence Rattigan's double bill of *The Browning Version* and *A Harlequinade,*

co-starring with Edna Best, but the Peter Glenville production lasted only 69 showings. After two unsuccessful plays—*Happy As Larry* and *The Bird Cage*—the Coronet had another hit revue with the Hartmans— *Tickets, Please!* in the spring of 1950. Their cast this time included Jack Albertson, Tommy Wonder, Larry Kert, Dorothy Jarnac, and many others. The Hartmans' formula paid off for 245 performances.

Other 1950s highlights at this theatre included Jessica Tandy, Beulah Bondi, Evelyn Varden, Eileen Heckart, and John Alexander in Samson Raphaelson's *Hilda Crane* (1950), staged by Hume Cronyn; Lillian Hellman's fascinating play about the middle-age crisis, *The Autumn Garden* (1951), with Fredric March, Florence Eldridge, Jane Wyatt, Ethel Griffies, and others, directed by Harold Clurman; Edna Best giving a memorable performance in S.N. Behrman's *Jane* (1952), based on a Somerset Maugham story; and a revival of Miss Hellman's explosive play *The Children's Hour* (1952), with Patricia Neal, Kim Hunter, Robert Pastene, and Iris Mann.

More hits of the 1950s: Burgess Meredith, Martha Scott, Glenn Anders, and Una Merkel in Liam O'Brien's *The Remarkable Mr. Pennypacker* (1953); Robert Anderson's *All Summer Long* (1954), with John Kerr, Ed Begley, June Walker, and Carroll Baker; Noël Coward's *Quadrille* (1954), starring the Lunts, Brian Aherne, and Edna Best, directed by Lunt, with striking sets and costumes by Cecil Beaton. Maxwell Anderson's hit thriller about a sweet little murderess, *The Bad Seed* (1954), with Nancy Kelly, Patty McCormack, Eileen Heckart, Henry Jones, and Evelyn Varden, moved here from the 46th Street Theatre. Then came Arthur Miller's *A View from the Bridge*, with Van Heflin, J. Carrol Naish, and Eileen Heckart, in tandem with a shorter play, *A Memory of Two Mondays* (1955).

The Lunts returned in *The Great Sebastians* (1956), which transferred from the ANTA Theatre. Barbara Bel Geddes, Michael Redgrave, and Cathleen Nesbitt starred

Top: From left: Van Heflin. Jack Warden (holding chair), Eileen Heckart (in background), Gloria Marlowe, and Richard Davalos, in Arthur Miller's *A View from the Bridge* (1955). *Above Left:* Steve Cochran comes up to see Mae West in a revival of her *Diamond Lil* (1949). *Right:* PLAYBILL cover for Paul and Grace Hartman's hit revue, *Tickets, Please!* (1950).

Patty McCormack and Nancy Kelly in Maxwell Anderson's homicidal thriller, *The Bad Seed* (1954).

in Terence Rattigan's *The Sleeping Prince* (1956). Siobhan McKenna transferred her *Saint Joan* (1956), from the Phoenix Theatre. Sir Ralph Richardson and Mildred Natwick had fun in Jean Anouilh's memorable play *The Waltz of the Toreadors* (1957), directed by Harold Clurman, followed by Katharine Cornell and Anthony Quayle in Christopher Fry's *The Firstborn* (1958), with songs by Leonard Bernstein.

Jason Robards, Jr. gave a Tony Award-winning performance as a writer (said to be inspired by F. Scott Fitzgerald) in *The Disenchanted* (1958), with Jason Robards, Sr., also in the cast, along with George Grizzard, Rosemary Harris, and Salomé Jens. The last show to play the Coronet before it had yet another change of name was a revival of Eugene O'Neill's play *The Great God*

Brown (1959), with Fritz Weaver, Robert Lansing, and Nan Martin, in a Phoenix Theatre production.

In November 1959 the Coronet was renamed the Eugene O'Neill Theatre, in honor of America's greatest playwright, who had died in 1953. The first play at the O'Neill was William Inge's *A Loss of Roses*, with Betty Field, Warren Beatty, Carol Haney, Robert Webber, and Michael J. Pollard, but the critics found the play dull and it closed after 25 performances.

After several quick failures, the theatre housed Carol Channing in Charles Gaynor's revue *Show Girl*, with Jules Munshin and Les Quat' Jeudis, a quartet of singing Frenchmen. It ran for 100 performances. John Mills starred in Terence Rattigan's *Ross* (1961), about Lawrence of Arabia; Jason Robards, Jr., and Sandy Dennis enjoyed a long run in Herb Gardner's comedy *A Thousand Clowns* (1962), which perfectly captured the growing anti-establishment spirit of the time.

The 1960s brought Hal Prince's production of the charming musical *She Loves Me* (1963), by Joe Masteroff, Sheldon Harnick, and Jerry Bock with Jack Cassidy, Daniel Massey, and Barbara Cook singing what became her signature tune, "Ice Cream"; plus two hits from other theatres—*The Odd Couple* and *Rosencrantz and Guildenstern Are Dead* (1966-67); and the London musical version of *The Canterbury Tales* (1969), with George Rose, Sandy Duncan, Hermione Baddeley, Martyn Green, and Reid Shelton.

In the late 1960s playwright Neil Simon bought this theatre, but did not change its name. A series of Simon plays were then staged here, beginning with the successful comedy *Last of the Red Hot Lovers* (1969), with James Coco, Linda Lavin, Marcia Rodd, and Doris Roberts; *The Prisoner of Second Avenue* (1971), with Peter Falk, Lee Grant, and Vincent Gardenia, who won a Tony Award for his performance; *The Good Doctor* (1973), a series of sketches and songs, which Simon adapted from Chekhov stories, starring Christopher Plummer, Marsha Mason, Rene Auberjonois, Barnard Hughes, and Frances Sternhagen; *God's Favorite* (1974), Simon's comedy version of the Biblical story of Job, with Vincent Gardenia, Charles Nelson Reilly, and Rosetta LeNoire, staged by Michael Bennett.

The Simon parade was interrupted in 1975 by the

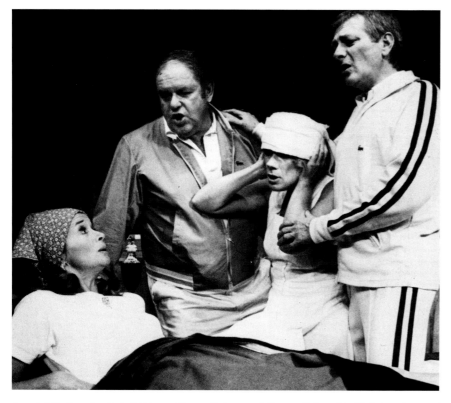

From left: Barbara Barrie, Jack Weston, Tammy Grimes, and George Grizzard, in Neil Simon's comedy, *California Suite* (1976). Right: PLAYBILL from *Big River*.

arrival of *Yentl*, a play by Isaac Bashevis Singer and Leah Napolin, starring Tovah Feldshuh, which stayed for seven months. Simon returned with *California Suite* (1976), an evening of four short plays, with Tammy Grimes, Jack Weston, and George Grizzard, which ran for 445 performances. Simon's hit play *Chapter Two* moved here from the Imperial in 1979, followed by another of his comedies, *I Ought to Be in Pictures* (1980), with Ron Leibman, Joyce Van Patten, and Dinah Manoff, who won a Tony Award for her performance. Simon's play *Fools,* with John Rubinstein, had a brief run in 1981, followed by *Annie,* which moved in from another theatre. A revival of Simon's musical *Little Me*, starring James Coco and Victor Garber, did not succeed in 1982 and the hit musical *The Best Little Whorehouse In Texas* returned from its tour and played at this theatre for a month.

In 1982 Jujamcyn Theatres bought the Eugene O'Neill from Simon and is currently operating the theatre. In October of that year, Beth Henley's play, *The Wake of Jamey Foster*, with Anthony Heald, played a short run here, followed by William Gibson's *The Monday*

After the Miracle, a continuation of his acclaimed play *The Miracle Worker*. Then came a legendary fiasco, *Moose Murders*, which closed on its opening night. Eve Arden, who had starred in it, wisely left the show after an early preview. It became a touchstone for Broadway flopdom.

Jessica Tandy, Amanda Plummer, Bruce Davison, and John Heard starred in a revival of Tennessee Williams' *The Glass Menagerie*, directed by John Dexter in 1983. In 1985, a musical called *Big River* based on Mark Twain's *The Adventures of Huckleberry Finn* opened and won the following Tony Awards: Best Musical, Best Book (William Hauptman), Best Score (Roger Miller), Best Direction (Des McAnuff), Best Featured Actor (Ron Richardson), Best Scenic Design (Heidi Landesman), and Best Lighting (Richard Riddell). Two years later, this hit was followed by *Tom Waits In Concert On Broadway* for a limited engagement.

Another hit arrived in 1988 when David Henry Hwang's controversial play, *M. Butterfly*, opened and won three Tony Awards: Best Play, Best Direction (John Dexter), and Best Supporting Actor (B.D. Wong).

211

into this production during its nearly four-year run: Brooke Shields, JoAnne Worley, Debby Boone, Sheena Easton, Jon Secada, Al Jarreau, Chubby Checker, and Darlene Love. Comedian Joe Piscopo was playing Vince Fontaine on January 8, 1996, when a blizzard shut down all of Broadway... except *Grease!* For that one night, Piscopo and *Grease!* had Broadway all to themselves.

The Herbal Bed, Peter Whelan's hit London drama about Shakespeare's daughter, was one of the most eagerly awaited events of spring 1998. Unfortunately it did not repeat its success in New York, and closed after 13 performances. In October of 1998, an even bigger disaster arrived. *More To Love* by radio comic Rob Bartlett and also starring him, received brutal notices. Subtitled "A big fat comedy," the play about obesity was dubbed "A stand-up dramedy" by Peter Marks of *The New York Times*. It vanished after 4 performances.

The fiftieth anniversary production of Arthur Miller's *Death of a Salesman* (from Chicago's Goodman Theatre) opened on February 10, 1999, and was acclaimed. Brian Dennehy and Elizabeth Franz won Tony Awards for their performances as Willy and Linda Loman. Robert Falls won a Tony as Best Director of a Play and the production received a Tony as Best Revival of a Play. It ran for 276 performances and was taped for broadcast on cable TV, where it won more awards.

Another bonanza opened at the O'Neill Theatre on October 26, 2000. *The Full Monty*, a musical comedy based on the popular film of the same name with music and lyrics by David Yazbek and a book by Terrence McNally, came to Broadway from the Old Globe Theatre in San Diego and proved an immediate hit. With its appealing story of six men who lose their jobs and decide to become male strippers to support their families, the show quickly (though briefly) became Broadway's hottest ticket. Not all theatregoers were impressed. Many older playgoers felt the musical had possibly the worst overture in theatre history and a mediocre score, but the general public embraced its warmhearted comedy. Following twenty years during which musical drama was king, *The Full Monty* was hailed for heralding a rebirth of musical comedy.

Arthur Miller outside the O'Neill for the opening of the fiftieth anniversary revival of *Death of a Salesman* (1999).

Kathleen Turner and Charles Durning opened in a revival of Tennessee Williams' *Cat On A Hot Tin Roof* in 1990 and Mr. Durning was rewarded with a Tony for his performance as Big Daddy.

David Hirson's verse drama *La Bête* was an interesting failure in 1991, followed by the New Vaudeville *Penn & Teller: The Refrigerator Tour;* the British hit revue *Five Guys Named Moe*, and a new production of the musical *Grease!* (exclamation point added for this production), which ran for 1,503 performances. Producers Fran and Barry Weissler opened the show with actress (and later talk show and Tony Awards host) Rosie O'Donnell as Rizzo. She began what became a signature Weissler policy of bringing in stars from other media for brief stints to extend the runs of their shows. Among those who stepped

BILTMORE THEATRE

The Chanin Brothers, construction moguls who were bitten by the showbiz bug in the 1920s, built six legitimate theatres. The Biltmore, at 261 West Forty-seventh Street, was their second project. When this theatre opened on December 7, 1925, *The New York Times* reported that it was the first theatre to be built on the north side of Forty-seventh Street, just east of Eighth Avenue. The theatre was designed by the busiest architect in town, Herbert J. Krapp, with a single balcony, just under 1,000 seats, and a color scheme of cerise and brown.

The opening show at the Biltmore was not new. It was an Owen Davis farce called *Easy Come, Easy Go*, which moved here from the George M. Cohan Theatre on Broadway. Otto Kruger and Victor Moore played bank robbers, with Edward Arnold also involved in the fracas. It had a run of 180 performances.

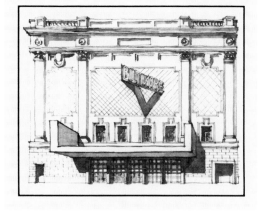

Next came a very steamy drama, *Kongo* (1926), with Walter Huston as "Deadleg Flint," a bitter man in the Belgian "Kongo" who gets even with a man who not only stole his wife but caused his legs to be paralyzed. This jungle rot lasted for 135 performances. A comedy called *Loose Ankles* (1926) followed, with Osgood Perkins, and it was sufficiently foolish to run for 161 performances. Walter Huston returned to the Biltmore in a solid hit, *The Barker* (1927), Kenyon Nicholson's play about carnival life. Huston played a tent show barker; Claudette Colbert played a snake charmer who vamps Huston's son, acted by Norman Foster. Colbert vamped Foster so well that they got married, for real, offstage. The critics admired Claudette's legs and this lively show ran for 225 performances.

A comedy called *Jimmie's Women* was a hit in 1927, but moved to another theatre after a month. Noël Coward's *The Marquise* was chichi nonsense about an errant society woman (Billie Burke) who returns to her family years later, just in time to save her daughter (Madge Evans) from mistakenly marrying her half-brother (Rex O'Malley). Coward's fans supported this fluff for 82 performances.

There were several flops in 1928, including another play, *Tin Pan Alley*, with Colbert and Foster returning to the scene of their first romance. There was also a cause célèbre at this theatre on October 1, 1928, when the incomparable Mae West opened her new play, *The Pleasure Man*. This time, Mae did not appear in her show, but her plot was sufficiently lurid to shock the populace, and the police closed the play after its second performance. *The Pleasure Man* was about an actor who has impregnated so many women that the brother of one of them decides to perform a brutal operation on him that will curtail his love life. The operation is performed at a party attended largely by transvestites and the lover dies under the knife.

Wall Street laid an egg in 1929 and so did the Biltmore Theatre. It housed seven flops, including *Man's*

BILTMORE THEATRE
47th STREET, WEST OF BROADWAY

Estate, a Theatre Guild production with Dudley Digges, Elizabeth Patterson, Earle Larimore, Armina Marshall, and Margalo Gillmore.

The 1930s began with an interesting but depressing play by Edwin Justus Mayer called *Children of Darkness*. Set in the notorious debtors' prison of Newgate in London, the drama dealt with the last days of the infamous criminal Jonathan Wild. The seamy play starred Basil Sydney, Mary Ellis, and Eugene Powers, and lasted ten weeks.

George Kelly's play *Philip Goes Forth* was a near-hit in 1931, playing for 98 performances. Madge Evans, Thurston Hall, Dorothy Stickney, Cora Witherspoon, and Harry Ellerbe were in the comedy about a young man who fails as a playwright and ends up in his father's business. From May 1931 until January 1934, the Biltmore housed a number of mediocre plays, such as *Her Supporting Cast, Zombie, Border-land*, and *The Scorpion*. One drama, a biographical study called *Carry Nation*, was unsuccessful, but featured this interesting cast: James Stewart, Joshua Logan, Mildred Natwick, Esther Dale, and Katherine Emery.

New Year's Day, 1934, brought a comedy hit at last to the Biltmore. It was called *Big Hearted Herbert* and starred J.C. Nugent as a mean miser who upsets all his family's plans until they turn the tables on him. It amused theatregoers for 154 performances. Emmet Lavery's religious play *The First Legion*, with Bert Lytell, John Litel, Charles Coburn, and Frankie Thomas, moved in from the 46th Street Theatre in October and stayed through December.

The Chanin Brothers lost all six of their Broadway theatres, including the Biltmore, during the Depression. In 1936 the Federal Theatre Project took over the theatre and presented some of its "Living Newspaper" productions. These consisted of a series of news sketches written by a staff of seventy reporters and writers and about sixteen dramatists. A cast of a hundred actors appeared in such striking productions as *Triple A Plowed Under* and *1935*. In June 1936 the Federal Theatre presented *Stars on Strings*, a marionette show, at this theatre.

The Biltmore was next taken over by Warner Brothers, the film studio, to serve as a showcase for the work of famed producer/playwright/director George Abbott. PLAYBILL magazines for the Biltmore, beginning

Above: Critics pronounced Claudette Colbert's gams one of the highlights of the 1927 hit *The Barker. Opposite:* Program cover for *Tin Pan Alley*, a 1928 play with Claudette Colbert and Norman Foster.

in 1937 and continuing into the 1940s, stated that the theatre was managed by Bernard Klawans.

Mr. Abbott's production of *Brother Rat*, a comedy about life at the Virginia Military Institute, by John Monks, Jr. and Fred F. Finklehoffe, was a huge hit in 1936. The sprightly cast included Eddie Albert, Jose Ferrer, Frank Albertson, and Ezra Stone. It turned out to be the Biltmore's longest-running show to that time, registering 577 performances. Abbott's next two shows, *Brown Sugar* and *All That Glitters*, were not successful,

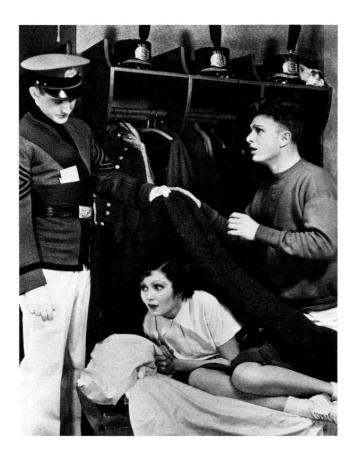

Top: George Abbot's hilarious production of *Brother Rat* with Richard Clark, Mary Mason, and Eddie Albert (1936). *Top Right:* Shirley Booth and Jo Ann Sayers in the rollicking hit *My Sister Eileen* (1940). *Above:* Ezra Stone, Vaughan Glaser, James Corner in another George Abbot winner, *What A Life* (1937).

but his production of Clifford Goldsmith's *What a Life*, a hilarious comedy about a squeaky-voiced high-schooler who is always in trouble (perfectly played by Ezra Stone), turned into a gold mine. Henry Aldrich became such a popular character that he ended up on a successful radio series and, years later, on TV. Eddie Bracken, Betty Field, Joyce Arling, Edith Van Cleve, and Butterfly McQueen were also in the cast of the play, which ran for 538 performances.

George Abbott's 1939 show was a shocker and quite unlike the type of farce comedy at which he excelled. Called *The Primrose Path*, it was based on Victoria Lincoln's sultry novel *February Hill*. The language was salty and the morals very loose in this saga of a slattern and her family. Helen Westley, Betty Field, Betty Garde, and Russell Hardie were in the cast of this moderate success.

In 1940, Warner Brothers and Bernard Klawans produced a play called *Jupiter Laughs*, by A.J. Cronin, starring Jessica Tandy, Alexander Knox, Mary Orr, Edith Meiser, and Philip Tonge. This drama about doctors ran for only 24 performances. But on December 26, 1940, the Biltmore welcomed a comedy that would bring it distinction. It was the fabulous *My Sister Eileen*, by Joseph A. Fields and Jerome Chodorov, based on *The New Yorker* stories by Ruth McKenney. Ms. McKenney had written charming vignettes about her adventures with her wacky blonde sister Eileen when they moved from Ohio to Manhattan. This uproarious comedy, skillfully staged by George S. Kaufman, played for 864 performances. The cast included Shirley Booth as Ruth, Jo Ann Sayers as Eileen, and Morris Carnovsky as their Greek landlord in Greenwich Village. Only one tragic note marred this joyous production. The real Eileen was driving from Ohio to attend the opening night of her sister's play when she was killed in an auto accident.

Another enormously successful comedy, *Janie*, moved here from another theatre for two months in 1942. On March 17, 1943, a play called *Kiss and Tell*, by F. Hugh Herbert, opened and broke all records at this theatre, running for 956 performances. The comedy about teenage pregnancy had in its cast Richard Widmark, Jessie Royce Landis, Joan Caulfield, and Robert Keith. It was produced and directed by the prolific George Abbott and was made into a hit movie and a successful radio series.

Bernard Klawans, who continued as manager of the Biltmore, presented (with Victor Payne-Jennings) an adaptation of Emile Zola's *Thérèse Raquin* by Thomas Job called simply *Thérèse* in 1945. Starring Dame May Whitty, Eva Le Gallienne, and Victor Jory, it played for 96 performances. In February 1946 Walter Huston returned once again to this theatre in *Apple of His Eye*, written by Charles Robinson and Kenyon Nicholson (who wrote Huston's big hit *The Barker* at this theatre in 1927). Jed Harris directed the comedy, which played for 118 performances, and coproduced it with Mr. Huston.

Mr. Harris produced another comedy here, *Loco*, with Jean Parker, Elaine Stritch, and Jay Fassett in 1946,

Richard Widmark and Joan Caulfield in the wartime comedy hit *Kiss and Tell* (1943).

but it ran for a brief 37 performances. Paul Bowles's adaptation of Sartre's play about three characters trapped in a room in hell, *No Exit*, played for only a month, but it was memorable for performances given by Claude Dauphin, Annabella, and Ruth Ford. One of the drama critics complained that movie star Annabella's performance gave him a stomach ache and she promptly sent him a laxative.

In March 1947 Russian playwright Konstantine Simonov's comedy *The Whole World Over*, with Uta Hagen, Sanford Meisner, and Jo Van Fleet, opened and managed to stay for 100 performances. It was directed by Harold Clurman. On September 29, 1947, Jed Harris returned to this theatre with a fine play—Ruth and Augustus Goetz's excellent adaptation of Henry James's novel, *Washington Square*. The play, called *The Heiress*, starred Basil Rathbone, Wendy Hiller, Patricia Collinge, and Peter Cookson and ran for 410 performances. It was directed by Jed Harris and produced by Fred F. Finklehoffe. Mr. Rathbone won a Tony Award for his chilling performance as Ms. Hiller's father.

Left: Basil Rathbone and Wendy Hiller in the Jed Harris production of *The Heiress* (1947). *Right:* Elizabeth Ashley and Robert Redford in Neil Simon's giant hit, *Barefoot in the Park* (1963).

More hits arrived at the Biltmore in the 1940s: José Ferrer, George Matthews, and Doro Merande in *The Silver Whistle* (1948), a comedy set in an old people's home, which ran for 219 performances; and *Clutterbuck* (1949), a British comedy by Benn W. Levy about a Don Juan named "Clutterbuck," which was one of David Merrick's earliest Broadway productions (in association with Irving L. Jacobs).

The 1950s brought a dramatic adaptation of Herman Melville's novel *Billy Budd.* This excellent play, with Charles Nolte in the title role and Dennis King, James Daly, and Lee Marvin in the cast, had an unfortunate opening-night incident. A critic for a major newspaper arrived at the theatre intoxicated. The management called the newspaper and the editor quickly sent another staff critic without telling the inebriated reviewer. Both critics wrote their reviews; the drunk raved, the sober critic panned it. Unfortunately, the pan appeared in the paper, which helped to shorten the run to 105 performances for this superb drama.

From 1952 to 1961, the Biltmore suspended its legitimate theatre policy. It was leased to the Columbia

Broadcasting System. On December 21, 1961, it reverted to being a legitimate house with Harold Prince's production of the hit comedy *Take Her, She's Mine*, directed by the old Biltmore genius George Abbott. Art Carney, Phyllis Thaxter, and Elizabeth Ashley starred in this play about a father's concern when his daughter is ready to go to college. It ran for 404 performances. Ms. Ashley won a Tony for her performance. The actress returned to this theatre in October 1963 in an even bigger hit comedy, *Barefoot in the Park.* Neil Simon's play about the problems of newlyweds (attractively portrayed by Ms. Ashley and Robert Redford, with brilliant support by Mildred Natwick and Kurt Kasznar) became the longest-running play at the Biltmore up to this time (1,530 performances). It played there from October 1963 to June of 1967. Mike Nichols won a Tony Award for his direction.

Several short-lived plays followed—Dyan Cannon and Martin Milner in *The Ninety-Day Mistress* (1967); Milo O'Shea and Eli Wallach as homosexuals in the British play *Staircase* (1968); and Joe Orton's black comedy, *Loot* (1968).

Perhaps the most famous production to play the

Biltmore, the seminal rock musical *Hair*, opened there on April 29, 1968. This freewheeling look at the Flower Power Generation had been an Off-Broadway hit at the downtown New York Shakespeare Festival, produced by Joseph Papp. It then moved to an uptown disco called Cheetah, but it failed, until a producer named Michael Butler took it over and hired director Tom O'Horgan. A very salable commodity was added to this show—total nudity, something that had not been seen on Broadway since some of the 1920s revues—and the show became the biggest hit in town, running a record four years and two months (1,750 performances) at the Biltmore. With book and lyrics by Gerome Ragni and James Rado, and music by Galt MacDermot, *Hair* became an icon of the 1960s. Among the many performers that the musical introduced were Melba Moore and Diane Keaton.

Some highlights of the 1970s at this theatre included Michael Moriarty in his Tony Award-winning performance as a homosexual in *Find Your Way Home* (1974); Jules Feiffer's farce *Knock, Knock* (1976), with Lynn Redgrave and Leonard Frey; Barry Bostwick winning a Tony Award in the musical *The Robber Bridegroom* (1976); Lily Tomlin in her dazzling one-woman show *Appearing Nitely*; an unsuccessful return engagement of *Hair* (1977); a revival of *The Effect of Gamma Rays on Man-in-the-Moon Marigolds* (1978), starting Shelley Winters; Claudette Colbert in her third appearance at this theatre, in *The Kingfisher* (1978), with Rex Harrison and George Rose; and Peter Allen in a spectacular personal appearance called *Up in One*.

The 1980s brought such divergent fare as an exciting courtroom drama, *Nuts* (1980), with Anne Twomey; Arthur Miller's play *The American Clock* (1980), which failed; Eva Le Gallienne and Shepperd Strudwick in *To Grandmother's House We Go* (1981); and Claudette Colbert one last time, in *A Talent for Murder* (1981), with Jean Pierre Aumont.

The Biltmore wasn't done with murder yet, however. Next came a transfer of the longest-running thriller in the American theatre, *Deathtrap* (1982), from the Music Box; and Anthony Shaffer's spoof of mystery plays, *Whodunnit* (1983).

Later in 1983, Pulitzer Prize-winning cartoonist Garry Trudeau turned his famous comic strip "Doonesbury" into a musical of the same name. He wrote the book and lyrics, and Elizabeth Swados supplied the music. In 1984, film actress Barbara Rush appeared in a one-woman show, *A Woman of Independent Means*, and the following year, John Pielmeier's play *The Boys of Winter* starring Matt Dillon opened here and shocked some with its realistic scenes of the Vietnam War. A musical called *Honky Tonk Nights*, about black vaudeville, arrived here in 1986. In 1987, a musical revue, *Stardust*, celebrated the famed songs of Mitchell Parrish. This was the last production of the twentieth century at the Biltmore.

Several factors made the Biltmore difficult either to book, to sell—or to demolish. Its relatively small size for a Broadway house made it uneconomical. Standing dark for several years, it soon was vandalized. With part of the interior open to weather and pigeons, it soon began to mildew and crumble. However, the interior design of the theatre's auditorium had been landmarked—but not its exterior or even its stage, which made repairs difficult and expensive. Unable to find a bidder, the theatre's owner defaulted on the mortgage and the theatre was seized by a bank. The Biltmore was purchased by James Nederlander

Gerome Ragni, one of the authors and stars of the American Tribal Love-Rock Musical, *Hair* (1968).

and Stewart Lane in 1993 for $550,000. With the late 1990s Times Square boom, several plans for refurbishment were considered but became tangled in legal and union conflicts.

The Biltmore enjoyed a momentary return to glory in 1999 when its marquee, festooned with 1930s-era posters, was used as a backdrop for the Oscar-nominated film *The Cradle Will Rock.*

On November 22, 2000, it was announced that the prestigious Manhattan Theatre Club, one of Manhattan's most prominent nonprofit theatres and producer of many successful Broadway transfers, would take part in a renovation of the Biltmore, and occupy it as MTC's new mainstage. The restoration is part of the plan to build a fifty-one-story apartment tower next door to the theatre by Biltmore 47 Associaties, a partnership of the Jack Parker Corporation and the Moinian Group, which owns the Biltmore. The plan is to reduce the seating capacity of the house from 950 to 650. The Manhattan Theatre Club plans to occupy the theatre upon completion of the work in 2003, and buy it from Biltmore 47 Associates within five years. Ground was broken for the $27 million renovation in a starry ceremony December 12, 2001, amid bare concrete and plaster. The theatrical community is looking forward to the restoration of this landmark Broadway theatre.

BROOKS ATKINSON THEATRE

The Brooks Atkinson Theatre at 256 West Forty-seventh Street opened in 1926 as the Mansfield Theatre, named in honor of the great classical American actor Richard Mansfield, who died in 1907. The theatre was another house built by the Chanin Brothers, construction tycoons, and it was designed by architect Herbert J. Krapp, who seemed to turn out a theatre a week in the Roaring Twenties. It followed the latest trends—only one balcony and an auditorium that was wide rather than deep. According to *The New York Times,* the attractive color scheme was old rose, gold, and light tan.

The opening bill at the Mansfield on the night of February 15, 1926, was a melodrama called *The Night Duel,* by Daniel Rubin and Edgar MacGregor, starring Marjorie Rambeau and Felix Krembs. *The Times* reported that there was an embarrassing bedroom scene in the second act, but that it seemed to please the audience. The play lasted only 17 performances. It was followed by three more failures: *The Masque of Venice,* with Arnold Daly, Osgood Perkins, Selena Royle, and Antoinette Perry (the Tony Awards were named in her honor); *Schweiger,* with Ann Harding as a wife who discovers that her husband (played by Jacob Ben-Ami) was a child murderer; and *Beau-Strings,* with Estelle Winwood as a flirt and Clarence Derwent (namesake of the theatre award for actors) as one of her interests.

The first moderate hit at the Mansfield opened on September 2, 1926: William Anthony McGuire's *If I Was Rich,* starring vaudeville/musical comedy favorite Joe Laurie, Jr. It ran for 92 performances.

Antoinette Perry again appeared at this theatre, in a long-running play with a curious history. *The Ladder,* a show about reincarnation, was disliked by the critics, but it was backed by a millionaire, Edgar B. Davis, who wanted the world to listen to the drama's message. So he kept the play running for 789 performances (often allowing people in free) and lost half a million pre-Depression dollars on it.

The Actors' Theatre revived Eugene O'Neill's Pulitzer Prize-winning play *Beyond the Horizon* (1926) and it ran for 79 performances. This production starred Robert Keith, Thomas Chalmers, and Aline MacMahon. The year ended with a revival of *The Dybbuk.*

Minnie Maddern Fiske revived Ibsen's *Ghosts* for 24 performances in January 1927, but the rest of the year brought undistinguished productions.

The year 1928 began with something called *Mongolia,* which transferred here from the Greenwich Village Theatre, but played for only three weeks. This was followed by *Atlas and Eva,* a comedy about a family called the Nebblepredders, which expired after 24 labored performances. Finally, on April 26, 1928, Rodgers and Hart came to the rescue with a sprightly musical about

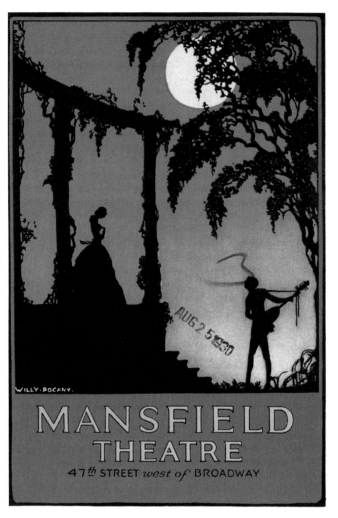

Program cover for the immortal 1930 Pulitzer-winning play *The Green Pastures*.

U.S. Marines stationed at Pearl Harbor. Called *Present Arms*, it produced one Rodgers and Hart classic: "You Took Advantage of Me." This song was sung in the show by none other than Busby Berkeley (who also did the dances for the musical), and on the opening night he forgot the lyrics and made up some of the most foolish words ever sung on the American stage. Lew Fields, originally half of the vaudeville team Weber & Fields, produced this musical. He was the father of Herbert Fields, who wrote the show's book. For the next year or so, this theatre was known as Lew Fields' Mansfield Theatre. *Present Arms* ran for 147 performances.

The next Rodgers/Hart/Fields musical at this theatre was a disaster. Called *Chee-Chee*, it was inspired by a novel called *The Son of the Grand Eunuch*, but critics did not find this musical comedy about castration amusing. St. John Ervine, critic for *The New York World,* snapped: "Nasty! Nasty! I did not believe that any act could possibly be duller than the first—until I saw the second."

Herbert and Dorothy Fields next provided a musical called *Hello, Daddy,* which was appropriate since their daddy, Lew Fields, again produced it and this time starred in it. It turned out to be the Mansfield's biggest hit so far, running for 198 performances. The catchy music was the work of Jimmy McHugh.

On February 26, 1930, a classic of the American theatre opened at the Mansfield and won the Pulitzer Prize for the season. It was Marc Connelly's magnificent adaptation of Roark Bradford's stories from the Old Testament, *Ol' Man Adam an' His Chillun.* Connelly's adaptation was called *The Green Pastures* and it had an enormous cast, consisting entirely of black actors. Many Broadway producers turned the script down, saying that a play about Bible incidents as viewed by Southern blacks would never make it on Broadway. They were wrong. Richard B. Harrison, a sixty-six-year-old man who had never acted before, gave an enthralling performance as de Lawd God Jehovah. *The Green Pastures* played for 640 performances and was also successful down South and wherever it was staged throughout the world.

During the Great Depression, the Chanin Brothers lost all six of the theatres they had built, including the Mansfield. From early March of 1932 until December of that year, the house was dark. Then, on December 26, it reopened with *Shuffle Along of 1933,* a successor to two former black musicals with similar titles. Once again the show was the work of Eubie Blake, Noble Sissle, and Flournoy Miller, who also appeared in the entertainment. Unfortunately, this edition ran for only 17 performances.

The Mansfield's bookings in 1933-34 were sparse and undistinguished. A comedy called *Page Miss Glory,* directed by George Abbott, was a moderate hit in November 1934. The cast included James Stewart, Charles D. Brown, Jane Seymour, Royal Beal, and Dorothy Hall. Another moderate hit, *Moon Over Mulberry Street,* moved in from the Lyceum in 1935. It was followed by Osgood Perkins giving an excellent performance as a playwright who dreams that he is a character in his latest drama. The play was called *On*

Left: Antoinette Perry in *The Ladder,* which ran for 789 performances. *Above:* Richard B. Harrison as "De Lawd" and Edna M. Harris as a "sinner" in the classic Marc Connelly play, *The Green Pastures* (1930).

Stage, but it did not stay there for very long. It had a short run of 47 performances.

In January 1937, a lurid exposé of a Manhattan prostitution ring on Park Avenue called *Behind Red Lights* opened and stayed for 176 performances.

In 1940 Barry Fitzgerald, Sara Allgood, and Effie

Shannon appeared in a successful revival of O'Casey's *Juno and the Paycock.* This was followed by *Separate Rooms,* a popular comedy that moved here from Maxine Elliott's Theatre. A West Coast revue, *Meet the People,* was a welcome Christmas present in 1940 and stayed for 160 performances. The cast included such bright talents as Jack Gilford, Nanette Fabares (later, Fabray), Jack Williams, Jack Albertson, Peggy Ryan, and many others.

The years 1942 and 1943 brought mostly failures to this theatre. A popular wartime comedy, *Janie,* which had already played at three other theatres, moved in for a few months in 1943-44. Then, on August 30, 1944, a bonanza arrived. *Anna Lucasta,* a play by Philip Yordan, was first done by the American Negro Theatre in Harlem (although the playwright wrote it for white actors). It was so successful that producer John Wildberg transferred it to the Mansfield Theatre with a few changes in the script.

Hilda Simms (standing), Earle Hyman, Georgia Burke in *Anna Lucasta* (1944).

Harry Wagstaff Gribble directed the superb cast, featuring Hilda Simms as the prostitute Anna, plus Canada Lee, Earle Hyman, and Frederick O'Neal. The drama ran for 957 performances.

Another hit arrived at this theatre on December 3, 1946. Actress Ruth Gordon switched to playwriting, and her autobiographical play, *Years Ago,* was warmly received. It starred Fredric March as her father, Florence Eldridge as her mother, and Bethel Leslie as Ruth Gordon Jones. The play recaptured Ms. Gordon's high

school days in Massachusetts when she startled her parents and friends by announcing that she was going to New York to be an actress. The nostalgic hit played for 206 performances.

A lively revival of Marc Blitzstein's proletarian musical *The Cradle Will Rock* opened during the famed blizzard of December 26, 1947. The cast included such luminaries as Alfred Drake, Will Geer, Vivian Vance, Dennis King, Jr., Estelle Loring, Jack Albertson, and Leonard Bernstein, but it lasted only for two weeks at this theatre before it moved to another house. Charles Boyer gave a powerful performance in *Red Gloves* in December 1948, but the Jean Paul Sartre play was too talky and full of messages for the public. The brilliant revue *Lend an Ear* moved in from another theatre in 1949 and played for three months. A mediocre play, *All You Need Is One Good Break,* was the last legitimate show to play the Mansfield. For the next decade, it functioned as a television playhouse.

When this theatre returned to legitimacy in 1960, producer Michael Myerberg was its owner/manager. The house was renovated and renamed the Brooks Atkinson Theatre in honor of the drama critic of *The New York Times,* who had retired from reviewing the previous spring. According to the PLAYBILL for that occasion, Mr. Atkinson was the first critic in recorded history to have a theatre named for him.

The Brooks Atkinson opened on September 12, 1960, with a revue called *Vintage '60.* Although it was produced by David Merrick, with Zev Bufman, George Skaff, and Max Perkins, it lasted only 8 performances. The next tenant, a comedy called *Send Me No Flowers,* with David Wayne and Nancy Olson, wilted after 40 performances.

On February 22, 1961, Neil Simon's first play, *Come Blow Your Horn,* opened, and it flourished for 677 performances. The cast featured Hal March, Sarah Marshall, Warren Berlinger, Lou Jacobi, and Pert Kelton. In late 1962, Sidney Kingsley's play *Night Life,* with Neville Brand, Walter Abel, Carmen Matthews, Carol Lawrence, Salomé Jens, and Bobby Short, presented a realistic nightclub onstage, but the drama lasted only 63 performances. Peter Ustinov's comedy, *Photo Finish,* offered Ustinov as a writer with alter egos played by

Dennis King, Donald Davis, and John Horton. Eileen Herlie, Jessica Walters, and Paul Rogers were also in the cast of this charade, which ran for 160 performances in 1963.

The year 1964 started out disastrously at the Brooks Atkinson. Tennessee Williams decided to rewrite his unsuccessful play *The Milk Train Doesn't Stop Here Anymore*, and this time he turned it into, of all things, a Kabuki-style drama. The great Tallulah Bankhead made her last Broadway appearance in this error, and Tab Hunter, Ruth Ford, and Marian Seldes all went down the drain with her. It played only 5 times.

Josephine Baker made a dazzling personal appearance here in 1964, followed by the very controversial play, Rolf Hochhuth's *The Deputy,* which accused Pope Pius XII of having failed to denounce the Nazi extermination of the Jews. Emlyn Williams played the pope. The drama was picketed by Catholic organizations, but it managed to run for 318 performances. Julie Harris, Estelle Parsons, and Lou Antonio were next in a comedy called *Ready When You Are, C.B.!* Ms. Harris was praised for her acting, but the show closed after 80 performances. A revival of *The Glass Menagerie,* with Maureen Stapleton, George Grizzard, Pat Hingle, and Piper Laurie, was well received and lasted 176 performances in 1965.

From November 1965 until November 1967 the Brooks Atkinson housed a series of undistinguished plays. Peter Ustinov's *Halfway Up the Tree*, a generation gap comedy—with the younger generation winning out—was moderately amusing, with Eileen Herlie, Anthony Quayle, Sam Waterston, and Graham Jarvis.

Peter Nichols's macabre comedy, *A Day in the Death of Joe Egg,* had memorable performances by Albert Finney, Zena Walker, and Elizabeth Hubbard. Ms. Walker won a Tony Award as Best Supporting Actress in a drama.

Lovers and Other Strangers, a quartet of revue-style playlets by Renée Taylor and Joseph Bologna, in which they appeared, was amusing in 1968, as was *Jimmy Shine*, a Murray Schisgal comedy starring Dustin Hoffman that ran for 153 performances in 1968-69.

After a series of mishaps, the Brooks Atkinson booked *Lenny*, a play about the late Lenny Bruce.

Top: Fredric March and Florence Eldridge in Ruth Gordon's autobiographical play *Years Ago* (1946). *Above*: Barry Fitzgerald and Sara Allgood in a revival of *Juno and the Paycock* (1940).

Written by Julian Barry, the stinging biographical study gave Cliff Gorman a part that won him a Tony Award for his tour de force performance. Brilliantly directed by Tom O'Horgan, who also wrote the play's music, *Lenny* presented a corrosive portrait of the drug-riddled,

Above: PLAYBILL covers for Albert Finney in *A Day in the Death of Joe Egg* (1968); Julian Barry's *Lenny* (1971), and Dustin Hoffman in *Jimmy Shine* (1968).
Below: PLAYBILL cover for the Pulitzer Prize-winning play *Talley's Folly* (1979).

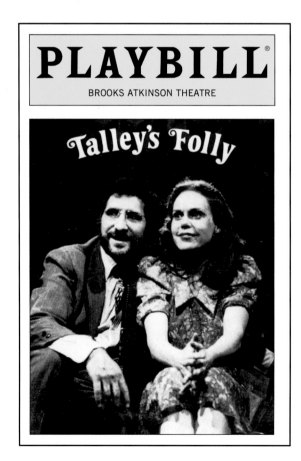

foulmouthed comic whose fame increased after he died. This "dynamite shtick of theatre," as critic Clive Barnes labeled it, played for 453 explosive performances and was made into a film with Dustin Hoffman, directed by Bob Fosse.

In 1973 the Negro Ensemble Company transferred its successful play, *The River Niger,* from Off Broadway to the Brooks Atkinson, where it remained for 280 performances. Written by Joseph A. Walker and directed by Douglas Turner Ward, who also appeared in the play, it won a Tony Award as the best drama of the season. In January 1974 Michael Moriarty gave a stunning performance as a homosexual hustler in *Find Your Way Home,* by John Hopkins, and was rewarded with a Tony. Jane Alexander costarred with him. The British comedy *My Fat Friend,* with Lynn Redgrave and George Rose, brought laughter to this theatre in 1974, and was followed by a revival of John Steinbeck's powerful play *Of Mice and Men,* with James Earl Jones as Lenny and Kevin Conway as George.

On March 13, 1975, a comedy with only two performers—Ellen Burstyn and Charles Grodin—opened at the Brooks Atkinson and stayed for 1,453 performances,

Ellen Burstyn and Charles Grodin in the smash comedy about infidelity, *Same Time, Next Year* (1975).

of *Lolita* (1981), with Blanche Baker as the nymphet and Donald Sutherland as Humbert Humbert; and *Wally's Cafe* (1981), with Rita Moreno, James Coco, and Sally Struthers.

The British play *The Dresser* (1981), by Ronald Harwood, starred Tom Courtenay as a dresser to an aging drunk actor, played by Paul Rogers, and the fascinating drama played for 200 performances. Christopher Durang's Off-Broadway hit *Beyond Therapy* did not repeat its success on Broadway in 1982. Liv Ullmann and John Neville appeared in a revival of Ibsen's *Ghosts* for a few weeks, and the British comedy *Steaming*, set in a women's steam room, won a Tony Award for Judith Ivey as Best Featured Actress in a Play. Patrick Meyers's thrilling *K2* was about two mountain climbers—Jeffrey DeMunn and Jay Patterson—trapped on an icy ledge

making it this theatre's record holder. It was Bernard Slade's *Same Time, Next Year*—a merry romp about a man and woman who meet every year in a motel for a sexual tryst, unknown to their respective spouses. Ms. Burstyn won a Tony Award for her beguiling performance.

Jack Lemmon returned to Broadway in another play by Mr. Slade—*Tribute*—in 1978, and his performance was rated better than the play. The British comedy *Bedroom Farce* had some hilarious moments and won Tony Awards for Michael Gough and Joan Hickson as Best Featured Actors in a play.

Teibele and Her Demon, a drama by Isaac Bashevis Singer and Eve Friedman, did not succeed in 1979, but *Talley's Folly,* one of Lanford Wilson's cycle of plays about the Talley family, moved here from Off-Broadway's Circle Rep with its original cast—Judd Hirsch and Trish Hawkins—and scored a triumph. Directed by Marshall W. Mason, the play won the Pulitzer Prize and the Drama Critics Circle Award for best play.

Four unsuccessful shows followed: *Tricks of the Trade* (1980), with George C. Scott and his wife, Trish Van Devere; *Mixed Couples* (1980), with Julie Harris, Geraldine Page, and Rip Torn; Edward Albee's adaptation

Tom Courtenay and Paul Rogers in the British play *The Dresser* (1981).

on the second highest mountain in the world. The incredible set for this drama won a Tony Award for its designer, Ming Cho Lee.

Ben Kingsley starred in a one-man performance of *Edmund Kean*, followed by an enormous British hit, *Noises Off*, with Dorothy Loudon, Brian Murray, and Victor Garber, which ran here from December 1983 to April 1985. Later that year, Rex Harrison, Claudette Colbert, Lynn Redgrave, and George Rose cavorted in a revival of Frederick Lonsdale's amusing trifle, *Aren't We All?* In December 1985 the British hit *Benefactors* by Michael Frayn set up shop here, starring Sam Waterston, Glenn Close, Simon Jones, and Mary Beth Hurt. The following December, *Jackie Mason's "The World According To Me!"* had a highly successful engagement with the stand-up comic receiving a Special Tony Award for his galvanic comic performance. He played his trenchant political romp for more than a year.

In 1989, a revival of the 1942 play *Café Crown* starring Eli Wallach and Anne Jackson won a Tony Award for the best scenic design of the season (Santo Loquasto). That same year, *Peter, Paul & Mary: A Holiday Celebration on Broadway* and *Stephanie Mills Comes "Home" To Broadway* brightened the Atkinson with limited runs, as did the *Victor Borge Holiday Show On Broadway*.

The Cemetery Club by Ivan Menchell had a short run here in 1990, and later that year, *Shadowlands*, by William Nicholson, starred Nigel Hawthorne as British author C.S. Lewis and Jane Alexander as American poetess Joy Davidman. Mr. Hawthorne won a Tony as Best Actor in a play.

In 1992, Glenn Close, Gene Hackman, and Richard Dreyfuss starred in *Death and the Maiden* by Ariel Dorfman, directed by Mike Nichols. Ms. Close won a Tony Award for her performance as a South American woman who captures and confronts the government agent who once tortured her.

On October 7, 1993, the delightful Roundabout Theatre Company revival of Bock & Harnick's witty *She Loves Me* moved here from Criterion Center/Stage Right Theatre and continued its run.

On December 8, 1994, *What's Wrong With This Picture?*, a new play by Donald Margulies, opened to mostly negative reviews, despite the presence of actress

PLAYBILL cover for the Elington/Shakespeare musical, *Play On!* (1997).

Faith Prince as a woman who returns to her family from beyond the grave. Jerry Stiller was in the cast and the offbeat comedy was directed by Joe Mantello. It closed after 12 performances.

In May 1995 a disastrous failure that seemed to be jinxed came to this theatre. It was a stage adaptation of the classic film, *On The Waterfront*, and bore the same title. Adapted by Budd Schulberg (who won an Academy Award for the film's screenplay) and Stan Silverman, the play had nothing but trouble during previews. The original director was replaced by Adrian Hall, one actor was fired and another suffered a heart attack and had to be replaced. It closed after 8 performances at a loss of $2.6 million.

On April 30, 1996, a revised version of Sam Shepard's 1979 Pulitzer Prize-winning play, *Buried Child*, was presented by Chicago's Steppenwolf Theatre Company,

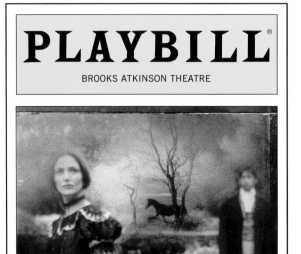

PLAYBILL cover for *Jane Eyre,* the musical (1997).

The next attraction at this theatre, in November 1997, was really more of a concert than a musical. Called *Street Corner Symphony,* it featured eight young singers/dancers performing pop and soul songs of the 1960s and 1970s under a street light in Gainesville, Florida. The show was performed without an intermission and with virtually no plot. It lasted for 79 performances.

A new production of Frederick Knott's 1966 thriller *Wait Until Dark* arrived in 1998, starring the Hollywood director Quentin Tarantino and film actress Marisa Tomei, but it failed to achieve the success of the original, which ran for 373 performances. Lee Remick had thrilled audiences in 1966 as a blind victim stalked by drug dealers, but the acting in this production, especially by Mr. Tarantino, was severely criticized. It closed after 65 performances.

On April 8, 1999, a highly praised production of Eugene O'Neill's *The Iceman Cometh* arrived from London where it had scored an enormous success, first at the Almeida, then at the Old Vic. Kevin Spacey, who was the acclaimed Hickey of the revival, repeated his performance on Broadway and was joined by four actors from the British cast. The production, scheduled for a limited engagement, received five Tony Award nominations: Best Actor (Spacey); Best Revival of a Play; Best Director (Howard Davies); Best Scenic Design (Bob Crowley); and Best Lighting Design (Mark Henderson).

Roundabout Theatre Company returned to the Atkinson in spring 2000 with a short-lived revival of *Uncle Vanya* starring Derek Jacobi. In December 2000, the Atkinson hosted a rare musical, *Jane Eyre,* with a sweeping score by Paul Gordon, and a grand performance by Marla Schaffel as Charlotte Brontë's resolute heroine.

The Brooks Atkinson is owned and operated by the Messrs. Nederlander. It has been refurbished in recent years and its intimate ambience makes it ideally suited for dramas and comedies.

directed by one of its leading actors, Gary Sinise. Most critics felt that the playwright had improved the play about a family with a terrible secret, and it ran for 71 performances.

Taking Sides, an engrossing play about Wilhelm Furtwangler, the famed orchestra conductor who refused to leave Germany but conducted for the Nazis, opened on October 17, 1996, and was praised for the electric performances of Daniel Massey as the conductor and Ed Harris as the American deNazification officer who confronts him. Taking place in the American sector of occupied Berlin, the play by Ronald Harwood was a bigger hit in London. On Broadway, it closed after 85 performances. It as followed in March 1997 by the musical *Play On!,* which updated Shakespeare's *Twelfth Night* to 1940s Harlem with a score of Duke Ellington standards. Toplining the cast were Andre De Shields and Tonya Pinkins.

ROYALE THEATRE

The Royale Theatre at 242 West Forty-fifth Street was one of the six legitimate theatres built by the Chanin Brothers in the 1920s. In describing the new house, *The New York Times* reported that it was "comfortable, with plenty of leg room around the seats." The theatre was done in modern Spanish style, had two murals, collectively titled "Lovers of Spain" by Willy Pogany, on the walls, and the general color scheme was cardinal red, orange, and gold. Not surprisingly, once again the architect was the busy Herbert J. Krapp.

With a seating capacity of a little over 1,000, the Royale opened on January 11, 1927, with a musical comedy called *Piggy*. The popular comic Sam Bernard played a monocled Englishman whose son (Paul Frawley) falls in love with an American girl. Brooks Atkinson in *The Times* called it an "average musical comedy" and highly praised the dancing of Goodee Montgomery, whom he identified as the daughter of the late and still lamented Dave Montgomery of the famed Montgomery and Stone team. The following day, *The Times* carried a correction. Miss Goodee was Montgomery's niece. Shortly after this show opened, the producer changed its title (a very rare practice in the theatre) to *I Told You So* and it ran for 79 performances.

The Royale's next musical, *Judy,* starred the bubbly Queenie Smith and the romantic Charles Purcell. One of the songs was titled "When Gentlemen Grew Whiskers

and Ladies Grew Old." *Judy* pleased the nostalgia crowd for 104 performances.

A musical version of Oscar Wilde's *The Importance of Being Earnest*, retitled *Oh, Earnest!,* did not last long, but a black revue called *Rang Tang* fared better in 1927, running for 119 performances. The dancing in this show was highly praised by the critics. *The Times* referred to the revue as "a blackamoor folderol."

Winthrop Ames's Gilbert and Sullivan Opera Company moved into the Royale in September 1927 and performed *The Mikado, Iolanthe,* and *The Pirates of Penzance* for a very successful three months. A popular (but aging) entertainer named Mitzi next appeared in *The Madcap,* a very silly musical about an older woman (Mitzi) who pretends to be much younger in order to win rich Lord Clarence Steeple (Sydney Greenstreet). Arthur Treacher was also in this nonsense, which ran for 103 performances.

After its yearlong musicals-only diet, the Royale played its first straight show in 1928. It was *Sh! The Octopus,* described by an overzealous press agent as a "sneaky, snaky, slimy mystery." The murderous doings took place in a lighthouse, and since there is little prospect that this show will be revived, it can be revealed that the plot turned out to be nothing but a dream.

The Royale had its first bona fide hit on April 9, 1928, when Mae West starred in her own play, *Diamond*

Top: Standard program cover for Royale in the 1920s and early 1930.
Above: From left: Freida Inescort and Selena Royle in Rachel Crother's comedy *When Ladies Meet* (1932).

Lil, a melodrama set in the 1890s Bowery. This devil's brew bubbled for 323 performances. The year 1929 ended at the Royale with an item called *Woof Woof,* a musical that featured not one, but two live whippet races onstage. They ran only 46 times.

The Second Little Show, a successor to the highly successful revue *The Little Show,* opened at the Royale on September 2, 1930, but did not measure up to the first edition. Although the score was by the illustrious Howard Dietz and Arthur Schwartz, it was a song by Herman Hupfeld that swept the nation—"Sing Something Simple." The show managed only 63 performances. A popular farce called *Stepping Sisters* played two engagements at this theatre in 1930-31. Mae West returned to the Royale in 1931 with her latest play, *The Constant Sinner,* but it wasn't sinful enough and ran for only 64 performances. Ms. West announced that she might do some matinees of *Macbeth* and play Lady Macbeth herself, but the project, unfortunately, never got off the ground. Instead, Fritz Leiber and his Chicago Civic Shakespeare Society arrived in *The Merchant of Venice* (1931). His company included Helen Menken, Tyrone Power (Sr.), William Faversham, Pedro De Cordoba, Viola Roache, and Whitford Kane.

Rachel Crothers had a hit play, *When Ladies Meet,* which opened at the Royale on October 6, 1932, starring Frieda Inescort, Walter Abel, Spring Byington, and Selena Royle.

The Theatre Guild production of Maxwell Anderson's exposé of corruption in the nation's capital, *Both Your Houses,* was brilliantly acted by Shepperd Strudwick, Morris Carnovsky, Walter C. Kelly, Mary Philips, J. Edward Bromberg, and others, but it managed to play for only 72 performances. A comedy called *Every Thursday,* starring Queenie Smith, opened in May of 1934, and it was the last play at the Royale before the theatre changed its name.

John Golden, the famous theatrical producer, owned the John Golden Theatre on West Fifty-eighth Street between Broadway and Seventh Avenue, but he lost it in 1933. In 1934 he leased the Royale and renamed it the Golden Theatre. The first production under the new management was Norman Krasna's comedy *Small Miracle,* which opened on September 26, 1934. Directed

by George Abbott, this unusual play took place in a theatre lobby and chronicled the lives of the theatre's patrons who congregated there. The large cast included Ilka Chase, Joseph Spurin-Calleia, Myron McCormick, Elsbeth Eric, and many others. It prospered for 118 performances.

In November, 1934, The Abbey Theatre Players from Dublin opened at the Golden in a repertory of plays that changed weekly. Headed by Barry Fitzgerald, the company presented such Irish classics as *The Plough and the Stars, The Far-off Hills, The Shadow of the Glen, The Playboy of the Western World,* and *Drama at Inish.* On Christmas Eve, the Theatre Guild presented one of S.N. Behrman's most thoughtful drawing room comedies, *Rain from Heaven,* with Jane Cowl, John Halliday, Lily Cahill, Ben Smith, and Thurston Hall. Contemporary issues—fascism, Nazism, communism, Lindbergh hero worship—were brilliantly discussed by intellectuals of

opposing viewpoints during a country weekend in England.

The remainder of 1935 was devoted to a comedy, *The Bishop Misbehaves,* starring Walter Connolly, which moved here from the Cort Theatre, and an acerbic play, *A Touch of Brimstone,* with Roland Young as a very nasty theatrical producer who took perverse delight in mistreating people. (Shades of Jed Harris?)

During 1936 the Golden Theatre had a series of short-run shows. Some of the more interesting ones were the return of eighty-year-old actor William Gillette, after four years of retirement, in a revival of *Three Wise Fools,* with Charles Coburn; Nazimova in *Ghosts,* which returned after a tour and played for a month at a $1.65 top (reasonable even for that time); and *Double Dummy,* a "farce-satire" about contract bridge, with Martha Sleeper, Dudley Clements, and John McGovern.

From 1937 until 1940 the Golden ceased functioning as

Top Left: John Halliday and Jane Cowl in S.N. Behrman's thoughtful comedy, *Rain from Heaven* (1935). *Above:* Herald for Ina Claire in George Kelly's romantic comedy *The Fatal Weakness* (1946).

Audrey Christie and Sam Levene in Moss Hart's theatre comedy *Light Up The Sky* (1948).

a legitimate playhouse. It became the CBS Radio Theatre. Undaunted, producer John Golden leased the Masque Theatre next door and rechristened it the John Golden Theatre. It has remained so ever since.

In October 1940 the former Golden Theatre was taken over by the Magoro Operating Corporation, which restored this theatre's original name: the Royale. Now owned by the Shubert Organization, the Royale has kept that name to this day. To review: first, this theatre was the Royale, then it became the Golden, then the CBS Radio Theatre, and, finally, the Royale again.

The hit Cole Porter musical *DuBarry Was a Lady* moved from the 46th Street Theatre to the Royale on October 21, 1940, minus one of its stars—Ethel Merman—who was succeeded by Gypsy Rose Lee. Bert Lahr was still the star of the show. It stayed for two months. This was followed by Elmer Rice's *Flight to the West* (1940), from the Guild Theatre, and Ethel

Barrymore in her hit *The Corn Is Green* (1940), which transferred from the National Theatre. Paul Muni returned in a revival of Elmer Rice's *Counsellor-at-Law* (1942), one of his earlier hits. It ran for 258 performances. The daffy ZaSu Pitts arrived in a melodramatic farce, *Ramshackle Inn* (1944), and her Hollywood fans supported this ramshackle play for 216 performances.

The critics scorned *School for Brides,* a Chicago hit that came East with Roscoe Karns and a bevy of beauties in the summer of 1944, but the public bought it for 375 performances. Michael Todd's spectacular production of *Catherine Was Great,* with the mistress of triple entendre, Mae West, moved here from the Shubert and pulverized the local yokels for three more months. Another sex comedy that was a smash in Chicago—*Good Night, Ladies* (1945)—came East and was assassinated by the New York drama critics. The public listened to the scribes this time and the farce left after 78 performances. A stage adaptation of Lillian Smith's best-seller *Strange Fruit* expired after 60 performances in 1945.

The distinguished veteran producer Arthur Hopkins presented Louis Calhern as Justice Oliver Wendell Holmes and Dorothy Gish as his loving wife in Emmet Lavery's *The Magnificent Yankee* in January 1946, and it ran a respectable 160 performances. Tennessee Williams's first Broadway play, *The Glass Menagerie,* with triumphant performances by the great Laurette Taylor, Eddie Dowling, Julie Haydon, and Anthony Ross, moved here from the Playhouse in 1946. This was followed by a moderately successful revival of *The Front Page,* with Lew Parker and Arnold Moss. The radiant Ina Claire returned to the stage in George Kelly's amusing comedy *The Fatal Weakness,* about a romantic woman (Ms. Claire) who loves to attend weddings, even if the groom happens to be a former husband of hers.

A stylish revival of Wilde's *The Importance of Being Earnest* starred John Gielgud (who also staged it), Margaret Rutherford, and Robert Flemyng in 1947 and achieved a run of 81 performances. Gielgud and Flemyng returned to the Royale in May in a revival of William Congreve's artificial bore *Love for Love,* which left town after 48 showings.

In December 1947 Judith Anderson returned from a triumphant tour in *Medea* and continued to kill her

Clockwise from above: Julie Andrews (center) and flappers in Sandy Wilson's spoof of the 1920s musicals, *The Boy Friend* (1954). Sir Laurence Olivier in John Osbourn's *The Entertainer* (1958). Bette Davis in Tennessee Williams's *The Night of the Iguana* (1961). Back cover of souvenir program for *New Faces of 1952.*

Top: Lauren Bacall in the long-running comedy *Cactus Flower* (1965). *Above:* Martin Sheen (seated), Irene Dailey and Jack Albertson in *The Subject Was Roses* (1964).

helpless babes for five more months. Moss Hart's acidulous comedy about theatre folks trying out a show in Boston, *Light Up the Sky,* arrived in November 1948 and provoked hilarity for 214 performances. Sam Levene played a vulgar producer, Audrey Christie acted his loudmouth wife, and Broadway insisted that the characters were modeled after Billy Rose and his then wife, Olympic swimmer Eleanor Holm.

Alfred de Liagre's memorable production of *The Madwoman of Chaillot* moved here from the Belasco in 1949 and stayed for four months. *Dance Me a Song,* an intimate revue, was not a hit, but it served to introduce the delightful comic Wally Cox, who wrote his own very funny monologues. This was followed by a revival of Shaw's *The Devil's Disciple,* with Maurice Evans, Dennis King, Victor Jory, and Marsha Hunt, staged by Margaret Webster for 111 performances. Next came a London hit, Christopher Fry's verse play *The Lady's Not for Burning,* starring John Gielgud (who also directed), Richard Burton, and Pamela Brown, which made pleasant rhymes for 151 performances. Sidney Kingsley's powerful dramatization of Arthur Koestler's novel *Darkness at Noon* moved here from the Alvin and played for three more months in 1951.

Borscht Capades, described as an "English Yiddish revue," pleased the critics and ran for 90 performances. Another revue—Leonard Sillman's *New Faces of 1952,* which opened here on May 16, 1952—turned out to be the best show of this series and one of the finest revues in Broadway history. Staged by the great revue director John Murray Anderson, the cast included such bright talents as Paul Lynde, Ronny Graham, June Carroll, Eartha Kitt, Robert Clary, Alice Ghostley, Carol Lawrence, and many others. The smash ran for 365 performances and was one of the few Broadway revues that was filmed by Hollywood.

Billy Rose presented a stage adaptation of André Gide's novel *The Immoralist,* with Geraldine Page as a woman who has married a homosexual, played by Louis Jordan. In the cast was the young James Dean as a North African homosexual who attempts to lure the husband to the local date grove. The daring play ran for 104 performances in 1954.

A British musical, *The Boy Friend,* by Sandy Wilson, opened at the Royale on September 30, 1954, and

Sharon Brown and David Cassidy in *Joseph and the Amazing Technicolor Dreamcoat* (1983).

captivated Manhattan. This diverting parody of 1920s musicals introduced Julie Andrews to Broadway and she was a delight. The spoof ran for 485 performances. This theatre had another smash hit in Thornton Wilder's *The Matchmaker,* which opened on December 5, 1955. The play had a very curious history. Wilder first wrote it as *The Merchant of Yonkers,* but it flopped on Broadway in 1938, despite direction by the famed Max Reinhardt, and Jane Cowl and Percy Waram in the leading roles. But this raucous version—staged by Tyrone Guthrie and vividly performed by Ruth Gordon, Loring Smith, Robert Morse, Eileen Herlie, and Arthur Hill—rang the cash register for 486 performances. Mr. Guthrie won a Tony Award for his galvanic staging of this comedy, which was later adapted as the celebrated musical, *Hello, Dolly!*

The Tunnel of Love, a minor comedy by Joseph Fields and Peter DeVries, managed to run for 417 performances in 1957, probably because of the popularity of its leading man, Tom Ewell. Nancy Olsen, Darren McGavin, and Elizabeth Wilson were also in this comedy about a childless suburban couple who wish to adopt a baby.

Laurence Olivier gave a memorable performance as a seedy vaudeville actor in John Osborne's rather boring play *The Entertainer* (1958). The cast included Olivier's wife, Joan Plowright, Brenda de Banzie, Peter Donat, and

Jeri Archer, who played Britannia as a topless statue who did not move. David Merrick, the producer of this British play, did not allow Ms. Archer to take a curtain call, stating that she would be too distracting to the audience.

The 1950s came to a dazzling close at this theatre with the lunatic French revue, *La Plume de Ma Tante,* which opened on November 11, 1958, and stayed for 835 performances. Robert Dhery conceived, wrote, and starred in this uproarious vaudeville explosion, and the entire cast won Tony Awards as the best featured performers in a musical.

Highlights of the 1960s at this theatre included Laurence Olivier and Anthony Quinn in Jean Anouilh's *Becket* (1960), which moved here from the St. James; *From the Second City* (1961), a hit Chicago revue with Alan Arkin, Barbara Harris, Paul Sand, and others; Tennessee Williams's *The Night of the Iguana* (1961), starring Bette Davis, Patrick O'Neal, Alan Webb, and Margaret Leighton, who won a Tony Award for her luminous performance; and Charles Boyer in S.N. Behrman's high comedy about an art dealer, *Lord Pengo* (1962), with Agnes Moorehead, Brian Bedford, and Henry Daniell.

Coral Browne and Keith Michell followed in Anouilh's *The Rehearsal* (1963); Margaret Leighton, John Williams, Alan Webb, Peter Donat, and Douglas Watson in Enid Bagnold's *The Chinese Prime Minister* (1964); Frank D. Gilroy's *The Subject Was Roses* (1964), the Pulitzer Prize-winning play with Jack Albertson (who won a Tony Award for his performance), Irene Dailey, and Martin Sheen; Jason Robards in Eugene O'Neill's *Hughie* (1964); and Lauren Bacall, Barry Nelson, Robert Moore, and Brenda Vaccaro in *Cactus Flower* (1965), adapted by Abe Burrows from a French comedy. It ran for 1,234 performances.

The last hit of the 1960s at the Royale featured Donald Pleasence starring in Robert Shaw's play *The Man in the Glass Booth* (1968), directed by Harold Pinter.

The 1970s brought Robert Marascois's chilling *Child's Play* (1970), with Ken Howard, Pat Hingle, Fritz Weaver, and David Rounds; Michael Weller's fascinating portrait of the 1960s generation, *Moonchildren* (1972); and the record-breaking musical *Grease*, which moved to the Royale from the Broadhurst in 1972 and stayed until April 13, 1980. It became the longest-running musical in Broadway history with 3,388 performances. (In September 1983, it was surpassed by *A Chorus Line*, and subsequently by others.)

An unusual event occurred at this theatre in February 1980. The British play *Whose Life Is It Anyway?*, in which Tom Conti had won a Tony Award for his performance as a man paralyzed from the neck down, was revised to make the hero a heroine. Mary Tyler Moore played the part in the revised version, which ran at the Royale for 96 performances. The experiment was considered a success.

Next came a screwball musical, *A Day in Hollywood/A Night in the Ukraine,* which moved here from the John Golden Theatre and won a Tony Award for Priscilla Lopez as Best Featured Actress in a Musical and another for co-choreographers Tommy Tune and Lopez' fellow *A Chorus Line* alumnus, Thommie Walsh. Actually a double-bill, the show consisted of a first-act tribute to movie musicals, and a second-act adaptation of a short Chekhov play as a vehicle for the Marx Brothers. The curious amalgam lasted 588 performances.

In December 1981, *Duet For One* by Tom Kempinski starred Anne Bancroft and Max von Sydow, and was directed by William Friedkin. The following month, *Joseph and the Amazing Technicolor Dreamcoat*, Andrew Lloyd Webber and Tim Rice's first musical (though not

Rosemary Harris in *An Inspector Calls* (1994). Photo by Joan Marcus.

their first on Broadway), moved here from the Entermedia Theatre and ran until September 1983. The following April, *The Human Comedy*, a musical version of Saroyan's novel of the same name (with music by *Hair*'s Galt MacDermot) had a brief run here. That fall, Alec McCowen played a limited engagement in his one-man show, *Kipling*. In 1985, Carroll O'Connor and Frances Sternhagen starred in *Home Front* for a brief run, followed by Rosemary Harris, Dana Ivey, George N. Martin, and Patrick McGoohan in the absorbing British play *Pack of Lies* by Hugh Whitemore. Ms. Harris received a Drama Desk Award for her performance.

September 1985 brought Bernadette Peters in a Tony Award-winning performance in *Song & Dance* by Andrew Lloyd Webber, Don Black, and Richard Maltby, Jr. Among the excellent dancers in this British import were Charlotte and Christopher d'Amboise, Scott Wise,

From left: Victor Garber, Alfred Molina, and Alan Alda in the Tony Award-winning play *Art*, by Yasmina Reza. Photo by Joan Marcus.

Victor Barbee, and Cynthia Onrubia. The offbeat musical, another double-bill at the Royale, ran for 474 performances. Next came a revival of the famed 1926 play *Broadway* by George Abbott and Philip Dunning. It coincided with Mr. Abbott's 100th birthday and he directed the production. Unfortunately, the critics found the play to be dated and it ran for only 4 performances.

It was succeeded at the Royale by *Roza*, a musical directed by Harold Prince and starring Georgia Brown, but this, too, had a short run: 12 performances. The story of a woman who cares for the unwanted children of Paris prostitutes was based on *La Vie Devant Soi* by French author Roman Gary.

Serious Money by Caryl Churchill, a devastating satire on the British stock market in the Thatcher era, moved here from the New York Shakespeare Festival in February 1988, but did not repeat its London successes, lasting only 15 performances. May 3, 1988, brought the Broadway debut of rock star Madonna in David Mamet's *Speed-the-Plow*, also starring Ron Silver (who won a Tony Award for his dynamic performance) and Joe Mantegna. Most critics were not impressed with Madonna's thespian abilities. Nevertheless, the play ran for 278 performances.

In March 1989, Ken Ludwig's hilarious farce, *Lend Me A Tenor* opened and played here for more than a year. The superlative cast included Philip Bosco (Tony Award), Victor Garber, Ron Holgate, Tovah Feldshuh, and Jane Connell, and the director was Jerry Zaks (Tony Award). Next, Herb Gardner's *Conversations With My Father* opened and won a Tony Award for Judd Hirsch. Also starring Tony Shalhoub and David Margulies, it ran here for a year.

The 1994 attraction was the acclaimed Royal National Theatre production of J.B. Priestley's thriller *An Inspector Calls* with dazzling direction by Stephen Daldry. It starred Rosemary Harris, Philip Bosco, and Kenneth Cranham and featured Jane Adams and Marcus D'Amico. Ms. Adams won a Tony Award as best featured actress in a play. Stunning stage effects included a pounding rain storm on stage in Act I, and an Act II climax in which the house set turned inside-out disgorging its contents. It closed in 1995 after 454 performances.

In 1996, Tony Randall's National Actors Theatre presented a well-received revival of the 1955 play *Inherit the Wind* by Jerome Lawrence and Robert E. Lee. This absorbing drama about the famed 1925 Scopes "Monkey Trial" in Tennessee, charging an educator with teaching evolution, was hailed for the savage performance of George C. Scott as Henry Drummond. Unfortunately, Scott became seriously ill during the short run and had to be replaced by Randall. The production closed after only 45 performances.

Blair Brown, Michael Cumpsty, and Philip Bosco in the Tony-winning play *Copenhagen* (2000). Photo by Joan Marcus.

On September 19, 1996, *Skylight*, a London hit, opened here with the stars of the British production, Michael Gambon and Lia Williams. The domestic drama by David Hare took place in a depressing flat in London and involved former lovers who attempt to rekindle their love. The production received four Tony Award nominations and ran for 116 performances.

Stars of the present and future were packed into the tiny seven-member cast of the November 1997 musical *Triumph of Love*, adapted by James Magruder, Jeffrey Stock, and Susan Birkenhead from the Marivaux play. Betty Buckley, F. Murray Abraham, Susan Egan, Kevin Chamberlin, Nancy Opel, Christopher Sieber, and Roger Bart were featured in the chamber musical-comedy, which managed a run of only 83 performances.

On March 1, 1998, *Art*, an international hit by Yasmina Reza, translated by Christopher Hampton,

opened to rave reviews. It starred Alan Alda, Victor Garber, and Alfred Molina, as longstanding buddies whose friendship is shattered over an expensive white-on-white painting that Mr. Garber's character has bought. Performed without intermission, the comedy gave Mr. Molina a show-stopping monologue about his battles with his mother-in-law over his impending wedding. During the play's long run, Mr. Alda was succeeded by Brian Cox, Judd Hirsch, and Buck Henry; Mr. Garber by Henry Goodman, Joe Morton, and George Segal; Mr. Molina was succeeded by David Haig, George Wendt, and Wayne Knight. *Art* won a Best Play Tony Award and received two other Tony nominations.

A new production of Arthur Miller's 1968 play, *The Price*, opened here on November 15, 1999, starring Jeffrey DeMunn, Bob Dishy, Lisbeth Mackay, and Harris Yulin. It was well received. The drama involves two brothers who have been estranged for sixteen years. One a successful doctor, the other a policeman, they meet again in an attic to dispose of their late father's belongings and to battle over the past that the furniture represents. The drama was directed by actor James Naughton and ran for 128 performances.

A lauded British play, *Copenhagen,* opened at the Royale Theatre on April 11, 2000. Starring Philip Bosco, Blair Brown, and Michael Cumpsty, it told the complex tale, based on actual people and events, of a 1941 meeting between two brilliant physicists—German Werner Heisenberg and Danish Niels Bohr—plus the latter's wife, Margrethe Bohr. The two men had collaborated on work that led to unlocking the power of the atom, but were now on opposing sides in World War II. The meeting ended in personal disaster—but may have prevented Hitler from developing nuclear weapons. Written by Michael Frayn and directed by Michael Blakemore, the drama won the following Tony Awards: Best Play, Best Direction, and Best Featured Actress (Blair Brown). The American production of this intellectual drama was hailed for its intelligent content and ran for 326 performances. The play was recorded with its original cast by Fynsworth Alley.

JOHN GOLDEN THEATRE

The John Golden Theatre at 252 West Forty-fifth Street was originally named the Theatre Masque. It was the fifth theatre built by the Chanin Brothers, and once again they chose Herbert J. Krapp as their architect. This house was their smallest, with 800 seats, and the Chanins announced that it aimed to be "the home of fine plays of the 'artistic' or 'intimate' type." They also reiterated their philosophy that their theatres were built to afford ease and comfort to actors as well as playgoers.

The New York Times reviewed the first production at the Theatre Masque, an Italian play called *Puppets of Passion,* which opened on February 24, 1927, and the paper liked the new playhouse more than the new play. "Like all the Chanin houses," wrote critic Brooks Atkinson, "the Theatre Masque is pleasing and comfortable. The architecture is modern Spanish in character, and the interior of the house is decorated in pastel shades, trimmed in grayish blues and reds." Of the play, which had Frank Morgan in the cast, Atkinson wrote that it moved along at a funereal pace. It expired after 12 performances.

The theatre's next attraction fared better. It ran for 15 performances. This was a play called *The Comic,* with J.C. Nugent, Patricia Collinge, and Rex O'Malley, and the program stated that it was written by one Lajos Luria, a pseudonym for a famous serious European dramatist who wouldn't use his real name on a comedy.

During the remainder of 1927 this theatre housed a revival of the Gilbert and Sullivan operetta *Patience*; a play about the corruption of the Harding administration in Washington, *Revelry*; Lionel Atwill in a sorry swashbuckler, *The King Can Do No Wrong*; and, finally, a misguided comedy called *Venus,* by the usually skillful Rachel Crothers, who, this time out, wrote a futuristic play about man's first flight to the planet Venus. Her play was visible for only 8 performances.

Things did not improve much in 1928. There were eight productions here and only one ran more than a hundred performances. This was an ethnic comedy called *Relations,* written by and starring Edward Clark. *The Scarlet Fox,* written by and starring Willard Mack, ran for 79 performances. *Young Love,* by Samson Raphaelson, starring Dorothy Gish and James Rennie, lasted for 87 performances.

Theatre Masque's biggest hit in 1929 was a macabre drama called *Rope's End,* by British playwright Patrick Hamilton. The play detailed the grisly murder of an Oxford undergraduate by two upperclassmen, just for kicks. Although the playwright denied it, he was obviously influenced by the similar murder of a young boy in Chicago by Leopold and Loeb, two intellectuals who also committed a thrill kill. In *Rope's End*, the murderers put their victim's body in a chest, then invite his father and aunt to dinner. The meal is served on the chest. Alfred Hitchcock made a rarely-shown film of this play and called it *Rope.*

In early 1930 the hit play *Broken Dishes,* with Bette Davis and Donald Meek, moved here from the Ritz and

Left: Osgood Perkins as a best-selling novelist besieged by female fans in *Goodbye Again* (1932). *Right:* Sir Cedric Hardwicke and Julie Hayden in *Shadow and Substance* (1938).

played for three months. A comedy about life in Greenwich Village, *Up Pops the Devil,* with Roger Pryor, Sally Bates, Brian Donlevy, and Albert Hackett (who co-authored the play with Frances Goodrich) ran for 146 performances that year. An interesting but unsuccessful drama, *Brass Ankle,* by DuBose Heyward (who later wrote *Porgy and Bess* with the Gershwins) starred Alice Brady in 1931.

A Norman Krasna farce about Hollywood, *Louder, Please!* was a moderate success in 1931. It starred Lee Tracy as a loudmouth publicity man, and it was directed at top speed by George Abbott. A much bigger hit was *Goodbye Again,* a comedy in which Osgood Perkins felicitously played a novelist who tries to renew an old affair while on a publicity tour for his latest book. This romantic trifle kept the Theatre Masque full for 212 performances in 1932-33.

Post Road, a hit 1934 play about kidnapping, featured delirious performances by Lucile Watson and Percy Kilbride. The following year brought J.B. Priestley's *Laburnum Grove,* starring Edmund Gwenn, Elizabeth

Risdon, and Melville Cooper, which moved here from the Booth. In 1936, *Russet Mantle,* a pleasant play about Santa Fe characters by Lynn Riggs, moved in and stayed for 116 performances. There was much praise for the actors—Evelyn Varden, John Beal, Martha Sleeper, Margaret Douglass, Jay Fassett, and others.

The last show to play the Masque before it changed its name was *The Holmeses of Baker Street,* in which Sherlock's daughter (Helen Chandler) proved that she was as good a sleuth as her old man. Cyril Scott played Sherlock, Conway Wingfield was Dr. Watson, and the wonderful mimic Cecilia Loftus was Mrs. Watson.

On February 2, 1937, the Masque became the John Golden Theatre, making it the third house named after the illustrious theatrical producer. Its first play was *And Now Good-bye,* a drama based on a James Hilton novel, starring Philip Merivale as a reverend who falls in love with a parishioner. It was not successful.

A radiant play, *Shadow and Substance,* by Paul Vincent Carroll arrived in January 1938 and was

audience in 1944 and ran for 255 performances. The play, which had a star-studded cast—Martha Scott, Frieda Inescort, Lili Darvas, Glenn Anders, and Myron McCormick—was not a war play. It was about a woman who wrote a best-seller and the problems it engendered for her family.

The remainder of the 1940s brought a number of shows to this theatre, but none was outstanding. Among them were: *The Rich Full Life* (1945), with Judith Evelyn and Virginia Weidler; S.N. Behrman's *Dunnigan's Daughter* (1945), with June Havoc, Dennis King, Richard Widmark, Jan Sterling, and Luther Adler; *January Thaw* (1946), with Robert Keith and Lulu Mae Hubbard; and *I Like It Here* (1946), with Oscar Karlweis and Bert Lytel.

From mid-1946 until February 1948 the John Golden

acclaimed by the drama critics. It had shining performances by the ethereal Julie Haydon as the servant to an intellectual snob, and by Sir Cedric Hardwicke, who played her employer. The spiritual play found favor and stayed for 206 performances. The following year, another memorable play by Paul Vincent Carroll, *The White Steed*, moved here from the Cort. It starred Jessica Tandy and Barry Fitzgerald.

On December 5, 1941, a Victorian thriller called *Angel Street* opened here, with Judith Evelyn, Vincent Price, and Leo G. Carroll. Produced by Shepard Traube, in association with Alexander H. Cohen, it was not expected to succeed, and consequently, only a three-day supply of PLAYBILL magazines was ordered. The producers underestimated their show. It played 1,295 times, making it the longest-running show in this theatre's history.

Rose Franken's comedy *Soldier's Wife* found an

Top Left: Sketch of Victor Borge in *Comedy in Music* on the souvenir program (1953). *Above*: Vincent Price and Judith Evelyn in the celebrated thriller *Angel Street* (1941).

243

Bert Lahr as "Estragon" in Samuel Beckett's surrealistic *Waiting for Godot* (1956).

gettable performances as Estragon in Samuel Beckett's parable of perpetual anticipation, *Waiting for Godot*. It was a radical departure for this famed clown of revues and musical comedies, and the critics hailed him. Also in the cast were E.G. Marshall, Kurt Kasznar, and Alvin Epstein.

Menasha Skulnik appeared in a comedy, *Uncle Willie*, in late 1956 and stayed for 141 performances. The play was a variant of *Abie's Irish Rose*, focusing on two neighboring families, one Irish, the other Jewish.

John Osborn's vitriolic hit *Look Back in Anger* moved here from the Lyceum in 1958 and stayed for six months. *A Party with Betty Comden and Adolph Green*, with the popular duo singing their witty lyrics from Broadway musicals and Hollywood films, was welcomed in 1958-59, as was the *Billy Barnes Revue* from the West Coast. The British duo of Michael Flanders and Donald Swann scored a hit in their two-man revue *At the Drop of a Hat* (1959).

One of the John Golden's most cherished entertainments was the brilliant Alexander H. Cohen production of *An Evening with Mike Nichols and Elaine May*. Even their PLAYBILL biographies, which they wrote themselves, were hilarious. The duo presented some of their classic comedy sketches that satirized everyday foibles, and they kept the John Golden Theatre quaking with laughter for 306 performances in 1960-61.

An Evening with Yves Montand (1961) also proved a hit, with the French actor/singer charming audiences in a one-man show. Robert Redford appeared here in *Sunday in New York*, a fair comedy by Norman Krasna that moved to the Golden from the Cort Theatre in 1962. On October 27, 1962, a tornado of mirth called *Beyond the Fringe* arrived from England and fractured audiences for 667 performances. This Alexander H. Cohen import was a delirious revue written and performed by Alan Bennett, Peter Cook, Jonathan Miller, and Dudley Moore; Mr. Cohen staged the uproar.

In 1964 Victor Borge returned to the Golden with *Comedy in Music, Opus 2*, which was good enough for 192 performances. Another hit revue, *Wait a Minim*, opened here in 1966, bringing eight extremely personable and talented performers from South Africa. Their zany entertainment delighted theatregoers for 457 performances. The remainder of the 1960s brought seven shows, but

was leased as a motion picture theatre. It returned to legitimacy on February 29, 1948, with Maurice Chevalier in a one-man show of songs and impressions.

Highlights of the 1950s at the John Golden included Grace George and Walter Hampden in *The Velvet Glove* (1950), which moved here from the Booth; Emlyn Williams in a solo performance of six scenes from the works of Charles Dickens (1952); Cornelia Otis Skinner in *Paris '90* (1952), a monodrama that moved here from the Booth; the long-running comedy *The Fourposter* (1952), which moved here from the Ethel Barrymore.

On October 2, 1953, the witty Victor Borge opened at this theatre in a one-man show called *Comedy in Music*. Mr. Borge played the piano and indulged in deadpan patter and lampoons that kept audiences in stitches for 849 performances.

In 1956, comic Bert Lahr gave one of his most unfor-

Above: PLAYBILL covers for *An Evening with Mike Nichols and Elaine May* (1960) and David Rabe's *Sticks and Bones* (1972). *Right:* Dudley Moore (at piano), Alan Bennett and Jonathan Miller (standing on piano), and Peter Cook in the British revue *Beyond the Fringe* (1962).

only two of them were of much interest: John Bowen's British play *After the Rain* (1967) with Alec McCowen, and the British actor Roy Dotrice in his one-man show, *Brief Lives*, about an English antiquarian named John Aubrey.

Highlights of the 1970s included *Bob and Ray—The Two and Only* (1970), a two-man show featuring the popular radio comics Bob Elliott and Ray Goulding; David Rabe's Vietnam War drama *Sticks and Bones* (1972), which won a Tony Award for best play of the season; *Words and Music* (1974), a revue featuring the songs of Sammy Cahn, who appeared in the show with Kelly Garrett, Jon Peck, and Shirley Lemmon; Robert Patrick's *Kennedy's Children* (1975), with Shirley Knight, who won

A pair of Pulitzer-winners. *Left:* Jessica Tandy and Hume Cronyn in *The Gin Game* (1977). *Right:* Kathy Bates and Anne Pitoniak in *'night Mother.*

a Tony Award as best supporting actress of the season; Tom Stoppard's *Dirty Linen* and *New-Found-Land* (1977), two plays in one, performed without intermission.

D.L. Coburn's Pulitzer Prize-winning *The Gin Game* (1977) starred husband-wife team Hume Cronyn and Jessica Tandy as two residents of a nursing home whose relationship is reflected in the games of cards they try to play. Ms. Tandy won a Tony Award for her performance.

The 1980s began with a revival of Lillian Hellman's *Watch on the Rhine*, soon followed by *A Day in Hollywood/A Night in the Ukraine* (1980), which transferred to the larger Royale Theatre; *Tintypes* (1980), a diverting revue of turn-of-the-century songs, which moved to the John Golden from the Off-Broadway Theatre at St. Peter's Church; Beth Henley's Pulitzer-winning play *Crimes of the Heart* (1981), which transferred from Off-Broadway's Manhattan Theatre Club; and Marsha Norman's Pulitzer-winning play *'night, Mother*, with Kathy Bates as a daughter who announces to her mother (Anne Pitoniak) that she intends to commit suicide.

In 1984, another Pulitzer-winning play opened here: David Mamet's *Glengarry Glen Ross*, making it three Pulitzer-winning plays in a row—four in seven years—a record for any Broadway theatre. Gregory Mosher won a Tony Award for his direction of the Mamet play about ruthless real-estate salesmen, which starred Ron Silver, Joe Mantegna (Tony Award), and Robert Prosky.

This was followed by a revival of Athol Fugard's play *Blood Knot*, starring the playwright and Zakes Mokae. Tandy and Cronyn returned in *The Petition*, a British play having its world premiere on Broadway. Another British production, *Stepping Out*, directed by Tommy Tune, arrived for a brief run in 1987; then came a revival of Arthur Miller's *All My Sons*; The Gate Theatre Dublin production of O'Casey's *Juno and the Paycock*, presented in a limited engagement by the Circle in the Square Theatre as part of the first New York International Festival of the Arts; *Paul Robeson* starring Avery Brooks; Richard Greenberg's Broadway debut, *Eastern Standard*, with Peter Frechette, Ann Meara and others; *Sid Caesar & Company: Does Anyone Know What I'm Talking About?*; and *Michael Feinstein in Concert—Piano and Voice*.

In 1992 the Golden hosted an unusual musical: *Falsettos*, an amalgam of William Finn's and James Lapine's two earlier Off-Broadway musicals, *March of the*

246

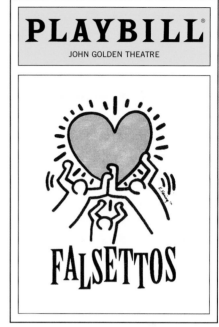

Left: David Loud accompanies Zoë Caldwell in her Tony-winning performance as Maria Callas in *Master Class* (1995). *Right*: PLAYBILL for William Finn's musical, *Falsettos* (1992).

Falsettos and *Falsettoland*. The combined show chronicled the misadventures of Marvin, a married man who comes out as gay, and tries to build a family that includes his son, his ex-wife, her new husband, and Marvin's lover, Whizzer. The combined show won Tony Awards for Best Musical Book and Score, and ran 487 performances.

In 1993, a play called *Mixed Emotions* by Richard Baer, with Katherine Helmond, played for 55 performances. It depicted a romance between a widow and a widower. This was followed by an evening of political comedy by Jackie Mason called *Politically Incorrect.* Hilariously performed by Mr. Mason, it ran for 347 performances.

The next tenant at this theatre scored a resounding hit. It was Terrence McNally's fascinating *Master Class*, which opened to rave reviews on November 5, 1995. Mr. McNally, who was a friend and great admirer of opera superstar Maria Callas, attended some of her master classes in which she tutored aspiring opera singers. In the play, Zoë Caldwell, who played Callas, dramatically coached three would-be singers with volcanic fury. Ms. Caldwell and Audra McDonald, who played one of her badgered students, both won Tony Awards for their dynamic performances, and the *Master Class* won the

Best Play Tony Award for the season. It ran for 601 performances. During its long run, Ms. Caldwell was succeeded by Patti LuPone and Dixie Carter. Ms. McDonald was succeeded by Helen Goldsby and Alaine Rodin-Lo.

On April 1, 1998, a revival of Eugene Ionesco's play *The Chairs*, translated by Martin Crimp, opened at this theatre. A production of Théâtre de Complicité and Royal Court Theater, the acclaimed absurdist play starred Geraldine McEwan and Richard Briers and filled the Golden's chairs for a 12-week limited engagement. The two stars played a very eccentric old couple who entertain a growing number of invisible guests each of whom needs a chair. Both stars made their Broadway debuts in this production, directed by Simon McBurney. *The Chairs* received six Tony Award nominations: Best Actor (Briers), Best Actress (McEwan), Best Revival of a Play, Best Director (McBurney), Best Scenic Designer (Quay Brothers), and Best Lighting Designer (Paul Anderson).

Side Man, a memory play by Warren Leight, had a fortunate career. It opened Off Broadway in March of 1998 and earned such glowing reviews that it moved to the uptown Roundabout Theater Company's Criterion Center Stage Right, where it again received rave notices.

Left: Geraldine McEwan and Richard Briers in Ionesco's *The Chairs* (1998). Photo by Joan Marcus. *Right*: Robert Sella and Frank Wood (Tony Award) play son and father in *Side Man*, an autobiographical play.

From there it moved to the Golden Theatre on November 8, 1998, and critics again hailed it. It was a deft examination of the troubled family life of a professional jazz trumpet player who is married to his music, with little emotion left for his wife and son. The son is the play's narrator, reviewing his life with father and mother in vivid flashbacks. One of the play's attributes was the use of the recordings of jazz greats in the background. In music circles, a side man is a musician who plays alongside the star performer, an anonymous artist to the audience. The autobiographical play won the Best Play Tony Award. Frank Wood, who played the father, won a Tony Award as Best Featured Actor in A Play. *Side Man* ran at the John Golden until October 31, 1999. During the run, Robert Sella, who played Clifford, was succeeded by Christian Slater. Mr. Sella returned to the role in March 1999 and was succeeded by Scott Wolf in May of that year. The cast also included a group of actors who played musicians and who enlivened the play with jazz slang.

The John Golden is currently a Shubert Organization Theatre. It has been very successful as a house for intimate revues, one- and two-person shows, and dramatic plays with small casts.

MAJESTIC THEATRE

The Majestic Theatre at 245 West Forty-forth Street, right off the corner of Eighth Avenue, was the sixth and last of the houses built by the Chanin Brothers. With a seating capacity of 1,800 (1,655 today), it was for decades the largest legitimate theatre in the Times Square district, suited primarily for the staging of lavish musical comedies and revues.

Architect Herbert J. Krapp used the same stadium-style design for this house as he had for the Chanins' first theatre, the 46th Street. The orchestra was built on a steep slope, and patrons had to climb stairs to reach the rear section of the orchestra. There was only one balcony. *The New York Times* described the architecture and decoration of the interior as being in the Louis XV style, with a color scheme of gold and ivory. "The house curtain, the valence, the box drapes and panels on the side walls are of gold and rose silk damask," the paper reported. "As in other Chanin houses, the seats are said to be three inches wider than the ordinary theatre chair."

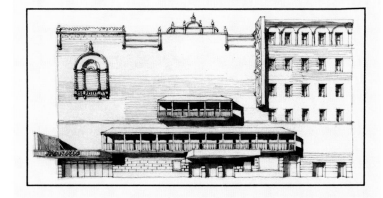

The Majestic Theatre opened on March 28, 1927, with a revue curiously called *Rufus LeMaire's Affairs,* after the show's producer, Rufus LeMaire. Despite such talents as Ted Lewis, Charlotte Greenwood, and Peggy Fears, the show was a dud and played only 56 times. This was succeeded by a black revue, *Rang Tang,* that moved here from the Royale Theatre and stayed for two months. A Sigmund Romberg musical play called *The Love Call* was next, but didn't tarry more than 88 performances. An extremely elaborate 1928 Gilbert Miller production, *The Patriot* had John Gielgud in the cast and, considering the reviews, should have run longer than 12 performances. George Kelly's play, *Behold the Bridegroom,* which critic Burns Mantle named one of the year's ten best plays, moved to the Majestic from the Cort Theatre in February 1928. It starred Judith Anderson, Jean Dixon, Mary Servoss, Thurston Hall, and Lester Vail, but it ran only 88 performances.

Ziegfeld's enormous hit, *Rio Rita* (1928), moved to the Majestic after playing some months at the splendid new Ziegfeld Theatre. Champion boxer Jack Dempsey made his Broadway debut at the Majestic September 18, 1928, in a drama called, aptly, *The Big Fight,* in which he had to knock out another boxer to win the hand of a manicurist named Shirley. The critics rated his boxing better than his acting and the novelty wore off after 31 rounds.

The Majestic's biggest hit thus far was a revue called *Pleasure Bound,* with Phil Baker, Jack Pearl, Grace Brinkley, and others. The young Busby Berkeley created the dances, and the show made it to 136 performances. The Shuberts produced a new version of *Die Fledermaus* called *A Wonderful Night,* and the star was a young stilt walker from England called Archie Leach, who became better known in Hollywood as Cary Grant. This Johann Strauss bauble played 125 performances.

In February 1930 *The International Revue* opened here and should have been a triumph. It cost $200,000 to mount (an exorbitant amount for the Depression) and it had such luminaries in the cast as Gertrude Lawrence, Harry Richman, Jack Pearl, ballet star Anton Dolin, the great Spanish dancer Argentinita, Moss and Fontana, and the Chester Hale Girls. It also had two song hits by Dorothy Fields and Jimmy McHugh that have become standards: "On the Sunny Side of the Street" and "Exactly Like You." But the revue was earthbound. On the opening night, it was so long that the second act did not begin until 11:00 PM, and the highly touted Argentinita laid an egg.

The Shuberts's next venture, an operetta called *Nina Rosa,* by Sigmund Romberg, Otto Harbach, and Irving Caesar, ran 137 times. It starred Ethelind Terry (the famed star of *Rio Rita*) and Guy Robertson and it had a novel setting—the Peruvian Andes. A revival of Romberg's *The Student Prince* in 1931 fared less well, running for 45 performances. The Depression was felt by this theatre in 1932, when it was dark for many months.

In January 1933 much was expected of *Pardon My English,* a musical by George and Ira Gershwin and Herbert Fields. The producers were Alex Aarons and Vinton Freedley, who had mounted a series of highly successful Gershwin shows. The stars were Jack Pearl, Lyda Roberti ("the Polish bombshell"), Josephine Huston, and the dance team of Carl Randall and Barbara Newberry. The net result was one of the Gershwins's biggest flops. It ran for only 43 performances. According to Gerald Bordman in his book *American Musical Theatre,* the fact that this musical was set in Germany disturbed many theatregoers, since Hitler was coming to power there.

The successful team of Ray Henderson and Lew Brown decided to give the Depression a kick in the slats by writing and producing an opulent revue, *Strike Me Pink,* at the Majestic in March 1933. The show, backed by gangster Waxey Gordon, smacked of the Roaring Twenties. Opening-night top was $25 (outrageous for those dark days), and the tickets were printed on gold

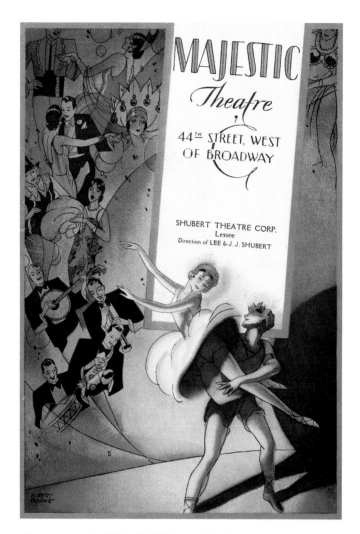

Program cover for *A Wonderful Night* with Archie Leach (Cary Grant) in the cast (1930).

stock. The stars included the ebullient Jimmy Durante, the vivacious Lupe Velez (then married to Tarzan, Johnny Weissmuller), and that cool socialite, Hope Williams. The result was neither a flop nor a smash, but a pleasant run of 122 performances.

An ingenious musical, *Murder at the Vanities,* moved to the Majestic from the New Amsterdam in November 1933 and stayed for four months. It focused on backstage murders during a performance of *Earl Carroll's Vanities* and thus combined thrills with lush scenes from a typical Carroll revue. Bela Lugosi was in the cast, but he wasn't the one who "dunnit." Since producers are constantly promising to revive this novelty, we shall not divulge the killer's identity.

The successful 1942 revival of George Gershwin's opera, *Porgy and Bess*, with J. Rosamond Johnson, Todd Duncan, and Anne Brown.

An impresario named S.M. Chartock took over the Majestic in the spring of 1934 and staged a festival of five Gilbert and Sullivan operettas. During 1935 a series of quick failures played at this theatre. The only show to stay longer than a few weeks was the *Earl Carroll Sketch Book,* described as an "Hysterical Historical Revue," or American history as seen through the eyes of a chorus girl. This amusing show, starring Ken Murray and the usual near-nude Carroll girls, moved here from the Winter Garden and stayed for almost three months.

Beginning in 1936 the Majestic booked more and more successful musicals that had opened in other theatres and would end their Broadway runs here, usually at reduced prices. In 1937 there was an unsuccessful attempt to revive two old thrillers, *The Bat* and *The Cat and the Canary.* A new operetta, *Three Waltzes,* employing the music of Johann Strauss, Sr. and Jr., was

a moderate success that year. It starred Kitty Carlisle, Glenn Anders, and Michael Bartlett, and ran for 122 performances.

At the end of 1938 Gertrude Lawrence moved into this theatre from the Plymouth with her hit *Susan and God,* and this was followed in February 1939 with the lively musical *Stars in Your Eyes,* with such personalities as Ethel Merman, Jimmy Durante, Richard Carlson, Mildred Natwick, and the Russian ballerina Tamara Toumanova. With a bright score by Arthur Schwartz and Dorothy Fields, a witty book about a lusty Hollywood star (Merman) trying to seduce her innocent leading man (Carlson), and direction by Joshua Logan, the show had a glittering opening night, which *Life* magazine photographed. But despite a rave review in *The New York Times,* it ran for only 127 performances. Producer Dwight Deere Wiman blamed the comparatively short run on the fact that the highly publicized World's Fair opened in Flushing Meadows that spring and presumably siphoned away audiences. Perhaps the most remarkable aspect of *Stars in Your Eyes* was its chorus line, which numbered such future ballet and Broadway luminaries as Alicia Alonso, Jerome Robbins, Nora Kaye, and Maria Karnilova.

The next musical at the Majestic, *Yokel Boy,* was not as good as *Stars in Your Eyes,* but ran longer. It also dealt with Hollywood studios—and not very kindly. Buddy Ebsen, Judy Canova, Lois January, and Phil Silvers led the cast and one hit tune emerged: "Comes Love."

Clare Boothe's hit anti-Nazi play, *Margin for Error,* moved here from the Plymouth in 1940; and Olsen and Johnson's *Hellzapoppin* transferred from the Winter Garden in 1941. In January 1942 producer Cheryl Crawford presented the first Broadway revival of the Gershwins's *Porgy and Bess,* and this production proved to be an artistic and a commercial success. Crawford removed the operatic recitative and made the work more of a Broadway musical than an opera, and the public flocked to it for thirty-five weeks. Many members of the

Jan Clayton and John Raitt in Rodgers and Hammerstein's memorable *Carousel* (1945).

original cast (Todd Duncan, Anne Brown, Warren Coleman, Ruby Elzy, and J. Rosamond Johnson) were in this revival, and they brought luster to a work that had failed in its premiere engagement in 1935.

Paul Green and Richard Wright's powerful drama, *Native Son,* directed by Orson Welles, played a return engagement at the Majestic in 1942, followed by the frothy hit comedy, *Junior Miss,* which moved here from the Lyceum Theatre in 1943.

One of the Majestic's biggest hits to this time opened on August 4, 1943: a new version of that favorite Franz Lehár/Victor Leon/Leo Stein operetta *The Merry Widow.* The cast included Marta Eggerth and her husband, Jan Kiepura, along with David Wayne, Gene Barry, Melville Cooper, and Ruth Matteson. It waltzed for 321 performances.

Cole Porter's *Mexican Hayride,* with Bobby Clark and June Havoc, moved here from the Winter Garden in 1945. But it soon made way for one of the treasures of the American Musical Theatre: Rodgers and Hammer-stein's lilting *Carousel.* A musical adaptation of Molnar's play *Liliom,* the work opened to rapturous reviews in April 1945. Critic John Chapman in *The New York Daily News* stated that it was one of the finest musical plays he had ever seen, and Richard Rodgers later confessed that of all the musicals he had written, this was his favorite. John Raitt was memorable singing his "Soliloquy," and he and Jan Clayton shared the lovely ballad "If I Loved You." The musical ran 890 performances and the Majestic established itself (with the St. James across the street) as one of the preferred theatres for Rodgers and Hammer-stein musicals.

The hit soldier revue *Call Me Mister* moved to this theatre in 1947 from the National, followed by another Rodgers and Hammerstein musical, *Allegro,* a rather pretentious chronicle of a man named Joseph Taylor, Jr., which critic Woollcott Gibbs described in *The New Yorker* as "a shocking disappointment." It ran for 315 performances.

On April 7, 1949, Rodgers and Hammerstein's *South Pacific* opened here, starring Mary Martin and Ezio Pinza, and immediately became the hottest ticket in town. Based on James A. Michener's Pulitzer-winning book *Tales of the South Pacific,* this parable of conflicting

Above: Mary Martin clowns in the Pulitzer Prize-winning musical *South Pacific* (1949). *Right:* Program cover sketch for the musical *Fanny* (1954).

production of some musicals of varying merit that enjoyed respectable runs. Rodgers and Hammerstein's backstage musical, *Me and Juliet,* was second-rate R&H, but ran for 358 performances in 1953-54; *By the Beautiful Sea,* a musical by Arthur Schwartz and Herbert and Dorothy Fields, starring Shirley Booth, ran a moderate 268 performances in 1954.

Fanny (1954), a musical adaptation of Marcel Pagnol's trilogy (*Marius, César,* and *Fanny*), by S.N. Behrman, Joshua Logan, and Harold Rome, ran for 888 performances. It starred Walter Slezak (who won a Tony Award for his performance) and Ezio Pinza.

The Majestic next hosted another musical theatre landmark, Meredith Willson's phenomenal *The Music Man* (1957), which won Tony Awards for Best Musical, Best Actor (Robert Preston), Best Supporting Players (Barbara Cook David Burns), Best Book (Willson and Franklin Lacey), Best Composer and Lyricist (Willson), Best Musical Director (Herbert Greene), and Best Producers (Kermit Bloomgarden, Herbert Greene, Frank Productions). This bonanza about a charismatic con man who tries to sell a small Iowa town on the fraudulent idea of a boys' band—but winds up falling in love with the place—ran for 1,375 performances.

Much was expected of *Camelot,* the Majestic's next

love and racial prejudice between American military and Polynesian locals during World War II also won the Pulitzer Prize for drama in 1950, plus the Tony Award, the New York Drama Critics Circle Award, and the Donaldson Award for best musical of the season. With direction by Joshua Logan (who co-authored the book with Oscar Hammerstein II) and with some of Richard Rodgers's most inspired melodies, the musical ran for 1,925 performances and won Tony Awards for Ms. Martin, Mr. Pinza, supporting performers Juanita Hall and Myron McCormick, director Logan, and Rodgers, Hammerstein, and Logan for their music, lyrics, and book.

The remainder of the 1950s at this theatre saw the

Julie Andrews charms Richard Burton in the Lerner/Loewe musical, *Camelot* (1960).

musical, in late 1960. Written by Alan Jay Lerner and Frederick Loewe, directed by Moss Hart, whose previous show had been the sensational *My Fair Lady,* it co-starred Julie Andrews of that show, plus movie star Richard Burton and newcomer Robert Goulet. The critics gave it very mixed reviews, and after a few weeks it appeared that the expensive musical was not long for Broadway. Then, a miracle happened. Ed Sullivan presented four musical numbers from the show on his popular TV variety show, and the following morning, there was a long line of ticket buyers at the Majestic Theatre. Mr. Burton won a Tony Award for his performance as King Arthur and the musical played for 873 performances.

The remainder of the early 1960s was devoted to a revival of *The School for Scandal* (1963), starring Ralph Richardson and John Gielgud (who also directed it), plus a remarkable series of flops with notable names attached:

Judy Holliday in her last Broadway show, the lamentable musical *Hot Spot* (1963); *Tovarich* (1963), the musical version of the play of the same name, which moved here from the Broadway Theatre with Tony Award winner Vivien Leigh and Jean Pierre Aumont; and Mary Martin in the flop musical *Jennie* (1963), supposedly based on the early career of actress Laurette Taylor.

The misguided musical *Anyone Can Whistle* (1964), with a beguiling score by Stephen Sondheim, a murky book by Arthur Laurents, and good performances by Angela Lansbury, Lee Remick, and Harry Guardino, lasted only 9 performances, but developed something of a cult following. Sammy Davis, Jr., starred in Strouse and Adams's unsuccessful musical version of Clifford Odets's *Golden Boy* (1964), followed by a transfer of the hit *Funny Girl* (1966), from the Winter Garden; and then the long-running classic *Fiddler on the Roof,* which moved here from the Imperial in 1967 and stayed until December 1970.

The 1970s saw a flop musical version of *The Teahouse of the August Moon* called *Lovely Ladies, Kind Gentlemen* (1970); the Tony Award-winning musical *1776* (1971), here from the St. James Theatre; and a fairly successful musical version of the popular movie *Some Like It Hot,* retitled *Sugar* (1972), with Robert Morse and Tony Roberts as the musicians who must masquerade as women to hide from gangsters, and Cyril Ritchard as the old tycoon who falls for one of them. *A Little Night Music* (1973), the Tony Award-winning musical, moved here from the Shubert Theatre.

Much was expected from *Mack and Mabel* (1974), the Jerry Herman/Michael Stewart musical about silent film icons Mack Sennett and Mabel Normand, but the show ran for only 65 performances despite the presence of Robert Preston and Bernadette Peters in the lead roles. *The Wiz,* an all-black take on *The Wizard of Oz,* won six Tony Awards—for Best Musical, Best Score (Charlie Smalls), Best Director (Geoffrey Holder), Best Supporting Performers (Ted Ross, Dee Dee Bridgewater), Best Costume Designer (Geoffrey Holder), and Best Choreographer (George Faison)—and ran for 1,672 performances.

In the late 1970s, Liza Minnelli and Barry Nelson starred in a pallid musical, *The Act* (1977), for which Ms.

Minnelli won a Tony Award. Henry Fonda and Jane Alexander played Supreme Court Justices in *The First Monday in October* (1978). Michael Bennett directed and choreographed *Ballroom* (1978). And Richard Rodgers presented his last show, *I Remember Mama,* a 1979 musical version of a John Van Druten play that Rodgers

and Hammerstein had produced in 1944. Liv Ullmann starred.

The next few years saw a series of short runs: a revival of *The Most Happy Fella* (1979); a personal appearance by Bette Midler (1979-80); the final performances of *Grease* (1980), from the Royale Theatre; *Blackstone!* (1980), a magic show; and a revival of the 1947 musical *Brigadoon* with Agnes de Mille recreating her dances that won a Tony Award in 1947.

In 1981, David Merrick's sumptuous production of the musical *42ⁿᵈ Street* (based on the classic movie musical of the same name) moved here from the Winter Garden where it had won Tony Awards for Best Musical and Best Choreography.

This lavish production stayed at this theatre until 1988, then moved across the street to the St. James to make way for the biggest hit in the distinguished history of the Majestic: *The Phantom of the Opera*, with three of its London stars, Michael Crawford, Sarah Brightman, and Steve Barton. This phenomenal success by Andrew

Left: Tiger Haynes, James Wigfall, Stephanie Mills, and Hinton Battle in the long-running hit *The Wiz* (1975). *Above:* Liza Minnelli gives a Tony Award-winning performance in *The Act* (1977).

Lloyd Webber, Charles Hart, and Richard Stilgoe won Tony Awards for Best Musical, Best Direction (Harold Prince), Best Actor in a Musical (Crawford), Best Featured Actress (Judy Kaye), Best Scenic and Costume Designer (Maria Bjornson), and Best Lighting Designer (Andrew Bridges). The great popularity of this spectacular musical kept it running beyond the end of the century, and may eventually make it a contender for the longest-running musical in Broadway history.

The Majestic Theatre is owned by the Shubert Organization and is one of the world's finest musical comedy houses. It has been renovated in recent years and its sloped orchestra section still offers better viewing than is available at most other theatres.

PLAYBILL cover for *The Phantom of the Opera.*

ST. JAMES THEATRE

The St. James Theatre at 246 West Forty-fourth Street was built by Broadway booking agent Abraham Erlanger and opened as Erlanger's Theatre in the fall of 1927. The theatre was designed by the architectural firm of Warren and Wetmore, with interiors by John Singraldi.

With an ample capacity of 1,600 seats, Erlanger's Theatre was aimed primarily for the production of musicals. According to *The New York Times*, it cost $1,500,000 to build and was the least ornate of all the theatres constructed in the Times Square district at the time. "In the auditorium," reported the paper, "there has been a studied attempt to create an intimate rather than a theatrical atmosphere. The interior design is Georgian, the color scheme coral and antique gold. Murals decorate the side walls and the proscenium arch.

Two large boxes on either side of the proscenium are known as the President's and the Governor's boxes. The main entrance is through wide doors to a spacious marble lobby extending all the way across the building. The façade, stretching along West Forty-fourth Street, is of marble, stone and stucco on a granite base and is also said to be representative of Georgian architecture."

The opening attraction at Erlanger's on the night of September 26, 1927, was George M. Cohan's musical *Merry Malones*, which, with typical Cohan modesty, he wrote, produced, and starred in. It was a hit and got the new theatre off to a good start. It played for 192 performances, strangely interrupted by a short engagement of a flop play called *The Behavior of Mrs. Crane*, then returned for 16 additional performances.

Erlanger's housed the last musical George M. Cohan wrote. It was called *Billie* and was based on Cohan's 1912 play, *Broadway Jones*. He did not appear in it, but it managed to run for 112 performances in 1928-29. This was followed by the popular musical *Hello, Daddy!* which moved here from the Mansfield Theatre. Herbert and Dorothy Fields wrote it for their father, vaudevillian Lew Fields, who starred in it. The remaining shows of 1929 were an unsuccessful revue, *John Murray Anderson's Almanac*, starring Jimmy Savo and Trixie Friganza, with Noël Coward as one of the contributors; and a moderately successful comedy, *Ladies of the Jury*, with Mrs. Fiske as an opinionated juror who sways the other jurors to her way of thinking.

Mrs. Fiske appeared again at Erlanger's in 1930 in a brief revival of Sheridan's comedy *The Rivals*, in which she played Mrs. Malaprop. Next came this theatre's biggest hit thus far, the infectious musical *Fine and Dandy*, with a funny book by Donald Ogden Stewart and a score by Kay Swift and Paul James that included two standards: "Can This Be Love?" and the rousing title tune. Comedian Joe Cook fractured theatregoers with his acrobatics, juggling, daffy gadgets, and inane patter. The hit thrived for 246 performances.

From May 1931 until March 1932 this theatre was

taken over by the Civic Light Opera Company, which presented a successful repertory of Gilbert and Sullivan operettas and other musical entertainments. Then a dark period followed, during which it was decided to rename the theatre the St. James, inspired by the St. James Theatre in London. On December 7, 1932, the theatre reopened with this new name. The star, appropriately, was London's favorite revue comedienne, Beatrice Lillie, in a new revue called *Walk a Little Faster.* Her co-stars were the famed comedy team of Bobby Clark and Paul McCullough, and the score was by Vernon Duke and E.Y. Harburg. The show was staged by Monty Woolley and Albertina Rasch, the production was designed and conceived by Boris Aronson, and the orchestrations were by the fabulous Robert Russell Bennett and Conrad Salinger. So what went wrong? Who knows, but the revue was only a moderate success, running for 121 performances. One gem has survived from this show: the beautiful Duke/Harburg song "April in Paris," which the notoriously tone-deaf drama critics didn't even mention.

After this sophisticated revue, the St. James reverted to Gilbert and Sullivan for several months. An event more balletic than theatrical occurred at this theatre in January 1934. Concert impresario Sol Hurok brought over the Ballet Russe of Monte Carlo and the famed company presented its repertoire from January through April. The

Top: Standard program cover in the early years, when the St. James was known as Erlanger's Theatre. *Above:* Ina Haywood and Robinson Newbold in this theatre's first production, *The Merry Malones* (1927). *Right:* Beatrice Lillie, Bobby Clark, and Paul McCullough cavort in the sleek revue, *Walk a Little Faster* (1932).

lead dancers included Leonide Massine, Irina Baronova, David Lichine, André Eglevesky, Tamara Toumanova, and Sono Osato. It was the beginning of America's ballet craze, and helped lay the groundwork for a more balletic style of Broadway choreography.

Bobby Clark and Paul McCullough returned to the St. James in another gilded revue, *Thumbs Up*, produced by Eddie Dowling, who also starred in the show with his comical wife, Ray Dooley. Two great dancers—Hal Le Roy and Jack Cole—were also in the show, as well as the popular Pickens sisters. It ran for 156 performances and introduced two song hits: James Hanley's "Zing Went the Strings of My Heart" and Vernon Duke's haunting "Autumn in New York."

On December 5, 1935, *May Wine*, a Sigmund Romberg, Oscar Hammerstein II, and Frank Mandel operetta that disguised itself as "a musical play," waltzed into the St. James for 212 performances. Among the large cast were Walter Slezak, Walter Woolf King, Leo G. Carroll, and Jack Cole.

John Gielgud moved his highly successful abridged *Hamlet* from the Empire Theatre to the St. James in January 1937, and Maurice Evans followed him in the title role of the highly praised revival of Shakespeare's *Richard II*, staged by Margaret Webster. This was the first revival of this tragedy in America since Edwin Booth played it in 1878 and it was a triumph. It ran for 132 performances.

A truly delightful fantasy called *Father Malachy's Miracle* opened here on November 17, 1937. The beloved comic Al Shean (of Gallagher and Shean fame) played Father Malachy, a kindly priest who tires of a noisy dance hall across the way from his church and prays for it to be transported to an island far away. It happens and he gets into a lot of trouble because he has not consulted the church hierarchy before working a miracle. Mr. Shean was hailed for his acting and the fantasy ran for 125 performances.

On October 12, 1938, another dramatic milestone occurred at this theatre. The first full-length production of *Hamlet* in America was presented by Maurice Evans, Joseph Verner Reed, and Boris Said. Staged by the Shakespearean expert Margaret Webster, it ran from 6:45 PM until 8:15, with a dinner intermission, then resumed

Top: Lillian Gish and John Gielgud in *Hamlet*, which moved to the St. James in 1937. *Above:* Maurice Evans and Henry Edwards in the uncut revival of *Hamlet* (1938).

from 8:45 until 11:15. Later, the dinner intermission was extended from a half-hour to an hour, bringing the final curtain down at 11:45. The production was a success,

Joan Roberts, Joseph Buloff, Betty Garde, and Celeste Holm in the Rodgers and Hammerstein blockbuster *Oklahoma!*

running for 96 performances. Ophelia was played by Katherine Locke, Gertrude by Mady Christians, and Rosencrantz by Alexander Scourby. Mr. Evans, of course, played Hamlet. In January 1939, Evans switched to playing the rotund Sir John Falstaff in a revival of Shakespeare's *Henry IV, Part 1* with Edmond O'Brien as Henry, Prince of Wales. It was another success, running for 74 performances.

Shakespeare was interrupted for a brief moment by the arrival from the West Coast of the last Earl Carroll *Vanities*, a sorry revue with Jerry Lester and, worst of all, microphones onstage! According to Gerald Bordman in *American Musical Theatre*, this was really the beginning of that monster of our present-day musical theatre: electronic amplification.

Shakespeare returned to the St. James in the fall of 1940 with a splendid production of *Twelfth Night*, co-presented by the Theatre Guild and Gilbert Miller. The cast included Helen Hayes (Viola), Maurice Evans (Malvolio), June Walker (Maria), Wesley Addy (Orsino), and Sophie Stewart (Olivia) in this delightful revival staged by Margaret Webster in the fall of 1940. In March 1941, a dramatic thunderbolt hit this theatre. It was *Native Son*, the dramatization of Richard Wright's novel

of the same name by Mr. Wright and Paul Green. Produced by John Houseman and Orson Welles and directed by Welles, this powerful drama stunned theatregoers with its story of a black man who accidentally kills a white woman. It ran for 114 performances and was chosen one of the season's ten best plays by critic Burns Mantle.

The Boston Comic Opera Company and the Jooss Ballet Dance Theatre presented an exciting season of their works (including Kurt Jooss's brilliant dance drama *The Green Table*) at the St. James from January to March 1942. This event was followed by the hit play *Claudia*, transferred from the Booth, which stayed at this theatre until November. The Theatre Guild then moved in with Philip Barry's comedy, *Without Love*, starring Katharine Hepburn, Elliott Nugent, and Audrey Christie. It was definitely not another winner like *The Philadelphia Story*, being a flimsy notion about a platonic marriage. After 110 performances, it departed. The best thing about the show was the stunning wardrobe designed for Ms. Hepburn by that supreme couturier, Valentina.

On March 31, 1943, a musical play opened at the St. James that was rumored to be hopeless. In fact, the opening night was not sold out, and that was astounding, considering that it was a Theatre Guild production and that it was the first fruit of a new collaboration between Richard Rodgers and Oscar Hammerstein II, with choreography by Agnes de Mille and staging by Rouben Mamoulian. The show was *Oklahoma!* and after the opening night, you needed powerful friends or powerful ticket brokers to get you into the St. James. It became the hottest ticket since *Show Boat* in 1927. At the first matinee the following day, the St. James lobby was jammed with blue-haired ladies and rabid musical comedy lovers all trying to get seats for the show that revolutionized the American musical theatre. Enough has been written about the significance of this musical—integrated book and musical numbers, ballets woven into the plotetera—not to warrant repetition. Notably, it launched the great team of Rodgers and Hammerstein, saved the Theatre Guild from bankruptcy (once again), and directed the course of musicals for decades to come. It ran for 2,212 performances.

Although the musical that followed *Oklahoma!* into this theatre—Frank Loesser's *Where's Charley?*—did not match the artistry of its predecessor, it featured a winning performance by Ray Bolger, who stopped the show at every performance with his engaging number "Once in Love with Amy." George Abbott wrote the libretto and directed the show, which ran for 792 performances. The choreography was by George Balanchine.

A successful revival of *Peter Pan*, starring Jean Arthur and Boris Karloff, with some songs by Leonard Bernstein, moved here from the Imperial Theatre in October 1950 and stayed until mid-January 1951. On March 29, 1951, Rodgers and Hammerstein presented their latest creation, *The King and I*, directed by playwright John Van Druten and choreographed by Jerome Robbins. With Gertrude Lawrence and a practically unknown actor, Yul Brynner, in the leads, the romantic musical based on the popular novel *Anna and the King of Siam* proved an immediate hit and played for 1,246 performances. It also proved to be Gertrude Lawrence's last Broadway show. She passed away while it was still running and was succeeded by Constance Carpenter. In tribute to the great British star, all theatre marquee lights were dimmed for one minute on the night after her death.

Two more successful musicals followed *The King and I* at this theatre. *The Pajama Game* opened in May 1954

Top: Jane Lawrence and Ray Bolger in Frank Loesser's delightful musical, *Where's Charley?. Above:* Jean Arthur enchants in the 1950 revival of *Peter Pan,* which moved here from the Imperial.

and stayed for 1,061 performances; *Li'l Abner* opened in November 1956 and ran for 693 performances.

In 1957 the Shuberts, who owned the St. James at this point, sold the theatre to Scarborough House Inc., which leased it to Jujamcyn Amusement Corporation. It

Yul Brynner dances with Gertrude Lawrence in *The King and I*, her last show.

was the first Broadway theatre owned and operated by Jujamcyn Theatres. In 1987 it was granted landmark status by New York City Landmarks Preservation Commission.

When *Li'l Abner* closed in 1958, the theatre was dark for almost six months and stripped to its skeleton. The

noted stage and interior designer Frederick Fox was engaged to rebuild the house and redecorate it from its original shell. He designed a new marquee and houseboards; new box office and lobby; new foyer walls and floors; a brand-new smoking loggia; a new lighting system and chandelier; sculpture; murals; specially woven fabrics for seats, walls, and carpeting; new house and asbestos curtains; new stairs; and an improved stage and dressing rooms. The latest equipment was installed, including a closed-circuit TV system so that technicians backstage could follow the action onstage. The new St. James was hailed as one of the most beautiful theatres in America.

The first production in the renovated theatre was Rodgers and Hammerstein's *Flower Drum Song*, one of their lesser efforts, which managed to run from December 1, 1958, until May 7, 1960. It was succeeded by *Once Upon a Mattress*, the popular musical starring Carol Burnett, which started at the Off-Broadway Phoenix Theatre and moved to Broadway when it turned into a hit. The score was written by Richard Rodgers's daughter, Mary, in collaboration with Marshall Barer. Ms. Burnett was praised for her zany performance.

Highlights of the 1960s at this theatre included Laurence Olivier and Anthony Quinn in Anouilh's *Becket* (1960); the Comden & Green, Jules Styne, Garson Kanin musical *Do Re Mi* (1960), starring Nancy Walker and Phil Silvers; *Subways Are for Sleeping*, another Comden/Green/Styne collaboration, with Sydney Chaplin, Carol Lawrence, Orson Bean, and Phyllis Newman (who won a Tony for her performance) in 1961; an uninspired Irving Berlin musical, *Mr. President* (1962), also his last Broadway show, starring Robert Ryan and Nanette Fabray; and the exciting John Osborn play *Luther* (1963), which won the Tony Award for best play of the season, starring Albert Finney.

On January 16, 1964, *Hello, Dolly!* exploded at this theatre and by the time it closed on December 27, 1970, it had chalked up 2,844 performances, making it the longest-running Broadway musical up to that time. The David Merrick production, with a score by Jerry Herman, book by Michael Stewart (based on Thornton Wilder's *The Matchmaker*), and direction and choreography by Gower Champion, won a then-record ten Tony Awards. During its run at the St. James, Carol Channing was

Left: Carol Channing sings the title song of *Hello, Dolly!* and wins a Tony Award for her performance (1964). *Above:* The PLAYBILL cover for the Tony Award-winning musical, *Two Gentlemen of Verona* (1971).

succeeded by the following stars: Ginger Rogers, Martha Raye, Betty Grable, Bibi Osterwald, Pearl Bailey, Thelma Carpenter, Phyllis Diller, and Ethel Merman.

In 1971 Joseph Papp then brought his musical success *Two Gentlemen of Verona* from Central Park to this theatre, where it stayed for 613 performances, winning a Tony Award for best musical. The cast included Raul Julia, Clifton Davis, and Jonelle Allen, and all three received Tony nominations.

A revival of *A Streetcar Named Desire* in 1973, with Lois Nettleton, Alan Feinstein, Barbara Eda-Young, and Biff McGuire, was well received, but lasted only 53 performances. A revival of the 1920s musical *Good News* (1974), with Alice Faye and John Payne (who was replaced by Gene Nelson during previews), fared even worse, with only 16 repetitions. A revival of Moliere's *The Misanthrope*, starring Alec McCowen, Diana Rigg, and others, played 94 performances in 1975, and *A Musical Jubilee*, a revue of popular American songs, ran for just 92

performances. A revival of *My Fair Lady* opened in March 1976, with Christine Andreas, Ian Richardson, Brenda Forbes, and George Rose, who won a Tony for his performance as Alfred P. Doolittle, and it had a run of 384 performances.

In February 1978 Comden & Green and Cy Coleman brought in their musical version of the play *Twentieth Century* and called it *On the Twentieth Century*. John Cullum and Kevin Kline won Tony Awards for their performances, and the musical played 453 times.

From the spring of 1979 to the following spring, this theatre booked four unsuccessful productions. They were the Alan Jay Lerner/Burton Lane musical *Carmelina*, *Broadway Opry '79*, *The 1940's Radio Hour*, and the British import *Filumena*, directed by Laurence Olivier and starring his wife, Joan Plowright, along with Frank Finlay.

On April 30, 1980, the hit musical *Barnum* arrived and won a Tony Award for its star, Jim Dale, as well as for its sets (David Mitchell) and costumes (Theoni V.

Left: Twiggy in the "new" Gershwin musical, *My One and Only* (1983). *Right:* Souvenir program cover for *Barnum* (Australian production).

Aldredge). The fanciful musical about the mighty circus impresario P.T. Barnum ran for 854 performances.

In 1982, *Rock 'n Roll! The First 5,000 Years*, a tribute to that genre of music, had a very short run, but it was followed by a solid-gold hit in *My One and Only*, a new version of the old Gershwin musical *Funny Face*. After many troubles on the road, this production opened on May 1, 1983, to some very enthusiastic notices, especially for its two stars, Twiggy and Tommy Tune, and for tap dancer Charles ("Honi") Coles. Mr. Tune won a Tony for his performance and another for his choreography with Thommie Walsh. The musical played here until March 3, 1985 (767 performances).

The next show at the St. James was a revue called *Jerry's Girls*, a tribute to the women who had starred in the musicals of Jerry Herman. It starred Dorothy Loudon, Chita Rivera, and Leslie Uggams, and had choreography by Wayne Cilento. During the run of this revue, Ms. Rivera had a tragic accident and her numbers were performed by a series of her understudies. Fortunately, after years of therapy, she recovered and was able to resume her career.

The hit musical *42nd Street* moved here in 1987 and stayed until 1989. It was followed by *Largely New York*,

starring the brilliant silent comedian Bill Irwin. Then came Tyne Daly in a well-received new production of the classic *Gypsy* for which the TV star won a Tony Award. The musical also won a Tony for Best Revival. In 1991, a musical version of the children's classic *The Secret Garden* opened here and won Tony Awards for Best Book of a Musical (Marsha Norman), Best Featured Actress (Daisy Eagan), and Best Scenic Designer (Heidi Landesman). The popular musical played for 706 performances.

On April 22, 1993, this theatre saw the Broadway premiere of *The Who's Tommy*, the legendary rock opera by Pete Townshend (with additional music and lyrics by fellow Who rockers John Entwistle and Keith Moon), directed by Des McAnuff. The show dazzled critics and audiences with its multimedia effects and driving force. It garnered the following Tony Awards: Best Direction of a Musical (McAnuff), Best Original Music Score (Townshend, tied with Kander and Ebb for *Kiss of the Spider Woman*), Scenic Design (John Arnone), Best Lighting Design (Chris Parry), and Best Choreography (Wayne Cilento). The musical ran for 900 performances.

On April 18, 1996, another hit opened at this theatre. It was the revival of the 1962 Tony Award-winning musical *A Funny Thing Happened on the Way to the Forum*. The

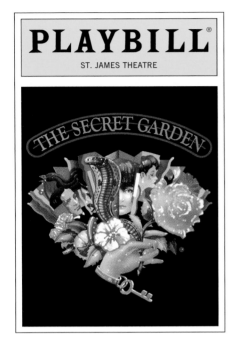
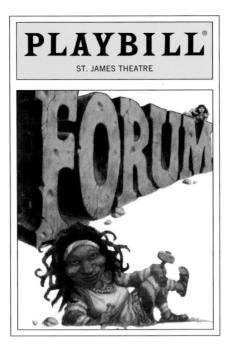

Left: PLAYBILL cover for *The Secret Garden* (1991). *Center: A Funny Thing Happened on the Way to the Forum* with Whoopi Goldberg (1997). *Right:* The stage adaptation of Cole Porter's film *High Society* (1998).

leading role of Pseudolus has been a lucky one for actors. It won the Tony Award for Zero Mostel in the original, Phil Silvers in the 1972 revival, and Nathan Lane in this revival. He was assisted by such skillful farceurs as Lewis J. Stadlen, Mary Testa, Mark Linn Baker, and Ernie Sabella. Mr. Stadlen was nominated for a Tony for his featured performance and Jerry Zaks for his choreography. The musical also received a Tony nomination for Best Musical Revival.

The musical had a novel cast change on February 11, 1997, when Whoopi Goldberg succeeded Mr. Lane as Pseudolus. Cleverly, she left it unclear whether her Pseudolus was supposed to be a man or a woman, but garnered much laughter with her raucous antics and ad-libs. Later in the run, she was succeeded by David Alan Grier. The show ran for 715 performances.

Pop singer Patti LaBelle played a brief engagement at this theatre in January 1998 in an entertainment called *Patti LaBelle on Broadway.*

The next tenant at the St. James seemed promising, but it proved a disappointment. It was a musical version of Philip Barry's classic high comedy, *The Philadelphia Story*, using Cole Porter songs from the film musical version of this property called *High Society*, the latter title

being retained for this stage adaptation. Some other Cole Porter songs from various of his vintage musicals were thrown in, but it was not enough. The production was doomed by the golden memories of the 1939 stage version and the 1940 film version, both starring Katharine Hepburn, and the 1956 movie musical starring Grace Kelly, Frank Sinatra, and Bing Crosby. The musical was directed by Christopher Renshaw, had a book by Arthur Kopit and a cast that included Melissa Errico, John McMartin, Daniel McDonald, Stephen Bogardus, Randy Graff, Marc Kudisch, and precocious youngster Anna Kendrick, who garnered the best reviews as Dinah Lord and was nominated for a Tony Award, as was stage veteran John McMartin. The musical had a short run of 98 performances. When it closed, Jujamcyn shuttered the theatre for eight months and embarked on a $3 million restoration of the St. James that harmoniously incorporated recreations of Beaux-Arts style architectural and design elements recovered from extensive research to return this illustrious house to its original 1927 splendor.

On April 22, 1999, *The Civil War* opened at the newly restored St. James. Frank Wildhorn wrote the music and lyrics and co-authored the book with Gregory Boyd and Jack Murphy. Adding it to his *Jekyll & Hyde*

Left: The cast of *The Civil War* takes a curtain call (1999). Photo by Joan Marcus. *Right:* PLAYBILL from *The Producers* with original stars Nathan Lane and Matthew Broderick (2001).

and *The Scarlet Pimpernel*, Wildhorn became the first American composer in 20 years—since Jerry Herman—to have three musicals on Broadway simultaneously. The moment was marked by a tribute to the composer that put all three casts on the St. James stage at one time. Unfortunately, although his first two musicals ran a long time, *The Civil War* received adverse reviews and lasted only 61 performances. Originally commissioned and produced by Houston's Alley Theatre, it was a song cycle that eschewed plot and dialogue to depict the experiences of Civil War soldiers in song, with occasional spoken lines taken from history. The musical was directed by Jerry Zaks.

The next tenant at this theatre had a run of 461 performances. It was the popular musical *Swing!*, an all-singing, all-dancing entertainment with Ann Hampton Callaway, Everett Bradley, Jennifer Shrader, and J.C. Montgomery. The explosive show showcased

more than thirty numbers directed and choreographed by Lynne Taylor-Corbett, supervised by Jerry Zaks, including such classic songs as "Boogie-Woogie Bugle Boy," "It Don't Mean A Thing," "Sing, Sing, Sing," "Stompin' At The Savoy," and "Blues In The Night." The musical received six Tony Award nominations.

It ran through winter 2001, then closed to make way for Mel Brooks's stage adaptation of his cult film comedy, *The Producers*, which brought back to Broadway a sight rarely seen in the era of telephone and internet ticket sales: a line of ticket buyers down Forty-fourth Street. The musical won a record 12 Tony Awards, including Best Musical and Best Actor in a Musical for star Nathan Lane. It soon set a record top ticket price of $100 for regular seats, and a whopping $480 for VIP seats. A segment of the audience was happy to pay that for the wacky, tuneful, hot-ticket musical comedy.

NEIL SIMON THEATRE

One of Manhattan's most illustrious musical comedy houses, the Neil Simon Theatre was known for most of its history as the Alvin. The theatre was named after the men who built it and produced shows there—Alex Aarons and Vinton Freedley. Having made considerable money producing musicals, Aarons and Freedley built their own playhouse at 250 West Fifty-second Street, facing the stately Guild Theatre (now the Virginia Theatre).

Critic Brooks Atkinson of *The New York Times* wrote about their theatre: "The new Alvin Theatre, set defiantly across the street from the scholarly Theatre Guild, seems to have all the best features of the modern playhouse—even an old English lounge where refreshments may be had. The auditorium is decorated with pastel shades of blue and gray, with ivory and gold decorations. The Alvin can serve 1,400 drama gluttons at one sitting."

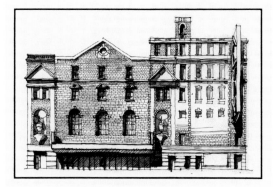

Designed by Herbert J. Krapp, the new house had three floors of offices above it where Aarons and Freedley had their headquarters. The theatre contained a spacious lobby in black marble, and an inner lobby of simple design. There was only one balcony. The ample orchestra pit could accommodate forty-eight musicians, and the stage was spacious enough to allow for the production and staging of the most elaborate musicals.

The Alvin opened auspiciously on November 22, 1927, with the Aarons/Freedley *Funny Face,* a hit musical by George and Ira Gershwin, Paul Gerard Smith, and Fred Thompson. The cast included Fred and Adele Astaire, Victor Moore, Allen Kearns, Betty Compton, William Kent, and the duo pianists Phil Ohman and Victor Arden. The memorable score featured such gems as "He Loves and She Loves," "'S Wonderful," "My One and Only," "The Babbitt and the Bromide," and the title song. The Astaires captivated theatregoers for 250 performances.

The following November, Aarons and Freedley tried again with another Gershwin musical, *Treasure Girl,* but this time they failed. The star was Gertrude Lawrence, and her supporting cast included Paul Frawley, Walter Catlett, Clifton Webb, Mary Hay, and Ohman and Arden at the ivories. But the show's book was uninspired and the critics complained that Ms. Lawrence had to play a disagreeable liar. Clifton Webb's and Mary Hay's dancing was applauded and the Gershwin tunes included "I Don't Think I'll Fall in Love Today," "Feeling I'm Falling," and "I've Got a Crush on You." The musical expired after 69 performances.

In 1929 the Theatre Guild production of *Wings Over Europe,* a startling drama that speculated about the destructive power of atomic energy, moved here from the Martin Beck Theatre. This was followed by two Rodgers and Hart musicals in succession. The first was *Spring Is Here,* with a book by Owen Davis from his play *Shotgun Wedding.* It was not one of Rodgers and Hart's triumphs,

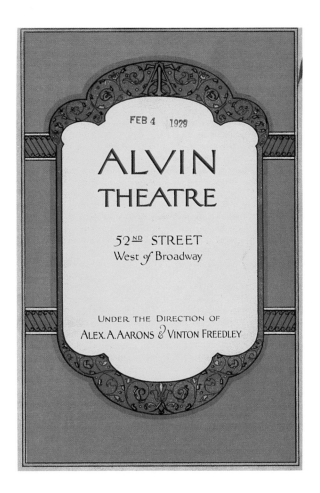

opened. It was the Aarons/Freedley production of George and Ira Gershwin's *Girl Crazy,* with a book by Guy Bolton and John McGowan. The cast included Ginger Rogers, Willie Howard, Allen Kearns, William Kent, and the Foursome. But it was Ethel Merman, making her Broadway debut, who shook the Alvin with her electrifying rendition of the classic "I Got Rhythm." The musical ran for 272 performances.

Eugene O'Neill's great trilogy, *Mourning Becomes Electra,* moved here from the Guild Theatre across the street in 1932.

Jerome Kern's *Music in the Air* was an enormous hit in 1932 at this theatre, which did not have another

Above: Standard program cover for the Alvin Theatre in the 1920s. *Right:* Helen Hayes loses her head in Maxwell Anderson's *Mary of Scotland* (1933).

but a pleasant show with two songs that lasted: "With a Song in My Heart" and "Yours Sincerely." In the cast were Inez Courtney, Glenn Hunter, Charles Ruggles, and Joyce Barbour. *Spring Is Here* lasted 104 performances. *Heads Up!,* the next Rodgers and Hart musical, had a book by John McGowan and Paul Gerard Smith and contained a lovely song that is sometimes heard in supper clubs—"A Ship Without a Sail." The cast included Ray Bolger, Victor Moore, Betty Starbuck, Jack Whiting, Barbara Newberry, and Lewis (later, Lew) Parker. Victor Moore won raves for his comedy routines. The musical ran for 144 performances.

In 1930 the Theatre Guild's production of Shaw's *The Apple Cart,* with Claude Rains and Violet Kemble Cooper, moved here from the Martin Beck. Then, on October 14, 1930, one of this theatre's historic musicals

theatrical booking until May 29, 1933, when The Players chose it as the house for their twelfth annual revival of a classic play. They scheduled a revival of *Uncle Tom's Cabin* for a week, but it was so popular that it stayed for three. The distinguished cast included Otis Skinner as Uncle Tom, Fay Bainter as Topsy, Thomas Chalmers as Simon Legree, Elizabeth Risdon as Eliza, Minnie Dupree as Aunt Ophelia, Cecilia Loftus as Aunt Chloe, and Gene Lockhart as Gumption Cute.

The Alvin housed a distinguished play in the fall of 1933. It was the Theatre Guild production of Maxwell Anderson's verse play *Mary of Scotland*, starring Helen Hayes in the title role, Helen Menken as Queen Elizabeth, and Philip Merivale as the Earl of Bothwell.

On the night of November 21, 1934, one of the Depression's most glittering first-night audiences gathered at the Alvin to roar its approval of Cole Porter's felicitous musical *Anything Goes*. This show had a very shaky history. The original libretto by Guy Bolton and P.G. Wodehouse involved a group of zany characters on a luxury liner that is shipwrecked. Just as the musical was about to go into rehearsal, the luxury liner S.S. Morro Castle burned off the coast of Asbury Park and the musical's plot seemed very unfunny. With Bolton and Wodehouse out of the country, producer Vinton Freedley turned in desperation to the show's director, Howard Lindsay, who hired press agent Russel Crouse to help him quickly write a new libretto. The show went into rehearsal with only a portion of the first act on paper. They kept the action on a luxury liner, but dropped the shipwreck notion. The result was a triumph of mirth and melody, with Ethel Merman as Reno Sweeney (a parody of Aimee Semple MacPherson) traveling with her band of singers, called "Angels." Victor Moore was Public Enemy No. 13, gangster Moon-Face Mooney, disguised as Reverend Dr. Moon (with a machine gun in his violin case), and William Gaxton was a playboy in pursuit of Hope Harcourt (Bettina Hall). Porter wrote his greatest score to that time, including "I Get a Kick Out Of You," "You're the Top," "All Through the Night," "Blow, Gabriel, Blow," and the infectious title song, The musical became the most representative show of the 1930s—glamorous, screwball, slightly risqué, very topical, and very sophisticated. It ran for 420 performances.

In October 1935, the Gershwins and DuBose Heyward brought their magnificent opera *Porgy and Bess* to the Alvin. The reception was mixed and it played only 124 times. George Gershwin went to his grave two years later thinking it was a failure, but revivals have helped audiences recognize it as his masterpiece and the capstone of his career.

In October of 1936, Vinton Freedley hoped to strike gold again with another Ethel Merman/Cole Porter show. This one was called *Red, Hot and Blue!* and there was trouble from the very start. Both Ethel and her co-star, Jimmy Durante, wanted top billing. After much haggling, Mrs. Porter came up with a solution: a criss-cross arrangement of the two names so that each could be construed as having top billing. The other star, Bob Hope, took to lying down and mugging during one of Ethel's song numbers and she threatened "to sit on the son of a bitch" if he didn't stop. He stopped. The show was not another *Anything Goes*. The plot, by Howard Lindsay and Russel Crouse, was about a national lottery. The winner was the person who could find one "Peaches Le Fleur," who had a distinctive mark on her behind because she once sat on a hot waffle iron. The Supreme Court got into the lottery and began examining show girls in cellophane skirts to see if they had the winning mark. The dippy show ran for 181 performances and the most memorable moments were provided by Durante, as a polo-playing convict, and three great Porter songs: "It's De-Lovely," "Ridin' High," and "Down in the Depths (On the Ninetieth Floor)."

On November 2, 1937, George M. Cohan returned to this theatre as President Franklin D. Roosevelt in the satirical musical *I'd Rather Be Right,* and the occasion turned into one of Broadway's most flamboyant opening nights. The fact that no living U.S. president had ever been portrayed onstage (and in a satire, no less) and the added lure that the show was the creation of Rodgers and Hart, George S. Kaufman, and Moss Hart made this a must-see event. Reported Lucius Beebe in *Stage* magazine: "Probably no theatrical event has occasioned such civic tumult since the Astor Place Riots. All New York wanted in, as the phrase has it. New York seemed completely overwhelmed by the return of Mr. Cohan, and popular rejoicing and Morris dancing in Longacre

Ethel Merman and chorus belt out Cole Porter's rousing "Blow, Gabriel, Blow" in *Anything Goes* (1934).

Square complemented the most insufferable crush, confusion, and amiable uproar Fifty-second Street has ever known."

Although *I'd Rather Be Right* was not as biting as *Of Thee I Sing,* Cohan's affectionate portrayal of F.D.R. and his delightful tap dancing made the show one of the season's sold-out delights. Only one Rodgers and Hart song was played beyond the show: "Have You Met Miss Jones?" The musical ran for 289 performances.

In November 1938, Rodgers and Hart and George Abbott brought to the Alvin their memorable musical *The Boys from Syracuse,* based on Shakespeare's *The Comedy of Errors,* with Eddie Albert and Ronald Graham as one set of twins, Jimmy Savo and Teddy Hart (brother of lyricist Lorenz) as the other set, and Muriel Angelus,

Marcy Wescott, Wynn Murray, Betty Bruce, and Burl Ives. With choreography by George Balanchine and such lilting songs as "This Can't Be Love," "Falling in Love With Love," and "Sing for Your Supper," the exuberant musical ran for 235 performances.

In February 1940, to aid the Finnish Relief Fund, the Lunts brought back their 1935 revival of *The Taming of the Shrew.* It was a short engagement but a notable one for a worthy war cause. In April of that year, they returned to this theatre in Robert E. Sherwood's *There Shall Be No Night,* which was awarded the Pulitzer Prize. It was a powerful denunciation of war and, in particular, Russia's invasion of Finland. The play showed the devastating effects of this attack on a Finnish family. The supporting cast included Montgomery Clift, Richard

Whorf, Sydney Greenstreet, Elizabeth Praser, and Phyllis Thaxter. It ran for 115 performances, took a vacation, then resumed for 66 additional performances.

On January 23, 1941, the Alvin housed one of the American Musical Theatre's finest works: *Lady in the Dark* by Moss Hart, Kurt Weill, and Ira Gershwin. Gertrude Lawrence scored one of her greatest triumphs in it, bumping and grinding to one of the musical's greatest tunes, "The Saga of Jenny." Danny Kaye also stopped the show with his tongue-twister "Tschaikowsky." The supporting cast included Bert Lytell, Macdonald Carey, Victor Mature, and Margaret Dale. The choreography by Albertina Rasch and the opulent sets and costumes made it one of the most memorable musicals ever seen on Broadway. Brooks Atkinson in *The New York Times* called it "a work of theatre art." It ran for 467 performances.

On January 7, 1943, there was a unique opening night at the Alvin for the latest Cole Porter/Ethel Merman musical, *Something for the Boys*. This was the

date that a new government ruling went into effect because of the war. Private automobiles could not be driven to places of entertainment, therefore Fifty-second Street was jammed with taxicabs, all honking to get through the crush. The musical, with Paula Laurence, Allen Jenkins, Betty Garrett, Bill Johnson, Jed Prouty, Betty Bruce, and—in the chorus—Dody Goodman, was a smash hit. Its plot, by Herbert and Dorothy Fields, was even more foolish than that of *Red, Hot and Blue!* Ms. Merman played a defense worker who got carborundum in her teeth fillings, which turned her into a radio receiving set. At the show's climax, she saved an army plane from crashing by receiving landing instructions via her teeth. Wartime audiences ate this up for 422 performances.

A series of failures played this theatre during 1944 and 1945. They were a musical called *Jackpot,* with Nanette Fabray, Benny Baker, Allan Jones, Wendell Corey, and Betty Garrett; *Helen Goes to Troy*, a new musical version of Offenbach's operetta *La Belle Hélène*, with Ernest Truex and Jarmila Novotna; *The Firebrand of Florence,* a musical version of the play *The Firebrand,* by Kurt Weill, Ira Gershwin, and Edwin Justus Mayer, with Lotte Lenya; and *Hollywood Pinafore*, George S. Kaufman's modern interpretation of Gilbert and

Above: Polo-playing convict Jimmy Durante taps Ethel Merman's wire in *Red, Hot and Blue!* (1936). *Top Right:* George M. Cohan as F.D.R. gives a fireside chat in *I'd Rather Be Right* (1937).

Lynn Fontanne, Montgomery Clift, and Alfred Lunt in the Pulitzer-winning play *There Shall Be No Night* (1940).

Sullivan's *Pinafore,* with Victor Moore, William Gaxton, and Shirley Booth. More successful was a revival of *The Tempest,* as interpreted by Margaret Webster and Eva Le Gallienne and starring Vera Zorina, Arnold Moss, Canada Lee, and Frances Heflin.

Betty Comden, Adolph Green, and Morton Gould combined talents on *Billion Dollar Baby,* an interesting musical about the Roaring Twenties. Mitzi Green, Joan McCracken, Helen Gallagher, Danny Daniels, William Tabbert, and David Burns gave vivid performances, and the show amused postwar audiences for 220 performances.

Ingrid Bergman scored a triumph in Maxwell Anderson's *Joan of Lorraine* (1946), with Sam Wanamaker and Romney Brent also giving memorable performances in this unconventional interpretation of the story of Joan of Arc.

In 1947 *Life with Father* moved to the Alvin from the Bijou Theatre and ended its record run here of 3,224 performances, making it the longest-running straight play in the history of the American theatre—a record that it still holds.

On October 8, 1947, Maurice Evans opened his highly successful revival of Shaw's *Man and Superman* and starred in it for 294 performances. This was followed by one of the Alvin's most fondly-remembered bookings: *Mister Roberts,* the navy comedy, which opened on February 18, 1948, and stayed in port at the Alvin until January 6, 1951, for a total of 1,157 performances. The Thomas Heggen/Joshua Logan play starred Henry

Fonda, who won a Tony Award for his performance in the title role. Other Tony Awards went to the play, to its producer, and to its authors.

Highlights of the 1950s at this theatre included Sidney Kingsley's adaptation of Arthur Koestler's novel *Darkness at Noon* (1951), which won a Tony Award for its star, Claude Rains; the musical version of Betty Smith's novel *A Tree Grows in Brooklyn* (1951), by Ms. Smith, George Abbott, Arthur Schwartz, and Dorothy Fields, starring Shirley Booth, Johnny Johnston, Marcia Van Dyke, and Nathaniel Frey: Henry Fonda again in *Point of No Return* (1951), Paul Osborn's dramatization of John P. Marquand's novel of the same name, with Leora Dana, Frank Conroy, and John Cromwell.

In 1952 Bette Davis rashly starred in a Vernon Duke revue called *Two's Company,* but the decision was ill-advised. It closed after 90 performances. Mary Martin and Charles Boyer starred in a humdrum comedy, *Kind Sir,* by Norman Krasna in 1953. The spring of 1954 brought the Phoenix Theatre production of *The Golden Apple,* based on Homer's *Iliad* and *Odyssey,* which won the New York Drama Critics Circle Award for best musical of the season, though it continued for only 173 performances. This was followed in December 1954 by *House of Flowers,* a musical by Truman Capote and Harold Arlen, directed by Peter Brook, and starring Pearl Bailey, Diahann Carroll, Ray Walston, Juanita Hall, and dancers Alvin Ailey, Geoffrey Holder, and Carmen de Lavallade. Although the score, sets, costumes, and cast were praised, the musical had a weak book and it did not recoup its large investment despite a run of 165 performances.

On October 20, 1955, *No Time for Sergeants* opened and convulsed theatregoers for 796 performances. Ira Levin's comedy, based on Mac Hyman's novel, starred Andy Griffith as an amiable southerner who throws the army into an uproar with his friendly simplicity; Roddy McDowall played his army buddy.

The late 1950s at this theatre housed some musicals that were only moderately successful: *Oh, Captain!* (1958), with Tony Randall, Abbe Lane, Susan Johnson, and Alexandra Danilova; and *First Impressions*, a musical version of *Pride and Prejudice* (1959), starring Hermione Gingold, Farley Granger, Polly Bergen, Phyllis Newman, and Ellen Hanley. During these years, there were also engagements of *Jerome Robbins' Ballet U.S.A.*, and *Bells Are Ringing*, the musical that moved here from the Shubert.

The 1960s brought Frank Loesser's unsuccessful musical *Greenwillow* (1960), starring Anthony Perkins, Ellen McCown, Pert Kelton, and Cecil Kellaway; the Ballets Africains and *West Side Story*, from the Winter Garden (1960): Lucille Ball in a moderately entertaining musical (and Cy Coleman's Broadway debut), *Wildcat* (1961); *Irma La Douce* (1961), the hit musical from the Plymouth Theatre; an unsuccessful revue, *New Faces of 1962*; and a huge hit, A *Funny Thing Happened on the Way to the Forum,* the Stephen Sondheim/Burt Shevelove/Larry Gelbart musical based on several plays by Roman playwright Plautus, directed by George Abbott and starring Zero Mostel, David Burns, Jack Gilford, John Carradine, and Raymond Walburn. This antic production tickled theatregoers for 964 performances.

Beatrice Lillie made her final Broadway appearance at the Alvin in 1964 in *High Spirits,* an uproarious musical version of Noël Coward's comedy *Blithe Spirit,* by Hugh Martin and Timothy Gray, staged by Coward. Miss Lillie was brilliant as the medium, Madam Arcati, and she was splendidly assisted by Tammy Grimes, Edward Woodward, and Louise Troy. The musical ran for 376 performances.

Maurice Chevalier at 77, a personal appearance by

Ingrid Bergman plays Saint Joan in Maxwell Anderson's play-within-a-play *Joan of Lorraine* (1946).

the French singer, came to the Alvin in 1965, as did the Broadway debut of Liza Minnelli in an unsuccessful musical, *Flora, The Red Menace*, the Broadway debut of Kander and Ebb as a team. Other unsuccessful shows followed: a musical version of the best-selling book *The*

Above: From left: David Wayne, Henry Fonda, and Robert Keith sample some homemade Scotch in *Mister Roberts* (1948). *Below:* Andrea McArdle as Little Orphan Annie is menaced by Dorothy Loudon, as Janine Ruane and Robyn Finn look on in *Annie* (1977).

Yearling (1965); a musical adaptation of the Superman comic strip called *It's a Bird It's a Plane It's Superman* (1966); an all-star revival of *Dinner at Eight* (1966); and a musical version of *The Man Who Came To Dinner,* called *Sherry!* (1967). Finally, a palpable hit arrived in October 1967, when Tom Stoppard's coruscating play *Rosencrantz and Guildenstern Are Dead* opened. The dazzling work, which offered *Hamlet* as seen through the eyes of two of its minor characters, won a Tony Award as the best drama of the season. It was brilliantly acted by John Wood, Paul Hecht, and Brian Murray. It played for 421 performances.

Another powerful drama, *The Great White Hope,* by Howard Sackler, opened here in 1968 and won the Pulitzer Prize, New York Drama Critics Circle Award, and Tony Award for best play. James Earl Jones and Jane Alexander won Tony Awards for their memorable performances as the first black heavyweight champion of the world and his tragic girlfriend. The play ran for 557 performances.

In the spring of 1970 Harold Prince arrived with an exciting, groundbreaking musical, *Company,* by Stephen Sondheim and George Furth. A popular bachelor (played by Dean Jones briefly, then succeeded by Larry Kert) takes a tour through the imperfect marriages of his

demanding friends in a series of musical sketches. *Company* won seven Tony Awards, including Best Musical, Best Book, Best Music, Best Lyrics, and Best Direction. Boris Aronson's magnificent set—a skeletal

Above: Zero Mostel chastises Raymond Walburn in the antic musical, *A Funny Thing Happened on the Way to the Forum* (1963). *Below:* Medium Beatrice Lillie in her last show, *High Spirits,* with ghostly Tammy Grimes (1964).

apartment house with running elevators—also won a Tony.

Shenandoah, a musical that arrived from the Goodspeed Opera House in Connecticut in 1975, starred John Cullum, who won a Tony Award for his performance in this Civil War musical. Next came a veritable gold mine for this theatre, another winner from the Goodspeed Opera House, called *Annie.* Martin Charnin, Thomas Meehan, and Charles Strouse's musical adaptation of the popular comic strip "Little Orphan Annie" played at the Alvin for almost five years before moving to another theatre. It received Tony Awards for Best Musical, Best Book, Best Score, Best Sets, Best Costumes, Best Choreography, and Best Actress (Dorothy Loudon, as the villainous Miss Hannigan). Young Andrea McArdle was highly praised for her acting of Annie and the beguiling orphans also received raves. It was a great family show and ran for 2,377 performances.

After *Annie* left the Alvin, the theatre had five musical failures in succession: *Merrily We Roll Along, The Little Prince and the Aviator* (which closed during previews), *Little Johnny Jones, Do Black Patent Leather Shoes Really Reflect Up?,* and *Seven Brides for Seven Brothers.*

Next came a revival of *Your Arms Too Short To Box With God* starring Al Green and Patti LaBelle. It was

followed by Neil Simon's *Brighton Beach Memoirs,* the first play of an autobiographical trilogy about his youth with his family, which won the New York Drama Critics Circle Award for the season's best play. Matthew Broderick won a Tony Award for his performance and Zeljko Ivanek, Elizabeth Franz, Peter Michael Goetz, Joyce Van Patten, and Mindy Ingber also sparkled.

On Wednesday, June 29, 1983, the Alvin was officially renamed the Neil Simon Theatre in honor of one of America's most prolific playwrights.

In 1985, the second play of Mr. Simon's trilogy— *Biloxi Blues*—opened here and won the following Tony Awards: Best Play, Best Featured Actor (Barry Miller), Best Director of a Play (Gene Saks). The play ran here for over a year. Next came an unlikely musical called *Into the Light,* about scientists testing the veracity of the Shroud of Turin. Starring Dean Jones, the show had a brief run of 6 performances.

In March, 1987, a revival of Noël Coward's *Blithe Spirit* starred Richard Chamberlain, Blythe Danner, Judith Ivey, and the admired actress Geraldine Page. Tragically, on June 13, 1987, in the midst of its run, Ms. Page died. Patricia Conolly succeeded her in the plum role of Madame Arcati. Ms. Page was nominated for a Tony Award for her performance.

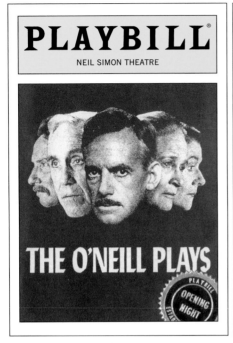 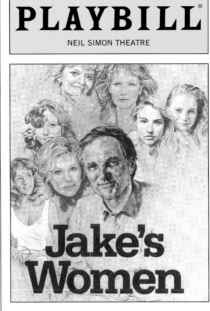 

Left: Opening night PLAYBILL cover for the paired booking of O'Neill's *Long Day's Journey Into Night* and *Ah! Wilderness* (1988). *Center:* Neil Simon's comedy *Jake's Women* (1992). *Right:* Matthew Bourne's *Swan Lake* (1998).

In October, 1987, *Mort Sahl On Broadway* played a limited engagement, followed by a London success, *Breaking the Code*, by Hugh Whitmore, a playwright who liked to use real-life situations in his plays (*Stevie* and *Pack of Lies*). Based on the book *Alan Turing, the Enigma* by Andrew Hodges, the play dealt with the brilliant, but eccentric British mathematician who broke Nazi Germany's "Enigma" code during World War II, saving millions of Allied lives. The play's title had two meanings: Turing not only broke the mathematical code, but the moral code, because he was a homosexual at a time when that was a criminal offense and branded him a security risk. Turing was brilliantly played by Derek Jacobi. He was nominated for a Best Actor In a Play Tony Award and his co-star, Michael Gough was nominated as Best Featured Actor in a play. The drama ran for 161 performances and was later televised.

In June, 1988, as part of the First New York International Festival of the Arts, two Eugene O'Neill plays were revived: *Long Day's Journey Into Night* and *Ah, Wilderness!* both starring Colleen Dewhurst and Jason Robards. Elizabeth Wilson and George Hearn also appeared in the latter play, O'Neill's only comedy. *Long Day's Journey Into Night* played for 28 performances; *Ah, Wilderness!* for 12. The latter play was nominated for a Best Play Revival Tony Award.

In the fall of 1988, *Kenny Loggins On Broadway* presented the singer-composer in a program of folk and rock songs. The engagement ran for 8 performances. In January, 1989, two musicals with music by Tom O'Horgan were announced to open at this theatre. One of them, *Senator Joe*, played only three days of previews, then closed before the official opening; the other one, *The Tower of Babel* never even had a preview.

From the Theatre Royal Haymarket in London came Peter Hall's revival of Tennessee Williams's *Orpheus Descending* in September, 1989. It starred Vanessa Redgrave and Kevin Anderson, with Tammy Grimes and Anne Twomey in the supporting cast. Ms. Redgrave's performance was admired by some and deemed "wrong-headed" by others. The revival lasted for 97 performances.

There was a limited engagement by the Don Cossacks, the State Academic Ensemble of Rostov, USSR in January, 1990. Later in the year, *Jackie Mason: Brand New*, another of his hysterical one-man shows of topical barbs, played from October 1990 to June 1991.

On March 24, 1992, Neil Simon's *Jake's Women* opened with an impressive cast: Alan Alda, Helen Shaver, Kate Burton, Joyce Van Patten, and Brenda Vaccaro. Directed by Gene Saks, the play dealt with the women in the life of Jake (Simon's alter-ego), acted by Mr. Alda. His relationships with six women were depicted both in actuality and in fantasy—in Jake's mind. The play received mixed reviews and it reminded one critic of the musical *Company*, which examines the relationships of the leading male character with his friends. Some critics felt that the play's philosophies were rather shallow. It ran for 245 performances.

Cyrano: The Musical, based on the classic play by Edmond Rostand, arrived here from the Netherlands on November 21, 1993. It did not receive enthusiastic reviews, but it ran for 137 performances and was praised for its sets, lights and costumes. It received the following Tony Award nominations: Best Musical, Best Original Score, Best Book of a Musical, and Best Costumes.

An odd play from London, *The Rise and Fall of Little Voice*, arrived on May 1, 1994, and lasted only until May 8. It depicted a shy girl (Hynden Walch) with a talent for impersonating famous singers (Judy Garland, Edith Piaf,

etc.). The critics judged it to be a tasteless, minor English comedy, but it was later filmed.

Another short run was achieved by another vocal acrobat, impressionist Danny Gans, who called himself "The Man of Many Voices." He claimed that he could impersonate more than 200 famous voices and one critic wrote that it seemed as if he did all 200 of them in his intermissionless show, which ran for only 6 performances in 1995.

A welcome hit opened on April 11, 1996: a handsome revival of Rodgers and Hammerstein's beloved *The King and I*. Donna Murphy played Anna and Lou Diamond Phillips played the King of Siam. Both received excellent reviews. It was a sumptuous production and it won Tony Awards for Ms. Murphy (Best Actress in a Musical), for Best Musical Revival, for Brian Thomson (Best Scenic Designer), for Roger Kirk (Best Costume Designer). It also received the following Tony Award nominations: Best Actor in a Musical (Phillips), Best Featured Actress in a Musical (Joohee Choi), Best Musical Director (Christopher Renshaw), and Best Lighting Designer (Nigel Levings). During its long run (807 performances) Ms. Murphy was succeeded as Mrs. Anna by Faith Prince and Marie Osmond; Mr. Phillips

Lou Diamond Phillips and Donna Murphy ask "Shall We Dance" in a sumptious revival of *The King and I* (1996). Photo by Joan Marcus.

PLAYBILL cover and a scene from Susan Stroman's revival of *The Music Man* (2000). Photo by Joan Marcus.

was succeeded as King by Kevin Gray.

An unusual and critically acclaimed dance entertainment came to this theatre from London and Los Angeles on October 8, 1998. It was Matthew Bourne's trendy version of *Swan Lake,* featuring a bevy of hirsute male swans. The plot featured a Prince with a smothering mother, who searches for love among the gay swans. Tony Awards were garnered by Matthew Bourne for Direction and Choreography, and by Lez Brotherston for Costumes. Adam Cooper was nominated as Leading Actor in a Musical. The popular spectacle had a limited engagement of 124 performances.

The last show at the Neil Simon Theatre before the celebration of the millennium was *The Scarlet Pimpernel,* nicknamed *Version 3.0* because it was the third version of

this musical by Frank Wildhorn and Nan Knighton. The first, in 1997, played 373 performances at the Minskoff Theatre, the second in 1998 played for 239 performances, and the last, at this theatre, lasted for 129 performances.

In spring 2000, Susan Stroman directed a major revival of Meredith Willson's classic, *The Music Man,* starring Rebecca Luker and Craig Bierko. The production was memorable for its finale, in which the entire cast appeared dressed as a marching band, toting trombones, and were led by Bierko in playing the show's signature tune, "Seventy-six Trombones."

The Neil Simon is currently owned by the Nederlander Organization, and is one of Broadway's most sought-after houses.

ETHEL BARRYMORE THEATRE

I n 1927, when Ethel Barrymore was appearing at Maxine Elliott's Theatre in Somerset Maugham's hit play *The Constant Wife*, playwright Zoe Atkins came to her with an irresistible proposition. Miss Atkins said that the Shuberts wanted Miss Barrymore to star in a new play for them—and were willing to build a theatre in her name if she consented. Miss Barrymore read the play, a religious drama called *The Kingdom of God*, liked it, and thereupon agreed to switch to Shubert management.

The Ethel Barrymore Theatre, designed by Herbert J. Krapp, opened on the night of December 20, 1928. The star played Sister Gracia, a character who aged from nineteen to seventy. Wrote Brooks Atkinson in *The New York Times*: "As the curtain raiser for a splendid new theatre that fittingly bears her own name, Ethel Barrymore has chosen a quiet and elusive piece by that dexterous Spaniard, G. Martinez Sierra. For Miss Barrymore, it serves as a vehicle." Critic Heywood Broun was more enthusiastic. He wrote: "Miss Barrymore's performance is the most moving piece of acting I have ever seen in the theatre."

With more than 1,000 seats, the Barrymore was ideal for dramas, comedies, and intimate musicals. Miss Barrymore chose for her next appearance at her theatre one of those Hungarian romances in which the lovers are named He and She. *The Love Duel*, as it was called, starred Barrymore as She and Louis Calhern as He, and it was directed (as *The Kingdom of God* had been) by E.M. Blythe (who happened to be Ethel Barrymore). This Hungarian trifle ran for 88 performances.

In 1929, John Drinkwater's hit comedy *Bird in Hand* moved to the Barrymore from the Morosco for three months. This was followed by a fascinating drama called *Death Takes a Holiday*, in which Philip Merivale played death on vacation, masquerading as Prince Sirki. Death falls in love with a young mortal named Grazia (Rose Hobart) and takes her with him (willingly) as he returns to "the other side." This fanciful play engrossed theatregoers for 181 performances.

Topaze, a popular comedy, moved here from the Music Box in 1930, with Frank Morgan, Catherine Willard, and Clarence Derwent. Miriam Hopkins appeared very fleetingly in another of those Hungarian romances, *His Majesty's Car*. Ethel Barrymore returned in blackface to do a play about blacks called *Scarlet Sister Mary*. The critics felt that whites should not attempt to portray blacks when blacks did it so much better, and this curious drama ran for only 23 performances. It did, however, serve to introduce Miss Barrymore's daughter, Ethel Barrymore Colt, in her Broadway debut.

The beautiful Billie Burke returned to the stage in Ivor Novello's 1930 play *The Truth Game*, in which the author also appeared. *The Times* labeled the work "a perfect matinee comedy" and audiences flocked to it for 105 performances. The following year brought Edna Best,

Left: Ethel Barrymore as Sister Gracia in *The Kingdom of God,* the play that opened the theatre built for her by the Shuberts (1928). *Right:* Philip Merivale as the Grim Reaper prepares to take Rose Hobart with him to the "other side" in *Death Takes a Holiday* (1929).

Basil Rathbone, and Earle Larrimore in a French triangle situation, *Melo,* but it was only moderately successful. Later in the year, Ethel Barrymore returned in Lee Shubert's revival of *The School for Scandal,* and this time the actress introduced her son, John Drew Colt, to Broadway.

Socialite/actress Hope Williams starred in something called *The Passing Present* in 1931, with Maria Ouspenskaya, but this made way after 16 performances for a more deserving production, *Whistling in the Dark.* Starring the amusing Ernest Truex as a detective story writer who is forced by a gang of gunmen to concoct a perfect crime, the comedy delighted Barrymore patrons for 144 performances.

Here Today, a "comedy of bad manners," by George Oppenheimer, directed by George S. Kaufman, amused first-nighters in September 1932 mainly because the acid-mouth character played by Ruth Gordon was supposed to be no less than acid-mouth Dorothy Parker. But the general public did not take to this evening of bitchiness and the play folded after 39 performances. John Van Druten's more civilized comedy hit, *There's Always Juliet,* moved here next from Henry Miller's Theatre.

On November 29, 1932, the Barrymore Theatre housed its first musical, Cole Porter's *Gay Divorce.* Fred Astaire, without his sister Adele for the first time, danced with the blonde Claire Luce, who once rode a live ostrich in the *Ziegfeld Follies.* Astaire and Luce singing and dancing Porter's haunting "Night and Day" helped to turn this into a hit. The scintillating cast included the

From left: Alfred Lunt, Lynn Fontanne, and Noël Coward in Coward's ménage-a-trois comedy *Design for Living* (1933).

venomous Luella Gear and the wry Eric Blore and Erik Rhodes, who would repeat their roles when Astaire appeared in the movie version, slightly retitled *Gay Divorcee*. The stage version had to move to the Shubert Theatre to make way for another event at the Barrymore, but rang up a total of 248 performances.

On January 24, 1933, Alfred Lunt, Lynn Fontanne, and Noël Coward dazzled first nighters in *Design for Living*, a comedy Coward had promised to write for them and himself as a starring vehicle. Mr. Coward, who did not relish long runs, limited this engagement to 135 performances, but it could have run all season. The play presented two men in love with the same woman, but when she was not available, in love with themselves. One critic described this as the most amoral situation ever viewed on the Broadway stage. It proved an acting triumph for this gilded trio.

A mystery play, *Ten-Minute Alibi*, with Bramwell Fletcher, John Williams, and Joseph Spurin-Calleia, was a moderate success in the fall of 1933. This was succeeded by *Jezebel*, a southern drama by Owen Davis, originally written for Tallulah Bankhead. When she became ill, Miriam Hopkins stepped in, but the play was not a success. It later made an excellent film for Bette Davis.

The year 1934 was not a bountiful one for this theatre. No fewer than seven failures paraded across its stage. Theatregoers looked forward to Noël Coward's *Point Valaine*, starring the Lunts, Osgood Perkins, Louis Hayward, and Broderick Crawford, in January 1935, but the play was sordid and overly melodramatic, with Lunt spitting in Fontanne's face in one scene. This turgid tale of tropical lust expired none too soon after 56 performances.

The hit play *The Distaff Side* moved here from the Longacre Theatre in March 1935. Later in the year, Philip Merivale and his wife, Gladys Cooper, brought their revivals of *Othello* and *Macbeth*, but they were not successful. A historical play, *Parnell*, with George Curzon as the Irish hero, fared better, playing for 98 performances. Irwin Shaw provided excitement in 1936 with his one-act war play *Bury the Dead*, paired with another short work, *Prelude*, by J. Edward Shugrue and John O'Shaughnessy, which moved theatregoers for 97 performances. In the fall of 1936, the British playwright/actor Emlyn Williams starred in his terrifying *Night Must Fall*, based on an actual case in the British courts. He played a charming psychopath who carries one of his victims' head around in a hat box. May Whitty (later Dame May Whitty) played his intended next victim.

On December 26, 1936, Clare Boothe Luce's play *The Women* opened at this theatre with about forty women in the cast and not one male. Critic Brooks Atkinson called it "a kettle of venom" in *The New York Times* and said he disliked it. It promptly became the Barrymore's longest running play to date, keeping that kettle bubbling for 657 performances, with such brittle actresses as Ilka Chase, Margalo Gillmore, Betty Lawford, Arlene Francis, Audrey Christie, and Marjorie Main.

In October 1938 the Playwrights' Company presented the Maxwell Anderson/Kurt Weill musical *Knickerbocker Holiday*, starring Walter Huston as Peter Stuyvesant. It is chiefly remembered today for Huston's magnificent rendition of the classic "September Song."

The spring of 1939 brought Katharine Cornell in a rarity—a modern comedy by S.N. Behrman called *No Time for Comedy*. Laurence Olivier costarred as her playwright husband who is swayed by his mistress

(Margalo Gillmore) to switch from writing hit comedies and instead attempt a stuffy drama. The public took to Cornell in high-fashion gowns by Valentina, and the comedy ran for 185 performances, with Olivier turning into a matinee idol.

The last show to play this theatre in the 1930s was Maxwell Anderson's *Key Largo*, a moderate hit with Paul Muni, Uta Hagen, José Ferrer, and Carl (later Karl) Malden. It ran for 105 performances.

Highlights of the 1940s at the Barrymore included Ethel Barrymore's last appearance at her theatre, in a weak play by Vincent Sheean called *An International Incident*. On Christmas night, 1940, Rodgers & Hart and John O'Hara brought in a landmark musical that shocked some of the critics. It was *Pal Joey*, the tough chronicle of a Chicago heel (Gene Kelly) who is kept by a rich adulteress (Vivienne Segal). The memorable score contained "Bewitched, Bothered and Bewildered," "I Could Write a Book," and some great musical comedy

numbers that stopped the show. The cast also included June Havoc, Van Johnson, Leila Ernst, and Jack Durant. It ran for 270 performances. When it was revived in the 1950s, it shocked no one and it had a triumphant run of 540 performances.

George Abbott, who produced and staged *Pal Joey*, brought another musical hit here on October 1, 1941: the prep-school show *Best Foot Forward*, detailing what happens when a movie queen visits a campus as a publicity stunt. The star was Rosemary Lane, but the show was stolen by Nancy Walker, June Allyson, and Maureen Cannon as students. It ran for 326 performances.

This was followed by a musical failure, *Count Me In*, written by Walter Kerr (before he was a critic) and Leo Brady, with such talents as Charles Butterworth, Luella Gear, Hal LeRoy, Mary Healy, and Gower and Jeanne (Champion).

The early 1940s are remembered for Katharine Cornell's production of Chekhov's *The Three Sisters*

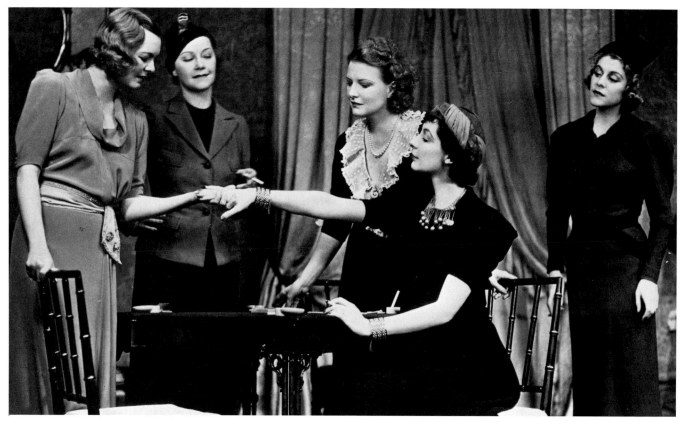

From left: Margalo Gillmore, Jane Seymour, Phyllis Povah, Ilka Chase (displaying her "Jungle Red" nail polish), and Adrienne Marden in Clare Boothe's witches' brew, *The Women* (1936).

Above: Vivienne Segal and Gene Kelly in the "amoral" *Pal Joey* (1940).
Botton Right: Gertrude Musgrove, Judith Anderson, Katharine Cornell in *The Three Sisters* (1942).

(1942), in which she starred with Ruth Gordon and Judith Anderson. The distinguished cast also included Gertrude Musgrove, Dennis King, Edmund Gwenn, Alexander Knox, McKay Morris, Kirk Douglas, Tom Powers, and Marie Paxton. This splendid production was directed by Ms. Cornell's husband, Guthrie McClintic, and played for 123 performances. Ralph Bellamy and Shirley Booth appeared in an enormous success, *Tomorrow the World,* by James Gow and Arnaud d'Usseau in 1943, which showed what happened to members of an American family who sheltered a twelve-year-old boy (Skippy Homeier) brought up in Germany as a Nazi.

A series of revivals played this theatre in the mid-1940s: Katharine Cornell and Brian Aherne in *The Barretts of Wimpole Street* (1945); Gertrude Lawrence, Raymond Massey, and Melville Cooper in *Pygmalion* (1945), Elisabeth Bergner, John Carradine, and Canada Lee in *The Duchess of Malfi* (1946); and José Ferrer in his acclaimed revival of *Cyrano de Bergerac*, which moved here from the Alvin Theatre (1946).

Gian-Carlo Menotti's twin opera bill, *The Telephone* and *The Medium* (1947), received high praise, especially for Maria Powers's electrifying performance in the latter.

On December 3, 1947, the Barrymore Theatre presented its most distinguished offering, Tennessee Williams's *A Streetcar Named Desire*, one of the greatest American plays of the 20th century. Jessica Tandy won a Tony Award for her unforgettable performance as Blanche DuBois, and the inspired acting of Marlon Brando, Kim Hunter, and Karl Malden made this a historic night in the American theatre. The haunting play won the Pulitzer Prize and the New York Drama Critics Circle Award for best play of the season and ran for 855 performances. During the run, Anthony Quinn and Uta Hagen succeeded Brando and Tandy.

Gian-Carlo Menotti returned in 1950 with another superb opera, *The Consul,* a harrowing work about postwar Europe, with magnificent performances by Patricia Neway and Marie Powers. Irene Mayer Selznick, who produced *A Streetcar Named Desire*, piloted another hit at this theatre in 1950 when she presented Rex Harrison and his then-wife, Lili Palmer, in John Van

Above: Marlon Brando rapes Jessica Tandy in *A Streetcar Named Desire* (1947). *Top Right:* Gertrude Lawrence makes a fair lady in Shaw's *Pygmalion* (1945 revival). *Right:* Hume Cronyn marries Jessica Tandy in the long-running comedy *The Fourposter* (1951).

Rex Harrison seduces Lili Palmer in *Bell, Book and Candle* (1950).

Druten's beguiling comedy about witchcraft, *Bell, Book and Candle.* The silken duo enchanted audiences for 233 performances. Another huge hit opened on October 24, 1951, when Jessica Tandy and her husband, Hume Cronyn, starred in Jan de Hartog's two-character comedy *The Fourposter,* which won a Tony Award as the season's Best Play and another Tony for its director, José Ferrer. The play, about events in the thirty-five-year married life of a couple simply named Agnes and Michael, ran for 632 performances. It was later adapted as the musical *I Do! I Do!*

A spirited revival of Shaw's *Misalliance,* with William Redfield, Roddy McDowall, Richard Kiley, Tamara Geva, and Jerome Kilty, moved here from the New York City Center in 1953. Later that year, Robert Anderson's first Broadway play, *Tea and Sympathy,* with Deborah Kerr, John Kerr, and Leif Erickson, presented a poignant study of a young prep-school student who is suspected of being gay in an extremely closeted era. One of the first broadly popular plays to deal with the formerly taboo subject, the drama ran for 712 performances. John Kerr won a Tony Award for his performance.

In February 1955 Paul Newman returned to the stage in a thriller by Joseph Hayes called *The Desperate Hours.* It was one of those plays in which criminals hide out in a pleasant family's house and terrorize them. The excellent cast also included Karl Malden, Nancy Coleman, Patricia Peardon, George Grizzard, James Gregory, and Mary

Orr. *The Desperate Hours* won a Tony Award as Best Play Production and also one for Robert Montgomery's direction.

Marcel Marceau played an engagement here in 1955, followed by another Irene Mayer Selznick production, the exquisite Enid Bagnold play *The Chalk Garden,* with sparkling performances by Gladys Cooper, Fritz Weaver, Siobhan McKenna, Betsy von Furstenberg, Percy Waram, and Marian Seldes. The unusual drama played for 182 performances.

The British actress Maggie Smith made her Broadway debut at the Barrymore in June 1956 as one of Leonard Sillman's *New Faces of 1956.* But it was female impersonator T.C. Jones who drew raves for his embodiments of Tallulah Bankhead, Bette Davis, and other stars, and who kept the revue running for 220 performances.

The Barrymore's next hit was Ketti Frings's 1957 dramatization of Thomas Wolfe's *Look Homeward Angel,* which was awarded the Pulitzer Prize and the New York Drama Critics Circle Award for Best Play. It starred Anthony Perkins, Jo Van Fleet, Arthur Hill, Hugh Griffith, Rosemary Murphy, and many others, and ran for 564 performances. Another fine drama, *A Raisin in the Sun,* by Lorraine Hansberry, opened here in March 1959, starring Sidney Poitier, Claudia McNeil, Diana Sands, Ruby Dee, and Louis Gossett. This drama, about a black family's struggles to take its place in the middle class in white America, won the New York Drama Critics Circle Award for best play and had a run of 530 performances.

The smash hit comedy *A Majority of One,* starring Gertrude Berg and Cedric Hardwicke, moved here in 1959 from the Shubert Theatre and stayed for eight months. Some highlights of the 1960s included Henry Fonda and Mildred Natwick in Ira Levin's comedy *Critic's Choice* (1960); Michael Redgrave, Sandy Dennis, and Googie Withers in Graham Green's comedy *The Complaisant Lover* (1961); Henry Fonda and Olivia de Havilland in Garson Kanin's play *A Gift of Time* (1962); James Baldwin's play *The Amen Comer* (1965); Lee Remick and Robert Duvall in Frederick Knott's thriller *Wait Until Dark* (1966); an engagement of *Les Ballets Africains* (1966); Peter Shaffer's offbeat twin bill—*Black Comedy* and *White Lies* (1967)—with Geraldine Page,

Deborah Kerr is kind to John Kerr in *Tea and Sympathy* (1953).

Lynn Redgrave, Donald Madden, Michael Crawford, Peter Bull, and Camila Ashland; *Noël Coward's Sweet Potato* (1968), a revue of Coward's songs with Dorothy Loudon, George Grizzard, Carole Shelley, and Arthur Mitchell; and a revival of *The Front Page* with Robert Ryan, Bert Convy, Doro Merande, Peggy Cass, and Julia Meade (Helen Hayes later joined the cast) in 1969.

The 1970s brought to this theatre *Conduct Unbecoming* (1970), the British thriller with Jeremy Clyde and Michael Barrington; Alec McCowen in *The Philanthropist* (1971); Melvin Van Peebles's vignettes of black life, titled *Ain't Supposed to Die a Natural Death* (1971); Pirandello's *Emperor Henry IV* (1973), with Rex Harrison; the New Phoenix Repertory Company with revivals of *The Visit, Chemin de Fer,* and *Holiday* (1973); Jessica Tandy, Hume Cronyn, and Anne Baxter in two plays by Noël Coward, *Noël Coward in Two Keys* (1974); John Wood's Tony Award performance in Tom Stoppard's *Travesties* (1975), which also won a Tony Award for Best Play; Robert Duvall in David Mamet's *American Buffalo* (1977), winner of New York Drama Critics Circle Award for Best Play; the inventive musical *I Love My Wife* (1977), by Michael Stewart and Cy Coleman; Anthony Perkins and Mia Farrow in Bernard

Slade's *Romantic Comedy* (1979); Jean Kerr's *Lunch Hour* (1980), with Sam Waterston and Gilda Radner; Katharine Hepburn and Dorothy Loudon in Ernest Thompson's *The West Side Waltz* (1981); and Jessica Tandy, Hume Cronyn, and Keith Carradine in *Foxfire*, by Mr. Cronyn and Susan Cooper. Ms. Tandy won a Tony Award for her performance in this play with music.

In December 1983, the musical *Baby* arrived, based on a story developed by Susan Yankowitz, with a book by Sybille Pearson, music by David Shire and lyrics by Richard Maltby, Jr. The interesting entertainment, about a group of expectant parents, received several Tony nominations and ran for 241 performances.

The following year, David Rabe's scabrous play about Hollywood vermin, *Hurlyburly*, transferred here from Off Broadway and starred William Hurt, Harvey Keitel, Ron Silver, Jerry Stiller, Sigourney Weaver, Cynthia Nixon, and Judith Ivey. Directed by Mike Nichols, the play ran for 343 performances and won a Tony Award for Ms. Ivey as Best Featured Actress. During its run, the following stars succeeded members of the original cast: Candice Bergen, John Christopher Jones, John Rubinstein, Christine Baranski, Frank Langella, and Danny Aiello.

In January 1986, Zoë Caldwell starred in *Lillian*, a one-woman show by William Luce about writer Lillian Hellman. When the curtain rose on the opening night, there was a gasp in the audience at Ms. Caldwell's remarkable makeup that made her the spitting image of the fiery authoress.

Social Security, a popular comedy by Andrew Bergman, arrived on April 17, 1986, with this interesting cast: Ron Silver, Marlo Thomas, Joanna Gleason, Kenneth Welsh, Olympia Dukakis, and Stefan Schnabel. Directed by Mike Nichols, the comedy about a senior citizen who embarks on her last fling with an artist, played here for a year.

An arresting, mystical play, *Joe Turner's Come and Gone* by August Wilson, opened March 27, 1988. Part of Wilson's epic cycle of plays about black life in America during the 20th century, it was directed by Lloyd Richards and won a Tony Award for L. Scott Caldwell as Best Featured Actress in a Play. The following year, ballet superstar Mikhail Baryshnikov made his Broadway

Left: PLAYBILL cover for *Lettice & Lovage. Right:* Katharine Hepburn at the ivories and Dorothy Loudon on the fiddle in *West Side Waltz* (1981).

debut in Kafka's *Metamorphosis* and was nominated for a Tony Award.

David Hare's play *The Secret Rapture* (October 26, 1989) caused a brouhaha, not as a play, but as an altercation between the playwright and *New York Times* critic Frank Rich, who wrote a devastating review of it. Mr. Hare wrote a scathing letter to the critic, which somehow got published in newspapers, and the result was much publicity for a play that ran for only 10 performances.

On March 25, 1990, a delirious theatrical event occurred at the Barrymore Theatre. The volatile actress Maggie Smith arrived in her London hit *Lettice & Lovage* by the British playwright Peter Shaffer. The scintillating comedy about a tour guide who embellishes history with fiction to make it more interesting, won Tony Awards for Ms. Smith and Margaret Tyzack (who had appeared in the play in London with Ms. Smith). This sparkling theatrical experience ran here for a sold-out ten months and could have run longer if the two actresses had continued to be available.

On February 14, 1991, *Mule Bone* received its long-delayed Broadway debut. Written in 1930 by Langston Hughes and Zora Neale Hurston, it had never been performed because of a dispute between authors. This production had a prologue and epilogue by George Houston Bass and music by Taj Mahal. It ran for 67 performances.

In 1992, the classic *A Streetcar Named Desire* returned to the Barrymore, this time starring Alec Baldwin and Jessica Lange with Amy Madigan and Timothy Carhart. Directed by Gregory Mosher, it had a limited run of four months and garnered a Tony nomination for Mr. Baldwin.

Wendy Wasserstein's popular Off-Broadway play *The Sisters Rosensweig* moved here on March 18, 1993 from the Mitzi E. Newhouse Theatre at Lincoln Center with its original cast, including Jane Alexander, Madeline Kahn (Tony Award) and Robert Klein. It enjoyed a long run at the Barrymore.

A curious play opened here on April 27, 1995. Called *Indiscretions,* it was Jeremy Sams's translation of Jean Cocteau's play *Les Parents Terribles.* It had an impressive

 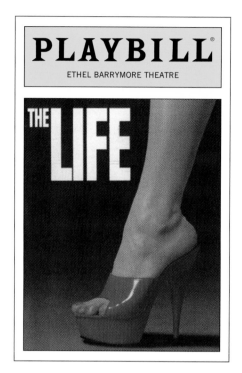

Left: PLAYBILL for Wendy Wasserstein's *The Sisters Rosensweig* (1993). *Right:* Cy Coleman and Ira Gasman's musical, *The Life* (1997).

cast: Kathleen Turner, Eileen Atkins, Jude Law, Roger Rees, and Cynthia Nixon, and was directed by Sam Mathias. According to *Variety,* the drama, which featured incest and male nudity, received 15 favorable reviews, 2 mixed and 4 unfavorable. It ran for 220 performances and received the following Tony Award nominations: Best Actor in a Play (Rees), Best Actress in a Play (Atkins), Best Featured Actor (Law), Best Featured Actress (Nixon), Best Play, Best Director of a Play (Mathias), Best Scenic Designer (Stephen Brimson Lewis), Best Costume Designer (also Mr. Lewis), and Best Lighting Designer (Mark Henderson).

The next tenant at the Barrymore was Oscar Wilde's *An Ideal Husband,* which had not been produced on Broadway since 1918. The 1895 play dealt with political blackmail in London's high society. This production found favor with critics and audiences for 309 performances. Martin Shaw, who played Lord Goring, was highly praised for his witty performance and was nominated for a Tony Award. Other Tony nominations went to Peter Hall for his direction and to Bill Kenwright for producing a Best Revival of a Play.

A raucous musical exploded next at the Barrymore on April 26, 1997. *The Life,* with music by Cy Coleman, lyrics by Ira Gasman, and a book by Mr. Gasman, David Newman, and Mr. Coleman, had been previously produced Off-Off-Broadway at the Westbeth Theater Center. It was a seamy look at the sordid life led by hookers in the Times Square area before the Disney-led late 1990s cleanup. *The Life* received what George S. Kaufman called "mixed reviews—good and lousy." One critic called it a morality tale in which everyone pays for their sins. Mr. Coleman's songs were praised and so was the gritty cast. The musical ran for 466 performances and won Tony Awards for two of its featured performers: Lillias White and Chuck Cooper. Other Tony nominations included Best Actress in a Musical (Pamela Isaacs), Best Featured Actor in Musical (Sam Harris), Best Musical Book (Gasman, Newman, and Coleman), Best Musical, Best Musical Director (Michael Blakemore), Best Costume Designer (Martin Pakledinaz), Best Lighting Designer (Richard Pilbrow), Best Choreographer (Joey McKneely), Best Score (Coleman and Gasman), and Best Orchestrations (Don Sebesky and Harold Wheeler).

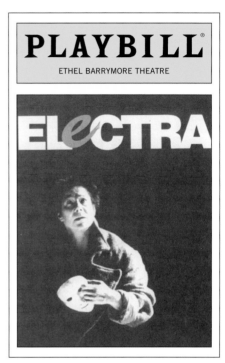

Left: The cast of *The Life* (1997) recreated the underworld of 1970s Times Square. *Right:* Zoë Wanamaker had an unusual hit with Sophocles' *Electra* (1998).

From Forty-second Street mayhem, the Barrymore went to ancient Greek violence for its next attraction. On December 3, 1998, a splendid production of Sophocles' *Electra* opened with a magnificent cast: Zoë Wanamaker, Claire Bloom, Michael Cumpsty, Pat Carroll, Stephen Spinella, and others. Ms. Wanamaker, who had won an Olivier Award in London for her commanding performance as Electra, was nominated for a Tony Award, as was Claire Bloom as her mother, Clytemnestra. With a new translation by Frank McGuinness, the play also received a nomination for Best Revival. Some critics found Ms. Wanamaker's costume—an oversized trench coat and a fright wig—somewhat bizarre, but her frenzied performance was praised, as were the startling, bloody stage effects. Due to overwhelming ticket demand, the limited engagement was extended an additional nine weeks. The 2,400-year-old play recouped its investment in six weeks, a record for a Greek classic.

Another London hit opened at the Barrymore on April 15, 1999. It was David Hare's *Amy's View* and it starred a radiant Judy Dench as a veteran actress who has problems with a grown daughter and with the irritations of contemporary society. For her acclaimed performance, Ms. Dench won a Tony Award as Best Actress in a Play. Samantha Bond, who played her daughter, received a nomination as a Best Supporting Actress in a Play. The show ran for 103 performances.

The next show at the Barrymore Theatre had a complex history. Called *Putting It Together—A Musical Review*, it showcased a rich collection of songs with words and music by Stephen Sondheim. The show originated in 1992 as a Cameron Mackintosh production in Oxford, England. He produced a revised version of the revue in 1993 at the Manhattan Theater Club Off Broadway, starring Julie Andrews. In the fall of 1998, he produced still another version of the musical at the Mark Taper Forum in Los Angeles. Starring Carol Burnett, it broke every one of that theatre's box office records. On November 21, 1999, it opened at the Barrymore with Ms. Burnett, George Hearn, John Barrowman, Ruthie Henshall, Bronson Pinchot—and at certain performances, talk show hostess Kathie Lee Gifford, substituting for Ms. Burnett. It did not repeat the success it had enjoyed at the Mark Taper Forum. Some critics did not feel that Ms.

Judi Dench won a Tony Award for her performance in *Amy's View* (1999).

Burnett was an ideal Sondheim singer and they also disliked the show's frame for Sondheim's celebrated songs. It ran for 101 performances.

The highly anticipated engagement of the new Donmar Warehouse production of Tom Stoppard's *The Real Thing* opened here on April 17, 2000, and repeated the great success it had achieved in England. The play starred the lauded Donmar cast led by Stephen Dillane, Jennifer Ehle, Nigel Lindsay, and Sarah Woodward, all making their Broadway debuts, and was directed by David Leveaux. The play dealt with marriage and writing, emotional fidelity and intellectual integrity, high art and pop culture, and truth and acting, both onstage and in real life. *The Real Thing* won the following Tony Awards: Best Revival, Best Performance by a Leading Actor in a Play (Stephen Dillane), and Best Performance by a Leading Actress in a Play (Jennifer Ehle).

In late fall 2000 the Barrymore hosted the transfer of a more successful Manhattan Theatre Club show: *The Tale of the Allergist's Wife*, which featured Linda Lavin, Michele Lee, and Tony Roberts, and marked the Broadway debut of Charles Busch, previously known for his Off-Broadway campfests, including *Vampire Lesbians of Sodom.*

The Barrymore was the last of the pre-Depression playhouses to be built, and remains one of the few Broadway theatres that has never changed name or owner.

MARK HELLINGER THEATRE

This theatre was one of the last opulent movie palaces built in Manhattan. It opened on April 22, 1930, as the Hollywood Theatre, one of Warner Brothers's flagship houses. The architect was Thomas W. Lamb, the distinguished designer of some of America's most magnificent movie houses. The Hollywood was typical of his style of ornate splendor, with columns, grand staircases, and baroque curlicues. The entrance to this theatre was originally on Broadway, but later it was switched to Fifty-first Street.

Hollywood returned to showing films, including a reserved-seat, two-a-day engagement of the Warner Brothers/Max Reinhardt movie *A Midsummer Night's Dream.*

In October 1936, the Hollywood Theatre became the 51st Street Theatre when it presented George Abbott's version of *Uncle Tom's Cabin,* called *Sweet River.* The play was spectacular, with a very large cast and choir and mammoth sets by Donald Oenslager, but the critics were not impressed and the epic achieved

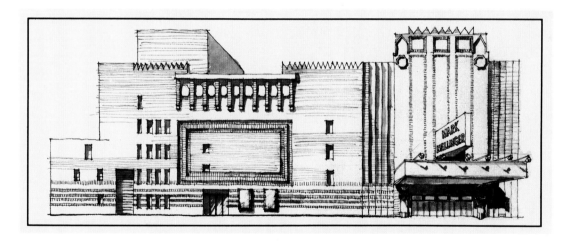

During the Depression, Warner Brothers experimented with live entertainment at this huge movie house and, with Lew Brown, presented a variety show, *Calling All Stars,* on December 13, 1934. The cast glittered with such headliners as Lou Holtz, Phil Baker, Jack Whiting, Martha Ray (later, Raye), Gertrude Niesen, Patricia Bowman, Mitzi Mayfair, and Ella Logan, along with Judy, Pete, Zeke, and Anne Canova, but the show registered only 35 performances. In 1935 the

only 5 performances.

The 51st Street Theatre went back to being the Hollywood Theatre to show major Warner Brothers releases until November 1939, when *George White's Scandals* moved here from the Alvin Theatre. The 1939 edition of this popular revue was the last of the series and it featured the Broadway debut of Hollywood's tap dancing star Ann Miller, who garnered raves. Other headliners in the show included Ella Logan, Willie and

Eugene Howard, Ben Blue, Collette Lyons, and Victor Arden and his Orchestra. The show ran for 120 performances.

In the spring of 1940 this theatre once again switched its name to the 51ˢᵗ Street Theatre when Laurence Olivier and Vivien Leigh opened in *Romeo and Juliet*. Olivier designed and directed the production and played Romeo, Ms. Leigh was Juliet, Dame May Whitty was the Nurse, Cornel Wilde was Tybalt (he also directed the dueling scenes), Edmond O'Brien was Mercutio, Wesley Addy was Benvolio, and Halliwell Hobbes was Capulet. Motley designed the sets and costumes; Robert Edmond Jones created the lighting. The play should have been a triumph, but it was a disaster. The leading stars had invested their own money in the revival, and lost all of it. Major blame was placed upon Olivier's direction, and the production managed only 36 performances.

The theatre went back to being the Hollywood and showing films until Christmas night, 1941, when Eddie Cantor returned to Broadway after a thirteen-year absence in Hollywood. He starred in the hit musical, *Banjo Eyes*, based on the popular comedy *Three Men on a Horse*. The impressive cast also featured Jacqueline Susann (yes, the future novelist), Virginia Mayo, Bill Johnson, Audrey Christie, June Clyde, Lionel Stander, and the dancing De Marcos. The score was by Vernon Duke and lyrics by John Latouche and Harold Adamson. The musical could have run longer than 126 performances but it closed due to Cantor's illness.

During the war years, the Hollywood Theatre reverted to showing films once more and in 1947 it renamed itself the Warner Brothers Theatre during the showing of the film version of *Life with Father*.

In 1949, tycoon Anthony B. Farrell bought the theatre and rechristened it the Mark Hellinger in honor of the esteemed Broadway columnist. The name stuck. Mr. Farrell, a manufacturer from Albany who got bitten by the show biz bug, paid $1.5 million for the theatre, and spent another fortune producing a revue called *All for Love*, which opened at the Mark Hellinger on January 22, 1949. The theatre, beautifully refurbished by Mr. Farrell, looked great, but the show did not. It managed to run for 121 performances but not at a profit. Farrell took a

Laurence Olivier and Vivienne Leigh in their star-crossed production of *Romeo and Juliet* (1940).

Bert Lahr as Queen Victoria and the leader of a space brigade in the 1951 revue *Two on the Aisle*.

$12,000 weekly loss, and when the revue closed in May, *Variety* estimated that its producer had lost $500,000 on it. The talented cast included Paul and Grace Hartman and Bert Wheeler.

S.M. Chartock presented a three-week season of Gilbert and Sullivan in the fall of 1949. Anthony B. Farrell fared better with his next musical in his theatre. Even though the critics were not wild about *Texas, Li'l Darlin'*, with Kenny Delmar, theatregoers disagreed with them and supported this show for 293 performances.

The Hartmans returned to Mr. Farrell's theatre in their hit revue *Tickets, Please!*, which moved here from the Coronet Theatre in 1950. A lavish revue, *Bless You All*, was produced at the Hellinger in December 1950 by Herman Levin and Oliver Smith. It starred Pearl Bailey, Jules Munshin, Mary McCarty, Donald Saddler, Valerie Bettis, and Gene Barry, but it was not a success. The score was by Harold Rome and the sketches by Arnold Auerbach.

A far more successful revue was *Two on the Aisle*, starring Bert Lahr and Dolores Gray, written by Betty Comden, Adolph Green, Jule Styne, Nat Hiken, and William Friedberg, which opened on July 19, 1951, and ran for 279 performances. Lahr's great clowning and Gray's belting were a dynamic combination. The following year brought another musical, *Three Wishes for Jamie*, with Bert Wheeler, John Raitt, Charlotte Rae, Anne Jeffreys, and Ralph Morgan, with a score by Ralph Blane. This fairy tale set to music ran for 91 performances.

Gilbert and Sullivan returned to the Mark Hellinger in the fall of 1952, followed by the National Theatre of Greece in their repertory of classical plays presented by Guthrie McClintic.

Hazel Flagg arrived in February 1953, a musical version of the satiric film *Nothing Sacred*, by Hecht and MacArthur. Hecht wrote the show's libretto to a score by Jule Styne and Bob Hilliard. Helen Gallagher played the title role and she was ably assisted by Jack Whiting, Benay Venuta, Thomas Mitchell, and Sheree North. One hit tune emerged from the show: "How Do You Speak to an Angel?", which became popular before the show opened. This was followed in March 1954 by *The Girl in*

Pink Tights, starring dancer Zizi Jeanmaire. It was Sigmund Romberg's last Broadway show and, unfortunately, it was not a success. It ran for 115 performances. *The Ballets Espagnols: Teresa and Luisillo* played a profitable engagement here later that year.

The charming musical about the Amish—*Plain and Fancy*—opened here on January 27, 1955, and proved an immediate hit. It starred Shirl Conway, Richard Derr, Gloria Marlowe, Barbara Cook, Nancy Andrews, Daniel Nagrin, Stefan Schnabel, and many others. The hit song was "Young and Foolish" and the musical ran for 461 performances.

On the evening of March 15, 1956, the Mark Hellinger presented its most distinguished and long-running production: Herman Levin's presentation of the Alan Jay Lerner and Frederick Loewe masterpiece *My Fair Lady,* adapted from Shaw's *Pygmalion.* Brilliantly directed by Moss Hart, Rex Harrison and Julie Andrews made theatrical history singing "The Rain in Spain." With choreography by Hanya Holm, sets by Oliver Smith, and costumes by Cecil Beaton, the musical was one of Broadway's finest moments. The tale of a cockney flower girl who yearns to become a lady by learning to speak better, this Cinderella story ran for 2,717 performances and is constantly revived. The show won the Tony Award and New York Drama Critics Circle Award for best musical, and countless other awards. *My Fair Lady* remains one of the landmarks of American musical theatre and is the most honored show ever to play the Mark Hellinger.

It was succeeded in 1962 by another great hit, *The Sound of Music,* which moved in from the Lunt-Fontanne and stayed for seven months. Next came an Italian import, *Rugantino* (1964), probably the first show ever presented on Broadway with running supertitles, since it was acted and sung in Italian. Despite the translation, which was flashed across the top of the proscenium, the musical was a flop. Another musical that did not pay off was the Comden/Green/Styne show *Fade Out—Fade In,* starring the popular TV star Carol Burnett and Jack Cassidy. George Abbott directed the show about a movie usher who becomes a movie star, but there were book problems, and Ms. Burnett became ill, which eventually closed the musical. She did not return to Broadway

for thirty-two years.

On a Clear Day You Can See Forever (1965) had a stunning score by Burton Lane and Alan Jay Lerner and brilliant performances by Barbara Harris and John Cullum, but this unusual musical about reincarnation and ESP had script troubles. Nevertheless, it ran for eight months.

During the latter 1960s, the Mark Hellinger housed a number of shows with illustrious stars and creators, but none was a commercial hit. This included a musical called *A Joyful Noise* (1966), choreographed by Michael Bennett. *Illya, Darling* (1967) starred Melina Mercouri in the same role she played in the hit movie *Never on Sunday.* It ran for 319 performances, but did not recoup its investment. *I'm Solomon,* a Biblical disaster starring Dick Shawn, came and went in 1968. Marlene Dietrich made one of her public appearances here in 1968, as did Les Ballets Africains.

Jerry Herman, who had enjoyed two smashes in the 1960s—*Hello, Dolly!* and *Mame*—came up with a clinker named *Dear World* (1969), based on the sparkling play *The Madwoman of Chaillot.* Angela Lansbury won a Tony Award for her performance and that was the only redeeming feature of this pretentious musical. In 1969 Katharine Hepburn made her musical comedy debut in *Coco* at this theatre. Her acting was far better than her guttural singing, but the Alan Jay Lerner/Andre Previn show ran for 332 performances because of her star power.

That power paid other dividends as well. When work began across 51st Street on what would eventually become the building that houses the Uris (later Gershwin) and Circle in the Square theatres, Hepburn visited the construction site and convinced those in charge to suspend their clanging and banging during her matinees.

A horror named *Ari* opened here in 1971, followed by *Man of La Mancha* from another theatre. Then came a musical that brought out New York's worst-dressed people for the opening. The show was *Jesus Christ Superstar* and every creep in Manhattan showed up for the first performance. It was a grisly sight: a Biblical spectacle onstage, the dregs of society in the audience, and protesters picketing outside. The musical by Andrew

Left: Souvenir program for *My Fair Lady. Below:* Julie Andrews and Rex Harrison in Lerner and Lowe's classic *My Fair Lady* (1956).

Lloyd Webber and Tim Rice, staged by Tom O'Horgan, ran for 720 performances on Broadway and had considerably more dignity than its audiences. The show introduced Andrew Lloyd Webber (*Evita, Cats, Phantom of the Opera, Sunset Boulevard*) and Tim Rice (*Evita, The Lion King, Aida*) to Broadway, and few who attended the opening had an inkling of what a profound impact the two would have for the rest of the century.

The remainder of the 1970s at this theatre was a mixed bag. Martha Graham brought her Dance Company for an engagement, which was always welcome. Then there was an all-male *As You Like It* from Britain that did not fare well in 1974. A revival of *The Skin of Our Teeth* folded its tents quickly in the same year, as did the horrendous musical *1600 Pennsylvania Avenue,* a clumsy musical history of the White House by no less than Alan Jay Lerner and Leonard Bernstein. It was

Bernstein's final work for Broadway. *Timbuktu!,* a musical revamp of *Kismet* with Eartha Kitt, was not much better in 1978, nor was *Platinum,* Bruce Villanch's musical about the pop world, starring Alexis Smith, that same year.

Saravà, a musical about a Brazilian woman who is beset by the ghost of her first husband, was another clinker in 1979. This was succeeded by an engagement of Nureyev with the Joffrey Ballet and another forgettable musical, *The Utter Glory of Morrisey Hall,* with Celeste Holm in 1979.

Finally, in October 1979, the Mark Hellinger housed a show worthy of its dimensions. The burlesque revue *Sugar Babies,* starring Mickey Rooney (making his Broadway debut at the same theatre where he once appeared as "Puck" on the screen in *A Midsummer Night's Dream*) and Ann Miller (who had appeared here in the

Katharine Hepburn as Coco Chanel in the spectacular musical *Coco* (1969).

Ann Miller and Mickey Rooney do some patriotic clowning in *Sugar Babies* (1979).

1939 *George White's Scandals*) turned into this theatre's biggest hit since *My Fair Lady*. Its combination of old-time burlesque sketches with musical favorites of yesteryear made it a winning combination. It ran for 1,208 performances.

After *Sugar Babies* completed its long run, George Hearn and Betsy Joslyn opened here in *A Doll's Life*, a new musical with book and lyrics by Betty Comden and Adolph Green, and music by Larry Grossman. It purported to show what happened to Ibsen's heroine Nora after she walked out on her husband in *A Doll's House*. It ran for only 5 performances.

Next came *Merlin*, a spectacular musical of magic starring the fabulous magician Doug Henning, plus Chita Rivera and Nathan Lane. The show played 69 previews and 199 performances before pulling a disappearing act.

In 1984, a revival of the British musical *Oliver!* had a short run, and the following spring Ben Vereen, Leilani Jones, Timothy Nolen, and Stubby Kaye starred in a new burlesque musical called *Grind*, with a book by Fay Kanin, score by Larry Grossman and Ellen Fitzhugh, and direction by Hal Prince. Although the musical won

two Tony Awards—for Ms. Jones (Best Featured Actress) and Florence Klotz (Best Costumes)—it ran for only 75 performances. Next came *Tango Argentino*, a musical revue in Spanish conceived by Claudio Segovia and Hector Orezzoli, which found favor for 198 performances.

August 21, 1986, brought a new musical, *Rags*, starring the Metropolitan Opera's Teresa Stratas and Broadway veteran Larry Kert, with Dick Latessa, Terrence Mann, and Lonny Price in the supporting cast. Although many admired the score by Charles Strouse and Stephen Schwartz, and Ms. Stratas's singing, the storylines in Joseph Stein's book were deemed unclear, and the production closed after just 4 performances. Another dance production, *Flamenco Puro*, played here for more than a month in the fall of 1986 and it was followed by such personal appearances as *Smokey Robinson Plus Jean Carne*, *Virsky's Ukrainian State Dance Company* and *Rodney Dangerfield on Broadway!* In the spring of 1988, Christopher Plummer and Glenda Jackson starred in *Macbeth* for three months and were followed by an engagement of the *Georgian State Dance Company*.

December 26, 1988, brought Peter Allen in *Legs Diamond*, a musical for which he supplied the score, with a book by Harvey Fierstein and Charles Suppon. Cabaret chanteuse Julie Wilson also starred in this musical about the 1920s gangster, but the show was beset with problems and closed after two months. One of the producers of this musical was George M. Steinbrenner III, owner of the New York Yankees.

In 1989, the Times Square Church took a five-year lease on this theatre and used it as a house of worship. In 1994, the Church purchased the theatre from the Nederlander Organization for a reported $17 million.

CITY CENTER

The New York City Center, with its unique neo-Moorish facade and interior, was built in 1923 as a meeting hall for members of the Ancient and Accepted Order of the Mystic Shrine. In 1943, the building was about to be demolished when it was saved by Mayor Fiorello H. LaGuardia and Newbold Morris, president of the City Council. They envisioned the almost 3,000-seat house as a "temple of the performing arts" for New Yorkers who could not afford to go to the Broadway theatre, Carnegie Hall, or the Metropolitan Opera.

With the energetic Jean Dalrymple as its volunteer director of publicity and public relations, the building became the New York City Center of Music and Drama. It opened auspiciously on December 11, 1943, with a concert by the New York Philharmonic (after LaGuardia himself took up the baton for the "The Star Spangled Banner"), followed two days later by Gertrude Lawrence in a revival of her comedy hit *Susan and God* by Rachel Crothers. Reported *The New York Times:* "Gertie opened the Center with a roar."

Another lauded revival presented that first season was Sidney Kingsley's *The Patriots*, starring Walter Hampden and Julie Hayden. The top ticket price for these productions was $1.65.

The City Center's second season (1944-45) was distinguished by music events and highly praised produc-tions: Helen Hayes in *Harriet*, Paul Robeson in *Othello*, *Carmen Jones*, *New Moon*, *The Merry Widow*, *Little Women*, *The Cherry Orchard*, and *You Can't Take It With You*. The 1946-47 season brought Maurice Evans in *Hamlet*, Nanette Fabray in *Bloomer Girl*, and Michael Todd's lavish production of *Up In Central Park*. Among the many revivals presented in 1947-48 were *Rip Van Winkle*; José Ferrer (who for three seasons was director of the Center's drama company), Richard Whorf and John Carradine in *Volpone*; Uta Hagen and José Ferrer in *Angel Street*; Mr. Ferrer and George Coulouris in *The Alchemist*; four one-act plays by Eugene O'Neill; and others.

The parade of sterling revivals continued in 1949-50. Celeste Holm and Brian Aherne starred in *She Stoops To Conquer*; Eva Le Gallienne shone in *The Corn Is Green*; Maurice Evans, Marsha Hunt, Dennis King, and Victor Jory headed the cast of *The Devil's Disciple*; Basil Rathbone, Margaret Phillips, and John Dall starred in *The Heiress*; *A Streetcar Named Desire* returned with Uta Hagen, Anthony Quinn, and George Matthews; and *Brigadoon* returned from the highlands.

Another highlight was the return of Judith Anderson in her Tony Award-winning performance as Medea.

Gems presented during the 1950-51 season included Martita Hunt and John Carradine in *The Madwoman of Chaillot*; Edna Best in *Captain Brassbound's Conversion*;

PLAYBILL
CITY CENTER

LOVE! VALOUR! COMPASSION!

Terrence McNally presented a portrait of gay men who create a family together in *Love! Valour! Compassion!* (1994) which moved to Broadway and won the Tony as Best Play after a Manhattan Theatre Club debut at City Center.

Ruth Hussey, J. Edward Bromberg, Peggy Ann Garner, and Ethel Griffies in *The Royal Family*; Maurice Evans, Kent Smith, and Betsy Blair in *King Richard II*; Claire Luce, Ralph Clanton, and Larry Hagman in *The Taming of the Shrew*; Judy Holliday, Don Defore, and Edmond Ryan in *Dream Girl*; and Ruth Chatterton and Lee Tracy in *Idiot's Delight*.

During 1951-52, Maurice Evans, Mildred Dunnock, Diana Lynn, and Kent Smith appeared in *The Wild Duck*; Celeste Holm, Kevin McCarthy, and Art Smith starred in *Anna Christie*; Judith Anderson and Marian Seldes revived *Come of Age*; Robert Preston, Martha Scott, and Elliott Nugent starred in Thurber and

Nugent's *The Male Animal*; Uta Hagen, Herbert Berghof, and Paula Laurence were in *Tovarich*; Helen Gahagan, Scott McKay, Peggy Ann Garner, and Edna Best sparkled in *First Lady*.

The 1952-53 season brought Kevin McCarthy, Meg Mundy, Joseph Schildkraut, and Nancy Marchand in *Love's Labour's Lost*; Luther Adler and Margaret Phillips in *The Merchant of Venice*; and a sparkling production of Shaw's *Misalliance* with Roddy McDowall, Barry Jones, Richard Kiley, Tamara Geva, William Redfield, and Jerome Kilty that was so successful that it moved to the Ethel Barrymore Theatre for an extended run.

In 1953-54 Barbara Cook and Florence Henderson appeared in a revival of *Oklahoma!*; José Ferrer, Arlene Dahl, and Paula Laurence were in *Cyrano De Bergerac* (also in the cast was the future novelist Tom Tryon); Ferrer and Judith Evelyn repeated their roles in Joseph Kramm's Pulitzer Prize play *The Shrike*; Mr. Ferrer next appeared in a revival of *Richard III* with Vincent Price, Jessie Royce Landis, Florence Reed, Margaret Wycherly, and Maureen Stapleton; Mr. Ferrer followed this classic with his famed cavorting in *Charley's Aunt* with Peggy Wood, Kent Smith, and Robert Lansing. The New York City Light Opera Company presented two productions: *Show Boat* and *Die Fledermaus*.

The 1954-55 season brought revivals of major Broadway musicals (which often transferred directly from their Broadway runs, with cast and designs intact): *Carousel, Guys and Dolls, South Pacific, Finian's Rainbow*, and *Damn Yankees* with the original leads: Gwen Verdon, Ray Walston, Stephen Douglass, and Jean Stapleton. Plays included two with Helen Hayes—*What Every Woman Knows* and *The Wisteria Trees*; Jessica Tandy and Hume Cronyn in *The Fourposter*; and William Saroyan's *The Time of Your Life* with Franchot Tone, John Carradine, Carol Grace, and Gloria Vanderbilt.

The 1955-56 season offered William Marshall as Othello; a revival of *Henry IV, Part 1*; Orson Welles and Viveca Lindfors in *King Lear*; and Tallulah Bankhead in a revival of *A Streetcar Named Desire*, which was marred by the hysterical behavior of her fans who shrieked uncontrollably when she told Stanley Kowalski (Gerald O'Loughlin) that she rarely touched liquor. Musical revivals included *The King and I, Carmen Jones*, and

Kiss Me, Kate.

In 1956-57, the City Center presented revivals of *The Teahouse of the August Moon* with Gig Young; Helen Hayes in *The Glass Menagerie* with James Daly; Charlton Heston, Orson Bean, and Dick Button in *Mister Roberts*; and such musicals as *The Beggar's Opera*; *Brigadoon*; *The Merry Widow*; *South Pacific*, and *The Pajama Game.*

During the 1957-58 season, the City Center concentrated on musical revivals: *Carousel* (Howard Keel, Barbara Cook, Marie Powers, and Victor Moore); *Annie Get Your Gun* (Betty Jane Watson, David Atkinson, Jack Whiting); *Wonderful Town* (Nancy Walker, Jo Sullivan, George Givot, Betsy von Furstenberg); *Oklahoma!* (Gene Nelson, Lois O'Brien, Helen Gallagher, Harvey Lembeck, Herbert Banke, Gemze De Lappe, George Church, and, from the original cast, Betty Garde as Aunt Eller).

The 1958-59 season began with Sylvia Sidney in *Auntie Mame*, followed by Art Lund, Paula Stewart, and Norman Atkins in *The Most Happy Fella*; Robert Morse, Mindy Carson, Orson Bean, Jack Waldron, and Betsy von Furstenberg in *Say, Darling*; Dolly Haas, Estelle Winwood, Clarence Derwent, Tonio Selwart, and Leueen MacGrath in *Lute Song.*

The City Center's 1959-60 season was distinguished by the last appearance on a New York stage of the famed couple Alfred Lunt and Lynn Fontanne in their Broadway hit, *The Visit*. Glenn Anders and Thomas Gomez were also in the cast. Other productions that season included the Piccolo Teatro Di Milano in its influential production of *The Servant of Two Masters*; and revivals of *Finian's Rainbow* with Anita Alvarez, Bobbie Howes, Jeanne Carson, Carol Brice, and Howard Morris; and *The King and I* with Barbara Cook, Farley Granger, and Gemze De Lappe.

The 1960-61 season brought productions by the City Center Gilbert and Sullivan Company of *The Mikado, The Pirates of Penzance, The Gondoliers. H.M.S. Pinafore*; the Deutsches Theater production of *Faust/Part I* in German; La Comédie Française in a repertory of five plays; revivals of *Show Boat*; *South Pacific, Porgy and Bess; Brigadoon*; and *Pal Joey*, the latter with Bob Fosse as Joey and Carol Bruce as his mistress, Vera Simpson.

During the 1961-62 season the City Center presented the Greek Tragedy Theatre in three classic plays. Mazowsze,

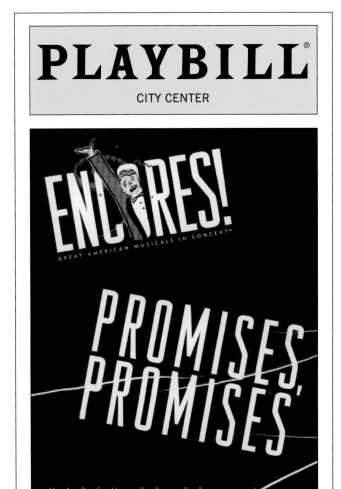

Martin Short and Christine Baranski starred in *Promises, Promises* (1997).

the Polish folk song and dance company, arrived with their unique show. And the Old Vic came from London with *Macbeth, Saint Joan*, and *Romeo and Juliet.*

The 1962-63 season brought more Gilbert and Sullivan; Marcel Marceau returned; and there were revivals: *Brigadoon* with Peter Palmer, Sally Ann Howes, Edward Villella, and Russell Nype; *Wonderful Town* with Kaye Ballard, Jacquelyn McKeever, and Jim Kirkwood (later one of the authors of *A Chorus Line*); *Oklahoma!* with Peter Palmer and Betty Garde again playing the part of Aunt Eller; and another revival of *Pal Joey* with Mr. Fosse and Viveca Lindfors, who slaughtered Rodgers and Hart's classic "Bewitched, Bothered and Bewildered."

In 1963-64, there was another revival of *The King and I*; another appearance by Poland's Mazowsze; The

Theatre De France in a repertory of five French classics directed by Jean Louis Barrault; and The City Center Gilbert and Sullivan Company in seven of the team's masterpieces.

During the remainder of the 1960s, the City Center continued to present revivals of plays and musicals and such companies as The Comédie Française, The Gilbert and Sullivan Company, The Grand Kabuki, La Compagnie Renaud Barrault, and others in repertory seasons. During the 1966-67 season four Frank Loesser musicals were presented; in 1967-68, a revival of the beloved classic *Life With Father* was produced with Dorothy Stickney and other members of the play's original cast.

During all these years, the City Center was also the official home for The New York City Opera and Balanchine's New York City Ballet, which were both born in this theatre. In the early 1970s, when many of its resident artists and companies moved to Lincoln Center for the Performing Arts, the City Center building was once again slated for demolition. Faced with the loss of their performing space, a group of artists banded together in 1976 to save the theatre. Under the forceful leadership of Howard M. Squadron, the City Center 55th Street Theater Foundation was formed to manage the Center and ensure its survival as a performing arts complex. Since then, annual performances have been given here by such distinguished companies as the Alvin Ailey American Dance Theater, The Paul Taylor Dance Company, Merce Cunningham Dance Company and the Martha Graham Dance Company (all of which are residents at City Center), as well as dozens of domestic and international troupes, earning City Center the title of America's premier dance theatre.

In July 1981, Mr. Squadron, a Manhattan lawyer, received a $700,000 Economic Development Administration grant to renovate the theatre. The cramped lobby was enlarged, the orchestra floor was rebuilt and steeply raked to improve sightlines and restroom facilities and acoustics were improved.

The extensive renovations took about six months to complete. They were carried out by architect Fred Lebensold and the firm of Rothzeid, Kaiserman & Thomson at the cost of $900,000. When the renovation was finished, the building won the prestigious City Club's Bard Award for Excellence in Architecture and Urban Design. In 1984, the resplendent theatre was designated a landmark by the New York City Landmarks Commission, protecting it from demolition.

In the fall of 1984, City Center became the performing home of one of Manhattan's most innovative and celebrated theatre companies, the Manhattan Theatre Club. MTC presented a full season of mainstage plays and its acclaimed "Writers in Performance" series in City Center's downstairs Stage I (299 seats) and a series of workshops and works-in-progress smaller works in Stage II (150 seats).

During the 1994 season, the Center began to broaden its offerings to meet Mayor LaGuardia's goal for the institution as a "People's Theatre," and focused its efforts on indigenous American art forms (including its modern dance companies). In Spring, 1994, City Center inaugurated a new and exciting series of performances called "Encores! Great American Musicals In Concert." The first three productions—*Fiorello!, Allegro,* and the previously never revived *Lady In The Dark*—were excitingly presented with striking staging and performances by leading musical comedy stars. "Encores!" shows received acclaim from both critics and audiences ("a runaway hit series" said *The New York Times*). The series was planned as an annual event and became one of the hottest tickets in town.

The 1995 "Encores!" series featured *Call Me Madam* with Tyne Daly in the Merman role, plus Melissa Errico, Christopher Durang, and Jane and Gordon Connell; *Out of This World* the 1950 Cole Porter flop with Ken Page, Marin Mazzie, Gregg Edelman, and Andrea Martin; and *Pal Joey* with Patti LuPone, Peter Gallagher, Daisy Prince, Bebe Neuwirth, and Arthur Rubin.

In 1996, "Encores!" presented the vulgar Cole Porter/Herbert Fields/Buddy DeSylva musical *DuBarry Was a Lady*, with Faith Prince in the Merman role and Robert Morse as the King of France. *One Touch of Venus* was a triumph for Melissa Errico in the part Mary Martin originally played, and she was ably supported by Carol Woods, Andy Taylor, Marilyn Cooper, and Jane Krakowski.

The 1996 season's final production was a triumph: a concert version of the 1975 musical *Chicago* with a brilliant score by Kander and Ebb and a acidulous book by Bob Fosse and Ebb. Ann Reinking recreated Mr.

PLAYBILL®
CITY CENTER

Do Re Mi

ENCORES!
Great American Musicals in Concert™

May 6 - 9 · 1999

Brian Stokes Mitchell, Nathan Lane, Heather Headley, and Randy Graff starred in the "Encores!" *Do Re Mi* (1999).

Fosse's original choreography, and the great cast—Bebe Neuwirth, Ms. Reinking, Joel Grey, James Naughton, and Marcia Lewis—turned this satire on our bizarre adoration of criminals into such a hit that it promptly moved to a commercial run at the Richard Rodgers Theatre, quickly making another shift to the Shubert Theatre where it was still playing at this writing. Although this musical was splendid in 1975 with Gwen Verdon, Chita Rivera, and Jerry Orbach, it was much more timely in 1996, after the travesty of the O.J. Simpson trial.

In 1997 the three "Encores!" musicals were *Sweet Adeline*, the 1929 musical by Jerome Kern and Oscar Hammerstein II, a mildly interesting antique; *Promises, Promises,* the 1968 musical by Neil Simon, Burt

Bacharach, and Hal David, which fared better with Martin Short and Christine Baranski; and Rodgers and Hart's 1937 triumph, *The Boys From Syracuse*, which went over best of all.

The 1998 trio included the Gershwins's dated *Strike Up the Band*; the cartoon musical *Li'l Abner* and the 1946 Harold Arlen, Johnny Mercer rarity, *St. Louis Woman*. The singing and dancing in the last were superlative. The cast included Alice Ripley, Burke Moses, Stanley Wayne Mathis, Vanessa L. Williams, and many others.

In 1999, one of Rodgers and Hart's best scores was heard in the "Encores!" series, the 1937 *Babes In Arms*, which boasted these gems in the score: "Where Or When," "The Lady Is A Tramp," "I Wish I Were In Love Again," "My Funny Valentine," and "Johnny One-Note." As a special treat, the production featured members of the original cast of *A Chorus Line* playing the old vaudevillians.

This was followed by a misguided attempt to revive the *Ziegfeld Follies of 1936*. A topical revue is very difficult to bring back after half a century. The sketches, mostly by David Friedman, were no longer funny. The Fanny Brice material acted by Mary Testa—even the famous Baby Snooks sketch—were passé. Even the great Vernon Duke/Ira Gershwin song "I Can't Get Started" did not register. And the dances performed in 1936 by Josephine Baker were meaningless. This was probably the most misguided of the usually astute "Encores!" series. Next came a more pleasing reconstruction of the 1960 musical *Do Re Mi* by Garson Kanin, Comden and Green, and Jule Styne. The concert version starred Nathan Lane, Randy Graff, Lewis J. Stadlen, Marilyn Cooper, Tovah Feldshuh, Brian Stokes Mitchell, and Heather Headley in a musical comedy about a hustler who hopes to make his fortune from jukeboxes.

The end of the 1990s brought these three offerings to the "Encores!" series: *On A Clear Day You Can See Forever, Tenderloin,* and *Wonderful Town.* The best was the concert staging of *Wonderful Town* with a Leonard Bernstein score and Comden and Green lyrics. Performed with gusto by Donna Murphy, Laura Benanti, and others, it was so excellent that it was slated to be moved to Broadway, but plans subsequently fell through.

One cannot mention "Encores!" without giving

credit to the Coffee Club Orchestra under the direction of Rob Fisher. This band plays the scores as they were originally orchestrated in these vintage musicals that young audiences might never otherwise get to see. It is a great pleasure to hear show music as it was heard in the Golden Age of Broadway musicals. Long live "Encores!" and the City Center!

The City Center "Encores!" series has won the following awards: the New York Drama Critics Circle, a Special Tony Honor, Lucille Lortel, Outer Critics Circle, and Jujamcyn Awards.

With Judith E. Daykin as Executive Director and President of the City Center 55th Street Theater Foundation, Inc., this historic theater is still the mecca for anyone who likes to be entertained at reasonable prices. Who could ask for anything more?

VIVIAN BEAUMONT THEATRE

The Vivian Beaumont Theatre at Lincoln Center, built at a cost of $9.7 million, opened on October 21, 1965. It was named for the philanthropist who donated half of its construction cost. A smaller performing space downstairs in the same building was first called the Forum, then later changed to the Mitzi E. Newhouse Theater, for another donor.

The Beaumont was designed by the distinguished set designer Jo Mielziner and the noted architect Eero Saarinen. It had 1,140 seats when proscenium staging was used and 1,083 when the thrust stage was employed. The color scheme was a pleasing red and brown.

When the Beaumont opened it was designated as the home of the Repertory Theater of Lincoln Center. Co-directed by Elia Kazan and Robert Whitehead, this company had been operating for two seasons downtown at the ANTA Washington Square Theater while the Beaumont was under construction. The troupe moved to the Beaumont under the management of Herbert Blau and Jules Irving. Their plan for the Beaumont was to create a "theatre of loud involvement" with plays that would fill the large stage with modern, social and emotional significance. Among the actors who regularly appeared in productions during those early years were Philip Bosco, Nancy Marchand, Aline MacMahon, and Robert Symonds.

The first production was George Buchner's *Danton's*

Death—certainly a large and loud play—about the French Revolution. It was directed by Mr. Blau, had magnificent sets by Mr. Mielziner and a cast that included James Earl Jones, Stacy Keach, and Mr. Symonds. The physical production was praised but the play was considered dull. (Orson Welles had also failed when his Mercury Theatre had produced the work.)

The three other plays produced that first season were Wycherley's *The Country Wife* with Elizabeth Huddle and Mr. Symonds (who also directed); the American premiere of Jean-Paul Sartre's *The Condemned of Altona* with George Coulouris; and the New York premiere of Brecht's *The Caucasian Chalk Circle*, adapted by Eric Bentley, in which actors wore masks. This surrealistic play, directed by Mr. Irving, was considered the best production offered by the company that season.

The first season was a financial success with most subscribers signing up for the next year, but it was not an artistic success. Otis L. Guernsey, Jr., editor of *The Best Plays* annual, complained that the company hadn't found itself yet, and criticized the fact that they presented no American plays.

For its second season, the company began with a revival of Ben Jonson's *The Alchemist* with Michael O'Sullivan, Ms. Marchand, Mr. Bosco, Ms. MacMahon, and Mr. Symonds. Next came Lorca's *Yerma* with Frank

Top: Souvenir program for *The Little Foxes* (1967) with Anne Bancroft, Margaret Leighton, E.G. Marhshall, George C. Scott, Austin Pendleton, William Prince, and Maria Tucci. *Above:* Souvenir program for *The Time of Your Life* (1969) with James Broderick, Susan Tyrrel, and Skip Hinnant.

Langella, Maria Tucci, Ms. MacMahon, and Ms. Marchand. The third offering was the group's first American play—*The East Wind* by Leo Lehman—with Estelle Parsons, George Voskovec, Mr. Bosco, and Ms. MacMahon. This satisfied the critics who complained that the company was not doing new or even old American plays. The fourth subscription play was a revival of Bertolt Brecht's *Galileo*, adapted by Charles Laughton. Anthony Quayle played the title character, supported by Ms. Parsons and others of the rep company. The play dramatized 1600s astronomer Galileo's battle for intellectual freedom against the Church, which forced him to recant his theory of the movement of the planets around the sun.

On January 13, 1967, Herbert Blau resigned as co-director of the Lincoln Center Repertory Theater and Mr. Irving remained as its sole director. During 1967 the Beaumont was rented twice. On July 8, 1967, Alexander H. Cohen presented Peter Ustinov's *The Unknown Soldier and His Wife,* directed by John Dexter. The cast of this war drama included Brian Bedford, Christopher Walken, Melissa C. Murphy, Howard Da Silva, Bob Dishy, and many others. It played at the Beaumont for 84 performances, then moved to the George Abbott Theatre for an additional 64.

On October 26, 1967, the Beaumont presented a special invitational production of Lillian Hellman's *The Little Foxes*. The all-star cast—Anne Bancroft, E.G. Marshall, George C. Scott, Margaret Leighton, Maria Tucci, Austin Pendleton, and Richard A. Dysart—was directed brilliantly by Mike Nichols. The production was so successful that it moved to a commercial run at the Ethel Barrymore Theatre. Critics were beginning to have more faith in the Beaumont.

On January 4, 1968, with Mr. Irving still the company's director, the Beaumont presented Shaw's *Saint Joan* with Diana Sands in the title role. It played for 44 performances. This was followed by Christopher Fry's adaptation of Jean Giraudoux's *Tiger At the Gates*, directed by Anthony Quayle and starring Diana Sands, Mel Dowd, Mr. Bosco, and Mr. Symonds. It also played for 44 performances. Mr. Symonds next starred as the title role in *Cyrano de Bergerac* with Suzanne Grossman as Roxane.

In June 1968, the Lincoln Center Festival '68 presented Paris' Compagnie de Theatre de la Cite de Villeurbanne in three plays: *The Three Musketeers, George Dandin,* and *Tartuffe* for a limited engagement of 24 performances. Also part of the festival was Brian Friel's *Lovers,* starring Art Carney, which ran for 149 performances. Lee J. Cobb starred next as King Lear, playing in repertory with William Gibson's *A Cry of Players.* The double bill stayed for 72 performances.

In April 1969, Heinar Kipphardt's *In The Matter of J. Robert Oppenheimer* opened with Joseph Wiseman in the title role. It closed that month, but returned in June with Paul Sparer as Oppenheimer. During the play's absence, Robert Symonds, Blythe Danner, and Philip Bosco cavorted in Moliere's *The Miser* for 52 performances.

On November 6, 1969, William Saroyan's whimsical comedy, *The Time of Your Life,* was revived with James Broderick, Philip Bosco, and Susan Tyrrell in lead roles. It played for 52 performances. It was followed by Tennessee Williams's curious play *Camino Real* with Jessica Tandy and Al Pacino in the lead roles. It mystified the subscribers for 52 performances. Next was a new play by Sam Shepard called *Operation Sidewinder* and it was staged with dazzling surrealism. The story involved a deadly military device—a large mechanical rattlesnake—and there was much violence and loud rock music onstage. George S. Kaufman and Marc Connelly's 1924 fantasy, *Beggar On Horseback,* arrived next with Leonard Frey as a struggling artist about to be trapped in a loveless marriage to a wealthy woman. Much of the action occurred in the hero's dreams. Critics saluted the Repertory Theater of Lincoln Center for presenting an all-American season of plays—both new and old. The Sam Shepard play was judged to be the most interesting.

Four plays were presented in the 1970-71 season. Colleen Dewhurst starred in *The Good Woman of Setzuan* by Bertolt Brecht. David Birney, Frances Sternhagen, Philip Bosco, and Tandy Cronyn were in Synge's *The Playboy of the Western World.* Arthur Miller's adaptation of Ibsen's *An Enemy of the People* was revived with Stephen Elliott, Mr. Bosco, David Birney, and Barbara Cason. The final production of the season was Sophocles's *Antigone,* adapted by Dudley Fitts and Robert Fitzgerald, with Martha Henry as Antigone, Ms. Cronyn as Ismene, and Mr. Bosco as Creon. The critics pronounced it to be a distinguished season for the Beaumont.

The 1971-72 season brought a revival of Schiller's *Mary Stuart* with Salomé Jens in the title role, and Nancy Marchand as Queen Elizabeth. A very promising actor, Andy Robinson (later to chill audiences as the sniper in the film *Dirty Harry*), appeared in this play as Sir William Davison and in many other productions of The Repertory Theater of Lincoln Center. This production also marked the American premiere of Stephen Spender's translation of the play.

Next came *Narrow Road To The Deep North* by Edward Bond, a boring, symbolic play set in Japan. It was followed by a revival of Shakespeare's *Twelfth Night* starring Blythe Danner as Viola, Rene Auberjonois as Malvolio, Leonard Frey as Sir Andrew Aguecheek, and Moses Gunn as Orsino.

The last production of the season was a revival of Arthur Miller's 1953 play, *The Crucible.* This production, with Robert Foxworth as John Proctor, was enthusiastically received, but somewhat dampened by Arthur Miller's denunciation of the Lincoln Center's Board of Directors as being ignorant of how to run a repertory company. This attack appeared in several publications including *The New York Times.* Wrote Mr. Miller: "The first order of business now is to get clear in our own minds what a repertory theater is, what it can do and what is financially needed to do it. Then, if we are convinced of its value, a considered serious attempt must be made to transform Lincoln Center into such a theater."

The 1972-73 season brought Gorky's *Enemies,* O'Casey's *The Plough and the Stars,* Shakespeare's *The Merchant of Venice,* and Tennessee Williams's *A Streetcar Named Desire.*

A dramatic event occurred during this season. Artistic Director Jules Irving announced he was leaving the Lincoln Center Repertory Theater. He was displeased with the Board's management of the company. The Forum Theater had been reduced to showing films; they nearly permitted the destruction of the company's storage space for scenery, and, most seriously, they failed to provide the necessary financing for a true repertory company—a staple of British theatre, but an elusive ideal in

American theatre to the time of this writing. A meeting was held and the board considered renting the Beaumont to outside productions. A touring company of *Man of La Mancha* had done very well the previous summer as an extra attraction at the Beaumont. (After all, it had started at the downtown ANTA Theater, the original home of the company.)

But no, something else was proposed and sanctioned. Joseph Papp, head of the New York Shakespeare Festival, would take over with his own Board. Mr. Papp immediately began raising financing for his project and when the Rockefeller Foundation granted $350,000 and Mrs. Samuel I. Newhouse donated $1 million, the name of the Forum Theater was changed to the Mitzi E. Newhouse.

Mr. Papp announced that he would continue to produce experimental plays downtown at his Public Theatre stages, and his Shakespeare summer productions at Central Park's Delacorte Theatre, but he would present more finished plays at the Beaumont. His company was in residence at the Beaumont from 1973 to 1977, presenting only new plays at first, rather than classics. During this time he also staged productions in the Newhouse. Among his offerings were David Rabe's *Boom Boom Room,* an expensive failure with Madeline Kahn; *The Au Pair Man* by Hugh Leonard with Julie Harris and Charles Durning; *What the Wine Sellers Buy* by Ron Miller; a revival of Strindberg's *The Dance of Death* with Zoë Caldwell, Robert Shaw, and Hector Elizondo; and a powerful prison drama called *Short Eyes* by Miguel Piñero, which transferred to the Beaumont from the downtown Public Theater. The latter was judged the strongest entry of Mr. Papp's inaugural season at this theatre. Otis L. Guernsey, Jr. wrote in *The Best Plays of 1972-1973*: "Joseph Papp's first season at the Vivian Beaumont was one of adventure for the Lincoln Center subscription audiences (and audiences who aren't adventurous don't belong at Papp productions)."

In 1974-1975, Papp presented *Mert & Phil* by Anne Burr, *Black Picture Show* by Bill Gunn, Ibsen's *A Doll's House* with Liv Ullman and Sam Waterston, and *Little Black Sheep* by Anthony Scully. Mr. Papp was upset by the public's lack of response to his new-play schedule at the Beaumont and announced that in the future he would mainly do revivals there.

His next season included *Trelawny of the "Wells"* by Arthur Wing Piñero, with Meryl Streep, John Lithgow, Walter Abel, Mary Beth Hurt, and Mandy Patinkin. The production received the following Tony Award nominations: Featured Actress in a Play (Hurt), Scenic Designer (David Mitchell), and Lighting Designer (Ian Calderon). *Hamlet* followed with Sam Waterston, Jane Alexander, Maureen Anderman, George Hearn, Larry Gates, and Mr. Patinkin. Shaw's *Mrs. Warren's Profession* was revived with Lynn Redgrave, Ruth Gordon, Edward Herrmann, and Milo O'Shea. Mr. Herrmann won a Tony Award (Featured Actor in a Play) and Ms. Redgrave was nominated for Best Actress in a Play. *Threepenny Opera* was next with Raul Julia as Mack the Knife, plus Elizabeth Wilson and Blair Brown performing a controversial new translation by Ralph Manheim and John Willett, replacing the familiar one by Marc Blitzstein. This production was highly successful, as was David Rabe's powerful army play, *Streamers,* which was nominated for a Best Play Tony Award.

In 1977, Mr. Papp presented a new adaptation of Chekhov's *The Cherry Orchard* by Jean-Claude van Itallie with Raul Julia, Meryl Streep, Irene Worth, Mary Beth Hurt, Max Wright, and Cathryn Damon. This was followed by a revival of *Agamemnon* by Aeschylus as conceived by Andrei Serban and Elizabeth Swados, using fragments of the original Greek, and Edith Hamilton's translation. Both revivals were judged to be outstanding. Despite this record, Mr. Papp's productions downtown at his theatre on Astor Place were judged to be superior to his uptown output and he decided to withdraw from the Beaumont. Plagued by complaints about poor acoustics and its unwieldy thrust stage, the Beaumont remained closed for 18 months.

From 1979 to 1984, producer Richard Crinkley was executive director of the Beaumont, which presented only one full season, in 1980-1981, including an unsuccessful revival of Philip Barry's celebrated high comedy, *The Philadelphia Story,* starring Blythe Danner as Tracy Lord, Meg Mundy as her mother, Frank Converse as C.K. Dexter Haven, Edward Herrmann as Mike Connor, Mary Louise Wilson as Liz Imbrie, Douglas Watson as Seth Lord, and George Ede as the lecherous Uncle Willie.

The play was lost in a gigantic set that resembled Pennsylvania Station and the charm of the 1939 original with Katharine Hepburn was missing.

Mr. Crinkley next presented *Macbeth* with Philip Anglim, Maureen Anderman, Dana Ivey, and Kelsey Grammer for 61 performances. The third offering that season was an inferior comedy by Woody Allen called *The Floating Light Bulb*, with Danny Aiello, Beatrice Arthur, Jack Weston, and Brian Backer, who received a Featured Actor Tony Award for his performance. Jack Weston was nominated for a Leading Actor Tony Award. This memory play was compared unfavorably to *The Glass Menagerie*.

In 1983, a memorable event occurred at the Beaumont. The theatre was rented to producer Alexander H. Cohen for Peter Brook's magnificent production of *La Tragédie de Carmen*, an 80-minute distillation of Bizet's opera *Carmen*. This production was originally aimed for the New Amsterdam Roof, but had to be switched to the Beaumont when the Roof was declared unsafe. The drama critics were jubilant at Brook's dynamic staging of the condensed opera on a thrust stage, but the music critics weren't. One of the fascinating aspects of the production was that the performance area was covered with dirt, like a bull ring. Not all the Bizet music was used, and three singers alternated in the lead roles. The work was subtitled "A Full Length Musical In One Act." It was a triumph, and thrilled playgoers for 187 performances. It received a Special Tony Award for its brilliance.

From 1985 to 1992, Gregory Mosher was director and Bernard Gersten was executive producer of the Lincoln Center Theater Company. In 1986 they produced *Juggling and Cheap Theatrics,* a variety revue devised by the incredible New Vaudeville troupe, The Flying Karamazov Brothers. In April they came up with a real winner: a revival of *The House of Blue Leaves* by John Guare, which had been a 1971 Off-Broadway delight. The revival starred John Mahoney, Stockard Channing, Swoosie Kurtz, Christine Baranski, and Danny Aiello. The comedy, about bedlam in the New York borough of Queens when the Pope pays a visit, won the following Tony Awards: Best Featured Actor (Mahoney), Best Featured Actress (Kurtz), Best Play Director (Jerry Zaks), and Best Scenic Designer (Tony

Walton). It also received the following Tony Award nominations: Best Featured Actress (Channing), Best Play, Best Costume Design (Ann Roth), Best Lighting Design (Paul Gallo).

In November 1986 the Beaumont had another hit revival: the Hecht/MacArthur classic *The Front Page* with Richard Thomas, John Lithgow, and Bill McCutcheon. It received two Tony Award nominations: Best Revival and Best Scenic Designer (Tony Walton).

In 1987, the theatre presented Earle Hyman in *Death and the King's Horseman*, a Nigerian drama by Wole Soyinka; *The Regard of Flight* and *The Clown Bagatelles*, entertainment by the superb mime Bill Irwin; and an antic version of *The Comedy of Errors* conceived by The Flying Karamazov Brothers and Robert Woodruff, which played for 148 performances.

On November 19, 1987, the Beaumont welcomed its greatest hit thus far—a jubilant revival of the 1934 Cole Porter musical *Anything Goes*. Patti LuPone had the famous Ethel Merman role of Reno Sweeney, Howard McGillin took the William Gaxton role, and Bill McCutcheon expertly acted the Victor Moore Public Enemy No. 13 part. The original Porter score was beefed up with interpolated numbers such as "Easy To Love," "It's De-Lovely," and others, and Tony Walton designed a deluxe shipboard set on which the show's band was perched. The stunning revival ran for 804 performances and won the following Tony Awards: Best Featured Actor in a Musical (McCutcheon), Best Choreography (Michael Smuin), and Best Musical Revival. It also received these Tony nominations: Best Musical Actress (LuPone), Best Musical Actor (McGillin), Best Musical Featured Actor (Anthony Heald), Best Musical Director (Jerry Zaks), Best Scenic Designer, and Best Costume Designer (Tony Walton), and Best Lighting Designer (Paul Gallo). This bonanza ran until September 3, 1989.

The last production of the 1980s was a revival of Paddy Chayefsky's *The Tenth Man* with Phoebe Cates. This was followed by a play transferred from Off Broadway called *Some Americans Abroad* by Richard Nelson, with Nathan Lane and Kate Burton. The play concerned a group of Anglophile American professors on a London theatre tour. In November 1990 another winner came to the Beaumont from Lincoln Center's

Left: PLAYBILL for John Guare's *Six Degrees of Separation* (1990). *Right:* Victor Garber and Blair Brown in Tom Stoppard's *Arcadia* (1995).

smaller theatre, the Newhouse. It was John Guare's fascinating *Six Degrees of Separation*, based on a true-life incident in which an imposter passed himself off as the son of actor Sidney Poitier and was able to invade the apartments of rich Manhattanites. The play was stylishly directed by Jerry Zaks, who won a Tony Award, and was voted the Best Play of the year by the New York Drama Critics Circle. It also earned these Tony Award nominations: Best Actress (Stockard Channing), Best Actor (Courtney B. Vance), and Best Play. It had a healthy run of 485 performances.

Another John Guare drama arrived next, but it was only fair. *Four Baboons Adoring the Sun* was an odd play and *The New York Times* called it the most controversial play of the season. Ms. Channing and James Naughton headed the cast.

Andre Bishop, who had successfully piloted Playwrights Horizons for many years, then succeeded Gregory Mosher and joined Bernard Gersten as Artistic Director of the Lincoln Center Theater. The Gersten/ Bishop team was to elevate this theatre to its pinnacle of artistic achievement.

During the 1992-1993 season, a musical version of the film *My Favorite Year* proved a failure, despite a score by Lynn Ahrens and Stephen Flaherty. It was based on a film about a real-life incident. In 1954, Errol Flynn arrived in New York to do a guest stint on Sid Caesar's "Your Show of Shows" and wound up wreaking havoc with his outra-

geous behavior. Although the musical did not work, it won a Tony Award for Andrea Martin as Best Featured Actress in a Musical. Other Tony nominees: Tim Curry (Best Actor in a Musical) and Lainie Kazan (Best Featured Actress in a Musical).

On November 29, 1993, a huge cast performed in a revival of Robert E. Sherwood's 1938 Pulitzer-winning play, *Abe Lincoln in Illinois*. Sam Waterston was praised for his performance as Lincoln, and Lizbeth Mackay played Mary Todd. The production received the following Tony Award nominations: Best Actor in a Play (Waterston), Best Play Director (Gerald Gutierrez), and Best Revival.

Jane Bowles's pretentious drama *In the Summer House* was next and it received mostly negative reviews. Dianne Wiest, Liev Schreiber, and Frances Conroy appeared in this misty fantasy, which was soon gone. The next tenant was such a huge success that it moved from the smaller Newhouse Theater to the larger Beaumont to accommodate the crowds. It was Wendy Wasserstein's autobiographical play, *The Sisters Rosensweig*, about her family of achievers. The setting was a luxurious house in London and the comedy had sparkling performances by Jane Alexander, Madeline Kahn, and Robert Klein. Ms. Kahn won a Tony Award for Best Actress in a Play and there were other Tony nominations: Best Play, Best Actress (Alexander), and Best Direction of a Play (Daniel Sullivan). The comedy was so successful that it trans-

Left: Michael Hayden and Sally Murphy on Bob Crowley's Tony-winning set for *Carousel* (1994). *Right:* Program image for the same production.

ferred to the Barrymore Theatre for an extended run.

Gray's Anatomy, a monologue about how an eye affliction literally changes one man's view of the world, was expertly delivered by actor Spalding Gray and played two engagements at the Beaumont in 1993 and 1994.

On March 24, 1994, London's Royal National Theatre sent New York its hit revival of *Carousel*, the Rodgers and Hammerstein classic. The cast included Audra Ann McDonald (who later dropped the "Ann"), Sally Murphy, and Michael Hayden. Bob Crowley's sets were outstanding, as was Nicholas Hytner's staging, especially the way the eponymous carousel assembled itself as if by magic in the musical's opening scene. The voices of Ms. McDonald and the other singers were superlative, giving new grandeur to the haunting score. The musical won the following Tony Awards: Best Musical Revival, Best Featured Musical Actress (McDonald), Best Musical Director (Hytner), Best Scenic Designer (Crowley), and Best Choreographer (Sir Kenneth MacMillan). *Carousel* revolved for 322 performances.

On March 30, 1995, a play arrived that was a masterpiece to some (especially critics) and a colossal bore to others. It was Tom Stoppard's play *Arcadia*, which had been an enormous success in London. The action in the play kept shifting from the present to 1809, which some found confusing. One critic wrote: "The night I saw it, large portions of the audience stood and cheered but others left looking wan and defeated. Stoppard's intellectual plays are like caviar—you either love it or loathe it." *Arcadia* won the New York Drama Critics Circle Award for Best Play. The cast included Billy Crudup, Jennifer Dundas, Lisa Banes, Victor Garber, Blair Brown, Robert Sean Leonard, and David Manis. It won no Tony Awards but was nominated in the following categories: Best Play, Best Scenic Designer (Mark Thompson), and Best Lighting Designer (Paul Pyant). The play ran for 173 performances.

David Hare, one of Britain's most prolific playwrights, supplied the next Beaumont attraction, *Racing Demon,* which attacked the politics of the Church of England. *Variety* felt it was "unsettling, deeply pessimistic play." The cast included Josef Sommer, Michael Cumpsty, Brian Murray, and Kathleen Chalfant. It ran for 48 performances and received a Best Play Tony Award nomination.

November 24, 1996, brought an imaginative novelty to the Beaumont: *Juan Darién,* subtitled *A Carnival Mass,* written and directed by the distinguished artist Julie Taymor, with composer Elliot Goldenthal. Taymor also designed the brilliant puppets, masks, and some of the sets and costumes that made this a stunning visual experience. Set in a South American jungle, this "music theatre" piece about a jaguar cub who transforms into a boy was praised more for its spectacular beauty than for

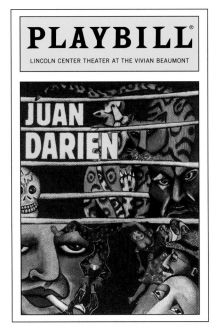 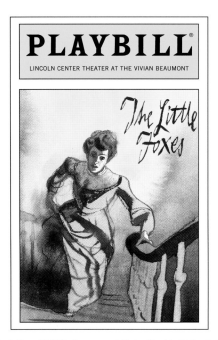 

Left: PLAYBILL for Julie Taymor's *Juan Darién: A Carnival Mass* (1996). *Center and Right:* Jim McMullen's beautiful poster designs on the opening night PLAYBILLs for *The Little Foxes* (1997) and *Twelfth Night* (1998).

its content.

Another revival of Hellman's *The Little Foxes* opened at the Beaumont in April 1997. It starred Stockard Channing in the Tallulah Bankhead role. *New York Times* drama critic Ben Brantley pronounced the revival "miscast and misconceived."

Chekhov's *Ivanov* was revived in November 1997 with Kevin Kline, Jayne Atkinson, Hope Davis, and Robert Foxworth. It received mixed reviews, but Mr. Kline's performance was praised. It ran for 51 performances. Eugene O'Neill's only comedy, *Ah, Wilderness!* was given a loving revival in March 1998 with Craig T. Nelson, Leo Burmester, Sam Trammell, and Jean Thompson in lead roles. It garnered mostly favorable reviews and received two Tony Award nominations: Best Play Revival and Best Featured Actor in a play (Trammell).

An eagerly-awaited musical in 1998 proved to be a letdown. *Parade*, a musical treatment of a very tragic real-life incident, turned out to be too grim for the musical stage. Co-conceived by Harold Prince, who directed it, the show had a book by Alfred Uhry and a score by Broadway first-timer Jason Robert Brown. The show recounted the harrowing lynching of the Northern-born

Jew Leo Frank, wrongly accused of murdering a thirteen-year-old girl in a pencil factory in Atlanta. This tragedy had been made into a superlative 1937 film, *They Won't Forget*, as well as an acclaimed TV movie, *The Murder of Mary Phagan*, but it did not work as a musical, despite the splendid performances of Brent Carver and Carolee Carmello, and an excellent score by Mr. Brown, captured on a superb RCA Victor cast album. The musical received the following Tony Awards: Best Musical Book (Uhry), and Best Musical Score (Brown). It also received the following Tony nominations: Best Musical, Best Choreography (Patricia Birch), Best Musical Direction (Harold Prince), Best Scenic Design (Ricardo Hernandez). It closed after 85 performances.

Next, Lincoln Center Theater co-produced a musical revue called *It Ain't Nothin' But The Blues*, as created by the Crossroads Theater Company of New Jersey. Music by various composers was used to trace the history of the blues.

The last new Broadway musical of the 1900s, *Marie Christine*, opened at the Beaumont on December 2, 1999. It was an odd work, based on Euripides' *Medea*. Michael John LaChiusa, who wrote the book and composed the score, set his version in New Orleans and Chicago. Audra

McDonald gave a thrilling dramatic and singing performance as Marie Christine, the Medea character, who dabbled in voodoo. Anthony Crivello played the charismatic sailor for whose sake she killed her brother, abandoned her home and fortune, and took off for Chicago. The music was dissonant and the libretto disjointed. Critics and audiences found the show cold, depressing, unmoving, and devoid of humor. It received the following Tony Award nominations: Best Musical Book (LaChiusa), Best Orchestrations (Jonathan Tunick), Best Lighting Design (Jules Fisher and Peggy Eisenhauer), Best Performance by the Lead Actress in a Musical (McDonald).

The Beaumont greeted 2000, however, with a great hit: Susan Stroman's triptych of one-act dance plays, collectively titled *Contact*, starring Boyd Gaines, Karen Ziemba, and Deborah Yates as the mysterious Woman in the Yellow Dress. The show prompted much debate over whether it fit the definition of a musical. It had just scraps of dialogue, and no singing whatever. All dancing was done to pre-recorded pop and classical music. Nevertheless, the production won the 2000 Tony Award as Best Musical, and settled in at the Beaumont for a long run.

The record of Bernard Gersten and Andre Bishop at the helm of Lincoln Center has been outstanding and has fulfilled many of the original hopes for an exemplary institutional theatre in Manhattan.

Boyd Gaines is haunted by Deborah Yates on the PLAYBILL for the Tony Award-winning dance musical, *Contact*.

CIRCLE IN THE SQUARE THEATRE

The new Circle in the Square Theatre opened on November 15, 1972, with Theodore Mann as artistic director and Paul Libin as managing director. The nonprofit organization was the uptown successor to the legendary Circle in the Square company in Greenwich Village, which helped to define the Off-Broadway movement. The handsome new theatre, with its distinctive U-shaped seating area around a true thrust stage, was designed by architect Allen Sayles and has lighting by Jules Fisher.

Located in the Uris Building at Fiftieth Street, west of Broadway, the Circle in the Square is situated below the former Uris Theatre, now renamed the Gershwin Theatre. It has 650 seats, more than double the number of its Off-Broadway parent. At the time of the new theatre's opening, Mr. Mann told PLAYBILL: "Every seat here has a perfect view. Essentially, the design is based on the old theatre—with almost exactly the same stage space. But we have the latest technical facilities—we can trap the stage, have enough height to fly the scenery—from an artistic and scenic point of view. And look at the ceiling in the auditorium. I don't know of any other theatre like this that has a visible grid above the audience where electricians and stage hands can walk about. All our lighting will come from there. This is a whole new innovation in the Broadway area—the arrival of institutional theatres."

The new theatre was much more cheerful than its predecessor on Bleecker Street, with bright red seats and red-and-gray checked carpet bearing the Circle in the Square cube symbol, which was repeated in the solid cube lights in the handsome lobby. Audiences enter the theatre by walking down a flight of stairs or riding escalators to a lounge below street level.

"We owe a lot to [the late *New York Times* critic] Brooks Atkinson for the design of this theatre," Mr. Mann stated. "When we were building the first one, I asked Mr. Atkinson what the essential ingredient should be. He replied, 'When you walk in the door, you should see the stage—that should predominate—not the audience.' So, when you walk into our theatre, the first thing you see is the stage—and it works."

Owing to the stature of Circle in the Square and its policy of offering a subscription season of short runs, the new theatre quickly amassed an impressive roll call of stars and productions, photographs of which were used to decorate the lounge and bar area.

The new Circle in the Square opened auspiciously with a revival of an edited version of Eugene O'Neill's *Mourning Becomes Electra,* with Colleen Dewhurst. Critics praised the production and the new theatre, expressing satisfaction that although the house was larger and more modern, it preserved the intimacy and ambiance of its downtown predecessor.

In 1973 the theatre presented Irene Papas in *Medea;*

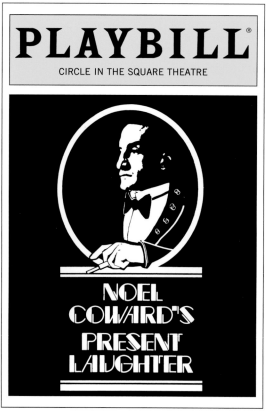

Left: Ellis Rabb (in wheelchair) berates Patricia O'Connell and Richard Woods in the 1980 revival of *The Man Who Came to Dinner. Above:* PLAYBILL cover sketch of George C. Scott in the scintillating 1982 revival of Noël Coward's *Present Laughter.*

Siobhan McKenna in *Here Are Ladies*; Lillian Gish, George C. Scott, Nicol Williamson, Barnard Hughes, and Julie Christie in *Uncle Vanya*; Anne Jackson and Eli Wallach in *The Waltz of the Toreadors*; and James Earl Jones in *The Iceman Cometh.*

The year 1974 offered a new play, *An American Millionaire*, by Murray Schisgal; Jim Dale in *Scapino*, which transferred to a commercial run at the Ambassador; Rita Moreno in *The National Health*; and Raul Julia in the musical *Where's Charley?*

In 1975, Circle in the Square staged Eugene O'Neill's *All God's Chillun Got Wings*, directed by George C. Scott; Arthur Miller's *Death of a Salesman*, starring Mr. Scott; *Ah, Wilderness!*, with Geraldine Fitzgerald; and Tennessee Williams's *The Glass Menagerie,* with Maureen Stapleton and Rip Torn.

The 1976 season highlighted Vanessa Redgrave in Ibsen's *The Lady from the Sea*; Rodgers and Hart's *Pal Joey*, with Christopher Chadman and Joan Copeland; Mildred Dunnock in *Days in the Trees,* by Marguerite Duras; and Tennessee Williams's *The Night of the Iguana,* starring Richard Chamberlain and Dorothy McGuire.

Four revivals were presented in 1977: Paul Rudd and Pamela Payton-Wright in *Romeo and Juliet*; Wilde's *The Importance of Being Earnest*; John Wood, Mildred Dunnock, and Tammy Grimes in Moliere's *Tartuffe*; and Lynn Redgrave in Shaw's *Saint Joan.*

In 1978 Circle in the Square staged Feydeau's *13 Rue De L'Amour*, with Louis Jourdan and Patricia Elliott; Kaufman and Hart's *Once in a Lifetime*, with John Lithgow, Treat Williams, Max Wright, and Jayne Meadows Allen; Gogol's *The Inspector General*, with

Theodore Bikel; and Shaw's *Man and Superman*, with George Grizzard, Philip Bosco, and Laurie Kennedy.

The 1979 season included two new plays: *Spokesong*, by Stewart Parker, with John Lithgow, Virginia Vestoff, Joseph Maher, and Maria Tucci; and *Loose Ends*, by Michael Weller, with Kevin Kline and Roxanne Hart.

The 1980 productions included *Major Barbara*, with Philip Bosco and Laurie Kennedy; *Past Tense*, by Jack Zeman, with Barbara Feldon and Laurence Luckinbill; and Ellis Rabb in *The Man Who Came to Dinner*.

In 1981 Irene Papas returned in *The Bacchae*; E.G. Marshall, Irene Worth, and Rosemary Murphy appeared

From left: William Atherton, Michael Moriarty, and John Rubinstein hold court in the 1983 revival of Herman Wouk's *The Caine Mutiny Court-Martial.*

in *John Gabriel Borkman*; Ralph Waite and Frances Sternhagen headlined *The Father*; and a new American play, *Scenes and Revelations*, by Elan Garonzik, was presented.

The 1982 season opened with Joanne Woodward in *Candida*, followed by *Macbeth*, starring Nicol Williamson. Next came Percy Granger's new play, *Eminent Domain*, with Philip Bosco and Betty Miller. In the summer of 1982, George C. Scott was hailed in a hilarious revival of Noël Coward's light comedy *Present Laughter*.

The year 1983 began with a scintillating revival of Molière's *The Misanthrope* with Brian Bedford, Carole Shelley, and Mary Beth Hurt. This was followed by an exciting revival of Herman Wouk's *The Caine Mutiny Court-Martial* with John Rubinstein, Michael Moriarty, and William Atherton. Later, Joe Namath joined the cast, making his Broadway debut. Next came a revival of Shaw's *Heartbreak House* starring Rex Harrison and Rosemary Harris, with Amy Irving.

The year 1984 brought a new production of Clifford Odets's *Awake and Sing!*; Noël Coward's *Design For Living* starring Jill Clayburgh, Frank Langella, Raul Julia, and Lisa Kirk; Shaw's *Arms and the Man* starring Kevin Klein and Mr. Julia, directed by John Malkovich; *The Marriage of Figaro* starring Christopher Reeve, Anthony Heald, Dana Ivey, Mary Elizabeth Mastrantonio, and Louis Zorich; and a limited engagement of *The Robert Klein Show*, starring the popular comic. Mr. Malkovich directed a 1986 production of Pinter's *The Caretaker*. George C. Scott and John Cullum starred in *The Boys in Autumn*, a play about the reunion after 50 years of Tom Sawyer and Huck Finn.

In the fall of 1986, a revival of Shaw's *You Never Can Tell* had a sterling cast headed by Uta Hagen, Victor Garber, Philip Bosco, and Amanda Plummer. In March, 1987, Tina Howe's play *Coastal Disturbances* opened and played for ten months. Next came a revival of *A Streetcar Named Desire*, starring Blythe Danner, Aiden Quinn, Frank Converse, and Frances McDormand. *An Evening With Robert Klein* played here in June 1988 and was followed by revivals of *Juno and the Paycock* and *The Night of the Iguana*. A revival of Shaw's *The Devil's Disciple* with Mr. Bosco, Mr. Garber, Rosemary Murphy, and Remak Ramsey played for 113 performances; and

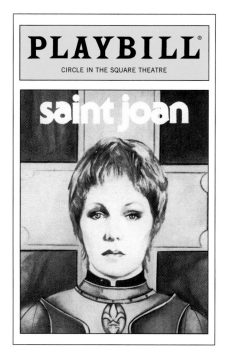  

Left: PLAYBILL for Lynn Redgrave's *Saint Joan* (1977). *Center:* Philip Seymour Hoffman and John C. Reilly alternated in the two main roles of *True West* (2000). *Right:* A revival of the sci-fi spoof, *The Rocky Horror Show* (2000).

Ghetto, by Joshua Sobol (English version by David Lan) gave 33 performances.

Susan H. Schulman's new production of the Stephen Sondheim/Hugh Wheeler classic, *Sweeney Todd*, which had previously been presented at the York Theatre in Manhattan, was brought to the Circle in the Square in September 1989 and played for 189 performances, starring Bob Gunton and Beth Fowler. Taking note of its dimensions (greatly reduced from the Broadway original) the parody revue *Forbidden Broadway* dubbed this production "*Teeny Todd.*"

May 1990 brought a new play, *Zoya's Apartment* by Mikhail Bulgakov (translated by Nicholas Saunders); the following October saw a lively revival of Molière's *The Miser* with Philip Bosco, Mia Dillon, and Carole Shelley. *Taking Steps*, a British farce by Alan Ayckbourn, enjoyed 78 performances in 1991.

On Borrowed Time, a loving 1991 revival of Paul Osborn's charming comedy about Death trapped up a tree, starred George C. Scott as Gramps and Matthew Poroc as Pud, his grandson, with Teresa Wright and Nathan Lane (as a dapper "Mr. Brink"). It received excellent notices.

Nevertheless, after this point increasing financial difficulties limited the number of shows presented by the Circle in the Square company at the uptown theatre.

Search and Destroy, a play by Howard Korder, played 46 performances in 1992 and was followed by Al Pacino in an evening of two very different plays: the overripe *Salomé* by Oscar Wilde and the spartan *Chinese Coffee,* a new play by Ira Lewis. Both received mixed reviews from the critics. In fall 1992, a musical version of Tolstoy's *Anna Karenina* by Peter Kellogg and Daniel Levine was also dismissed by the critics, with one of them rating it "One Czar." Better received was the 1993 *Wilder, Wilder, Wilder*, three one-act plays by Thornton Wilder, which received a Tony nomination as the season's Best Revival.

After standing dark for more than a year, the theatre relit in November 1994 for a revival of the Pulitzer-winning play *The Shadow Box* by Michael Cristofer, starring Marlo Thomas, Estelle Parsons, and Mercedes Ruehl, the latter of whom received a Tony Award nomination as Featured Actress in a Play. The revival received lukewarm reviews and played for 48 performances. In February, 1995, Chekhov's *Uncle Vanya*, in an English version by Jean-Claude van Itallie, opened with Tom Courtenay,

Werner Klemperer, Elizabeth Franz, and others, played for 29 performances. Another revival, Tennessee Williams's *The Rose Tattoo*, followed, with Ms. Ruehl and Anthony La Paglia in the leads. It was nominated for the Best Revival of a Play Tony Award and ran for 36 performances.

The following season, Circle in the Square presented the following revival: Tennessee Williams's *Garden District*, which consisted of two plays: *Something Unspoken* and *Suddenly Last Summer*. The first, short play starred Myra Carter and Pamela Payton-Wright and was considered "slight" by critics. The second was judged a better play, but marred by overacting. It starred Elizabeth Ashley, Jordan Baker, Celia Weston, and Victor Slezak, with critics singling out Baker for praise. The production was compared unfavorably with the movie version of *Suddenly Last Summer*, which starred Elizabeth Taylor, Katharine Hepburn, and Montgomery Clift. The unsavory theme of cannibalism soured some critics and theatregoers. It ran for 31 performances.

Philip Barry's delightful high comedy *Holiday* starred Laura Linney, Tony Goldwyn, Kim Raver, and Reg Rogers, whose performance as an alcoholic won him a Tony Award nomination for a Featured Actor in a Play. The comedy ran for 49 performances. Next came William Inge's *Bus Stop* starring Mary-Louise Parker and Billy Crudup. The play received mixed reviews with some critics feeling that it was dated. Mr. Crudup received excellent reviews as the boisterous cowboy. The revival ran for 29 performances. *Tartuffe: Born Again,* a new version of Moliere's 1664 satire, starred John Glover as the archetypal religious hypocrite, with the action transposed from France to the American South. But the reviews were not encouraging. It opened in May 1996 and ran for 29 performances.

In August 1996, this theatre presented Al Pacino in a revival of Eugene O'Neill's one-act, *Hughie,* with only one other actor in the cast, Paul Benedict. It's primarily a monologue for Pacino's character, talking to a night clerk in a New York hotel lobby in 1928. The star's performance received favorable reviews, boosting the show to a 56-performance run.

During that run an era ended at this theatre. Founders Theodore Mann and Paul Libin resigned, and Circle in the Square filed for bankruptcy protection.

The company seemed to be healing its financial wounds under their successors, Gregory Mosher and M. Edgar Rosenblum. On February 20, 1997, it hosted the Royal National Theatre of London's production of *Stanley,* starring Anthony Sher as the artist Stanley Spencer. Publicity over a brief nude scene almost overshadowed author Pam Gems's study of whether artists are subject to the same rules as the rest of society. The critics admired Mr. Sher's performance more than the play and he received a Tony Award nomination as Best Actor in a Play. Other nominations: Best Play

Above: Finbar Lynch and Dion Graham share a prison cell in Tennessee Williams's *Not About Nightingales* (1999). Photo by Joan Marcus.
Below: The Circle in the Square Theatre when it opened in 1972.

Tom Hewitt and Jarrod Emick in the raucous revival of *The Rocky Horror Show* (2000). Photo by Carol Rosegg.

(Gems) and Best Director of a Play (John Caird). The play ran for 74 performances.

But financial difficulties persisted, leadership changed again, and the Circle in the Square remained closed until 1999 when it reopened as a regular commercial rental theatre. The first tenant was *Not About Nightingales*, an early Tennessee Williams play, said to have been rediscovered among the author's papers by Vanessa Redgrave. Presented to considerable acclaim, it was the harrowing true story of a notorious incident in an American prison in 1938 in which a brutal prison warden punished some rebellious convicts by locking them in a section of the jail where radiators made the heat unbearable and scalded the men until they died. The warden was played by Corin Redgrave (Vanessa's brother) who received a Tony Award nomination, as did Finbar Lynch as one of the inmates. The play received a Best Play Tony Award nomination and ran for 125 performances.

The Circle in the Square Theatre was leased to the HBO cable service in fall 1999, which used it for taping the comedy-interview program "The Chris Rock Show." It returned to legitimacy in spring 2000 with a revival of Sam Shepard's *True West*, in which actors Philip Seymour Hoffman and John C. Reilly alternated performances in the two primary roles.

The theatre had its longest-running hit starting in fall 2000. Christopher Ashley staged a stylish revival of Richard O'Brien's cult rock musical *The Rocky Horror Show*, with a cast that included rock star Joan Jett, plus Dick Cavett, Alice Ripley, Jarrod Emick, and Tom Hewitt. The production, for which the interior of the theatre was redecorated with eerie casts of human figures hung on the walls, earned a Tony nomination as Best Revival of a Musical.

At this writing, The Circle in the Square was again under the direction of Theodore Mann and Paul Libin.

GERSHWIN THEATRE

The Gershwin Theatre was originally named the Uris. When it opened in 1972 it was the first large Broadway theatre to be built since the Earl Carroll in 1931. Occupying six stories of the new Uris Building on the site of the old Capitol movie palace at Broadway and Fifty-first Street, the huge theatre, with more than 1,900 seats (the most of any regularly-used theatre on Broadway), was devised by set designer Ralph Alswang. At the time of the theatre's opening, Mr. Alswang told PLAYBILL: "The Uris represents what I think is the total philsophy of a modern musical comedy house—seating, sight lines, acoustics—the economy and aesthetics of this kind of theatre. I was given a completely free hand by the Uris people and by the Nederlanders and Gerard Oestreicher, who have a thirty-year lease on the house."

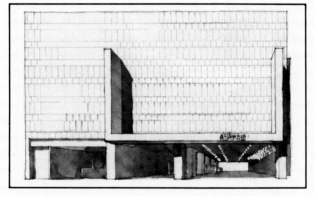

The designer said that the whole theatre was done in a sensuous Art Nouveau style. The auditorium is on the second floor and is reached by escalators. "The bar, the plaster wall running 200 feet on a reverse curve and the Lalique lighting fixtures are all Art Nouveau shapes," Alswang stated. "Most people want to sit in the orchestra, so we have 1,280 seats downstairs and a very small balcony with 660 seats with projecting side sections to replace box seats. We have dark proscenium panels that serve as light towers and that are removable if the production demands it. The flexible stage floor can be taken apart like a Tinkertoy or be extended as a thrust stage. And for the first time in theatre history, there is a water curtain instead of an asbestos curtain in the event of an onstage fire."

Another "first" for a legitimate theatre was a revolutionary automatic rigging system called Hydra-Float. Mr. Alswang estimated that the building cost would amount to about $12.5 million.

A special feature of the theatre is the inclusion of a Theatre Hall of Fame with the names of stage greats inscribed in bas-relief on the walls of an impressive rotunda. Another rotunda on the theatre's other side may be used for theatrical exhibitions. The Hall of Fame rotunda was suggested to the Nederlanders by Earl Blackwell.

The Uris opened on November 28, 1972, with Galt MacDermot's spectacular rock musical, *Via Galactica,* starring Raul Julia and Virginia Vestoff as space beings in the year 2972. Unfortunately, the special effects were more dazzling than the show, and it closed after only 7 performances.

The theatre's next tenant was much more successful. *Seesaw,* a musical version of William Gibson's hit comedy *Two for the Seesaw,* had music by Cy Coleman, lyrics by Dorothy Fields, a book credited to Michael Bennett, and starred Ken Howard and Michele Lee. Tommy Tune won a Tony Award as Best Supporting Actor in a Musical and Mr. Bennett received another for his choreography.

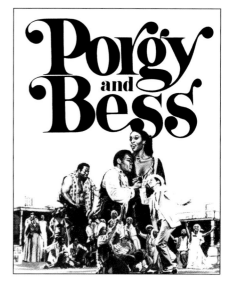

PLAYBILL covers for the opening production, *Via Galactica* (1972), the musical *Seesaw* (1973), and the Tony Award-winning revival of *Porgy and Bess* (1976).

On March 23, 1973, Mayor John V. Lindsay replaced Ken Howard in the opening "My City" number for seven minutes. The musical ran for 296 performances.

In September 1973 the Uris presented a revival of the operetta *The Desert Song*, but its 1920s appeal was lost on 1970s audiences. It closed after 15 performances. The next booking was unusual. The brilliant movie musical *Gigi* was converted to a stage show, not the usual order of creativity at that time, but one that would become increasingly frequent in ensuing years. Alan Jay Lerner and Frederick Loewe added some songs to the score, which won a Tony Award. The cast included Alfred Drake, Agnes Moorehead (later succeeded by Arlene Francis), Karin Wolfe, Daniel Massey, and Maria Karnilova. It ran for 103 performances.

During 1974, the Uris housed personal appearances by a series of celebrated artists, including Sammy Davis, Jr.; the rock group Mott the Hoople; Enrico Macias and his La Fete Orientale Co.; Andy Williams and Michel Legrand; Anthony Newley and Henry Mancini; Johnny Mathis; The Fifth Dimension; Raphael in Concert; and Nureyev and Friends.

These concert bookings continued in 1975 with the Dance Theatre of Harlem, Count Basie, Ella Fitzgerald, and Frank Sinatra. The first New York production of Scott Joplin's opera *Treemonisha* opened here in October of that year. The Houston Grand Opera Association production of this work, which had been lost for many years, was conceived and directed by Frank Corsaro and it ran for 64 performances. This was followed by the American Ballet Theatre, Margot Fonteyn and Rudolf Nureyev, Paul Anka, Dance Theatre of Harlem, D'Oyly Carte Opera Company, and Al Green.

The Houston Grand Opera and Sherwin M. Goldman presented an acclaimed revival of George Gershwin's opera, *Porgy and Bess,* in 1976, and the production received a Tony Award as the Most Innovative Production of a Revival, as the award was then called. Clamma Dale was especially praised for her singing and acting as Bess.

Bing Crosby made a rare appearance on Broadway at the Uris in 1976 with his wife, Kathryn, and other members of his family, plus Rosemary Clooney, Joe Bushkin, and others. *Bing Crosby on Broadway* played a limited engagement of 12 performances during the Christmas holiday season. Nureyev appeared next in a dance concert, followed by the Ballet of the Twentieth Century.

A splendid revival of Rodgers and Hammerstein's *The King and I* opened here on May 2, 1977, starring Yul Brynner and Constance Towers. Produced by Lee Guber and Shelly Gross, it was an immediate hit and became the Uris's longest-running show to that time: 719 performances.

On March 1, 1979, a thrillingly ghoulish event occurred at this theatre. It was *Sweeney Todd, The Demon Barber of Fleet Street*, the grisly musical by Stephen Sondheim and Hugh Wheeler, based on a version of *Sweeney Todd* by Christopher Bond. The work received critical acclaim and won Tony Awards for Best Musical, Best Score (Sondheim), Best Book (Wheeler), Best Musical Actress (Angela Lansbury), Best Musical Actor (Len Cariou), Best Director (Hal Prince), Best Scenic Design (Eugene Lee), and Best Costume Design (Franne Lee). The Grand Guignol-style shocker about a London barber who slits his customers' throats in revenge for an injustice suffered by him was not

Above: (From left): Willard White, Carmen Balthrop, and Betty Allen in the first New York production of Scott Joplin's opera, *Treemonisha* (1975). *Below:* Angela Lansbury and Len Cariou as the murderous twosome in the multi-award-winning *Sweeney Todd* (1979).

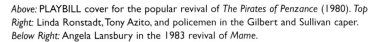

Above: PLAYBILL cover for the popular revival of *The Pirates of Penzance* (1980). *Top Right:* Linda Ronstadt, Tony Azito, and policemen in the Gilbert and Sullivan caper. *Below Right:* Angela Lansbury in the 1983 revival of *Mame.*

everyone's cup of blood, but the highly imaginative production ran for 557 performances.

In 1980, the Uris presented Roland Petit's Ballet National de Marseilles, Makarova and Company, and Nureyev and the Boston Ballet. On January 1, 1981, Joseph Papp presented the New York Shakespeare Festival production of *The Pirates of Penzance*, which had been a hit in Central Park the preceding summer. The cast included Kevin Kline (who received the Tony Award as Best Actor in a Musical), Linda Ronstadt, Estelle Parsons, Rex Smith, George Rose, and Tony Azito. The production received additional Tony Awards for Best Revival and Best Direction (Wilford Leach). It ran for 772 performances.

On August 18, 1981, the Uris presented a revival of Lerner and Loewe's classic *My Fair Lady,* with its original star, Rex Harrison. Nancy Ringham played Eliza Doolittle, Milo O'Shea played her father, and Cathleen Nesbitt, also from the original cast, recreated her role as Mrs. Higgins. The revival ran for 124 performances.

The long-running musical *Annie* moved into the Uris from the Eugene O'Neill Theatre in January 1982 and stayed here for a year. It ended its run at the Uris, having chalked up 2,377 performances.

Barry Manilow made a personal appearance here in February 1983, followed by a Houston Grand Opera revival of the Jerome Kern/Oscar Hammerstein II classic *Show Boat,* starring Donald O'Connor.

On the evening of June 5, 1983, during the annual Tony Award telecast, the name of the Uris was officially changed to the Gershwin Theatre, in honor of composer George Gershwin and his lyricist brother, Ira, who contributed many distinguished musicals and the opera *Porgy and Bess* to the Broadway theatre.

A month later, Angela Lansbury returned in a revival of the hit musical *Mame,* in the title role, which she had originated. Other repeaters in the show: Jane Connell as Agnes Gooch, Anne Francine, Willard Waterman, and Sab Shimono.

In 1984, *Wayne Newton on Broadway* and *Twyla Tharp Dances on Broadway* were seen here, followed by the long-running *Beatlemania,* which moved here from another theatre. Later in the summer, singer Patti LaBelle took the stage.

Robert Goulet as Arthur in the 1993 revival of *Camelot.*

In October 1984, the Royal Shakespeare Company arrived with two productions: *Much Ado About Nothing* and *Cyrano De Bergerac.* Among the players were Derek Jacobi and Sinead Cusack. Mr. Jacobi was awarded a Tony for his performance as Benedick in *Much Ado.* The actor reported at a PLAYBILL luncheon that on the opening night of *Cyrano*, José Ferrer, who won a Tony for playing that role in 1947, went backstage and said to the British Jacobi: "Your performance proves my point that only a Latin can play Cyrano."

Patti LaBelle returned to the Gershwin in January 1985. That summer, the lavish *Singin' in the Rain* opened here after many difficulties. It was a stage incarnation of the classic MGM musical, with Comden and Green adapting their original screenplay about Hollywood's bumpy transition from silent films to talkies. The songs were mostly by the MGM team of Nacio Herb Brown and Arthur Freed. Don Correia played the Gene Kelly role and danced the title song in a heavy stage downpour

Left: The PLAYBILL for the 1997 revival of *Candide. Center: Show Boat* (1994). *Right:* Opening night PLAYBILL for *Sweeney Todd: The Demon Barber of Fleet Street* (1979).

created by a system of pipes above the stage. The choreography was by Twyla Tharp, who also directed the musical. It ran for ten months.

The next production at this theatre, the British spectacular *Starlight Express* (1987), required the theatre to be turned into a gigantic roller rink, with the cast rollerskating on ramps and bridges around the stage to give the impression of being railroad cars. One of the costliest productions ever staged on Broadway to that time, the Andrew Lloyd Webber/Richard Stilgoe musical ran for nearly two years and won a Tony Award for John Napier's elaborate costumes. However, it did not achieve the success of the London production, nor did it recoup its enormous investment.

In 1989, *Barry Manilow at the Gershwin* played for two months. That fall, another MGM screen musical, *Meet Me in St. Louis*, took to the stage with some additional songs by Hugh Martin and Ralph Blane, who had written the famed movie score for this charming musical. The stage version starred George Hearn, Milo O'Shea, Charlotte Moore, and Betty Garrett (who was welcomed back by the critics), and featured Donna Kane in the Judy Garland role. The musical ran for seven months.

Bugs Bunny On Broadway played for several weeks in 1990, followed by a handsome revival of *Fiddler on the Roof*, starring Topol, recreating the role of Tevye which he had played both on stage (in London) and in the highly praised film version of the musical. This production won the Tony Award for Best Revival of the season, and ran for seven months. In 1991 and 1992, *The Moscow Circus* and *Tommy Tune Tonite!* played here, followed by a 1993 production of the Lerner/Loewe musical *Camelot*, starring Robert Goulet, the show's original Lancelot, who this time took the role of King Arthur.

In the fall of 1994, the highly anticipated Hal Prince production of *Show Boat* steamed in after a hugely successful run in Canada. The new production of this classic was rapturously received. A program note stated that this revival was based on the original 1927 Ziegfeld production, the London production, the 1936 film version, and the 1946 Broadway revival. Additional credit was given to musicologist John McGlinn and archivist Myles Kreuger, who had written an acclaimed book on the history of all productions of *Show Boat*.

Produced by the Garth Drabinsky's Livent (US) Inc., the sumptuously mounted production made some interesting departures from other versions of the show.

Mr. Prince restored six songs that had been dropped from other *Show Boat* productions, including "Mis'ry's Comin' Aroun'," which had been considered too depressing for a musical. He ameliorated some racial stereotypes that were felt to be too "Uncle Tom."

The cast included John McMartin (Cap'n Andy), Elaine Stritch (Parthy), Rebecca Luker (Magnolia), Mark Jacoby (Ravenal), and Michel Bell (Joe) whose rendition of the classic "Ol' Man River" stopped the show at every performance. One change that irritated some playgoers was having Ms. Stritch sing the lovely "Why Do I Love You?," instead of the traditional trio of Magnolia, Ravenal and Cap'n Andy. Ms. Stritch's voice at this time was particularly harsh.

Show Boat received ten Tony Award nominations and won the following five: Best Musical Revival, Best Director of a Musical (Prince), Best Costume Designer (Florence Klotz), Best Choreographer (Susan Stroman), and Best Featured Actress in a Musical (Gretha Boston). *Show Boat* ran for 949 performances, closing on January 5, 1997.

The next Livent production, also directed by Hal Prince, did not fare as well. It was a revival of the musical version of Voltaire's *Candide*, with a book by Hugh Wheeler, music by Leonard Bernstein, lyrics by Richard Wilbur, Stephen Sondheim, and John Latouche, and choreography by Patricia Birch.

This revival was based on three earlier versions of the musical, the most successful being the 1974 production, also directed by Prince, which ran for 740 performances. The 1997 cast starred Jim Dale, who played a variety of parts; Mal Z. Lawrence and Arte Johnson, who also played multiple roles; Harolyn Blackwell as Cunegonde (spelled by Glenda Balkan at some performances); Jason Danieley as Candide; Andrea Martin as the Old Lady; and Stacey Logan as Paquette.

The musical traced the marvelous adventures and appalling tribulations of the innocent Westphalian hero, Candide, who faces great hardships in his travels but remains loyal to the optimistic lesson of his teacher, Dr. Pangloss: "All is for the best in this best of all possible worlds." Critics praised (as usual) the great score by Bernstein, but disliked the show's book and the circusy staging that overwhelmed Voltaire's sharp-edged satire. Critic Howard Kissel wrote: "Bernstein's sublime score

lacks best of all books." Critic David Patrick Stearns' review stated: "New *Candide* low-voltage Voltaire." The musical received four Tony Award nominations—Best Musical Revival, Best Actor in a Musical (Dale), Best Featured Actress in a Musical (Martin), and Best Costumes (Judith Dolan)—but won none. The musical ran for 103 performances.

The next booking at the Gershwin Theatre was the successful revival of the 1969 Tony Award-winning musical *1776*, about the events that swirled around the signing of the Declaration of Independence in that year. This production by the Roundabout Theatre moved to this theatre on December 3, 1997, from the Criterion Center Stage Right Theatre, where it had played from August 14, 1997, to November 16, 1997. It was directed by Scott Ellis. The cast included Pat Hingle as Benjamin Franklin, Michael Cumpsty as John Dickinson, Richard Poe as John Hancock, Brent Spiner as John Adams, Tom Aldredge as Stephen Hopkins, Paul Michael Valley as Thomas Jefferson, Gregg Edelman as Edward Rutledge, Lauren Ward as Martha Jefferson, and many others.

The production received the following Tony Award nominations: Best Musical Revival, Best Featured Actor in a Musical (Edelman), and Best Director of a Musical (Ellis). It ran for 333 performances.

On November 19, 1998, a new production of the celebrated 1944 musical *On the Town* opened here. George C. Wolfe staged the New York Shakespeare Festival production, which originated as an August 1997 Central Park revival. The musical, inspired by Jerome Robbins' epic ballet, *Fancy Free,* had music by Leonard Bernstein, and book and lyrics by Comden and Green. It depicted the joyous shore leave of three sailors in Manhattan, and their adventures with three girls they encounter.

The most imaginative feature of this revival was the set by Adrienne Lobel, which contained a replica of the Brooklyn Bridge overhead, on which the orchestra was placed. The Manhattan skyline loomed behind the bridge. Some critics objected to this scenic device, saying that it took up too much space and resulted in a cramped stage for the dancers.

The new choreography by Keith Young was

Pat Roddy, Eileen Martin, and the Irish Dance Troupe in *Riverdance on Broadway* (2000). Photo by Joan Marcus.

compared unfavorably with Jerome Robbins' original dances, and Mr. Wolfe's direction was considered bland.

The cast received decent reviews, especially Lea DeLaria as the rowdy cab driver and Mary Testa as a tipsy singing instructor. The revival played only 65 performances and lost a lot of money for the New York Shakespeare Festival. It received only one Tony Award nomination: Ms. Testa for Best Featured Actress in a Musical.

The next tenant at the Gershwin was a return of the popular 1985 music and dance revue *Tango Argentino*. The entertainment, conceived by Claudio Segovia and Hector Orezzoli, featured Argentine artists interpreting the tango in song, story, and dance. It played for 63 performances.

On March 16, 2000, *Riverdance on Broadway* made its long-delayed Broadway debut, having originally proved a sensation at Radio City Music Hall in 1998 and having played around the world and even on PBS before returning to New York at last at a legitimate Broadway house. The extravaganza presented Irish step dances, and choral and solo songs by sparkling international performers. It had a long and highly successful engagement.

The Gershwin is a Nederlander Organization theatre, under the direction of the Messrs. Nederlander. Its large seating capacity makes it ideal for lavish musicals and dance events.

MINSKOFF THEATRE

The Minskoff Theatre, perched on the third floor of One Astor Plaza, the fifty-five-story office tower on the site of Broadway's old Astor Hotel, derives its name from Sam Minskoff and Sons, builders and owners of the high-rise. The modern theatre, with a very large 1,621-seat capacity, was designed by the architectural firm of Kahn and Jacobs and offers a spectacular view of the Great White Way from the glass front of the building on all levels of the theatre.

The theatre features a pedestrian arcade that runs from Forty-fourth to Forty-fifth streets, parallel to Shubert Alley. Inside the spacious, lobby, dual escalators take playgoers to the third level of the Grand Foyer of the house. Here there are coat-check concessions and bars. Additional escalators rise to the fourth, or orchestra, level, and above.

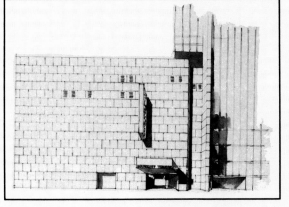

At the time of the theatre's opening in 1973, Robert A. Jacobs, partner-in-charge of Kahn and Jacobs, told PLAYBILL: "A theatre that is thirty-five feet in the air is quite an innovation. According to the old building code in Manhattan, a theatre's orchestra floor had to be within three feet of the sidewalk. We think we've created one of the most exciting, three-dimensional processional routes for the theatregoers—a series of forms, changes in ceiling heights, and spatial explosions. The whole processional, from the moment you enter and rise thirty-five feet to the theatre level, is a theatrical event in itself. Our forms are purely architectural, beautifully proportioned in relation to the processional drama you're going through."

Mr. Jacobs stated that his firm had kept everything simple in the theatre's decor, without hiring what he called "exotic interior desecraters." The theatre was done primarily in white and gold, with charcoal-gray seats that are roomy, comfortable, and offer an excellent view. The orchestra floor rakes steeply up from the stage. Hundreds of small, clear bulbs sparkle in the lobbies, and crystal-basket lights glow in the auditorium. The ceiling is broken into two sections with a narrow grid between them for the stage lights. The proscenium has removable mesh panels on both sides, and the mezzanine, with 590 seats, has narrow side projections instead of box seats. The stage has an innovation: all the flies are on the upstage wall instead of on the side wall. Part of the stage is trapped and can be extended out over the orchestra pit. The dressing rooms are sumptuous and the restrooms are large, cheerful, and comfortable.

The Minskoff Theatre opened on March 13, 1973, with a lavish revival of the 1919 musical *Irene*. Debbie Reynolds played the title role and sang the show's classic, "Alice Blue Gown." The cast also included Patsy Kelly, Monte Markham, Janie Sell, Ruth Warrick, Carmen

Debbie Reynolds parades her "Alice Blue Gown" for the ensemble in a revival of the 1919 hit *Irene* (1973), the inaugural production at the Minskoff. Note her daughter, future *Star Wars* star Carrie Fisher, to her left, on floor.

Alvarez, and George S. Irving, who won a Tony Award for his performance. The musical ran until the fall of 1974. It was succeeded by two concert shows: *Charles Aznavour on Broadway* and *Tony Bennett and Lena Horne Sing.*

The 1975 season at the Minskoff was extremely varied. It began on a sober note with Henry Fonda in his one-man show, *Clarence Darrow.* The raucous Bette Midler was next in her salty *Clams on the Half Shell Revue.* In the fall of that year, Pearl Bailey and Billy Daniels brought their version of *Hello, Dolly!* to the theatre. The 1976 attractions included a short-lived rock version of *Hamlet* called *Rockabye Hamlet,* with Meat Loaf playing a priest, and an Ophelia who committed suicide by wrapping her microphone cord around her neck. This was followed by the Dutch National Ballet and the Chinese Acrobats of Taiwan.

The 1977 season brought Merce Cunningham and

Dance Company, followed by the long-running musical *Pippin,* which moved here from the Imperial. The year ended with engagements of Cleo Laine and *Star Wars Concert Live.*

Rudolf Nureyev made a dance appearance at the Minskoff in 1978 with the Murray Lewis Dance Company. Next came a musical version of the play *Look Homeward, Angel,* called simply *Angel.* Its cast included Fred Gwynne, Frances Sternhagen, Don Scardino, Leslie Ann Ray, Patti Allison, and Joel Higgins, but the Thomas Wolfe classic did not succeed as a musical and it closed after 5 performances. Another unsuccessful musical opened in 1978: *King of Hearts,* adapted from the cult film of the same name, about a group of sweet-natured mental patients who escape into a small town during World War I. The cast included Donald Scardino, Millicent Martin, Pamela Blair, Gary Morgan, Timothy Scott, and Michael McCarty. It expired after 48 performances.

Pearl Bailey in a revival of *Hello, Dolly!* (1975).

In late 1978 an elaborate spectacle, *Ice Dancing*, opened here. It was followed by *Bejart—Ballet of the Twentieth Century*. A musical called *Got Tu Go Disco* tried to capitalize on the disco dance craze, but was a quick failure in 1979. Appearances by Shirley Bassey and the Chinese Acrobats and Magicians of Taiwan followed.

A revival of *West Side Story* in 1980 was moderately successful, running for 341 performances. A revival of Cole Porter's *Can-Can*, however, proved a disaster in 1981, despite the dancing of Zizi Jeanmaire and the choreography of Roland Petit. It folded after 5 showings.

In the fall of 1981 the successful revival of *The Pirates of Penzance* moved here from the Uris Theatre and stayed for more than a year.

In the spring of 1983, *Dance a Little Closer*, an ill-advised musicalization of Robert E. Sherwood's Pulitzer-winning play, *Idiot's Delight*, closed on its opening night, despite the fact that the book and lyrics were by Alan Jay Lerner and the music by Charles Strouse. The title song was especially lilting, but that didn't stop wags from dubbing the production *Close a Little Faster*. Starring Len Cariou and Liz Robertson, and featuring George Rose, the updated musical sadly was Lerner's last show.

Next came *Marilyn: An American Fable*, another fiasco. It purported to be a musical biography of the late sex goddess Marilyn Monroe, but the critics were not kindly disposed toward the enterprise. It vanished after two weeks.

The Tap Dance Kid moved here from the Broadhurst on March 27, 1984, and stayed until August 11, 1985, winning Tony Awards for Best Featured Actor in a Musical (Hinton Battle) and Best Choreography (Danny Daniels). Late in its run, the title role was assumed by an amazing child dancer named Savion Glover, who went on to help redefine tap a decade later in *Bring in 'da Noise, Bring in 'da Funk*.

In early 1986, personal appearances were made here by Patti LaBelle, TNT, and Peter, Paul & Mary. In April of that year, a new production of Cy Coleman's *Sweet Charity* opened with Debbie Allen, Bebe Neuwirth, and Michael Rupert. The revival won the following Tony Awards: Best Revival, Best Featured Actor in a Musical (Rupert), Best Featured Actress (Neuwirth), and Best Costumes (Patricia Zipprodt). It ran for 368 performances.

On February 9, 1988, a new production of *Cabaret* moved here from the Imperial Theatre with Joel Grey recreating his Tony Award-winning role as the Emcee, and with Alyson Reed, Gregg Edelman, Regina Resnick, and Werner Klemperer in other leading roles. It had a run of 262 performances. The next musical at this theatre was an elaborate patriotic spectacle called *Teddy & Alice*, set to tunes by John Philip Sousa with book by Jerome Alden and Lyrics by Hal Hackaday. Original songs were provided by Richard Kapp. Len Cariou played Teddy Roosevelt, Nancy Hume was Alice Roosevelt, and Ron Raines was Nick Longworth. It had a short run of 77 performances.

More successful was the next Minskoff musical, *Black and Blue*, a lavish revue using standard blues and hit songs of the past. It won Tony Awards for Ruth

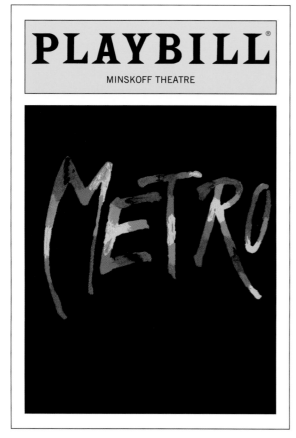

On November 10, 1993, a sumptuous new production of the Andrew Lloyd Webber/Tim Rice musical *Joseph and the Amazing Technicolor Dreamcoat* opened and had a successful run, starring Michael Damian in the title role.

Another Lloyd Webber musical arrived next: the highly anticipated London production of *Sunset Boulevard*. Controversy surrounded the production. Patti LuPone starred in it in London and was supposed to repeat her performance on Broadway. Unfortunately, a *New York Times* critic was unenthusiastic about her London performance and Glenn Close was hired to replace her. (Since Ms. LuPone had a contract to star in it on Broadway, she was paid a handsome sum for her dismissal.) The musical, based on the famous 1950 Billy Wilder film, was a dark look at Hollywood that infuriated the movie colony when the movie was released. It depicted a has-been actress (Norma Desmond) vainly trying to make a movie comeback via a penniless screenwriter who becomes her gigolo.

Brown (Best Actress in a Musical), Claudio Segovia and Hector Orezzoli (Best Costume Design) and the four choreographers. It played here until January 20, 1991, achieving 829 performances. In November 1991 Cathy Rigby played a return engagement in the title role of *Peter Pan,* which she had played at the Lunt-Fontanne Theatre the previous season.

A spectacular, multimedia production from Poland, *Metro,* did not repeat its success on Broadway. The youthful cast included a former miner and other blue-collar workers who had been scouted by the director at open auditions around Poland. A year later they found themselves opening on Broadway in a blaze of laser effects. But Frank Rich of *The New York Times* opened his review, "What's the Polish word for fiasco?" And they stayed only 13 performances.

Special PLAYBILL given out at the 1995 Tony Awards ceremony, which was held at the Minskoff.

The settings by John Napier were staggering. The palatial Hollywood villa Norma occupied was a gigantic set that resembled the lobby of the old Roxy theatre in Manhattan. At one point, the entire set was elevated and another set rose into place below it. Projections were used to simulate a car chase. The physical production received better reviews than the show, which had music by Lloyd Webber, book and lyrics by Don Black and Christopher Hampton, and direction by Trevor Nunn. Also in the cast were Alan Campbell, George Hearn, and Alice Ripley.

Two of Lloyd Webber's songs enjoyed popularity: "With One Look" and "As If We Never Said Goodbye," both of which were recorded by Barbra Streisand. The musical won the following Tony Awards: Best Musical, Leading Actress/Musical (Close), Best Supporting Actor

(Hearn), Best Musical Book (Black and Hampton), Best Score (Lloyd Webber, Black, Hampton), Scenic Design (Napier). and Lighting Design (Andrew Bridge), though book and score were won by default, as there were no other eligible nominees in those categories in a very lean Broadway season. *Sunset Boulevard* ran for 977 performances—still the house record at this writing. During its long run, Ms. Close was succeeded by Betty Buckley, who was followed by British musical comedy star, Elaine Paige, making her Broadway debut.

The next musical to open here had a complex history. *The Scarlet Pimpernel,* a spectacular production with music by Frank Wildhorn and book and lyrics by Nan Knighton, opened on November 9, 1997, Based on Baroness Orczy's popular novel, which Leslie Howard had glorified in a 1935 film, the musical followed the adventures of a British nobleman who poses as a fop in order to rescue French aristocrats from the guillotine. Unfortunately, the musical received mostly negative reviews, with most critics branding it boring. The charismatic Douglas Sills was praised as the Scarlet Pimpernel and he received a Tony Award nomination as Leading Actor in a Musical. Other Tony nominations: Best Musical and Best Musical Book (Knighton). The producers decided to make changes and the musical went on hiatus for several months of rewriting and restaging that reduced the scope of the production. When it reopened at the Minskoff Theatre, critics felt the show had been improved—but not enough, and it closed after 643 performances. Surprisingly, yet a further revised version, nicknamed "*The Scarlet Pimpernel Version 3.0,*" opened at the Neil Simon Theatre on September 10, 1999, and ran another 129 performances, for a total of 772 in all.

In fall of 1999, the producer of the 1977 disco film *Saturday Night Fever,* brought over the hit London stage adaptation, with extra songs by the Bee Gees, and a book by *The Scarlet Pimpernel's* Nan Knighton. It ran for 500 performances.

The Minskoff Theatre is under the direction of James M. Nederlander and Myron A. Minskoff. It is an ideal house for large-scale musicals, dance companies, and personal-appearance shows.

The company of Andrew Lloyd Webber's *Sunset Boulevard* (1994).

MARQUIS THEATRE

The Marquis Theatre opened in July 1986 as part of the new Marriott Marquis Hotel on Broadway between Forty-fifth and Forty-sixth Streets. Just before its unveiling, John C. Portman, Jr., the theatre's architect and designer, told PLAYBILL: "Our dream was to create a new theatre for the Broadway of today that could handle any type of production, any kind of light and sound equipment, provide maximum comfort for audience and actors and still convey a feeling of intimacy."

The Morosco, Hayes, and Bijou theatres (along with the shells of the old Astor and Gaiety theatres) were demolished to make way for the hotel, which occasioned protests and pickets. In return, Broadwayites got a second walk-through arcade a block north of Shubert Alley, and this splendid new musical-size state-of-the-art theatre that has quickly become a favorite with actors and audiences. It is also one of the few Broadway theatres that actually fronts on Broadway.

Leased by the Nederlander Organization for thirty-five years, the Marquis boasts many unique features. It is Broadway's only legitimate theatre built specifically as part of a new hotel, it has an extraordinary ceiling that masks lighting and sound equipment (with no ugly pipes in view of the audience), the orchestra floor is steeply raked with three separate aisles that offer perfect viewing from all seats, and there's a ramp for wheelchair patrons and a special area for the handicapped.

The auditorium can be reached by escalator from the Broadway box office, or by escalators or elevators inside the hotel. The hotel's enclosed portico is ideal for arriving by car or cab or for catching a cab after the performance, especially in cold and inclement weather. The theatre is on the hotel's third floor and there are two stunning spiral stairways leading to the mezzanine.

The theatre's lobby has a magnificent marble bar with a brass rail. As you enter the house, the stage is directly in front of you, offering a splendid view of the dazzling main curtain of many colors designed by artist Bjorn Wimblad. There are 1,000 seats in the orchestra and 600 in the mezzanine, with no seat farther than 80 feet from the stage.

"The theatre's interior is very straightforward, very understated and simplified," Mr. Portman said. "There are no chandeliers. The lighting emanates essentially from the walls. The house's color scheme is rose and different shades of burgundy." The architect's designs were executed by the project architect, Bob Jones.

Roger Morgan, the Tony Award-winning lighting designer, was retained as Theatre Design Consultant, and Chris Jaffe of Jaffe Acoustics, Inc. was the acoustical consultant, assisted by Abe Jacob, one of Broadway's leading

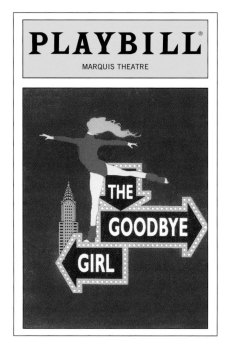
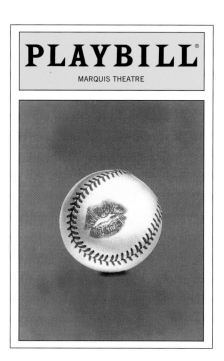
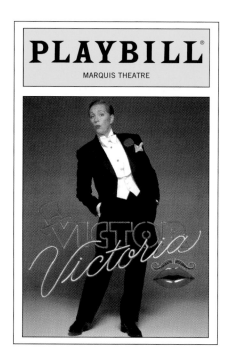

Left: Neil Simon adapted his film *The Goodbye Girl* as a musical (1993). *Center: Damn Yankees* (1994) opened with Victor Garber as the Devil, but then brought Jerry Lewis into the role. *Right:* Julie Andrews returned to Broadway after a quarter century absence to star in *Victor/Victoria* (1995).

sound designers. "The Marquis," said Mr. Morgan, "rates very high with other musical theatres in terms of backstage area. The first show there—*Me and My Girl*—had eight huge sets, which meant we could do anything. There are 75 dressing room stations and three Green Rooms for the actors, musicians, and stage hands. Chris Jaffe and Abe Jacob have been able to integrate the latest technology in acoustical system and we know that audiences will be happy with the sound in this theatre. My firm added the lighting."

A concert appearance by Shirley Bassey and George Kirby inaugurated the theatre on July 8, 1986. But the legitimate opening came on August 10, 1986, with the spectacular debut of the British musical *Me and My Girl*. Robert Lindsay recreated his award-winning London performance in the role of Bill Snibson, adding a Tony Award for his effort. Tonys were also bestowed on his co-star Mary Ann Plunkett and on Gillian Gregory for her choreography.

Me and My Girl was a new production of a 1937 Noel Gay musical, and it delighted 1986 audiences with its broad humor, music hall turns, glamorous sets and costumes, and rousing musical score, including the 1930s

dance craze, "The Lambeth Walk," which spilled out into the audience and raised the roof. The jubilant import ran for 1,420 performances and got the beautiful new theatre off to a flying start.

Next came a spirited Brazilian song-and-dance revue called *Oba Oba '90*. The near-nude dancing by a large cast enlivened the extravaganza.

The scenic resources of the Marquis were tested to their fullest by *Shogun: The Musical*, which opened in November 1990. Based on the best-selling novel by James Clavell, the musical had book and lyrics by John Driver and music by Paul Chihara. But scenic effects were not enough and the show played here for only two months.

Tyne Daly, who had won a Tony Award the previous season for her starring role in *Gypsy*, the celebrated musical by Arthur Laurents, Jule Styne, and Stephen Sondheim, brought the show back in 1991 at the Marquis, repeating her acclaimed performance as Rose, with Crista Moore again playing the title role.

Mr. Laurents was back at the Marquis later that year as librettist and director of the musical *Nick & Nora*, with a score by Charles Strouse and Richard Maltby, Jr. Based on the beloved characters Nick and Nora Charles, created by Dashiell Hammett in *The Thin Man* series, the musical murder spoof cast Barry Bostwick and Joanna Gleason as the husband/wife sleuths, and Faith Prince as a very comical murder victim. Unfortunately, the musical did not recapture the charm of the old MGM *Thin Man* films and ran for only 9 performances.

On April 24, 1992, a new production of *Man of La Mancha* opened here, starring Raul Julia as Cervantes/Don Quixote and pop singer Sheena Easton as Aldonza/Dulcinea. The revival ran for three months.

The next musical here was *The Goodbye Girl*, based on Neil Simon's film of the same name. With a book by Mr. Simon and a score by Marvin Hamlisch and David Zippel, the show starred Bernadette Peters and TV comic Martin Short, with Carol Woods, Scott Wise, and Cynthia Onrubia. The critics were unenthusiastic about most aspects of the show, except for Mr. Short's hilarious antics, and the musical managed a six-month run.

A splendid revival of the 1955 musical, *Damn Yankees*, by George Abbott and Douglas Wallop with a score by Richard Adler and Jerry Ross, opened here on March 3, 1994. One of the delights of the opening night was that Mr. Abbott (106 years old) attended. The new production, starring Bebe Neuwirth and Victor Garber, with Jarrod Emick, Dennis Kelly, Dick Latessa, Vicki Lewis, Linda Stephens, and Scott Wise, pleased most of the critics, especially the crusty John Simon, who gave it a surprisingly glowing review. Mr. Emick won a Tony for his performance. The Faustian baseball musical also garnered the following Tony Award nominations: Best Musical Revival, Leading Musical Actor (Garber), and Best Choreographer (Rob Marshall).

On March 12, 1995, Jerry Lewis made his Broadway debut when he succeeded Mr. Garber as Applegate. His excellent tomfoolery and good reviews helped to prolong the show's run to 533 performances.

On October 25, 1995, the red carpet was rolled out at the Marquis Theatre for the return of Julie Andrews to Broadway in a stage adaptation of her hit 1982 film, *Victor/Victoria*. Before the curtain rose, Mayor Rudolph Giuliani appeared onstage to make a welcoming speech for the star, who was making her first Broadway appearance since *Camelot* in 1960.

Ms. Andrews' husband, Blake Edwards, had written and directed the film, and he repeated these services for the stage version. Henry Mancini's songs from the movie were retained, with new tunes added by Frank Wildhorn. The critics were happy to have Ms. Andrews back, but compared the show unfavorably with the film. The lyrics by Leslie Bricusse were declared inept. The supporting cast included Tony Roberts, Rachel York, Michael Nouri, and Gregory Jbara.

The show earned a niche in Broadway history for the controversy that erupted when the Tony Awards failed to nominate anything about the production for an award, with the notable exception of Ms. Andrews's performance. She responded with a vehement curtain speech from the Marquis stage following a May 1996 matinee of the show, denouncing the snub, declining her nomination, and declaring solidarity with the rest of her cast and company, whom she said had been "egregiously overlooked." The phrase became a favorite in ensuing years whenever the Tonys ignored a favorite actor or show. Ms. Andrews also boycotted the Tony Awards ceremony—where the award for Best Actress in a Musical went to Donna Murphy of *The King and I*.

During Ms. Andrews' vacation and frequent illness, her replacements included Ann Runolfsson and Liza Minnelli. She was eventually succeeded in the role by Raquel Welch. The stormy run ended after 734 performances.

The next musical to arrive was controversial in a very different way. Pop composer Paul Simon made his Broadway debut with *The Capeman*, the story of Salvador Agron, the Puerto Rican-born real-life killer who made headlines for wearing a cape during his murder of two young men in 1950s New York. Simon said the musical was about the need for "forgiveness," but families and friends of his victims resented the depiction of Agron as a product of poverty and environment. They picketed the theatre on opening night, January 29, 1998. Much had been expected of this musical since it had music by Grammy-winner Simon and book and lyrics co-written by Nobel laureate Derek Walcott. Three actors portrayed the murderer at different stages of his life, including Latin pop stars Marc Anthony and Ruben Blades. But critics were not impressed and the musical played for only 68 performances. *The Capeman* received no Tony Awards, but was nominated for the following: Best Score,

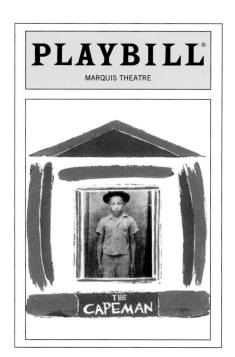

Left: Bernadette Peters won a Tony in the 1999 revival of *Annie Get Your Gun. Right:* Paul Simon and Derek Walcott collaborated on the interesting failure *The Capeman* (1998).

Best Orchestrations, and Best Scenic Designer. Mr. Simon was bitter about the failure of his first Broadway musical and vowed to rewrite the show and bring it back. To date it hasn't returned.

A concert performance by 74-year-old French singer Charles Aznavour was next at this theatre and had a pleasant engagement of 24 performances.

Cathy Rigby brought her revival of *Peter Pan*, in which she played the flying sprite, from November 1998 to January 1999. She reopened it at the Gershwin Theatre in April and it ran until August, having played 214 performances. This was the popular 1954 musical version of *Peter Pan* with a score by Jule Styne, Comden and Green, "Moose" Charlap, and Carolyn Leigh, and choreography by Jerome Robbins.

Another musical classic had even greater success at the Marquis starting March 4, 1999, with the revival of Irving Berlin's beloved *Annie Get Your Gun*, starring Bernadette Peters as sharpshooter Annie Oakley. The original book by Herbert and Dorothy Fields was revised by Peter Stone to remove material deemed offensive, including the song, "I'm An Indian, Too." Ethel Merman, who immortalized the role in the 1946 original produc-

tion and in the 1966 revival, proved a tough act to follow. Peters's singing was excellent, as usual, but some critics felt that she wasn't "country" enough for the part, and that her accent varied. Still, she won a Tony Award as Best Leading Actress in a Musical for her performance. Also nominated was her co-star Tom Wopat, who played rival marksman (and love interest) Frank Butler. The show also won the Tony as Best Musical Revival. Some critics were disappointed with the directorial concept of staging it as a play-within-a-play being presented by Buffalo Bill's Wild West Show, and that it lacked visual splendor. The Berlin score, however, remained his best. The musical had a long run with Ms. Peters succeeded by Susan Lucci, Cheryl Ladd, and country singer Reba McEntire, the latter of whom received the best reviews of all as Annie Oakley.

It was followed by a short-run musical adaptation of Mark Twain's *Tom Sawyer*, and a stage version of the film musical *Thoroughly Modern Millie*, with new songs by Jeanine Tesori and Dick Scanlan.

The Nederlanders's Marquis Theatre has achieved its goal of providing maximum comfort for audiences and actors while conveying a feeling of intimacy.

INDEX

T